The Book of David

An Exhaustive Study of the Life of David

By Bro. Ron Miller

An exhaustive study of the life of David

Note from the author:

The study method implemented here is to start with the first mention of David in the scripture and proceed with every verse in which his name is mentioned. Each verse will have a commentary, either short or long, depending on what is gleaned from the verse. When verses are the same or almost the same, we may reference our commentary on the first verse that is like it. For instance, many verses in 2 Samuel are found in 1 Chronicles as another account of the same record, so we may reference the commentary on the first mention in 2 Samuel. However, we will point out the differences in the accounts for the purpose of exhausting as much as possible the study of the life of David.

From time to time we will reference commentary from well proven commentators and expositors. In the pages ahead there is not the least effort to endorse or pacify doctrinal positions, nor is there the least effort to make this work an entertaining read. There are portions of David's life that thrill the serious Christian and parts that are disgusting. There are times and seasons in the life of David that are much more interesting than others. The life in general of David is amazingly worthy of all of the study we have given. I believe I have been firmly edified by my feeble effort to write this book and trust those who read it will likewise be blessed and edified.

Introduction

David is not mentioned in the scripture until the last part of the last chapter of Ruth. However, there are 968 verses in the entire Bible in which David is mentioned. This compared to the 784 verses that mention Moses, the 230 verses that mention Abraham, and the 159 verses that mention the Apostle Paul, tends to give us an idea of the significance of David's life. Even Jesus' name is mentioned in fewer verses (942), although God is mentioned in 3894 verses. There are also hundreds of verses that do not mention David by name but refer to him as king. From the sheer fact that David is mentioned and referred to so many times in the scripture, we can see that such a study that we hereby embark on is certainly legitimate.

David was the king that excelled beyond all others in the three Kingdom dimensions God instituted before man was ever created -- worship, word, and warfare. The Lord had even set an angelic leader over these three dimensions. Michael was over warfare; Gabriel was over word, or messages; Lucifer was over worship. David was the passionate worshipper whose zeal for worship has never been matched by mortal man. There was no greater warrior than King David. He never lost a military conflict. David delivered the Word of the Lord with accuracy and messianic insight. His messianic prophecies number more than any of the Major Prophets. So in all three Kingdom dimensions, David excelled above all others. No wonder that David will be the vice king of all the earth during the millennium.

As amazing as his life was, his failures were almost unfathomable. David's failures were indeed paramount and certainly were of a great cost to him and his family. Yet no one exemplifies true repentance and Godly sorrow more than David.

Again, the study of David's life is worthy of a genuine effort to look intently at every verse that mentions his name. We believe in so doing we will clearly see the entire life and legacy of this one whom God said is "a man after mine own heart" (Acts 13:22).

Thus we begin

Ruth

Ruth 4:17, *"And the women her neighbours gave it a name, saying, There is a son born to Naomi; and they called his name Obed: he is the father of Jesse, the father of David."*

Here we find the first mention of David in the declaration of his lineage. These neighbors advised Naomi of the name Obed which means servant. Then the verse tells us who Obed was in connection to David. This shows us clearly that Ruth was written historically to include the lineage of the tribe of Judah that would produce both King David and the coming King of Kings, the Lion of the tribe of Judah, Jesus Christ. So it is that David is mentioned as the result of Obed's birth, just as those sons of David down through generations mention him as a reference point in their past lineage. You will notice in this study that whether you move forward or backwards in Bible history, David is a pivotal point.

Ruth 4:22, *"And Obed begat Jesse, and Jesse begat David."*

The preceding verses give the patriarchs in sets of three. Ruth 4:19-22, *"And Hezron begat Ram, and Ram begat Amminadab, And Amminadab begat Nahshon, and Nahshon begat Salmon, And Salmon begat Boaz, and Boaz begat Obed, And Obed begat Jesse, and Jesse begat David."* There is a very good reason for this. Jews wrote in mathematical order, strongly utilizing the number three. Three is both the number of confirmation and the number of the release. The release of the Abrahamic promise was in Jacob; therefore we often read Abraham, Isaac, and Jacob. Here we see the release of the prophecy concerning the tribe of Judah is in David. Genesis 49:10, *"The sceptre shall not depart from Judah."* Numbering David's lineage in sets of three is a Jewish footnote of the magnitude of power released in David!

I Samuel

1 Samuel 16:13, *"Then Samuel took the horn of oil, and anointed him in the midst of his brethren; and the Spirit of the LORD came upon David from that day forward. So Samuel rose up, and went to Ramah."*

This was the climax of the life of Samuel. He had finally lived to pour the oil on the one God had ordained to be the king of Israel and the forerunner of the King of Kings. Samuel knew that Saul of the tribe of Benjamin was not the right king. Many people believe that the Lord was against Israel's having a king at all. But His real problem was the people wanted a king like other nations. Saul was a king like other nations. Saul was a king of the wrong tribe of Israel. Saul was the Ishmael; David was the Isaac! David was the right king of the tribe of Judah!

Imagine the pain that Samuel endured as he watched the pitiful life of Saul implode and bring Israel to the brink of destruction. But Samuel was allowed to live to anoint the right king.

The scene before this first anointing of David was quite amazing. Samuel was shown by the Lord that one of the sons of Jesse would be anointed king in the place of Saul. However, Samuel was not shown exactly which son of Jesse he would be anointing. When all of the sons of Jesse came to the feast except David, Samuel began to examine them, expecting the Lord to confirm one of them. When none of them was picked by the Lord, Samuel inquired of Jesse if there was yet another. David, the youngest son, was left out of the feast and told to watch the sheep while they ate. However, the one they left out is the one they had to wait for. This very experience speaks of the Christ. The one rejected is the one who will rule over them. The one they left out of the feast was the one they had to wait for because Samuel would not let them eat until David got there.

This is the first mention of the name of the eighth son of Jesse. Eight is the number of new beginnings, and this anointing began the new beginning of Israel that would ultimately lead to the 40 years of bliss in Solomon's reign, which is a type of the millennium.

The Spirit of the Lord came on David, and so is there always an outpouring when the right priest and the right king come together. Samuel was the right priest, and David was the right king.

1 Samuel 16:19, "*Wherefore Saul sent messengers unto Jesse, and said, Send me David thy son, which is with the sheep.*"

Saul was desperate because he was troubled by an evil spirit that the Lord allowed to attack him. In Saul's agony, his advisors tell him he needs someone to play a harp for him and drive the evil spirit away. Saul agrees, and the advisors recommended none other than David to him.

Here are the recommendations and acclamations ascribed to David for the king. I Samuel 16:18, "Then answered one of the servants, and said, Behold, *I have seen a son of Jesse the Bethlehemite, that is cunning in playing, and a mighty valiant man, and a man of war, and prudent in matters, and a comely person, and the LORD is with him.*"

Those who try to read the scripture placing every verse in chronological order have trouble with this verse because of its timing in the text. They seem to forget, ignore, or simply do not know that Jewish writers are not much concerned with writing in chronological order. The reason for this is that their method of study requires the concept of "here a little, there a little" (Isaiah 28:9-10).

These wonderful attributes ascribed could have been in part prophetic, for as yet David had not engaged in war. There are some who place this event after the slaughter of the giant because it was apparent that Saul didn't recognize him at that battle (1 Samuel 17:55). However, Saul was a tormented mad man and could have easily not remembered him.

Perhaps the most important of the list of attributes assigned to David is *"the LORD is with him."* This is a reference to the Spirit of the Lord being upon him. One's gift will make room for him, but that doesn't mean that he can drive demons out. David didn't drive demons away from Saul with his skill, but with his anointing. His skillful playing did not argue with his anointing but enhanced it. Thus they sent for David who was just finishing his seminary of solitude with the sheep, although David would return for a season to the sheep after this assignment.

1 Samuel 16:20, *"And Jesse took an ass laden with bread, and a bottle of wine, and a kid, and sent them by David his son unto Saul."*

David did not come to Saul empty handed. Jesse made sure of this. David here brings a gift to the one he is coming to serve. This shows respect and homage. David probably didn't realize at that time that the anointing in him would cause many kings and ambassadors to bring him gifts and tributes in the same manner.

1 Samuel 16:21, *"And David came to Saul, and stood before him: and he loved him greatly; and he became his armourbearer."*

It is most likely in Saul's condition of heart, that he loved David, not with *agape* love nor with *phileo* love, but with *eros* love. He loved David for what he could do for him. However, the spirit of the Lord on David brings with it a great attraction. Men are attracted to the anointing, and some don't even know why. The anointing also caused David to be promoted speedily.

1 Samuel 16:22, *"And Saul sent to Jesse, saying, Let David, I pray thee, stand before me; for he hath found favour in my sight."*

Saul desperately needs David to assist him because of the demonic attacks, so he asks permission from Jesse to allow David to come. He wants David to stand beside him as an amour bearer. Favor is an attribute from the Spirit of God that rested upon David. Like Joseph, who was promoted everywhere he went, so it is with David. Lightfoot said the anointing of God will cause people to be drawn to you who wish they weren't!

1 Samuel 16:23, *"And it came to pass, when the evil spirit from God was upon Saul, that David took a harp, and played with his hand: so Saul was refreshed, and was well, and the evil spirit departed from him."*

There was a belief among many in those days that music had a mysterious healing influence on mental disorders. There is a belief in these days that mental disorders are often caused by evil spirits. The power of God is able to heal them both. In this case we know that the evil spirit only departed when David addressed it with what was probably worship music he made in the solitude of his shepherding. It is evident that the spirit returned, and that Saul's condition worsened when he took into his spirit another spirit, the spirit of jealousy toward David (1 Samuel 18:9).

1 Samuel 17:12, *"Now David was the son of that Ephrathite of Bethlehemjudah, whose name was Jesse; and he had eight sons: and the man went among men for an old man in the days of Saul."*

Here we find a recap of who David is and the status of his father. His father was a well-established elder of his region of which the prophet Micah is definitely referring to as the place where Messiah will be born in Micah 5:2, *"But thou, Bethlehem Ephratah, though thou be little among the thousands of Judah, yet out of thee shall he come forth unto me that is to be ruler in Israel; whose goings forth have been from of old, from everlasting."* There are two Bethlehem's, as the name itself means House of Bread. Jesse hailed from the Bethlehem that was of the tribe of Judah. The fact that Jesse had eight sons is another reference to his greatness.

1 Samuel 17:14, *"And David was the youngest: and the three eldest followed Saul."*

David is now twice established as the youngest. This is more than information concerning his position in the family; it also establishes the amazement of his achievements. Also in the case of great men used of God, it seems the elder serves the younger. Romans 9:12, *"It was said unto her, The elder shall serve the younger."* This is to bring more glory to the Lord and to humble those who despise authority. The brothers of Joseph had to bow down to their younger brother. David's older brothers later became his subjects! Here we see three of them had already joined the army of Saul.

1 Samuel 17:15, *"But David went and returned from Saul to feed his father's sheep at Bethlehem."*

David had gone home, most likely to feed the sheep, because the enlistment of his three brothers in the army left the family shorthanded. A country at war causes changes and adjustments for everybody. Also it is likely that David remained on call at all times due to the nature of Saul's condition and never knowing when he would fall under attack.

1 Samuel 17:17, *"And Jesse said unto David his son, Take now for thy brethren an ephah of this parched corn, and these ten loaves, and run to the camp to thy brethren";*

David's journey from Saul's court to his home was evidently a different route than to pass along the war zone. After some days with the sheep, David receives the assignment from his father to take supplies to the three of his brothers who were in the army. There seems to be some haste in the matter, though we are not told what, and yet David didn't depart until the next morning. Perhaps the haste part is the anxiety of a father desiring to know the welfare of his sons, as verse 18 says, *"and look how thy brethren fare."*

Little did David know that this errand would change his life forever by bringing him in to instant fame. We never know as we carry out one errand what door might open for the fulfillment of our destiny.

1 Samuel 17:20, *"And David rose up early in the morning, and left the sheep with a keeper, and took, and went, as Jesse had commanded him; and he came to the trench, as the host was going forth to the fight, and shouted for the battle."*

David made his way to the trench of the battle which is translated the place of parked chariots or carriages. The timing of his arrival as the army marched out seems to be providential more than coincidental. The shout for the battle was most likely participated in by David himself. Sometimes wives of the soldiers were allowed to come this close to participate in the battle shout.

1 Samuel 17:22, *"And David left his carriage in the hand of the keeper of the carriage, and ran into the army, and came and saluted his brethren."*

It is seen here that David was allowed to go beyond the trench to salute his brethren and find out how they fared. He most likely told the keeper of the carriages that Jesse had told him to do so and thus was granted permission. All this was for the will of the Lord to be fulfilled in that David had to be positioned to hear the threats of Goliath.

1 Samuel 17:23, *"And as he talked with them, behold, there came up the champion, the Philistine of Gath, Goliath by name, out of the armies of the Philistines, and spake according to the same words: and David heard them."*

Goliath did this day what he had been doing every day for forty days. He challenged the nation of Israel, defied their army and blasphemed their God. Is this not the same noise secularism makes, though ever so subtle?

The one difference on this day was this -- the anointed of God heard it. The giant had been successful in terrifying the army of Israel every day including this day. But David was unafraid, not because of his strength, but he had felt the power of God on his body before. Killing the bear and the lion was just preliminary training for this nearly ten foot giant.

1 Samuel 17:26, *"And David spake to the men that stood by him, saying, What shall be done to the man that killeth this Philistine, and taketh away the reproach from Israel? for who is this uncircumcised Philistine, that he should defy the armies of the living God"?*

David had no doubt heard the announcement of what would be given the man who dispatched this Philistine. When he asks about it, it seems he is clarifying what he heard, "Now what shall be given?"

The thing he says next proved his love for the Lord and the love for his country. These are both important attributes, especially when you are in a country set forth for the glory of the Lord. The reward offered was the trailer, not the driver of motive. However, David had probably seen Saul's daughter while playing the harp at the king's court. As for as his father's house being free, that would mean Jesse and his posterity would pay no taxes or levies.

David gets the only kind of anger you can have without sinning, righteous indignation. This righteous anger however is seen on at least two fronts here. David is angry at the blasphemy coming out of the mouth of the giant. He is also angry at the fear and the complacency in his own ranks. Both are fairly common experiences for warriors who love the Lord and their country.

1 Samuel 17:28, *"And Eliab his eldest brother heard when he spake unto the men; and Eliab's anger was kindled against David, and he said, Why camest thou down hither? and with whom hast thou left those few sheep in the wilderness? I know thy pride, and the naughtiness of thine heart; for thou art come down that thou mightest see the battle."*

Like Joseph's older brothers, Eliab spoke with envy. Favor of God on one's life seems to pull this out of those around them. No better word on this subject than those of Wesley, "See the folly and wickedness of envy! How groundless its jealousies are, how unjust its censures, how unfair its representations? God preserve us from such a spirit!"

1 Samuel 17:29, *"And David said, What have I now done? Is there not a cause"?*

Two questions to the questioner reveal the whole matter. As of yet David had not revealed his intention to take on the Giant, but this kind of zeal can be seen in the eyes of a warrior.

David was asking, "What is wrong with my inquiry" and was probably insinuating, "Shouldn't somebody be asking this question?" Then David asks a question that has been one of the most preached texts in the scripture, "Is there not a cause?"

David's legitimate question was sufficient to prove his objective as well as his objection, his objective in fighting the giant and his objection to their do nothing behavior.

1 Samuel 17:31, *"And when the words were heard which David spake, they rehearsed them before Saul: and he sent for him."*

As soon as David's intention was known to more of the soldiers, they thought Saul needed to know about this. The aspect of the fear in this camp seems to be forgotten in many commentaries and needs at this point to be reiterated. For forty days this 9'9" monster had successfully frightened to the core of their being Saul and his entire army. By now they are more than ready to rid themselves of this fear and shame. This probably seemed like a long shot to them, but it was their only offer from anyone to take on the giant.

Saul sent for David in haste, no doubt because he could only surmise that because he stood a head and shoulders above the other Israeli soldiers, sooner or later he would be drafted to fight the giant.

1 Samuel 17:32, *"And David said to Saul, Let no man's heart fail because of him; thy servant will go and fight with this Philistine."*

David seems to be careful not to take a jab at Saul's cowardice. He speaks in a general term, *"Let no man's heart fail because of him."* David kindly submits to Saul by calling himself his servant, and then assures him that he need not take a further concern for finding someone who would fight the giant. However, when Saul received the news that someone was coming to fight the giant, he no doubt expected a seasoned warrior to appear. Saul's heart most likely sunk when young David appeared for the task.

1 Samuel 17:33, *"And Saul said to David, Thou art not able to go against this Philistine to fight with him: for thou art but a youth, and he a man of war from his youth."*

Saul was absolutely correct in the natural sense of the word. This stripling, as he calls David later, wouldn't have a chance of defeating Goliath in the natural. Saul didn't know how many times he was going to observe the supernatural anointing upon the youth standing in front of him. And then how forgetful was he of the past anointing on this young man as he played the harp and drove back the evil spirits! There are many who prefer to face a physical giant than the hordes of hell. Usually they that fear not the spirit world will fear not the natural.

1 Samuel 17:34, *"And David said unto Saul, Thy servant kept his father's sheep, and there came a lion, and a bear, and took a lamb out of the flock"*:

David most gladly gives Saul the testimony of the power of the Lord coming upon him to defeat the lion and the bear. These were no doubt the first results of the anointing of the Lord after Samuel poured oil upon him. These battles with the lion and the bear proved to provide David with the understanding that the sheep he was watching were to be protected by the anointing. Thus David perceived that the sheep of God, Israel, would likewise be protected by the same anointing. Like the lion and bear to his sheep was Goliath to the Lord's sheep. He knew the anointing was upon him and assured Saul it was a done deal, but did so carefully, giving glory to the Lord.

1 Samuel 17:37, *"David said moreover, The LORD that delivered me out of the paw of the lion, and out of the paw of the bear, he will deliver me out of the hand of this Philistine. And Saul said unto David, Go, and the LORD be with thee."*

As David's testimony of the power of God upon his life persuaded Saul to permit him to go and fight the giant, so should our testimony persuade those around us of the overcoming power of God. Notwithstanding, Saul was greatly relieved that someone would finally take the giant on. Saul at least blessed him and said, *"The LORD be with thee."*

1 Samuel 17:38, *"And Saul armed David with his armour, and he put an helmet of brass upon his head; also he armed him with a coat of mail."*

One must remember that Saul was by far the largest man in Israel. 1 Samuel 10:23b, *"he was higher than any of the people from his shoulders and upward."* Now imagine his armor on the young and ruddy David. Not only was it a misfit for David, but it was an insult to the anointing David trusted in to defeat Goliath. In David we see absolutely no hint of either depending upon his own strength or taking the least bit of glory for the victory. The one who is proud of his own strength will most certainly attempt to take the glory; therefore, that one can be trusted with very little results.

1 Samuel 17:39, *"And David girded his sword upon his armour, and he assayed to go; for he had not proved it. And David said unto Saul, I cannot go with these; for I have not proved them. And David put them off him."*

This is a unique situation for David. In honor of the king, he put it on. David had no skill with that kind of machinery and could hardly move. Yet, his main point is that he had not proved the equipment. Here David seems to be referring to the battle with the lion and the bear, and the fact that the weapons he used there were proven. It is better to enter into warfare with that which we know will work. Intense warfare is no time to learn to use new equipment.

Here we also see that though David trusted in the supernatural, it gave him no license to throw away common sense. Probably Saul was shamed somewhat because young David, instead of a seasoned warrior, answered the challenge of Goliath. If David was killed it would probably be even worse embarrassment on both Saul and the men of war.

1 Samuel 17:41, *"And the Philistine came on and drew near unto David; and the man that bare the shield went before him."*

After David had rid himself of the cumbersome and unproven armor of Saul, he pressed toward Goliath. David then stopped at the brook and chose five smooth stones for his sling. Many theologians have used the number five to prove a type or shadow of many things. David only used one stone to dispatch Goliath, so for what were the other four smooth stones? Some say David picked up a stone for the four brothers of Goliath (2 Samuel 21:16-22). This does seem logical, especially in the anointing David was operating. He most likely had heard of the four brothers of Goliath by listening to all of the talk while he was trying on armor.

Now at a certain point David stopped, and the giant moved forward. In so doing was saying, "I accept the challenge." As the Philistine custom was for a great warrior, he had an armor bearer going before him.

1 Samuel 17:42, *"And when the Philistine looked about, and saw David, he disdained him: for he was but a youth, and ruddy, and of a fair countenance."*

As soon as he was close enough to realize that David was not a runner or an ill equipped armor bearer, he was insulted. That is how ridiculous it looked in the natural. Here stands a nine foot, nine inch man who is a seasoned warrior, a warrior that the bravest of Israel feared. Now a ruddy fair complexioned kid with no armor, carrying nothing but a sling and a few rocks (which Goliath probably couldn't see) is his challenger.

1 Samuel 17:43, *"And the Philistine said unto David, Am I a dog, that thou comest to me with staves? And the Philistine cursed David by his gods."*

The diabolical discourse between two champions was a Middle East custom, especially Arab. Goliath is thoroughly insulted and asked if he was going to fight with him with a stick as he would a dog. This would indicate that David had a staff with him. Commentators usually don't mention this, but either Goliath was making mention of his staff or simply using phrases that were a part of his proverbial trash talk.

Goliath, like the pagan idolatrous heathen he was, used his gods to curse David. Of course this was to no avail, due to the fact that the gods of the Philistines were no gods. Even if Goliath could invoke the power of sorcery, witchcraft, or demonic forces, they are no match for the anointing on David.

1 Samuel 17:44, *"And the Philistine said to David, Come to me, and I will give thy flesh unto the fowls of the air, and to the beasts of the field."*

Emboldened by his apparent favorable odds, the giant encourages David to keep on coming. How foolish are those who trust in the arm of the flesh! How foolish to come to a spiritual fight with a physical sword.

1 Samuel 17:45, *"Then said David to the Philistine, Thou comest to me with a sword, and with a spear, and with a shield: but I come to thee in the name of the LORD of hosts, the God of the armies of Israel, whom thou hast defied."*

David does not engage in the customary war of words before the champions begin their contest. David speaks forth the prophetic words that are hung around the work of faith in his heart. Faith in God must speak without intimidation, and so it did.

David reminds Goliath of his equipment and how flimsy it is compared to the name of the God of Israel. He was saying to the giant, "I am representing the very God of Israel that you have offended, and your equipment is useless before the One I serve." Then he informs Goliath that not only is he about to lose his head, but the entire army of the Philistines is going to provide a great feast to the buzzards and the wild animals (verse 46).

David lays all of his zeal and purpose on vengeance for the name of the Lord God of Israel. Out of this position always come both the prophetic words he spoke and the sure victory. David was a worshipper, and in so being he knew two things: 1) God is very pleased with and desires to be glorified by those He created. 2) He has the opportunity to see many others give Him the glory He deserves, both His own and the Philistines.

David knew how to trust in God in the battle. If you were an enemy of God, you were an enemy of David. Great spiritual warriors must learn to ride upon the zeal of an indignant God who is the God of vengeance on His enemies.

David knew not to fear fleshly enemies. Later in another battle with Goliath's brothers, his words are recorded in Psalms 56:4, *"I will not fear what flesh can do unto me."* Generations later, his posterity practiced the same faith and had the same results. Hezekiah said concerning his enemies in 2 Chronicles 32:8, *"With him is an arm of flesh; but with us is the LORD our God to help us, and to fight our battles."* May the legacy of David the mighty warrior, the passionate worshipper, and lover of the Word live on forever!

1 Samuel 17:48, *"And it came to pass, when the Philistine arose, and came and drew nigh to meet David, that David hasted, and ran toward the army to meet the Philistine."*

The posturing and the preliminaries are now done and the Philistine begins to move toward David. The giant was accustomed to most of his enemies at this point either standing still in dread or turning and running in fear. David's response was quite different. So far from fear, he runs toward the whole army of the Philistines, and especially Goliath. David's action here is the ultimate picture of faith, courage, and an abiding resolve, accompanied by the absolute assurance of victory. Such attributes are needed in our own hearts as we seek to advance the Kingdom of God for His glory.

1 Samuel 17:49, *"And David put his hand in his bag, and took thence a stone, and slang it, and smote the Philistine in his forehead, that the stone sunk into his forehead; and he fell upon his face to the earth."*

David, like many young men in the Mid-East, was highly skilled in the use of the sling. However, the skill of David with his sling kissed the power and destiny of God for his life. Thus the smooth stone found its mark in the hard forehead of the blasphemer, and he fell on his face. Never again would Goliath speak against Israel or Israel's God. David not only brought the Lord much glory but stopped the mouth of the blasphemer, and a warrior knows these two cannot be separated.

After a study of the Philistine armor of that day, one would wonder if the pride of the Giant caused him to lift his helmet somewhat. If not, it would mean that God's power on David allowed him to sling the stone with enough velocity to go through his armor and sink in the forehead!

1 Samuel 17:50, *"So David prevailed over the Philistine with a sling and with a stone, and smote the Philistine, and slew him; but there was no sword in the hand of David."*

David prevailed, and always will, over the uncircumcised and the infidels. The type of David is a remnant after the heart of God, and the type of the giant is the proud, arrogant, and blasphemous Christ rejecter. The strength of Goliath was no match for the Sweet Psalmist of Israel who was walking in the anointing of God. Even to this present hour when wickedness is flexing its arm, parading its debauchery on the streets, and challenging the Davids of this hour, David will prevail. Not with the conventional weaponry, for it is not by power or might, but by the Spirit of the Lord resting on His people.

1 Samuel 17:51, *"Therefore David ran, and stood upon the Philistine, and took his sword, and drew it out of the sheath thereof, and slew him, and cut off his head therewith. And when the Philistines saw their champion was dead, they fled."*

The scripture doesn't say David was small, but refers several times to his youth. Here it appears he could not have been too small.

Some say David ran to cut off Goliath's head because he was only stunned by the stone. However, there is ample evidence in the preceding verses that Goliath was dead. 1) *The stone sunk into his forehead (*verse 49). 2) He was smitten and slain before David cut off his head (verse 50). Both of these terms are most used for those who are killed. 3) It was common to behead the enemy after killing them, especially those who were of the highest profile.

David's haste was that of the victor's excitement and anxiety to prove as he had said in his prophecy in 1 Samuel 17:46b, *"that all the earth may know that there is a God in Israel."*

It was Goliath's own sword that took his head and his own blasphemies that sealed his doom. Those who once had great confidence in the giant now had great fear at his death. So it is with all misplaced faith. Their rock was slain, never to rise except to be judged and thrown in the lake of fire. Our Rock was slain only to rise with the keys of death and hell jingling from His side! The Philistines fled in panic at the death of their champion, but the Christian rejoices in the death of their Champion. Our Champion's death, burial, and resurrection brought life and abundant life to all who receive Him (John 1:12).

1 Samuel 17:54, *"And David took the head of the Philistine, and brought it to Jerusalem; but he put his armour in his tent."*

Upon the fleeing of the Philistines the Israelites routed their enemies. Just as fear and unbelief had adversely affected the whole army of Israel, now the faith and valor of David had given them the shout of victory. They rightly took the steps to dismantle the Philistines.

Upon the finishing of the battle, David took the head of Goliath to Jerusalem, but the armor became his for the wars ahead. The sword of Goliath was at some point and time dedicated as a memorial offering to the Lord because we find it later in the headquarters of the priesthood at Nob (1 Samuel 21:9).

1 Samuel 17:55, "*And when Saul saw David go forth against the Philistine, he said unto Abner, the captain of the host, Abner, whose son is this youth? And Abner said, As thy soul liveth, O king, I cannot tell.*"

This verse does not follow the preceding verse in chronological order but begins a recap of the events of the war and brings forth an interesting and controversial point. Saul did not recognize David; neither did Abner, the captain of the host.

Thus the controversy as to how this could be. Commentators who are quick to question the scripture will at once say this proves there is a mix up in the chronological structure of the verses concerning David's service in the court of Saul with his harp. There is no need for the controversy or question, considering these points. 1) Abner said, "*I cannot tell.*" Abner would not necessarily have ever met David, as Abner's job was not in the court but in the field. 2) It had now been a length of time since David was employed in the court with his harp. At David's youthful age, it is not uncommon for there to be a great spurt of height growth. 3) The anointing for this task could have very possibly changed his countenance considerably. 4) Saul's mental condition could have affected his ability to recognize David. 5) God could have holdened the eyes of Saul and others for the purpose of actually getting him into the battlefield. If Saul had recognized David as the one God used to drive back the demons in his most desperate time, he may have decided not to take the chance on his being destroyed.

1 Samuel 17:57, "*And as David returned from the slaughter of the Philistine, Abner took him, and brought him before Saul with the head of the Philistine in his hand.*"

This amazing day will hereafter be celebrated by everyone who hears of it. The young untrained shepherd with a sling in his hand has defeated the giant and led the nation of Israel into total victory over the Philistines! Now Abner, the captain of the host of Israel, brings David before the king with the head of Goliath in his hand. Abner shows no jealousy, but rather great appreciation for David. Abner also knew that the king was inquiring of his identity earlier.

1 Samuel 17:58, "*And Saul said to him, Whose son art thou, thou young man? And David answered, I am the son of thy servant Jesse the Bethlehemite.*"

Most likely Saul now recognizes David, as he asks for his father's name instead of David's name. Now Jesse, David's father, had more sons in Saul's army, but none this young, and the attire of David would show that he was not an enlisted man.

Bedford has David's age at twenty-two at this time. However, he seems to have failed to consider the well-established draft age of the Israeli men to be twenty. Numbers 1:3, "*From twenty years old and upward, all that are able to go forth to war in Israel*": Many other verses verify twenty as the official draft age for Israeli men. Therefore, David had to be visibly younger than the draft age, for Saul has now called him a young man. Most likely David is eighteen years old at the most.

David has identified himself now, but this was not the sum of their conversation, as we see by the first verse of the following chapter. However this is that which is needful to be recorded.

1 Samuel 18:1, *"And it came to pass, when he made an end of speaking unto Saul, that the soul of Jonathan was knit with the soul of David, and Jonathan loved him as his own soul."*

There seems to be an abruptness to the immediate love that David and Jonathon found for each other. In all of the scripture there is not such an example of this level of friendship. Thus, the sodomites have tried to distort the verses describing their relationship with the agenda of justifying their wicked homosexuality. Their efforts are futile here, as they are throughout the verses. Sodomites will not convince one Biblicist of their purported sanction of God concerning their sin. Not to mention the total absurdity of accusing David of all people, of being a homosexual.

In this verse we have mention of Jonathan's love for David, but later David relates in his eulogy for Jonathan, as recorded in 2 Samuel 1:26, *"I am distressed for thee, my brother Jonathan: very pleasant hast thou been unto me: thy love to me was wonderful, passing the love of women."* This proves their love was a mutual love, not just one sided or based on Jonathan's admiration of David's exalted position after his victory over the giant.

1 Samuel 18:3, *"Then Jonathan and David made a covenant, because he loved him as his own soul."*

David was not permitted to go back to his shepherding. The king drafted him in a very strong fashion, thus making the possibility of Jonathan and David's becoming even closer in their relationship. The strong love they had between them resulted in a covenant. True love has no fear of commitment. True commitment has no real merit outside of love. Such covenants of brotherhood are fairly common in the Mid-East. Here we find no certain ceremony. Perhaps there was none, but most likely there was some sort of outward symbolism performed, such as the generous transfer of clothing and weaponry Jonathan enacted. Possibly the Mid-East loyalty Covenant of Salt was utilized. However this loyalty covenant is not to be confused with the Levitical Covenant of Salt found three times in the Bible.

1 Samuel 18:4, *"And Jonathan stripped himself of the robe that was upon him, and gave it to David, and his garments, even to his sword, and to his bow, and to his girdle."*

While this doesn't appear ceremonial, it does seem to be a spontaneous act of love and affection between the two princes. Jonathan not only gives David his royal apparel but also his royal weaponry. Prophetically Jonathan saw David as a warrior prince and his equal. Because of this amazing love, Jonathan never showed the least bit of jealousy or wavering toward David, even though it cost Jonathan his father's blessing.

In the Mid-East at that time it was considered a great honor to have upon your back that which was worn by a king or his heir. Remember Haman's dreadful assignment of placing the king's apparel on his sworn enemy Mordecai because the king wanted to honor him (Esther 6:8).

1 Samuel 18:5, *"And David went out whithersoever Saul sent him, and behaved himself wisely: and Saul set him over the men of war, and he was accepted in the sight of all the people, and also in the sight of Saul's servants."*

The favor of the Lord rested abundantly upon David. His victory over the giant elevated him quickly in not only the military, but also in Saul's immediate cabinet. The anointing of God accomplished this ability to walk wisely. The prophecy said that the anointing rested upon him from the day he was anointed forward. We find this in 1 Samuel 16:13, *"Then Samuel took the horn of oil, and anointed him in the midst of his brethren; and the Spirit of the LORD came upon David from that day forward."* The anointing that gave him the victory over the giant also enabled him to walk wisely in and out of the court.

Some have the mentality that the anointing is only for the intense moment of battle, but that is not so. The anointing is abiding and becomes more intense as each episode of life may demand. Even the day to day activities are affected by true anointing.

1 Samuel 18:6, *"And it came to pass as they came, when David was returned from the slaughter of the Philistine, that the women came out of all cities of Israel, singing and dancing, to meet king Saul, with tabrets, with joy, and with instruments of musick."*

This verse is not saying that David is now returning from the slaughter of the giant, though I have never read a commentary on this verse that didn't say so. The verse is saying *"as they came, when David was returned from the slaughter of the Philistine,"* meaning they came this day in the same manner as they came the day of the slaughter of the giant. It was the same victorious home coming as the day the Philistines were defeated after the slaughter of Goliath. 1) Would David have been promoted as it speaks of in the preceding verse if Saul had developed the jealousy right after the battle with the giant? 2) How could there have been time for him to go wherever Saul sent him, as it speaks of in the preceding verse, if this is referring to the return of the slaughter of the giant? 3) How could the people have observed his wise behavior coming in and out if this verse is referring to the return from the slaughter of the giant?

Evidently it was a custom among the Jewish women to sing the praises of God in the streets when victory was celebrated, as in Exodus 15:20, *"And Miriam the prophetess, the sister of Aaron, took a timbrel in her hand; and all the women went out after her with timbrels and with dances."* These Hebrew women were merely paying tribute to the gallantry of Saul the king, David his new captain, and the men under them.

1 Samuel 18:7, *"And the women answered one another as they played, and said, Saul hath slain his thousands, and David his ten thousands."*

These women in their excitement and joy committed a great indiscretion. They exalted the servant higher than the king. Yet they were most likely innocent in motive on at least two accounts. 1) They would have expected Saul and David's relationship to be more of a father-son order. What true father doesn't desire that his son do better than he himself has done? 2) David was wearing the clothing of Saul's son Jonathan. This indicated to the people that David's exploits were to be honored, not only as a warrior, but as a part of the family royal.

1 Samuel 18:8, *"And Saul was very wroth, and the saying displeased him; and he said, They have ascribed unto David ten thousands, and to me they have ascribed but thousands: and what can he have more but the kingdom"?*

Anger and wrath will sooner or later manifest from the heart where fear and jealousy live. In this case Saul's fit was most likely met with shock as the people would have expected him to rejoice with them.

"And what can he have more but the kingdom?" Here is the speech of fear and insecurity. Deep in Saul's gut was the overwhelming fear that David would be the king that would replace him. Jonathan knew it by the prophetic voice of God, while Saul knew it by the torment of fear and jealousy.

1 Samuel 18:9, *"And Saul eyed David from that day and forward."*

From this day Saul, was consumed with jealousy. The green-eyed monster he harbored opened the door for the evil spirit to come again and torment him the very next day. Proverbs 27:4, *"Wrath is cruel, and anger is outrageous; but who is able to stand before envy?"* And the evident answer is, no one can.

1 Samuel 18:10, *"And it came to pass on the morrow, that the evil spirit from God came upon Saul, and he prophesied in the midst of the house: and David played with his hand, as at other times: and there was a javelin in Saul's hand."*

This verse involves two great controversies. 1) Does God send an evil spirit? 2) How does Saul prophesy through an evil spirit? First, Saul is actually attacked by an evil spirit from God. However the rendering here is an evil spirit permitted by God. Otherwise there would be a conflict with several other verses, namely James 1:13, *"Let no man say when he is tempted, I am tempted of God: for God cannot be tempted with evil, neither tempteth he any man."* Secondly, Saul was not prophesying from the Lord, but this rendering is referring to his antics and apparent loss of control, like the verse that compares drunkenness with spiritual fullness (Ephesians 5:18).

Lightfoot says that Saul was actually possessed by an evil spirit, and that through it he spoke some sort of demoniac predictions. This is most likely correct, as his state of mind is much worse now than before. This we know by the fact that David's harp delivered Saul before but now seems to only aggravate the matter. The spirit that had oppressed Saul before now controlled him, so much that it performed the false prophetic utterances, and then tried to use Saul to kill David.

1 Samuel 18:11, *"And Saul cast the javelin; for he said, I will smite David even to the wall with it. And David avoided out of his presence twice."*

Saul made several attempts to kill David, to no avail. Here are two instances. Some believe this is referring to the attempt recorded in 1 Samuel 19:10 as well as here. It is more reasonable that this day contains two attempts, and the one recorded in 1 Samuel 19:10 is the third attempt, confirming that David had to flee. In each case it is apparent that David was divinely protected from the demonized Saul. Oh, the madness of the soul filled with jealousy and empowered by the agents of hell!

1 Samuel 18:12, *"And Saul was afraid of David, because the LORD was with him, and was departed from Saul."*

Saul was now convinced of the power of the anointing on David's life that even protected him from his powerful use of the javelin. This is a sick type fear that comes with the realization of sure doom, and Saul's words prove it. Saul is a type of religion, and David is a type of the remnant. Even as religion persecutes the remnant, it knows that God's anointing rests upon it. Throughout history, religion has always persecuted the remnant, even while it fears it. The night Samuel experienced the theophany in 1 Samuel 3:10, Eli knew he was finished and the Lord was resting upon Samuel. Once Caiaphas saw the real High Priest, John the Baptist, he feared him, even while he persecuted him with a jealous hatred.

1 Samuel 18:14, *"And David behaved himself wisely in all his ways; and the LORD was with him."*

Saul moved David out of his immediate cabinet and away from the king's court, where everyone, including his own son, seemed to be smitten with admiration for him. This might have eased the horrible spirit of envy, but it only set David in a place where he would be even more proven and respected. So as David went out to war, he also came back, which is a reference to a victory. He behaved himself wisely in every way, and this he also accomplished by the good hand of God which was upon him.

One might take notice of the humility David operated in and also the unfeigned loyalty he expressed for Saul, who deserved not an ounce of it. Perhaps David pitied the sorry spiritual state of Saul and blamed his behavior toward him on the demon itself. Whatever the case, there is no instance we find in all of the verses that would indicate any vengeance in David's heart for Saul.

1 Samuel 18:16, *"But all Israel and Judah loved David, because he went out and came in before them."*

David's wise behavior and his coming in and out in successful military campaigns was enough to cause the jealousy of Saul to increase, as well as his fear of David. However, the fact that all of Israel and Judah loved him so much was even worse for Saul. How much of the general population knew that Saul had attempted to kill David we don't know. At this point Saul would have a difficult time disposing of David without losing his people. He was like John the Baptist, Jesus, and Paul, whose persecutors feared the people, because with the same degree they hated them, the people loved them and regarded them highly. Luke 22:2, *"And the chief priests and scribes sought how they might kill him; for they feared the people."*

Thus Saul has another diabolical plan to rid himself of David.

1 Samuel 18:17, *"And Saul said to David, Behold my elder daughter Merab, her will I give thee to wife: only be thou valiant for me, and fight the LORD'S battles. For Saul said, Let not mine hand be upon him, but let the hand of the Philistines be upon him."*

Saul's wicked plan shows the insanity of jealousy. He gives his own daughter to David, even while his plans will make her a widow at a young age. Caring nothing for her, he encourages David to step up his efforts against the Philistines in hopes that they will kill him so he won't have to. This would get rid of David and allow him to remain a great hero in the sight of the people.

1 Samuel 18:18, *"And David said unto Saul, Who am I? and what is my life, or my father's family in Israel, that I should be son in law to the king"?*

Oh the humility and total admiration David expresses for Saul. After he tried twice to kill him? Surely this also is a manifestation of the anointing and power of God upon his life. One commentator said David was young and stupid for falling for such flattery. How wrong! The flattery of guile from Saul's lips actually failed to puff David up or cause him to think of himself as some great one. Just as well the admiration of all of Israel failed to smite David with pride and haughtiness.

1 Samuel 18:19, *"But it came to pass at the time when Merab Saul's daughter should have been given to David, that she was given unto Adriel the Meholathite to wife."*

Like Laban did to Jacob, Saul deceived David and gave his daughter to another. Also like Laban, Saul changed the wages for David's hand in marriage and made a new arrangement with David for the next daughter. This was a horrible affront to David. We do not know how David handled the matter, but there is no recorded animosity or vengeance from David. There did not seem to be an outrage from the people or Jonathan, although this would have been much more a known thing among the people of Israel.

1 Samuel 18:20, *"And Michal Saul's daughter loved David: and they told Saul, and the thing pleased him."*

No doubt some time had elapsed from the time of the Saul performed jilt. However, it seemed a very convenient thing for Saul that Michal would now love David because Saul now could make another attempt at getting David killed.

1 Samuel 18:21, *"And Saul said, I will give him her, that she may be a snare to him, and that the hand of the Philistines may be against him. Wherefore Saul said to David, Thou shalt this day be my son in law in the one of the twain."*

Saul immediately launches his plan to get David killed by making the dowry such that he would surely be killed. This is how Michal was to be a snare unto him. From this statement we can see that Saul has premeditated and schemed the death of David very carefully. Oh the hatred lying latent in a heart of jealousy!

Saul thinks it necessary to assure David that this time he would receive his bride and become the king's son in law. Saul did not want David to shy from the assignment that Saul was hoping would mean his death. The term *"be my son in law in the one of the twain"* refers to the high regard the Jews have for betrothal, which will be transferred instead of renewed, because David was betrothed to Merab but will marry Michal.

1 Samuel 18:22, *"And Saul commanded his servants, saying, Commune with David secretly, and say, Behold, the king hath delight in thee, and all his servants love thee: now therefore be the king's son in law."*

Saul now uses his position to employ his servants in his efforts to murder David. He trained his servants to utilize his flattery by instructing them to tell David how much the king, as well as his whole cabinet, delighted in him. This effort was to insure that David would not back out because of his last affront.

It is notable that when David backslid in the matter of Bathsheba, he used his servants to carry out the death of Uriah, her husband. He occasioned Uriah's death, just as Saul attempted his death. David's attempt was to cover his fall to lust and adultery, while Saul's was made from fear and jealousy. Saul seemed to be sorry for his treatment on two occasions but never really came to full repentance. David's repentance was so deep and complete that it has become the very model for contrition and Godly sorrow (Psalms 51).

1 Samuel 18:23, *"And Saul's servants spake those words in the ears of David. And David said, Seemeth it to you a light thing to be a king's son in law, seeing that I am a poor man, and lightly esteemed"?*

This second attempt at feigned flattery from the king to David also failed. David was overwhelmed at the opportunity to be the king's son in law, but here he apparently is concerned about the price of the dowry. He would have expected that the higher the class, the more he would have to pay. He tells them that he is a poor man and not royalty. This was his honest thinking on the matter and it was reasonable. However, Saul didn't want money for the dowry, but David's very life.

1 Samuel 18:24, *"And the servants of Saul told him, saying, On this manner spake David."*

The servants of Saul reported to him that David would be honored to be the king's son in law but was not in a financial condition to be so. This was great tidings to Saul for now he knew that he could proceed in his plan to get David killed in battle. Saul was consumed with getting rid of the one whom he feared and whom he envied.

1 Samuel 18:25, *And Saul said, Thus shall ye say to David, The king desireth not any dowry, but an hundred foreskins of the Philistines, to be avenged of the king's enemies. But Saul thought to make David fall by the hand of the Philistines."*

Saul instructed his servants to tell David not to worry about the dowry, but one hundred foreskins of the Philistines would be sufficient and at the same time destroy more of his enemies. This was very shrewd of Saul by not asking for their heads as it was accustomed. All of his enemies had heads but only the non-Jews had foreskins! Saul also knew that the Philistines in general would be more enraged to discover that David had performed a Jewish circumcision on their fallen soldiers. Saul also knew that such an affront to the Philistines would elevate David to be their number one most wanted.

1 Samuel 18:26, *"And when his servants told David these words, it pleased David well to be the king's son in law: and the days were not expired."*

Saul was no doubt delighted to hear that David was excited about becoming his son in law. He probably felt sure at this point that his diabolical scheme would work. The phrase *"and the days were not expired"* from the Hebrew refers to the ample amount of time allotted for David to gather the dowry required. Yet as we see from the following verse, the connotation here is beyond that, because the phrase also indicates that David is excited, accepts the challenge, and will get right on and have it done before the time expires.

1 Samuel 18:27, *"Wherefore David arose and went, he and his men, and slew of the Philistines two hundred men; and David brought their foreskins, and they gave them in full tale to the king, that he might be the king's son in law. And Saul gave him Michal his daughter to wife."*

Immediately David and his men go hunting for Philistines. He slays two hundred instead of one hundred. He has them all circumcised and brings the full amount to Saul. The heart of Saul probably sank down when he saw the men coming back from this crusade with the dowry doubled and David leading the way. His plan didn't work, and Saul knew exactly why.

1 Samuel 18:28, *"And Saul saw and knew that the LORD was with David, and that Michal Saul's daughter loved him."*

Saul realized he had lost on two accounts: 1) This third unsuccessful attempt to rid himself of David had convinced him that the supernatural protection of God was resting upon David. 2) His daughter now loves the one he hates.

1 Samuel 18:29, *"And Saul was yet the more afraid of David; and Saul became David's enemy continually."*

The anointing on one's life will torment those who oppose them. Here Saul is dismantled by the favor of God on David, without David lifting a finger against him. Notice Saul became David's enemy, but never was Saul the enemy of David. The historicity of David reveals clearly what happened to David's enemies. The enemies of God were the enemies of David, not the anointed of God, which David considered Saul to be. This is why David spared Saul's life so passionately. 1 Samuel 24:10b, *"and some bade me kill thee: but mine eye spared thee; and I said, I will not put forth mine hand against my lord; for he is the LORD'S anointed."* Herein is a great standard for church folks!

1 Samuel 18:30, *"Then the princes of the Philistines went forth: and it came to pass, after they went forth, that David behaved himself more wisely than all the servants of Saul; so that his name was much set by."*

The Philistines went to war against Israel, probably enraged by the acts of David. At the first of their going forth, Saul might have had a little glimmer of hope that perhaps they would kill David. If so, it was short lived, for the God given military skill of David prevailed greatly so that all of the servants of Saul were amazed. David's fame and notoriety grew even more than ever.

1 Samuel 19:1, *"And Saul spake to Jonathan his son, and to all his servants, that they should kill David."*

Saul now orders the death of David. The last military campaign of David convinced Saul to do so. We recall the miracle Jesus performed in raising Lazarus convinced the Jews that they would have to kill Jesus to stop such a move. John 11:48, *"If we let him thus alone, all men will believe on him: and the Romans shall come and take away both our place and nation."* The only thing more insane than jealousy is religious anger.

1 Samuel 19:2, *"But Jonathan Saul's son delighted much in David: and Jonathan told David, saying, Saul my father seeketh to kill thee: now therefore, I pray thee, take heed to thyself until the morning, and abide in a secret place, and hide thyself"*:

Jonathan comes to the aid of David to save his life rather than obey his father Saul and take his life. Jonathan knows now that the matter is quite urgent if he is to succeed in delivering David from his father's madness. This is true love that Jonathan has, not just an admiration for David's powerful exploits. Here Jonathan becomes an intercessor as well as a friend. An intercessor will stand in the gap for the one they intercede for. Out of that intercession comes forth the instruction that will save David's life; then Jonathon proceeds to speak to his father on behalf of his friend.

1 Samuel 19:4, *"And Jonathan spake good of David unto Saul his father, and said unto him, Let not the king sin against his servant, against David; because he hath not sinned against thee, and because his works have been to thee-ward very good":*

The points Jonathan makes in his intercession for David are perfectly positioned in reasonability. 1) You will sin if you shed innocent blood. 2) David has never tried to hurt you or do one thing against you. 3) David has been a faithful servant to you in good works. 4) He risked his life to deliver the very nation that you are king over. 5) David's victory brought the people of Israel, including you, from depression and fear to rejoicing. 6) What good reason do you have to kill David?

The good intercession of Jonathan delivered David temporarily.

1 Samuel 19:5, *"For he did put his life in his hand, and slew the Philistine, and the LORD wrought a great salvation for all Israel: thou sawest it, and didst rejoice: wherefore then wilt thou sin against innocent blood, to slay David without a cause"?*

Though Jonathan in his great intercessional effort for his friend David is telling Saul that David risked his life, it is doubtful that David ever felt that he did. It seems from his utterance that he was very sure of the results of his battle with Goliath.

1 Samuel 19:7, *"And Jonathan called David, and Jonathan shewed him all those things. And Jonathan brought David to Saul, and he was in his presence, as in times past."*

This was probably a most jubilant time for Jonathan to be able to go get his friend and bring him back to the court of the king. David never forgot this day, and later when he was king of Israel, he brought Mephibosheth, the son of Jonathan, to the king's table. 2 Samuel 9:3, *"And the king said, Is there not yet any of the house of Saul, that I may shew the kindness of God unto him? And Ziba said unto the king, Jonathan hath yet a son, which is lame on his feet."* David was restored to the king's table and most likely all of his admirers were appeased, but only for a very brief time. The torment of jealousy does never rest long in whose heart it has a stronghold.

1 Samuel 19:8, *"And there was war again: and David went out, and fought with the Philistines, and slew them with a great slaughter; and they fled from him."*

The war with the Philistines begin to rage again, and of course David was the go to man. And once again the Lord gave David a powerful victory over his enemies. Now Saul would have been fine with David at his table as long as David didn't do anything great. This is exactly what religion is to the remnant. No need for religion to be jealous if it can persuade the remnant to be still. The problem is that you can't be remnant and remain still or quiet. David is a warrior, and as long as there is a war, he will be on the front lines. And as long as the Davids win wars, and they will, they will infuriate the Sauls.

1 Samuel 19:9, *"And the evil spirit from the LORD was upon Saul, as he sat in his house with his javelin in his hand: and David played with his hand."*

David was very confident in the protection of God upon his life. Or perhaps, he had confidence in the ability of the anointing to disarm the evil spirit; otherwise, he would be quite silly to go in and play his harp again for Saul, who is holding a javelin in his hand. After all, Saul had already thrown it at him twice. Perhaps he considered Saul to have gone deeper into repentance at Jonathan's intercession than he actually did. Lovers of mercy always show mercy and are the first to give someone a second chance.

1 Samuel 19:10, *"And Saul sought to smite David even to the wall with the javelin; but he slipped away out of Saul's presence, and he smote the javelin into the wall: and David fled, and escaped that night."*

Once again Saul tries to kill David with the javelin, and once again the Lord spared his life. David slipped away just in time as the javelin pierced the wall. David was no doubt watching closely because of his last experience with the javelin. The devil driving Saul wanted to destroy the seed of the tribe of Judah, for he knew the scepter was in the tribe of Judah from which would come the One that would bruise his head. David fled and escaped to his house, probably thinking the fit would pass from Saul.

1 Samuel 19:11, *"Saul also sent messengers unto David's house, to watch him, and to slay him in the morning: and Michal David's wife told him, saying, If thou save not thy life to night, to morrow thou shalt be slain."*

The diabolical craze Saul was in made him relentless. He directed his servant to set a watch on David's house and kill him in the morning, probably so as not to take a chance on his daughter's getting hurt in the episode.

This is a clear display of the absolute void of reasoning, demon-driven Saul to destroy David. Had he not seen enough of the power of the Lord on David to know that the anointing of God that took down the bear, the lion, and the giant could also destroy his men or himself? Nevertheless, Michal entreated David to flee by telling him if he didn't he would surely be slain.

1 Samuel 19:12, *"So Michal let David down through a window: and he went, and fled, and escaped."*

Two of the most choice of God's servants were let down through a window. Michal and Jonathan her brother had no doubt talked of the need to risk their own lives in order to save David. Certainly Michal goes the limit. David not only gets away from Saul, but Michal devised a plan to allow David some time to put a distance between his killers and himself. She builds a resemblance of a man lying in the bed to feign an illness had struck David.

1 Samuel 19:14, *"And when Saul sent messengers to take David, she said, He is sick."*

The plan of Michal worked. The messengers went back to Saul to report the matter after they were told he was sick. This allowed David even more time to get away, for the messengers were sent back to Saul, but Saul sends them back to get what he thought was David lying in the bed. By this time the agile David was very gone. The deceptive plan of Michal's doesn't mean that God sanctions deception as an activity in our lives. Some have used this, and the matter with Rahab, to declare it is all right to lie in order to achieve the safety of someone the Lord intends to use. However the Bible is simply reporting the method Michal and Rahab used to deliver the spies and King David. In both cases there would have been deliverance regardless.

1 Samuel 19:15, *"And Saul sent the messengers again to see David, saying, Bring him up to me in the bed, that I may slay him."*

Here is the savagery of a satanic driven mind. Bring him, bed and all. Saul was desperate to kill David, just as the spirit of antichrist is always desperate to destroy the Messianic seed. How could Saul, who at one time was anointed of God to fight the Amorites (1 Samuel 11:6) fall to such a sad state?

When the messengers arrive, they find that what they thought to be a sick man was in fact a dummy. Saul confronts Michal and asks her why she would conspire against him and deceive him. She deceives him yet again and tells him that David threatened to kill her if she didn't do what she did.

1 Samuel 19:18, *"So David fled, and escaped, and came to Samuel to Ramah, and told him all that Saul had done to him. And he and Samuel went and dwelt in Naioth."*

David fled for a spiritual refuge with Samuel. He needed that one who had poured the oil upon his head and prophesied over him. It seems Naioth was the name of the suburb in Ramah where Samuel trained the prophets and where the Word of the Lord was studied. David knew if there was any regard for God or man at all left in Saul, he would be safe with Samuel. There is ample proof in the verses that Saul feared Samuel. However, Saul is not deterred, because he is wholly given to jealous anger.

1 Samuel 19:19, *"And it was told Saul, saying, Behold, David is at Naioth in Ramah."*

Saul got the word that David was abiding with Samuel at the school of the prophets. It most likely caused him grief. He knew the Spirit of the Lord was upon both Samuel and David. He also knew his own heart was void of God's power. Saul lived in abject misery, just as anyone who takes his path.

1 Samuel 19:20, *"And Saul sent messengers to take David: and when they saw the company of the prophets prophesying, and Samuel standing as appointed over them, the Spirit of God was upon the messengers of Saul, and they also prophesied."*

Saul has lost all regard for God and man. He sends his messengers to arrest David right out of the school of the prophets. Most fail to consider David as a prophet, but in fact, there are more messianic prophecies from his pen than even Isaiah. David came to Samuel for comfort and support, but he also came to place himself under Samuel's fatherhood. Herein is proof that Samuel was the spiritual father of the prophets. He was over them as though he was appointed. Such is the amazing bond of the father son order in the Lord. When you see this order, you will also see a release of great power. Such power and anointing that when the messengers of Saul arrived, the Spirit of the Lord came on them as well. Actually three times the messengers came for David, and each time the spirit of prophecy came upon them and they prophesied. And yet this was overshadowed by Saul's experience when he himself finally comes.

This seems to be the point of great controversy. How could Saul's hatchet men prophesy? They knew they were aiding in the murder of an innocent man. But there need not be a controversy or amazement; even Judas cast out devils and performed healings. In God's sovereignty, he allows and performs matters we cannot begin to understand. In this case it seems to be the manner in which God protected David, for they forgot about David and left without him.

1 Samuel 19:22, *"Then went he also to Ramah, and came to a great well that is in Sechu: and he asked and said, Where are Samuel and David? And one said, Behold, they be at Naioth in Ramah."*

Saul finally had to go himself to try to dispatch David. As he comes to the general area, he stops at what at that time was the information center, the well of Sechu. Though Saul is the king at that time, he actually asks for the whereabouts of the legitimate king (David, already anointed so) and the priest, Samuel. The power of the proper king and the priest goes back to Melchizedek himself who was King and Priest, as well as the pre-incarnate Christ. Saul was not a king of the tribe of Judah and had no real relationship with Samuel, who walked in three offices of Israel -- prophet, priest, judge.

Unlike the messengers Saul sent, Saul started prophesying before he ever got to the school of the prophets. He was overcome by the Spirit of God and took off his outer clothes and lay before the Lord, speaking prophetically. This experience was noised abroad so that some asked if he had joined the school of the prophets.

1 Samuel 20:1, *"And David fled from Naioth in Ramah, and came and said before Jonathan, What have I done? what is mine iniquity? and what is my sin before thy father, that he seeketh my life"?*

While Saul is actually arrested by the Holy Spirit for a day and a night, David flees and goes back to Jonathan. David rightly asks, "What have I done, and why is he hunting me down?" The meeting with Jonathan proves the faith David placed in his covenant with him. David was safe with Jonathan, and yet Jonathan could not believe that his father had broken his word to him (1 Samuel 19:6). Jonathan's unwillingness to believe that his father would proceed to kill David is actually a tribute to his character and proof of his love and loyalty to his sick father.

1 Samuel 20:3, *"And David sware moreover, and said, Thy father certainly knoweth that I have found grace in thine eyes; and he saith, Let not Jonathan know this, lest he be grieved: but truly as the LORD liveth, and as thy soul liveth, there is but a step between me and death."*

David now has to emphatically tell Jonathan that his father was deceiving him because he knew that Jonathan loved him. It was Jonathan who had stood in the gap for David with his dad. However, the foremost reason for Saul's secrecy concerning his attempts to kill David remains the fact that Saul promised Jonathan he would not kill him. David presses upon Jonathan just how serious the matter is and that he is very close to death.

1 Samuel 20:4, *"Then said Jonathan unto David, Whatsoever thy soul desireth, I will even do it for thee."*

The covenant between Jonathan and David stood the tremendous test of a loyalty battle between his father and his friend. Jonathan knew David was innocent and that his father was insane. Jonathan is the most overlooked giant of the faith in the scriptures. He was a great warrior in his own right. He was courageous and consistent. He had the discernment to know that David was the anointed king of Israel. He died in loyalty to his father but never sanctioned his faults. Jonathan is a true biblical hero worthy of much study.

1 Samuel 20:5, *"And David said unto Jonathan, Behold, tomorrow is the new moon, and I should not fail to sit with the king at meat: but let me go, that I may hide myself in the field unto the third day at even."*

It seems amazing that David would even consider eating again with Saul but most likely for two reasons: 1) David was quite safe at the table of the king. Saul would be afraid to attack him at this most public setting. Evidently the messengers he had been sending to attack were secret operatives, for even Jonathan didn't know it. 2) This particular feast was a three day family feast held each new moon. The culture was very strong in the matter of everyone in the family that served in the kingdom was expected to be there, without exception. David, being the king's son in law, and not attending the feast would be out of the question. For this reason David and his friend devised a plan to keep David from taking the chance that Saul would try to kill him at the table.

1 Samuel 20:6, *"If thy father at all miss me, then say, David earnestly asked leave of me that he might run to Bethlehem his city: for there is a yearly sacrifice there for all the family."*

It was customary that even soldiers could be dismissed to attend their yearly tribal feast. Therefore, David hoped that if Jonathan told his daddy that he had made a very earnest plea, perhaps he would be excused. Then David would come back the third day for Saul's family feast. Of Course, David wasn't really attending the yearly tribal feast but was in hiding until he found out how it was to go. If Saul went into a rage because he was absent, he would know that he was going to go so far as to attack him at the very feast of new moon.

David asks Jonathan to deal kindly with him if Saul publicly orders his execution because of the covenant they have in the Lord. He bares his heart to his covenant friend and tells Jonathan to kill him himself if he sees anything in him that is wrong instead of taking him to Saul. Here we are beginning to see a certain fear of Saul developing that will cost David greatly later on.

Jonathan assures David once again of his steadfast love and loyalty to David.

1 Samuel 20:10, *"Then said David to Jonathan, Who shall tell me? or what if thy father answer thee roughly"?*

David asks the obvious question, "Who can we trust to come to me in hiding to tell me as to whether I need to flee or stay?" David here also shows a concern both for Jonathan and also the stoutness of the scheme by raising the question, *"What if thy father answer thee roughly?"* If Jonathan sent an informant to tell David, he knew it would be quite risky for his own life should the informant defect from the king's son and tell the king the whole matter.

1 Samuel 20:11, *"And Jonathan said unto David, Come, and let us go out into the field. And they went out both of them into the field."*

This trip to the field begins one of the sweetest scenes found in the Bible. One author called it the covenant field. David and Jonathan had already entered into a covenant relationship, but here in the field, it is Jonathan who declares before God the promise and the extremities of the vow. They no doubt chose the field for the privacy it would afford. If certain people saw them together it would not only ruin their plan but could very well cost them both their lives.

1 Samuel 20:12, *"And Jonathan said unto David, O LORD God of Israel, when I have sounded my father about to morrow any time, or the third day, and, behold, if there be good toward David, and I then send not unto thee, and shew it thee"*;

This is an amazing decree before God to not only David but to his house or posterity. Jonathan is invoking God to hear and judge his heart toward David. The declaration becomes quite prophetic as Jonathan continues. It is as though Jonathan in his spirit can look down through the annals of time and even see the day when the Messiah will come from the root of Jesse and reign upon the whole earth and make all of his enemies his footstool. Jonathan did a most wise thing here by connecting himself for ever with the anointing on David which he could see as a perpetual kingdom.

1 Samuel 20:15, *"But also thou shalt not cut off thy kindness from my house for ever: no, not when the LORD hath cut off the enemies of David every one from the face of the earth."*

Jonathan continues his prayerful declaration of his covenant with David by moving even deeper into the prophetic realm. Jonathan speaks partially to David, partially to the Lord, and partially to himself. Critics of the inerrancy of Scripture have said that the words of Jonathan and David were lost and therefore gathered in pieces making it seem sporadic. This is not the case at all. He is moving in the realm of the Spirit and seeing all the way until the end of time.

1 Samuel 20:16, *"So Jonathan made a covenant with the house of David, saying, Let the LORD even require it at the hand of David's enemies."*

Jonathan finishes his covenant declaration by asking the Lord, the supreme witness of the covenant, to punish by death any who would breach it. This was common in the Jewish vows as to display their severity and seriousness.

1 Samuel 20:17, *"And Jonathan caused David to swear again, because he loved him: for he loved him as he loved his own soul."*

After the covenant declaration had reached such a crescendo, Jonathan required a second confirmation. This was all conducted with the highest level of agape love between the two. Actually there existed between them a total desire to rather die than disappoint one another. Also there was a great surrender on Jonathan's part of his own sure position of someday being king of Israel. Jonathan knew he wouldn't be king, and even before David was king, he submitted to him as though he was already king. True love fears no commitment and true commitment has no merit outside of love.

1 Samuel 20:18, *"Then Jonathan said to David, To morrow is the new moon: and thou shalt be missed, because thy seat will be empty."*

Jonathan realizes the time has come to proceed with his plan to either save David's place in the present dynasty of his father or save his life from the wrath of his father. The plan was evidently well thought out so that David could hide in a certain place and take his cue from the particular instructions Jonathan gives to a lad servant. This would insure that not only would he have a witness that he was not with David should he need to escape but neither would he at this time be seen as the facilitator of the reunion to the king's table, and the new moon feast in particular.

1 Samuel 20:24, *"So David hid himself in the field: and when the new moon was come, the king sat him down to eat meat."*

Yes, David is hiding in the field in the early part of his life from a demonized King Saul, even as Jesus in the early part of life was hidden in Egypt from a demonized King Herod. Saul was a Jew and at one time anointed. Herod was pagan with an antichrist force to hunt down and kill Jesus. In his attempt to do so, he murdered thousands of innocent children two years old and under who went to heaven. Saul, if he had succeeded, would have destroyed the seed of the Messiah, which would have sealed the doom of all of mankind, thus explaining the tremendous level of spiritual warfare involved herein.

1 Samuel 20:25, *"And the king sat upon his seat, as at other times, even upon a seat by the wall: and Jonathan arose, and Abner sat by Saul's side, and David's place was empty."*

The account of the seating at the king's table indicates four places. 1) The king by the wall which is still customary in most countries in the Middle East for a king or president; 2) Jonathan the son of the king often standing as we see here, and most likely facing the king; 3) Abner, the general, at his one side; 4) An empty seat at the other side which was reserved for David.

The first day of the feast, David's absence brought no reaction from Saul, who supposed he may have been sick or failed to meet the Mosaic ceremonial standard for cleanness required before such a feast.

1 Samuel 20:27, *"And it came to pass on the morrow, which was the second day of the month, that David's place was empty: and Saul said unto Jonathan his son, Wherefore cometh not the son of Jesse to meat, neither yesterday, nor to day"?*

Where is David? This is the second day he is missing. What an audacious question to ask, after the three times Saul threw the javelin at him. This is the absolute proof that the only sorrow Saul had for his deeds was the difficult position his hatred placed him in due to his son and his daughter both being lovers and admirers of David. His daughter is bound to David by marriage covenant and his son by a solemn oath.

1 Samuel 20:28, *"And Jonathan answered Saul, David earnestly asked leave of me to go to Bethlehem":*

Jonathan proceeds with the plan he and David had agreed by telling Saul that David asked permission to go to the tribal feast at Bethlehem. Jonathan makes every attempt to make Saul blame him for permitting David to go instead of blaming David for going. Reasoning with such a spirit is impossible. Saul went into a fit of rage and cursed Jonathan and basically called him a wicked and ignorant traitor. He also reminded him that as long as David was alive, Jonathan would never be able to be the king. Saul then did the worst possible thing to Jonathan he could have done. He ordered Jonathan to bring him in so that Saul could kill him. Hatred has no sense. By this time he should have known that he could not succeed in any effort to kill David, for his God was protecting him.

1 Samuel 20:33, *"And Saul cast a javelin at him to smite him: whereby Jonathan knew that it was determined of his father to slay David."*

Jonathan makes one more attempt to plead for David in asking His father what crime has David committed. This is the answer he receives. Saul threw the javelin at him to kill him. In his deranged thoughts he thinks, "First my daughter assists in the escape of David, and now my son dismisses him from the feast where he was to be killed." Now Jonathan, who hated so badly to believe David's account of Saul's behavior, has no choice. He is convinced David is going to be hunted down.

1 Samuel 20:34, *"So Jonathan arose from the table in fierce anger, and did eat no meat the second day of the month: for he was grieved for David, because his father had done him shame."*

Having been seated, most likely right before the javelin was cast at him; he now rises very angrily and leaves the table. This was a travesty and an ill for the entire kingdom because of the severity of the royal family not even being able to complete the New Moon Feast together. Jonathan's anger is here recorded as very disinterested and benevolent. His interest was for the welfare of David instead of himself. Now Jonathan realizes that he too is in danger for assisting his friend, though it seems he stayed the night at his house.

1 Samuel 20:35, *"And it came to pass in the morning, that Jonathan went out into the field at the time appointed with David, and a little lad with him."*

Jonathan goes to the field of covenant to carry out the plan to give the message to David concerning the state of Saul and his intentions against him. The message was not good for either of them because they knew that this would probably be the last time they would see each other for a while. Jonathan shot the arrows, and his instructions for retrieving them revealed to David hiding in the field, what his next options would be.

1 Samuel 20:39, *"But the lad knew not any thing: only Jonathan and David knew the matter."*

Little did the lad retrieving Jonathan's arrows know that the whole of Israel was at stake. However, Jonathan and David realized that not only was the situation grim, but the God of their covenant would bless them and protect them. They knew not only the matter at hand but they literally knew the matter in the spirit, as both of them had either prophesied or been prophesied to concerning the dynasty of David.

1 Samuel 20:41, *"And as soon as the lad was gone, David arose out of a place toward the south, and fell on his face to the ground, and bowed himself three times: and they kissed one another, and wept one with another, until David exceeded."*

This meeting wasn't included in their initial plan. David was to take the cue from Jonathan's instruction to his arrow carrier, and if evil was determined against him from Saul, he was to flee immediately. Evidently, Jonathan loved David so much and didn't know if he would ever see him again, so he sent his lad on. When he did so, David took that opportunity to come to him. David fell on his face and bowed three times before Jonathan. They kissed each other and wept over each other. Both have much reason for doing so. Jonathan had quite an uncertain future because of the stormy relationship with his father, and David was losing not only Jonathan, but also his wife and all that he held dear. "David exceeded" means that his grief was unbearable and manifested even more than Jonathan's.

1 Samuel 20:42, *"And Jonathan said to David, Go in peace, forasmuch as we have sworn both of us in the name of the LORD, saying, The LORD be between me and thee, and between my seed and thy seed for ever. And he arose and departed: and Jonathan went into the city."*

After gaining their composure, Jonathan sends David away. But not before assuring him of the covenant between them and even strengthening it by adding to the covenant. Jonathan decreed all of their posterity as a witness of their friendship and commitment to each other. Then they departed.

1 Samuel 21:1, *"Then came David to Nob to Ahimelech the priest: and Ahimelech was afraid at the meeting of David, and said unto him, Why art thou alone, and no man with thee"?*

David is a political fugitive, and just as he ran to the school of the prophets, he again turns to the lovers of God. This time he turns to the priests. He knew that Samuel was both prophet and priest, and probably figured that the priesthood would know that Samuel favored him. Also the Ark was at Nob and likely David was seeking spiritual counsel until he ran into Doeg the Edomite.

Ahimelech was afraid because David didn't have an army with him. Alone in this case means that his army was not present, for in verse 4 young men with him are mentioned. Also Mark 2 gives an account stating that David fed those that were with him. Also, Abiathar is mentioned as the high priest instead of Ahimelech, his father. However the account should say, "In the days of Abiathar who later became the high priest." Ahimelech could have been afraid because he had heard something of the dysfunction in the royal family, but later he told Saul he knew nothing in the matter. 1 Samuel 22:15, *"for thy servant knew nothing of all this, less or more."*

1 Samuel 21:2, *"And David said unto Ahimelech the priest, The king hath commanded me a business, and hath said unto me, Let no man know any thing of the business whereabout I send thee, and what I have commanded thee: and I have appointed my servants to such and such a place."*

David lies to the high priest. He tells Ahimelech that he is on a special operation and in a very big hurry. He also excuses the lack of soldiers by saying there are others stationed in certain places. It is doubtful that David planned this out. The puzzled and fearful countenance of Ahimelech added to the presence of the detained Doeg. He knew he must move on. Therefore he abruptly asks him for victuals.

1 Samuel 21:4, *"And the priest answered David, and said, There is no common bread under mine hand, but there is hallowed bread; if the young men have kept themselves at least from women."*

It is clear that the priest doesn't want to deny David the food he needs because under conditions he offers the bread that came from the table of showbread which is only to be eaten by priests. This is allowable by David for two reasons: 1) The bread had already been on the table for a day. The priest baked fresh bread each day to go on the table. They replaced it each morning and though it belonged to the priests and was their portion, it was not in the same state as that which was presently on the table of showbread. David points this out to the priest in the next verse. 2) David as the messianic line was allowed to operate as a priest three other times: 1) Wearing the linen ephod and the moving of the Ark; 2) Offering the sacrifice at the threshing floor of Ornan; 3) Pouring the pour offering from the water out of the well in Bethlehem. David moved in the king and priest order of Melchizedek which relates to the pre-incarnate visit of our Lord Jesus who is both our King and our High Priest.

Ahimelech did require that David and the young men had kept themselves from women for the last three days, which seems to be the very least of Levitical requirements.

1Samuel 21:5, *"And David answered the priest, and said unto him, Of a truth women have been kept from us about these three days, since I came out, and the vessels of the young men are holy, and the bread is in a manner common, yea, though it were sanctified this day in the vessel."*

David affirms to Ahimelech that he and the young men were clean from sexual behavior for three days and that their vessels were holy. Exodus 19:15, *"And he said unto the people, Be ready against the third day: come not at your wives."* Of course, David lied about his being there at Nob and later lied to get the sword of Goliath. Anyone would wonder if in fact David is lying about his purity and the purity of his men. His journey from Saul's court to Nob was nowhere near three days. He was married to Saul's daughter and lived there with her. However, the tumultuous time at the end of his stay in the court could have prevented any time of intimacy, not to mention that she could have been unclean at the time being in her cycle. It seems a stretch, however, to so readily attest that his young men were also clean. The priest gave them the bread and Doeg, one of Saul's chief servants saw it.

1 Samuel 21:8, *"And David said unto Ahimelech, And is there not here under thine hand spear or sword? for I have neither brought my sword nor my weapons with me, because the king's business required haste."*

Now David is asking for a weapon, and again he lies to gain it. Weapons were still quite scarce in the land. David is now quite the warrior known for his slaughtering of the Philistines and his many military campaigns. Therefore, the excuse David gives the high priest for not having a weapon should have alarmed Ahimelech even more. A warrior is never in too big of a hurry to take his weapons lest he could not be a warrior.

1 Samuel 21:9, *"And the priest said, The sword of Goliath the Philistine, whom thou slewest in the valley of Elah, behold, it is here wrapped in a cloth behind the ephod: if thou wilt take that, take it: for there is no other save that here. And David said, There is none like that; give it me."*

The sword of Goliath was quite famous and evidently had been taken to the same site as the sacred Ark of the Covenant. Most likely seen as a trophy, it was wrapped and laid right behind the ephod. The ephod was often used when seeking direction from the Lord and herein is a message for David. He had no time to seek the Lord but had come to trust in his own persuasion to get the sword which was right beside the ephod. The fearlessness he had when he gained that sword was gone and in its place is a fear accompanied by lies and deceit. Could not the one who gave him strength to kill Goliath give him victory of the glare of Doeg and the pursuit of Saul?

1 Samuel 21:10, *"And David arose, and fled that day for fear of Saul, and went to Achish the king of Gath."*

These pitiful words tell the story of the miserable failure of David: He *fled that day for fear of Saul* and he *went to Achish.* His failure brought him right back to the land and home of the giant he had killed, and even while carrying the very sword he took from Goliath. Did he think no one would recognize him or the sword he was carrying, or did he think that they might have heard him to be the enemy of Saul and therefore show him mercy?

1 Samuel 21:11, *"And the servants of Achish said unto him, Is not this David the king of the land? did they not sing one to another of him in dances, saying, Saul hath slain his thousands, and David his ten thousands"?*

David had no sooner arrived at the headquarters of King Achish until they recognized him, or at least thought they knew him. The men of King Achish even quoted the song that drove Saul mad: *"Saul hath slain his thousands, and David his ten thousands."*

1 Samuel 21:12, *"And David laid up these words in his heart, and was sore afraid of Achish the king of Gath."*

When David heard them quote the song, he knew his life was in danger. Out of fear once again he turns to deceit in an attempt to save his life. He begins to mimic a deranged man. He slobbers and claws at the gate in such a theatrical way that Achish even scolds his men for bringing a crazy man into his presence. Again David is protected, but no doubt the hand of God accomplished it instead of his trickery.

1 Samuel 22:1, *"David therefore departed thence, and escaped to the cave Adullam. and when his brethren and all his father's house heard it, they went down thither to him."*

After such a close call with death at the garrison of Achish and Saul right on his heels, David escapes to the cave of Adullam. His family is in danger and comes to him, both as a comfort to David and a refuge from Saul. Most likely Saul had strengthened his position against David by declaring him a traitor and defector which spells certain death. Often kings would put to death both the one that committed treason and also his whole family, as we will soon see in the case of Ahimelech who helped David at Nob.

It is in this cave that David makes a fort for a season and here he seems to have written several of the Davidic psalms. In these psalms he confesses fear and despair but also writes with a deep faith in his help and restoration coming from the Lord. Four hundred social misfits come to David here at Adullam. The whole ration was in love with David, and every person in some sort of trouble would come and identify with David who also was in trouble.

This is the picture of the remnant that identifies with the suffering of Christ and the army who has been delivered from sin and now has a captain they can identify with. Heb 4:15, *"For we have not an high priest which cannot be touched with the feeling of our infirmities; but was in all points tempted like as we are, yet without sin."* This army later grew to 600 men and became the most feared army in the known world under the leadership of David to whom they were committed to live with or die with.

1 Samuel 22:3, *"And David went thence to Mizpeh of Moab: and he said unto the king of Moab, Let my father and my mother, I pray thee, come forth, and be with you, till I know what God will do for me."*

David's loving care for his family is here illustrated by his seeking asylum for them in Moab. He knew they could not withstand that which was coming, and the life of a refugee soldier would not serve them well.

David wisely understood the king of Moab's issue with Saul which took place before he ever served in Saul's army (1 Samuel 14:47). Also his great grandmother Ruth was a full blooded Moabite, and he could probably use that for some leverage in his request for his family.

At this point perhaps his brothers felt they were correct in their protest against David's getting involved in the war. They could be saying, "If David had listened to us, we wouldn't be in this mess."

1 Samuel 22:4, *"And he brought them before the king of Moab: and they dwelt with him all the while that David was in the hold."*

There are some theologians who declare that Ruth was from the royal family of Moab and that is why the king himself was so congenial. Nevertheless, David's request for asylum for his family was granted, and they stayed with the king of Moab the entire time he was in exile.

1 Samuel 22:5, *"And the prophet Gad said unto David, Abide not in the hold; depart, and get thee into the land of Judah. Then David departed, and came into the forest of Hareth."*

The appearing of the prophet Gad seems quite abrupt, which in itself is not uncommon. Elijah and other prophets seemed to appear from nowhere. Gad was most likely a student of Samuel and knew that Samuel had anointed David as king. He knew also that David had come to the prophets' school when he first ran from Saul. Gad was probably even taught to pray for David. While David exercised good wisdom, he was about to make a fatal mistake. Therefore the divine wisdom came to his aid through the prophet. No doubt David was greatly consoled to find Gad to be at his service and was most gladly willing to obey the words he brought. He would leave the cave and go to the forest of Hareth, southwest of Jerusalem and well inside the boundaries of his own tribe Judah which adored him as a national hero.

1 Samuel 22:6, *"When Saul heard that David was discovered, and the men that were with him, (now Saul abode in Gibeah under a tree in Ramah, having his spear in his hand, and all his servants were standing about him)";*

It seems that David is aware at this point that Saul has heard about his general whereabouts and that the 400 man army of misfits was with him. Saul was under a tree with a spear in his hand, which means he had set up his temporary field office. The custom seemed to be that the spear in a field office was the same to the people as a scepter in the court. It is from this position that Saul makes his speech which is full of fear, jealousy, hatred, and unrighteousness.

Saul addresses those in his army who are in the tribe of Benjamin by name. He was most concerned that these of his own tribe might defect first. Saul asks then if they think David would take care of them like he has done. Jonathan was also a most beloved military hero who was a sort of deliverer by the fact that only he and his armor bearer brought to Israel a great victory, related in 1 Samuel 14:1-23. Saul in his fear and envy is convinced that Jonathan was against him, and if so, the Benjamites might follow. He questions his own men about disloyalty. It is clear that Saul was not even considering that he could be close to a tribal war because David had resorted to Judah.

Doeg the Edomite who was a chief servant of Saul, told Saul what he had seen at Nob when Ahimlech the high priest had given David food and the sword of Goliath. Saul, in a fit of rage, sends for Ahimelech and all of his posterity. Then Saul asks the high priest why he had conspired against him in aiding David. In this setting and in such rage as he saw on Saul, Ahimelech knew he and his were in great trouble. Upon their arrival, the temporary office of Saul becomes a temporary judgment seat.

1 Samuel 22:14, *"Then Ahimelech answered the king, and said, And who is so faithful among all thy servants as David, which is the king's son in law, and goeth at thy bidding, and is honourable in thine house"?*

Ahimelech gives Saul an honest answer by asking him a question that should have brought Saul to remember the very words of his son Jonathan who had asked, "What hath David done?" Although Ahimelech was curious and somewhat suspicious as to David's coming to Nob, he actually did know nothing of his fleeing from the presence of Saul. Ahimelech assures Saul that he did not inquire of the Lord for David, as Doeg charged him in verse 10. Ahimelech then pleads with him not to charge him or his family with any form of treason, as he was innocent of any such thing, not knowing of the matter at all. Nevertheless, the most horrible and wicked words ever uttered against innocent humanity came forth from Saul's mouth, the death sentence: "Thou shalt surely die, Ahimelech, thou, and all thy father's house." Just think, this one who once had the anointing of God, now is so unbelievably cruel and ruthless.

1 Samuel 22:17, *"And the king said unto the footmen that stood about him, Turn, and slay the priests of the LORD; because their hand also is with David, and because they knew when he fled, and did not shew it to me. But the servants of the king would not put forth their hand to fall upon the priests of the LORD."*

Saul's own footmen refused to carry out such a wicked command to execute the innocent priesthood. Saul had lost all fear of God, but the men with him knew this was wrong and feared God more than man. These were actually quite courageous men, for they risked their lives to resist the king, especially at the moment of his rage. Nonetheless, Doeg the Edomite, so anxious to advance himself with Saul, murdered them. This whole horrific site was prophesied by the unnamed prophet in 1 Samuel 2:31-33.

1 Samuel 22:20, *"And one of the sons of Ahimelech the son of Ahitub, named Abiathar, escaped, and fled after David."*

Eli's posterity has now been cut off except for the one who escaped, Abiathar. Yet even his escape and his miserable life were prophesied by the unnamed prophet in 1 Samuel 2:33, *"And the man of thine, whom I shall not cut off from mine altar, shall be to consume thine eyes, and to grieve thine heart: and all the increase of thine house shall die in the flower of their age."* This Abiathar served with Zadok the faithful priest. Fourteen times in the verses Zadok and Abiathar are mentioned in the same verse. They shared the office of the High Priest. Abiathar was appointed by guilt, while Zadok was anointed by God.

1 Samuel 22:21, *"And Abiathar shewed David that Saul had slain the LORD'S priests."*

As Abiathar escapes, he seems to come straight to David in the land of Judah. He gives the gruesome report of the murder of his entire family. Because Samuel was of the school of the prophets and because the time was so near between the prophetic words of the unnamed prophet and his own prophetic ministry, it is most likely that Samuel was aware of the prophecy concerning Eli. If Samuel knew, it is most likely that David knew, for they abode together during the time of David's first exile from Saul.

1 Samuel 22:22, *"And David said unto Abiathar, I knew it that day, when Doeg the Edomite was there, that he would surely tell Saul: I have occasioned the death of all the persons of thy father's house."*

David sadly realizes that because he didn't deal with Doeg, the priests of the Lord were slain. In spite of the prophetic words against them by the unnamed prophet, David took full responsibility. He said, *"I have occasioned the death of all the persons of thy father's house."* One should note that the Jews never used prophecy and predestination to excuse themselves of wrong doing. David did the only thing he could for Abiathar, and that is to give him refuge and meaning of life. But as far as putting him in the priesthood because of his guilt, herein he made a great mistake. David seemed to ignore the prophetic curse resting on Abiathar and his posterity.

1 Samuel 23:1, *"Then they told David, saying, Behold, the Philistines fight against Keilah, and they rob the threshing floors."*

David would have but a short distance to take his army from the forest of Hareth to Keilah, both of them being in Judah (Joshua 15:44). The robbing of the threshing floors was often the agenda of a nation whose intent was to make their enemy suffer. The Philistines, as well as the

Midianites, were guilty of waiting and watching until their neighboring nations had labored so hard to bring in the harvest, and then try to steal it from them (Judges 6:11).

1 Samuel 23:2, *"Therefore David enquired of the LORD, saying, Shall I go and smite these Philistines? And the LORD said unto David, Go, and smite the Philistines, and save Keilah."*

David and his army were in a very precarious situation with Saul breathing down their necks, and David wanted to be sure that the Lord was going to protect him and go before him. Therefore David inquires of the Lord as to whether or not he should go and deliver the little city of Keilah. We do not see a prophet or priest involved here, and David is in direct communication with the Lord. Later in verse 9, David uses the priest and the ephod, but it is not recorded here. The Lord answers David by telling him to go and smite the Philistines and save Keilah.

God's commandments are our enablements. David knew that if God told him to smite the Philistines, he would be able to do exactly that. David also needed to get the full sanction from the Lord for this military campaign because it was normally unacceptable for one to go on such a mission without the king's blessing. It seems that David could envision the separation of the tribe of Judah that would later occur, or perhaps he was operating in the king's office which had been spoken over him prophetically.

1 Samuel 23:3, *"And David's men said unto him, Behold, we be afraid here in Judah: how much more then if we come to Keilah against the armies of the Philistines"?*

David's men remind him of the fact that they are in hiding and treading very fearfully. They bring a good point in asking David how much sense it makes for them to come out of hiding to help Keilah. They all knew of the wrath of Saul and his now fitful determination to kill David. Yet they were loyal to their leader and just wanted their leader to be sure before he went. This proves the point that being loyal doesn't make you blind.

1 Samuel 23:4, *"Then David enquired of the LORD yet again. And the LORD answered him and said, Arise, go down to Keilah; for I will deliver the Philistines into thine hand."*

The question his men brought forth concerning the campaign caused David to seek the Lord again as to whether or not to depart. The Lord's answer was sufficient to satisfy both David and his men. There is nothing wrong with seeking a second or even a third confirmation, as we see in the case of Gideon. This is much different from offending the Lord through unbelief by asking, *"Can God furnish a table in the wilderness?"* This question is referred to in Psalm 78:18-19 as tempting God with unbelief. David's question was seeking confirmation for a very dangerous mission and was yet benevolent. Judah was in trouble and had requested his help.

1 Samuel 23:5, *"So David and his men went to Keilah, and fought with the Philistines, and brought away their cattle, and smote them with a great slaughter. So David saved the inhabitants of Keilah."*

This little army, moving by the power and direction of the Lord of Hosts, easily defeated the invading Philistines. It should be noted that David took their cattle, which most likely means the cattle they had just stolen from Keilah. It is not likely that the Philistines would be conducting an invasion with their cattle at hand. David delivered the people of Keilah by the power of the Lord and probably took the spoil of the Philistine's property, while returning the property the Philistines had taken back to the owners. This was a great mercenary work toward the people of Keilah.

1 Samuel 23:6, *"And it came to pass, when Abiathar the son of Ahimelech fled to David to Keilah, that he came down with an ephod in his hand."*

At first notice it seems there is a contradiction as to when Abiathar first came to David. There is no contradiction here at all. Abiathar came to David in Hareth and when David inquired of the Lord to go to deliver Keilah there was no ephod mentioned. When he inquired again there is no mention of it. So it seems that as David left to go to Keilah, Abiathar went back to Nob which by then would have been in a state of mourning and burials, but Saul would have been gone. Abiathar, being the only priest, left would have no opposition in taking the ephod to the rightful king and performing the priestly duties therewith. The high-priest's Ephod had the Urim and the Thummim, which Saul was unworthy of and David would greatly appreciate.

1Sa 23:7, *"And it was told Saul that David was come to Keilah. And Saul said, God hath delivered him into mine hand; for he is shut in, by entering into a town that hath gates and bars."*

Of course, Saul would hear of such a feat as David's little army defeating the Philistines. He no doubt was happy to hear of David's entering into Keilah. How sick is Saul to think that God was working in his behalf to capture David! This is nothing but guile, the wicked deception that hides sin and prevents people from moving into true repentance.

Saul knew this fortified city and thought to take an army quickly to surround it, making David's capture and no doubt execution, easy. How can Saul continue to be unconvinced of the supernatural protection on David's life?

1 Samuel 23:8, *"And Saul called all the people together to war, to go down to Keilah, to besiege David and his men."*

Most likely the people he called together here were in the immediate area where he was. Saul would not have taken the time to send throughout all of Israel for soldiers, which would have defeated his effort to catch David in the city. However, when kings called for war, the men twenty years old and up were expected to go unless they had attained fifty years of age, their jubilee.

1Sa 23:9, "And David knew that Saul secretly practised mischief against him; and he said to Abiathar the priest, Bring hither the ephod."

We don't know exactly how David found out about Saul's plan. Dr. Lightfoot indicates that a large number of the people were knit to David and only tolerated Saul out of the national guilt of asking for a king like other nations, as recorded in 1 Samuel 8:5. Most likely one of those loyal to David informed him; however the wording here, *"David knew"* affords the knowledge could have come prophetically. Many forget that David was also a prophet, and more messianic prophecies came from his pen than any of the Major Prophets.

David is now in full use of the office of the priest as he calls for Abiathar to bring the ephod which has the Urim and the Thummim.

1 Samuel 23:10, "Then said David, O LORD God of Israel, thy servant hath certainly heard that Saul seeketh to come to Keilah, to destroy the city for my sake."

Now David is praying for the direction he desperately needs. And though the Lord already knows Saul is coming to Keilah, David reminds him of the danger he is now in. The Lord doesn't mind us telling Him things He already knows as we bring forth our petitions. Psalms 142:2 says, *"I poured out my complaint before him; I shewed before him my trouble."* We can take great comfort in telling our Heavenly Father our discomfort. The Lord assured David that Saul would come down. Some have an issue here because it turns out that Saul didn't come. However, Saul didn't come only because David fled at the Lord's directive information. Saul would have come had David stayed, and there is no contradiction or false prophecy here.

1 Samuel 23:12, "Then said David, Will the men of Keilah deliver me and my men into the hand of Saul? And the LORD said, They will deliver thee up."

David needs to know what the men of Keilah will do under the pressure of Saul's demanding them to release him. He asks that question of the Lord, and the Lord tells David that they will turn him over to Saul. This is not much reward for the one who saved their lives. Isn't this an accurate picture of the sorry believers who reward the One who saved them from their sins by caving in to the pressures of the world? The men of Keilah probably figured the one who saved them was also about to get them all killed. Everybody all over the land had heard about Saul's killing the priests of Nob, and therefore they knew very well that Saul would kill anyone that helped David in any way. So once again, by calling on the Lord, David escapes the hand of Saul.

1 Samuel 23:13, *"Then David and his men, which were about six hundred, arose and departed out of Keilah, and went whithersoever they could go. And it was told Saul that David was escaped from Keilah; and he forbare to go forth."*

By now David's army had grown to about six hundred. This shows us that more and more were coming to David's aid. This number continued to grow. Saul offered the entire nation of Israel a most horrific affront when he had the priests of Nob slaughtered. The severity of Saul's rage against David would cause the fainthearted to stay far away from him so that only the extreme lovers of David would fight in his army.

This is a most accurate example of the remnant church on the earth. David's men scattered out in the wilderness so as to evade Saul should he come, but when Saul found out that David had escaped, he decided not to go to Keilah. The men of Keilah most likely had many days of discomfort for even allowing David in their city. They probably wondered if Saul would deal with them as he did the priests of Nob.

1 Samuel 23:14, *"And David abode in the wilderness in strong holds, and remained in a mountain in the wilderness of Ziph. And Saul sought him every day, but God delivered him not into his hand."*

David decided to stay in his own tribal country, for Ziph was a small city in the southern portion of Judea fairly close to Carmel. The wilderness surrounding Ziph was hilly and at that time wooded. The region herein described is not that large, so we should surmise that the hand of God was protecting David every day. This experience of David's living by faith, being every day a step away from death, proved to be the source of so many of the psalms we read. Living on the edge, and yet in divine protection, is always the breeding ground for the deepest manifestations of praise and prose.

1 Samuel 23:15, *"And David saw that Saul was come out to seek his life: and David was in the wilderness of Ziph in a wood."*

David often fought deep seated fears that he would die by the hand of Saul. We read in 1 Samuel 27:1, *"And David said in his heart, I shall now perish one day by the hand of Saul"*: Even after all of the ways God had shown him protection, the pressure of being hunted down by thousands, and living in the wilderness, would often add to the factor of the battle against fear. Even the great Apostle Paul confessed that he had seasons of "fears within" in 2 Corinthians 7:5.

1 Samuel 23:16, *"And Jonathan Saul's son arose, and went to David into the wood, and strengthened his hand in God."*

This is a very daring and moving act on Jonathan's part. How he knew exactly where to find David is not told us, but the covenant between them was stronger than fear. The participants of the covenant have the latent ability to strengthen each other. In true covenant, there is always one that is strong when the other is weak. Therefore we have these most powerful words concerning Jonathan's meeting with David. He *"strengthened his hand in God."* This is the result of such disinterested benevolence. Though Jonathan's heart yearned to be with his friend, his purpose was not to satisfy his own heart but to strengthen his friend.

1 Samuel 23:18, *"And they two made a covenant before the LORD: and David abode in the wood, and Jonathan went to his house."*

This no doubt means that together they solemnly renewed their covenant before the Lord; their covenant that already existed was as strong as man could make with one and another. This is the last recorded meeting between these two, for we find no proof that they ever saw each other again. The next time Jonathan is mentioned in the scripture is to report his death by the Philistines in 1 Samuel 31:2, *"And the Philistines followed hard upon Saul and upon his sons; and the Philistines slew Jonathan, and Abinadab, and Malchishua, Saul's sons."* Perhaps they both sensed this, for David goes back to the woods and Jonathan goes to his house, evidently by protesting to assist Saul in his hunt for David.

1 Samuel 23:19, *"Then came up the Ziphites to Saul to Gibeah, saying, Doth not David hide himself with us in strong holds in the wood, in the hill of Hachilah, which is on the south of Jeshimon"?*

From the city of Ziph one could see well the entire region, even the outskirts of the wilderness to their south. It stands to reason that this enabled the Ziphites to see David and his men coming and going. Evidently there was an appearance precisely on the hill of Hachilah of David or some of his men. These Ziphites came to report the matter to Saul. It isn't clear why these from a city of Judah would hand over one of their own tribe to a king from Benjamin. However, it is very possible that they were trying to avoid a civil war because of the great love and admiration of the people of Israel for David their war hero.

Saul is trying to portray David as a very dangerous traitor and one who desires to steal from him the kingdom. In all of Israel, including the Ziphites, there was not one so faithful to Saul as David. The whole effort to kill David was born out of jealous fear and a demonic driven mentality. David had not done one thing to harm Saul.

Saul tries to bless the Ziphites for coming to tell him of David's whereabouts. Saul gives the people of Ziph instructions to go and document all of the places where the men of David could be hiding. He knows their heart would be too faint to actually engage in an attempt to arrest David. Saul therefore assures them that when they get the information, they should return to him, and he will go with them to capture David, though Saul readily admits as to David's stealth.

1 Samuel 23:24, *"And they arose, and went to Ziph before Saul: but David and his men were in the wilderness of Maon, in the plain on the south of Jeshimon."*

Before the Ziphites could get back to do their bidding for Saul, David had learned of the procedure against him. Again, he may have known this by the spirit of prophecy, or his intelligence department could have gained the information. Nonetheless, David moves quite a distance to the wilderness of Maon, which is closer to the border but still within the boundaries of Judah (Joshua 15:55).

1 Samuel 23:25, *"Saul also and his men went to seek him. And they told David: wherefore he came down into a rock, and abode in the wilderness of Maon. And when Saul heard that, he pursued after David in the wilderness of Maon."*

Verse 24 gives the report as to where David and his men went when they heard that Saul was coming, and this verse tells how it happened. *"They told David,"* meaning David's spies told David that Saul was coming, and David moved quickly to this wilderness and the rocky area close to Mount Carmel. This area is also full of caves both small and large. Saul heard of their escape and followed close behind, ever closing in on his imagined adversary.

1 Samuel 23:26, *"And Saul went on this side of the mountain, and David and his men on that side of the mountain: and David made haste to get away for fear of Saul; for Saul and his men compassed David and his men round about to take them."*

Saul was close to surrounding David's little army of six hundred men and would have succeeded had he been in a normal military setting. However Saul could not achieve his goal, for the Lord of Hosts was against him, and He is never lacking in ways and means for protecting His own. The Lord simply stirs up the Philistines to attack Saul on another front. While David and his men are in incredible danger, the messenger for Saul comes to tell him of the invasion of the Philistines. Saul has no choice but to leave off chasing his jealously perceived enemy and to go and fight a real one.

1 Samuel 23:28, *"Wherefore Saul returned from pursuing after David, and went against the Philistines: therefore they called that place Sela-hammahlekoth."*

This *Sela-hammahlekoth* means the place or stone where the two armies divided. Saul's army had to make haste to leave. Saul could never have survived in his position as king had he neglected to protect the nation of Israel from a murderous uncircumcised heathen army while trying to catch and kill one who remained a national hero.

1 Samuel 23:29, *"And David went up from thence, and dwelt in strong holds at Engedi."*

Engedi is still within the boundaries of Judah, and it seems clear that David doesn't want to cross over any tribal boundary. He just moves from place to place inside the territory of Judah. The tribal friction was growing over the person of David, and Judah was the first one to accept David as King.

Historical proofs reveal that there was much talk of tribal war even at this time, and the Bible confirms it finally did happen with David's grandson. Engedi was not far from the Dead Sea. Solomon writes of the vineyards in Engedi in Song of Solomon (Song 1:14). The balm of Engedi was also of note but David was not there for either. The region of Engedi was like Maon, having mountainous terrain with many caverns. This is why the reference is for strongholds, not man-made, but these natural strongholds that David was so good at utilizing.

1 Samuel 24:1, *"And it came to pass, when Saul was returned from following the Philistines, that it was told him, saying, Behold, David is in the wilderness of Engedi."*

Evidently this was not a large army of the Philistines that had invaded Israel, for Saul chased them out rather quickly. Saul was quick to renew his quest for innocent blood by gathering information as to the whereabouts of David. I am sure the news that David was in Engedi was not good news for Saul. Not only was it still in Judah, but it was much more treacherous terrain and more dangerous for his men in the matter of ambush.

1Samuel 24:2, *"Then Saul took three thousand chosen men out of all Israel, and went to seek David and his men upon the rocks of the wild goats."*

Saul makes his odds great against David by taking three thousand men, almost five to one. Saul knew the area and knew he would need a large portion of his army in the search department to ever find David in such terrain. This action of Saul adds to the already abundant truth that he would stop short of nothing to hunt down and kill David.

1 Samuel 24:3, *"And he came to the sheepcotes by the way, where was a cave; and Saul went in to cover his feet: and David and his men remained in the sides of the cave."*

The sheepcotes are the caves where shepherds would lodge their sheep in the winter. The caves were large enough according to Josephus to accommodate many herds of sheep, and one is mentioned by Lightfoot that would house an army of 4,000.

Saul was no doubt near total exhaustion after chasing David, then rushing back to chase the Philistines, then rushing back to apprehend David. It could hardly be coincidental that Saul and his men came in to sleep in the very cave where David and his men were hiding.

1 Samuel 24:4, *"And the men of David said unto him, Behold the day of which the LORD said unto thee, Behold, I will deliver thine enemy into thine hand, that thou mayest do to him as it shall seem good unto thee. Then David arose, and cut off the skirt of Saul's robe privily."*

As soon as Saul and his men entered the cave complex, David's men began to speak to him in an attempt to persuade David to take this opportunity to kill Saul, no doubt for two reasons: 1) They were probably tired of being on the run and living in the woods and in caves like animals. 2) They knew they would most likely be the men that would be advanced in David's dynasty, for they perceived that if Saul was gone, David would be the king. They knew Jonathan would not pursue his father's throne but would instead serve his covenant friend David.

These men were not wrong and had probably had this conversation before, for David must have told them the prophetic word that they are quoting back to him. The prophecy came completely true, like all true prophecies, without David's having to slay one who has had the anointing oil poured upon his head.

After David listens to the men, he arises, and instead of killing Saul, he cuts off his skirt. Either the Lord put a deep sleep on Saul and his men, or they were so exhausted from their pursuit that they didn't know of David's deed.

1 Samuel 24:5, *"And it came to pass afterward, that David's heart smote him, because he had cut off Saul's skirt."*

Not only did David fail to take this opportunity to kill Saul, but his heart smote him because he cut off his skirt. This is amazing, to say the least. How many times had Saul tried to kill him? Yet David has absolutely no ill feelings for him and is convicted because he humiliated him by cutting off his skirt. When you read the psalms that came out of this particular time of exile, you may begin to see the depth of relationship between the Lord and David. Out of this relationship came the heart from God displayed here by David in being free from every ounce of vengeance.

1 Samuel 24:7, *"So David stayed his servants with these words, and suffered them not to rise against Saul. But Saul rose up out of the cave, and went on his way."*

The men of David knew of David's great love for God. They understood his compassion for Saul that was born out of the worshipper's heart, even though they were intent on killing Saul. Probably to the man they would have done so but they were loyal to their king. Here is proof of the bond David had with his men and the anointed leadership David operated in. Some commentators count this release of Saul to be a fault in David by charging that he put his own feelings above the men. Though David's life had faults and failures in it, this is not one of them. David knew the timing was not right, and that Jonathan could be in great danger of being executed by rebels before he could get to him.

By allowing Saul to live, David accomplished the following: 1) Innocence against the Lord's anointed 2) Safety for his covenant friend Jonathan 3) the sure testimony throughout Israel that he was not the aggressor 4) Passing a critical leadership test as they watched Saul leave the cave unharmed.

1 Samuel 24:8, *"David also arose afterward, and went out of the cave, and cried after Saul, saying, My lord the king. And when Saul looked behind him, David stooped with his face to the earth, and bowed himself."*

This could be one of the most amazing scenes in the entire Bible. David follows Saul out of the cave then raises his voice to gain his attention. When Saul looks back, David actually bows to even put his face to the earth in honor of Saul.

Both Saul and David were anointed by Samuel, the only one in the history of Israel to hold all three offices of prophet, priest, and judge. Saul was anointed by protest, and David was anointed by providence. Saul was picked by the people, and David was picked by the Lord. Saul was operating in a diabolical plan, and David was operating in supernatural power. Yet David is bowing down before Saul. Wescott declares it mockery, but he is far from right. Others declare David to be showing reverence, and that he was. But remember David's heart was smitten with conviction.

David followed Saul out of the cave to surrender to being put to death. He was there discovered of Saul, who had three thousand soldiers. David could have been taken right then and there. This is a Messianic picture of Jesus before his executors. Jesus didn't resist. This is the picture of Jesus in Samaria without a place to stay when his disciples asked if they should pray down fire and destroy the city. They didn't understand that it was not in His heart to hurt, but to heal. David's emotional surrender smote the heart of Saul, but not for long.

1 Samuel 24:9, *"And David said to Saul, Wherefore hearest thou men's words, saying, Behold, David seeketh thy hurt"?*

David asks him, not in sarcasm, but in brokenness, "Why have you believed that I wanted to cause you harm?" David tells Saul that now he can see clearly that if he had an intention to hurt him, he would have. David holds up the skirt of Saul's robe to prove he was close enough to kill him if he wanted to. Then David gives proof of his surrender by saying, *"The LORD judge between me and thee, and the LORD avenge me of thee: but mine hand shall not be upon thee."* Thus David makes it clear to Saul that he would not resist him. This is surrender by David and trusting nothing but the power of God to help him. David even quotes an ancient psalm that is a discerner of the aggressor and then humbles himself once again in brokenness before the king. David didn't want to die but had placed himself in the hands of God.

1 Samuel 24:16, *"And it came to pass, when David had made an end of speaking these words unto Saul, that Saul said, Is this thy voice, my son David? And Saul lifted up his voice, and wept."*

The fact that Saul asked if it was David's voice doesn't mean that David was out of reach of Saul and his army. Neither does it mean David had no intention of surrendering. Saul is asking, "Is this your voice," which is the Hebrew word *qowl,* which means, "Is this your sound?" This is why Saul is accosting him by calling him son and wanting him to be restored, followed by loud weeping. Saul, even in his degenerate state, could not resist the power and anointing of David's words pouring from his smitten heart and brokenness. It is like Esau who intended to destroy Jacob, but when he saw a limping Jacob coming with the afterglow of a night wrestling with Jesus, he could do nothing but fall on his neck and weep.

1 Samuel 24:17, *"And he said to David, Thou art more righteous than I: for thou hast rewarded me good, whereas I have rewarded thee evil."*

Saul's confession was accurate and true. David never had an ounce of malice toward Saul and only desired to serve him with his family. David operated in Agape love by doing Saul good, while Saul was trying to do him bad. Romans 12:21 says, *"Be not overcome of evil, but overcome evil with good."* This verse David fulfilled and filled full. The jealous and angry spirit of Saul was no match for the broken and contrite spirit of David. Saul totally conceded to David and even confessed that he knew that David would be king of Israel. Saul proved he really believed David would be king by asking David to swear that he would have mercy on the posterity of Saul when he took over.

1 Samuel 24:22, *"And David sware unto Saul. And Saul went home; but David and his men gat them up unto the hold."*

David did swear to Saul that he would not harm his family when he became king of Israel, and the scripture bears witness that in fact he kept his solemn word.

Saul went home and David could have gone with him, but instead he goes back to the hold at Engedi. David had seen Saul do this before, and though I am sure he genuinely hoped Saul was into true repentance, he would wait in safety in the land of Judah until he was sure.

1 Samuel 25:1, *"And Samuel died; and all the Israelites were gathered together, and lamented him, and buried him in his house at Ramah. And David arose, and went down to the wilderness of Paran."*

This must have been a terrible time of loss for David. Samuel was his spiritual father. David had spent time with Samuel at Ramah. Samuel had poured the anointing oil on David's head. Now Samuel had lived a good long life, most estimate between 96 and 100 years. They buried him in his prepared sepulcher (house). One of the honors of older national figures was to build and maintain their sepulchers sometime before they died. He lived a noble life and died a noble death. Samuel was dedicated to the Lord from conception to the grave. He was nationally lamented. Though he didn't get to see David on the throne physically, he saw it in his spirit. "Hardly a dry eye in Israel for days," says Dr. Lightfoot. Tears should accompany the loss of spiritual and faithful leaders.

David thought it wise to move after Samuel's death, not necessarily because he felt more danger, but most likely he was restless and contemplative. He may have simply moved to have better possibilities of obtaining the resources needed for his growing army. The grassy wilderness of Paran in Judea near Carmel would offer that and more, for here he would meet Abigail and the miserable Nabal.

1 Samuel 25:4, *"And David heard in the wilderness that Nabal did shear his sheep."*

The time of shearing of the sheep was usually a time of feasting and celebration and often the bigger the herds, the bigger the celebration. In Nabal's case it would have been a huge feast for he was a wealthy man.

1 Samuel 25:5, *"And David sent out ten young men, and David said unto the young men, Get you up to Carmel, and go to Nabal, and greet him in my name"*:

David sent these men with very explicit instructions. They were to go to Carmel and greet Nabal in David's name and pronounce to him a blessing. David wanted Nabal to know that he and his men had not stolen one thing as they dwelt in Paran, neither did they allow anyone else to steal from the house of Nabal. This is the preface for the request for supplies that will follow. During that time there were bands of Arabs roaming and robbing, and David is most likely referring to that particular situation. The fact that David had dealt so kindly concerning Nabal was not normal for an army abiding in an area. But David was a very noble man in these respects and Abigail is told this in verses 15-17.

1 Samuel 25:8, *"Ask thy young men, and they will shew thee. Wherefore let the young men find favour in thine eyes: for we come in a good day: give, I pray thee, whatsoever cometh to thine hand unto thy servants, and to thy son David."*

David wanted his young men to be sure to tell Nabal that he was more than willing for him to speak to these messengers concerning the whole time of his stay in Paran. David shows them exactly how to make this request for supplies and makes sure that the young men arrive at a good time. The good time means the time of the shearing because there would be a great store of goods laid up for the event. David is very intelligent in his natural gifting from the Lord. His savvy in dealing with people is most amazing.

1 Samuel 25:9, *"And when David's young men came, they spake to Nabal according to all those words in the name of David, and ceased."*

David's young men came and did as they were told. They delivered their message in the name of David and waited for the response from Nabal.

1 Samuel 25:10, *"And Nabal answered David's servants, and said, Who is David? and who is the son of Jesse? there be many servants now a days that break away every man from his master."*

Nabal's answer was full proof of the accuracy of the description Abigail gives later concerning her husband. She says in 1 Samuel 25:25, *"Let not my lord, I pray thee, regard this man of Belial, even Nabal: for as his name is, so is he; Nabal is his name, and folly is with him: but I thine handmaid saw not the young men of my lord, whom thou didst send."*

Nabal's words will infuriate David more than almost anything he could have said. He accuses David of being a breakaway rebel, when in fact no one on earth was more loyal to Saul than David. After Nabal delivers such a grievous insult in such a haughty way, he then flatly refuses the young men any help at all and asks them why he should help anybody when he doesn't even know whose side they are standing on.

1 Samuel 25:12, *"So David's young men turned their way, and went again, and came and told him all those sayings."*

David's young men probably were in great anticipation as far as telling David what Nabal said, knowing David's pure heart toward Saul. These men of David knew first hand that David was loyal to Saul for they were unable to persuade David to kill Saul in the cave. It is possible that the young men took unto themselves the offense of David and were in great hopes that David would avenge himself and go deal with Nabal.

1 Samuel 25:13, *"And David said unto his men, Gird ye on every man his sword. And they girded on every man his sword; and David also girded on his sword: and there went up after David about four hundred men; and two hundred abode by the stuff."*

Immediately David was ready to go and wipe out the entire work force of Nabal. This seems to be hasty, but one must remember the accusation of David being a rebel was more than David could handle. As it turns out David later admits it was a hasty matter of indignation, but not righteous indignation, the difference being difficult for most warriors to discern (1 Samuel 25:32-34). David leaves 200 warriors with the stuff and takes 400 with him to destroy Nabal and his men.

1 Samuel 25:14, *"But one of the young men told Abigail, Nabal's wife, saying, Behold, David sent messengers out of the wilderness to salute our master; and he railed on them."*

Just as David's young men told David about the insults of Nabal toward him, one of Nabal's young men told Abigail, Nabal's wife, how Nabal had extremely insulted David. The young man gave Abigail testimony as to the way David had not only treated them well, but actually protected them. The young man pressed on Abigail that the scene was very bad, that nobody could tell Nabal anything, and that David would most likely respond harshly, due to such a foolish and extreme affront.

Abigail responds hastily and wisely by taking the victuals, without Nabal's permission, and sending them directly to David. Abigail, a type of intercession between the innocent people in her vast household and the insulted warrior who had slain his ten thousands, sent to David what Nabal should have given him. She planned to arrive herself to make her petition shortly after David saw the victuals. This was so David could see her heart before he heard her voice.

1 Samuel 25:20, *"And it was so, as she rode on the ass, that she came down by the covert of the hill, and, behold, David and his men came down against her; and she met them."*

It is said that Abigail came down from Mount Carmel while David was coming down from Mount Paran, and they met in the valley between the hills. David and his 400 men were on foot and Abigail was riding the donkey behind the animals laden with the supplies for David and his men. This meeting is of the utmost importance in so many ways just as the spot they met. David was on his way to do something out of the will of God, while Abigail was on her way to plead for the lives of all she loved and held dear.

1 Samuel 25:21, *"Now David had said, Surely in vain have I kept all that this fellow hath in the wilderness, so that nothing was missed of all that pertained unto him: and he hath requited me evil for good."*

Here we have the sum of David's words when he first discovered Nabal's ridiculous accusatory rant toward him. David could have said the same thing concerning Saul but did not. Saul definitely rewarded David evil for the good he did to Saul. The difference for David is the anointing. David had respect for both Samuel and the oil that Samuel placed on Saul. But as for Nabal, "this fellow" as David calls him, David felt he owed him nothing but the wrath of his mighty sword.

1 Samuel 25:22, *"So and more also do God unto the enemies of David, if I leave of all that pertain to him by the morning light any that pisseth against the wall."*

David had made such a vow in his hasty anger as to say. "Let my enemies destroy me if I don't destroy Nabal and all of the men of his house." The term *pisseth against the wall,* is found six times in your Bible and in each case it is referring to every man. The term also meant there was no intention to kill the little male children or the women, as neither would or could perform the conditions of the term. David was a seasoned warrior by now, and a very fit guerrilla fighter, so he could have easily accomplished his intention of making the house of Nabal totally matriarchal.

1 Samuel 25:23, *"And when Abigail saw David, she hasted, and lighted off the ass, and fell before David on her face, and bowed herself to the ground,"*

As soon as she saw David, she knew that what she feared was about to come to pass. The urgency she displays and the aggression she possesses does not give way to the need for humility. Herein is the picture of true intercession, as Abigail throws herself between the judge and the one being judged, then asks for an audience. Evidently David made some sort of gesture, for she then poured out her heart. Just as she spared not herself in this discourse, she spared not her husband, calling him a man of Belial, a foolishly vile person, and one that is judged already (verse 26b).

Abigail makes perfect intercession by 1) Assuring David that if she had seen the young men he sent, things would have been different; 2) Asserting that the Lord is using her to stop David from shedding innocent blood; 3) Insisting that David receive the bountiful supplies she has brought; 4) Asking for David's forgiveness in the matter and never count it against them, even when he comes to be the king; 5) Acknowledging that the Lord is fighting David's battles for him; 6) assuring David that she also considers him innocent in the matter of Saul. This is of great importance for David to hear, as Saul had purported throughout Israel that David was an insubordinate rebel, which evidently Nabal believed. Abigail also acknowledged that David will be the king by asking for his favor, not *if* but *when* he becomes king.

1 Samuel 25:32, "*And David said to Abigail, Blessed be the LORD God of Israel, which sent thee this day to meet me*":

As soon as David heard the intercession of Abigail, he completely acknowledged his hastiness in determining to destroy the males of the household of Nabal. David commends Abigail for the accuracy of her words and considers her coming to meet him as an act of mercy from God. David assures Abigail that had she not come, he would surely have carried out his plan. There is no record of David's attraction to Abigail here at this time.

1 Samuel 25:35, "*So David received of her hand that which she had brought him, and said unto her, Go up in peace to thine house; see, I have hearkened to thy voice, and have accepted thy person.*"

David receives the supplies and tells her to go in peace which means he has agreed to all that she is and all that she has said. We have seen that when David gives someone his word it is good, and so it is here in this matter of Nabal.

As so often the case, while intercessors are working, the ones in the danger are partying. When Abigail returned, she found her husband throwing a party like a king and so drunk that she had to wait until the next day to tell Nabal what almost happened. As soon as Nabal heard the words of his scrape with death and the near loss of all he had, he became like a stone. Perhaps he had a stroke. Nevertheless, he failed to recover and was dead in ten days.

1 Samuel 25:39, "*And when David heard that Nabal was dead, he said, Blessed be the LORD, that hath pleaded the cause of my reproach from the hand of Nabal, and hath kept his servant from evil: for the LORD hath returned the wickedness of Nabal upon his own head. And David sent and communed with Abigail, to take her to him to wife.*"

We don't know what length of time there was between the time of Nabal's death and David's sending for Abigail, but most likely just a few days at the most. Wesley, whose commentaries, like his life, gave each person the most benevolent cause, believed there was a good length of time that passed before David sent for her. We do suspect the time of mourning would have been respected. However, the scripture doesn't even afford that confirmation.

To David's credit, he had probably heard that Saul had given his wife Michal to Phalti in order to make sure David didn't inherit so much as a single shoelace from him. If David knew that Saul had done so, it would have caused him to feel justified in marrying this new widow. David also saw this as the judgment of God on Nabal, and Abigail as part of the spoil, because by marrying her David most likely became a very rich man, though he would remain a fugitive for some time yet. Certainly he was domestically wealthy with the abundantly prudent character of Abigail at his side. David soon gave over to wholesale polygamy in disrespect to Abigail, which cost him greatly.

1 Samuel 25:40, *"And when the servants of David were come to Abigail to Carmel, they spake unto her, saying, David sent us unto thee, to take thee to him to wife."*

It is not known why David did not go himself to propose to Abigail. Perhaps he thought she might refuse. He sent his men to talk to her, which even they might have considered an awkward assignment.

1 Sammuel 25:42, *"And Abigail hasted, and rose, and rode upon an ass, with five damsels of hers that went after her; and she went after the messengers of David, and became his wife."*

Abigail seemed most eager to become David's wife. Her five damsels that accompany her is yet more proof of her vast wealth. She had probably assigned the servants to the watch care of the vast estate.

1 Samuel 25:43, *"David also took Ahinoam of Jezreel; and they were also both of them his wives."*

David was wrong for this polygamy, even though it was practiced among kings. God did not want David to be a king like other nations which is what Saul was chosen for. God chose David, not man; and man, not God, influenced David to take two wives. This practice brought abundant grief to the house of David. It is thought by some that he had already married Ahinoam, but we can find no proof of this. The only apparent support for the thought is that she is listed before Abigail in 1 Samuel 27:3.

1 Samuel 25:44, *"But Saul had given Michal his daughter, David's wife, to Phaltiel the son of Laish, which was of Gallim."*

Here is the record of what Saul had already done, which David most likely knew before he took Abigail. The loss of Michal was most likely a great grief to David, as he loved her and had paid a heavy dowry for her. Later David recovers her, and the grief that he had was then upon Phaltiel.

1 Samuel 26:1, *"And the Ziphites came unto Saul to Gibeah, saying, Doth not David hide himself in the hill of Hachilah, which is before Jeshimon?"*

This is now the second time that these Ziphites have turned in the information to Saul that could allow Saul to apprehend David. They must have been successful in luring Saul from his promise to leave David alone by telling Saul, "We know this time we have him for sure." The hill of Hachilah by Jeshimon is not a place that affords David a great deal of options to evade Saul. David's army continues to grow, making it harder to hide, plus he continues to gain more stuff.

1 Samuel 26:2, *"Then Saul arose, and went down to the wilderness of Ziph, having three thousand chosen men of Israel with him, to seek David in the wilderness of Ziph."*

Here Saul plays the fool even more. He slides back further than ever by going against the grace the Lord showed him when David spared his life. He also shows himself to continually depend on physical strength by choosing his best three thousand men to go and find David. This act also shows some well deserved respect for the little army of six hundred David had by him.

1 Samuel 26:3, *"And Saul pitched in the hill of Hachilah, which is before Jeshimon, by the way. But David abode in the wilderness, and he saw that Saul came after him into the wilderness."*

Saul stops short of coming to the very spot the Ziphites reported David to be and camps with his men. David understood through his intelligence that Saul had digressed into his old self and was in pursuit of him.

1 Samuel 26:4, *"David therefore sent out spies, and understood that Saul was come in very deed."*

David wisely sends out spies to verify what he had learned. This is a wise thing for him to do. He could therefore gauge his distance between himself and Saul, as well as develop military plans accordingly.

1 Samuel 26:5, *"And David arose, and came to the place where Saul had pitched: and David beheld the place where Saul lay, and Abner the son of Ner, the captain of his host: and Saul lay in the trench, and the people pitched round about him."*

David does a daring thing by actually going to Saul instead of waiting for Saul to come to him. He knows the terrain inside and out, so in this he has an advantage. However, it is well established that David operated his military by divine guidance and protection. The more times we are supernaturally delivered from our enemies, the more boldness we operate in. He finds out exactly where Saul lay in the midst of the three thousand mighty men he had with him. The trench spoken of here is the middle of the circle of supply carts or wagons needed for the army's sustenance. Kings and captains often slept surrounded by this type of a makeshift garrison.

1 Samuel 26:6, *"Then answered David and said to Ahimelech the Hittite, and to Abishai the son of Zeruiah, brother to Joab, saying, Who will go down with me to Saul to the camp? And Abishai said, I will go down with thee."*

David's perch of observance is probably where he received the inspiration to go and do the daring deed that follows. Many are shocked to find the Hittite so close to David, especially with the Levite named Ahimelech. This provides ample proof that this army of misfits was also a multicultural people. Yet the Jewish name of the Hittite proves the influence of the Jews if not his being a full proselyte. One of David's nephews is there as well (1 Chronicles 2:16), and it is Abishai that volunteers to go with David.

1 Samuel 26:7, *"So David and Abishai came to the people by night: and, behold, Saul lay sleeping within the trench, and his spear stuck in the ground at his bolster: but Abner and the people lay round about him."*

This is the boldness of the righteous and further proof of David's revelation from God as to how He would deliver him. It is most likely that the Lord showed David He would put a deep sleep upon the three thousand men who were responsible to protect their king. Remember that David and Jonathan are covenant friends, and David would have known that his covenant brother went alone with his armor bearer only, up to defeat the Philistines through divine guidance and protection (1 Sam 14:1-15).

1 Samuel 26:8, *"Then said Abishai to David, God hath delivered thine enemy into thine hand this day: now therefore let me smite him, I pray thee, with the spear even to the earth at once, and I will not smite him the second time."*

Abishai, it seems, might have been the one talking in the cave in Engedi for the words are close to identical (1 Samuel 24:4). It is easy to see the fervent desire Abishai has to rid his uncle David, also his captain, of his enemy forever.

1 Samuel 26:9, *"And David said to Abishai, Destroy him not: for who can stretch forth his hand against the LORD'S anointed, and be guiltless"?*

This we find most amazing, that David would again allow Saul to live after Saul had repented twice already for trying to kill him. 1) Upon the intercession of Jonathan (1 Samuel 19:5-6) 2) Outside the cave of Engedi (1 Samuel 24:16-22). The Jewish number of confirmation is at play here. David full well knows that if Saul doesn't fully repent this time, it will be over for Saul. David wisely rejects the counsel of his nephew and refuses to kill Saul himself, referring again to the anointing that once rested upon Saul.

1 Samuel 26:10, *"David said furthermore, As the LORD liveth, the LORD shall smite him; or his day shall come to die; or he shall descend into battle, and perish."*

This is not a prophecy from David's lips, proven by the fact that David didn't know how Saul would die. David's words are more of a sad realization that Saul is coming to the end of his opportunity to really repent. How sad when one goes past the point of grace, and how incorrect is the doctrine that doesn't believe you can. David instructs Abishai to take his spear and cruise of water to once again prove to Saul that he was close enough to take his life if he wanted to.

1 Samuel 26:12, *"So David took the spear and the cruse of water from Saul's bolster; and they gat them away, and no man saw it, nor knew it, neither awaked: for they were all asleep; because a deep sleep from the LORD was fallen upon them."*

David's amazing exploit could not have been possible were it not for the Lord's placing Saul and his army under a deep sleep. The word *sleep* here is the same Hebrew word used to describe Adam's condition when the Lord extracted from him a rib (Genesis 2:21). The power of God brought the victory for David over and over again. It is amazing that Saul would be so ignorant as to chase him all over Judah, in a manner similar to Pharaoh's following the children of Israel, except Pharaoh was never the anointed of the Lord as Saul was.

1 Samuel 26:13, *"Then David went over to the other side, and stood on the top of an hill afar off; a great space being between them":*

This time David puts a great distance between him and Saul's army before he addresses them, unlike the time in Engedi when David cuts off Saul's skirt while he is in the cave, then comes out as soon as Saul leaves. This is recorded in 1 Samuel 24:8, *"David also rose afterward, and went out of the cave, and cried after Saul, saying, My lord the king. And when Saul looked behind him, David stooped with his face to the earth, and bowed himself."* In the case at Engedi David is broken over cutting off part of Saul's skirt and actually is surrendering. Here David puts a distance between himself and Saul, most likely because this time David addresses the army instead of the king.

1 Samuel 26:14, *"And David cried to the people, and to Abner the son of Ner, saying, Answerest thou not, Abner? Then Abner answered and said, Who art thou that criest to the king"?*

David cries first to the people and then to Abner, Saul's nephew and captain of his army (1 Samuel 14:50). Abner must be taken aback because it takes him a time to answer. They were probably trying to discern who it was before asking the question. Then Abner asks who it is that is addressing the king, meaning the camp of the king. David plainly addresses Abner and begins to chide him sharply.

1 Samuel 26:15, *"And David said to Abner, Art not thou a valiant man? and who is like to thee in Israel? wherefore then hast thou not kept thy lord the king? for there came one of the people in to destroy the king thy lord."*

David takes this opportunity to mock Abner by landing him one of the harshest insults, that of not protecting his master. David knew full well that Abner was not able to resist the power of God that had caused him to sleep, and yet he bears upon him. It is not known exactly why David chose this course of action, but it is a striking contrast from the words for the one Abner was subject to. David tells him he is worthy to die because of his neglect. David proves later that he does not really believe Abner should have died for this, because he makes great lamentation over Abner when Joab, David's captain, kills him to avenge his brother whom Abner killed.

1 Samuel 26:17, *"And Saul knew David's voice, and said, Is this thy voice, my son David? And David said, It is my voice, my lord, O king."*

Notice still how tenderly David answers Saul as once again he shows outward signs of repentance. It seems this time that David was not moved by Saul's confession and repentance. However, David clearly shows once again that he is guiltless toward Saul. This will be the last time David will make an effort to plead his case to Saul, but we find many psalms from this period of time in David's life that amply prove how much and how often David poured his complaint out before the Lord. David explains to Saul that if it was the Lord stirring up his heart against him, he could offer a sacrifice. David was proving to Saul that he was operating under the influence of demons and of men influenced by demons.

It seems here by these words of David to Saul, that David had contemplated leaving the coasts of Israel if God didn't deliver him from Saul. In fact in the very next chapter, he did just that. David was resolved that he would not and could not kill Saul or allow someone else to do so while in his presence. Therefore, David felt he was driven out of the land of Israel. This shows David's extreme position of praying on any land but the land of Israel. He later prayed in the ashes of Ziklag in the land of the Philistines, but it was in great desperation. As far as serving other gods, David is the only king in Israel or Judah who never practiced or allowed any form of idolatry.

1 Samuel 26:21, *"Then said Saul, I have sinned: return, my son David: for I will no more do thee harm, because my soul was precious in thine eyes this day: behold, I have played the fool, and have erred exceedingly."*

The confession here is even greater than the last time, and this time there is a plain request for David to return to the king's court. Saul seems very sincere and even alludes to himself as a fool, which is the strongest of words to condemn both himself and his horrible wicked actions.

1 Samuel 26:22, *"And David answered and said, Behold the king's spear; and let one of the young men come over and fetch it."*

Again David realizes that he is supernaturally protected and knows Saul is not going to command all of his army to pursue him. It should be noted that this knowledge did not come to David through Saul's temporary repentance, but through his relationship with the Lord. David graciously allows one of Saul's young men to come and get the spear of Saul, which is the symbol of Saul's authority. David testifies again how he is blessed of the Lord and is careful to give the Lord the glory for his longevity.

1 Samuel 26:25, *"Then Saul said to David, Blessed be thou, my son David: thou shalt both do great things, and also shalt still prevail. So David went on his way, and Saul returned to his place."*

Each time Saul comes to his senses, he immediately prophesies as to the hand of the Lord upon David and the exploits David is destined to do. It seems however that David abruptly left, not desiring to hear any more lofty words from Saul. Saul returned home.

1 Samuel 27:1, *And David said in his heart, I shall now perish one day by the hand of Saul: there is nothing better for me than that I should speedily escape into the land of the Philistines; and Saul shall despair of me, to seek me any more in any coast of Israel: so shall I escape out of his hand."*

Almost every theologian faults David in the direction he now takes. Why would such a warrior allow fear to grip him to the degree that he would make such a wicked confession, *"I shall now perish one day by the hand of Saul":* There are four amazing things to consider here: 1) David had a moment like John the Baptist, who after he had announced Jesus as the very Messiah, began to question whether or not it was really Him and suffered with deep doubt (Matthew 11:3). 2) He had constant weariness of living from camp to camp, having to deal with the demonic spirit in Saul, and maintaining his army in hiding. 3) He forgot the last clear command from the prophet Gad (1Samuel 22:5), who told him to go to the land of Judah. 4) He ignored the ample proof of God's constant protection in every situation while in exile.

1 Samuel 27:2, *"And David arose, and he passed over with the six hundred men that were with him unto Achish, the son of Maoch, king of Gath."*

David had already made one frightful attempt of going to Gath, and now he is going there again, most likely under another king than was there in his first visit. Because David was such a famous warrior, it is possible that Achish invited him there to strengthen himself against Saul. Whether or not Achish invited David does not lighten the darkness of David's inexcusable, and it seems, premeditated sin (1 Samuel 26:19). David is totally defenseless now because he is 1) Leaving the very calling of God on his life; 2) Actually placing himself under a false and totally inadequate covering of a heathen king; 3) Leading the men entrusted to him into the very judgment of God.

1 Samuel 27:3, *"And David dwelt with Achish at Gath, he and his men, every man with his household, even David with his two wives, Ahinoam the Jezreelitess, and Abigail the Carmelitess, Nabal's wife."*

Like David, the other men had their families with them. This is not the custom of the Israelis but the Arabs and their roving bands of invaders and pirates. However the length of time in exile from Saul and the uncertainty of their future may have been factors. Most likely it was Saul's treatment of the priests of Nob that caused the soldiers to be afraid to leave their wives and little ones with others.

1 Samuel 27:4, *And it was told Saul that David was fled to Gath: and he sought no more again for him.*

Saul is either giving up from the ever increasing difficulty of the task, or he is fulfilling his last pledge. From the words in 1 Samuel 26:19, Saul may have understood that David has backslidden completely and will never pursue his destiny as king. Most likely it is the latter. For in fact David is backsliding in coming to Achish, but if Saul considers David's failure a finality of his life, he has like many others, underestimated the mercy and restoration of God.

1 Samuel 27:5, *"And David said unto Achish, If I have now found grace in thine eyes, let them give me a place in some town in the country, that I may dwell there: for why should thy servant dwell in the royal city with thee"?*

We may wonder how many times the Lord tried to speak to David to keep him from deepening his alliance with the enemies of God. Where is Abiathar and the Ephod? Why is David seeking favor in the sight of God's enemies? Why is David asking for a permanent dwelling place among the enemies of God? This instance is the very closest David came to idolatry, and were it not for the burning of Ziklag (which once belonged to Judah), it would have been the case. Watts spoke the pitiful proverb "Lot in Sodom, poor gain, poor gain. Lot in Sodom, what shame, what shame!" What one compromises to gain, he will someday lose. Ziklag is called by Bishop Lightfoot "The city of the spoiled spoils of compromise."

1 Samuel 27:7, *"And the time that David dwelt in the country of the Philistines was a full year and four months."*

Sixteen months of wasted days. Sixteen months of rebellion. For sixteen months the most gifted warrior in the history of Israel used his skills to murder and rob innocent people (Verses 8-9). For sixteen months we have no record of David's penning a single psalm. For sixteen months there is no record of even one experience between David and his Lord. For sixteen months David ran from his calling to be king of the greatest people on earth. Where was his harp?

1 Samuel 27:8, *"And David and his men went up, and invaded the Geshurites, and the Gezrites, and the Amalekites: for those nations were of old the inhabitants of the land, as thou goest to Shur even unto the land of Egypt."*

David probably tried to justify his murdering rampage by saying these were the enemies of the Lord. These people were in fact included in the list of heathens appointed to be cleansed from the land by the judgment of God. However, God didn't tell David to do such. When David left his land in Carmel that he had gained by marrying Abigail, he didn't have the sustenance that he formerly had, so he spoiled the people around him to gain what he needed. In the sixteen months

David abides with the Philistines at Ziklag, we find no mention of any agricultural efforts by his people.

1 Samuel 27:9, *"And David smote the land, and left neither man nor woman alive, and took away the sheep, and the oxen, and the asses, and the camels, and the apparel, and returned, and came to Achish."*

Most likely David was bringing a portion of the spoil to Achish, as was probably prearranged at David's coming. From the following language of Achish, he showed neither shock of David's action nor any sort of disapproval. It seems that David has now gone in to the full merchandising of his anointing for successful war campaigns. But he has even stooped so low as to murder women and children. It is believed by many that this activity later prohibited David from building the Temple, as recorded in 1 Chronicles 22:7-8, *"And David said to Solomon, My son, as for me, it was in my mind to build a house unto the name of the LORD my God: But the word of the LORD came to me, saying, Thou hast shed blood abundantly, and hast made great wars: thou shalt not build a house unto my name, because thou hast shed much blood upon the earth in my sight."*

It is not likely that the Lord is holding David responsible for killing the enemies of the Lord such as Goliath, but for these women and children while he was in Gath. David was forgiven and yet knew very well that there is a strong recompense for sin. One can suffer without sinning, but one cannot sin without suffering.

1 Samuel 27:10, *"And Achish said, Whither have ye made a road to day? And David said, Against the south of Judah, and against the south of the Jerahmeelites, and against the south of the Kenites."*

It is no wonder that David lied to Achish as to where he had made the raid. Any one that will murder women and children for profit and self projection will certainly lie and deceive. David actually convinced Achish that he had brought this bounty from his own tribal people (1 Chronicles 2:9).

1 Samuel 27:11, *"And David saved neither man nor woman alive, to bring tidings to Gath, saying, Lest they should tell on us, saying, So did David, and so will be his manner all the while he dwelleth in the country of the Philistines."*

Lightfoot told of a reader of David's life who when he came to the account of this horrible failure, exclaimed in anger at David, "I will never speak or read of David again." This man made a horrible mistake, as David's name is found in the verses more than any other person. God redeemed such a wretch in such a high fashion that He declared David to be both the forerunner and true type of the Messiah of Israel.

1 Samuel 27:12, *"And Achish believed David, saying, He hath made his people Israel utterly to abhor him; therefore he shall be my servant for ever."*

David, who was called of God to defend his people Israel, actually made Achish believe he had destroyed them; therefore, Achish thought David would never, nor could ever, return to his people. Nobody who ever served him was like David as far as he was concerned. However, there are indications that the men of Achish and the Philistines in general were not convinced of David's loyalty to Achish.

1 Samuel 28:1, *"And it came to pass in those days, that the Philistines gathered their armies together for warfare, to fight with Israel. And Achish said unto David, Know thou assuredly, that thou shalt go out with me to battle, thou and thy men."*

I find no fault at all in King Achish for presuming that David would fight beside him against David's own people. David had deceived him to think he had been raiding Judah, so now he is expected to perform the thing he told Achish he was doing. Oh, the trap of deception and lies! How much farther can David degenerate than to strap on his sword and march with the uncircumcised Philistines against the covenant people of God? It is no wonder God had prepared the Amalekites to take Ziklag and wake David out of his pitiful backsliding.

1 Samuel 28:2, *"And David said to Achish, Surely thou shalt know what thy servant can do. And Achish said to David, Therefore will I make thee keeper of mine head for ever."*

It seems David clearly succeeded in impressing Achish, for now he intends for David to be his armor bearer for the rest of his life. Calmuet defends David by stating that David would not have carried through with actually killing his own people, but would have done as the lords of the Philistines warned and would turn on the Philistines. Calmuet is wrong, for David was visibly angry when he was prohibited by the lords of the Philistines to continue with them.

Here the verses leave the marching army of the Philistines, with David and his men as soldiers on their way to attack Israel, in order to cover another very sad story. We now see that Saul hears of the coming army and knows he is in trouble. We read in 1 Samuel 28:5-6, *"And when Saul saw the host of the Philistines, he was afraid, and his heart greatly trembled. And when Saul enquired of the LORD, the LORD answered him not, neither by dreams, nor by Urim, nor by prophets."*

We find no proof that Saul was aware that David and his men were in the company of the Philistines. Saul desperately needs direction from the Lord, but the Lord is not talking to him. So Saul goes to the witch of Endor. What a state Israel is in! Samuel is dead. David is backslidden. Saul is seeking counsel from a witch.

The witch brings up Samuel from the dead at Saul's request. There is great but needless controversy as to whether it was Samuel or a demon impersonating Samuel. The scripture says it was Samuel. Samuel could resurrect early without violating one single verse. Saul received no relief from the mouth of the disquieted Samuel.

1 Samuel 28:17, *"And the LORD hath done to him, as he spake by me: for the LORD hath rent the kingdom out of thine hand, and given it to thy neighbour, even to David":*

Samuel told Saul that he would die the next day and David would eventually be the king of Israel. It is quite amazing that at the very time David is marching in the wrong army, running from his destiny, and deceiving Achish, Samuel is confirming to Saul that David will be the king of Israel. Sovereign grace is sometimes near to unbelievable, but God knew that David would fully repent. Upon hearing Samuel's words, Saul is scared into a semi coma and remained there in Endor for the night.

1 Samuel 29:2, *"And the lords of the Philistines passed on by hundreds, and by thousands: but David and his men passed on in the rereward with Achish."*

The armies of the Philistines have moved into the land of Israel, as Aphek is a part of Issachar close by Gilboa. Yet David is still with the Philistines. However, his position in the ranks prove the low ranking of Achish king of Gath who some ascribe to be the general in charge. Yet Achish couldn't even over rule the princes of the Philistines concerning their desire to send David away. In the land of Israel, there was only one king over the entire nation, but the Philistines often placed kings over just one city. David was accustomed to leading large armies, not following along in the rear. This degradation is just a small part of the great price David paid for his sin. He had through deception, murder, and lies worked his way into a position with Achish that was much less than his calling.

1 Samuel 29:3, *"Then said the princes of the Philistines, What do these Hebrews here? And Achish said unto the princes of the Philistines, Is not this David, the servant of Saul the king of Israel, which hath been with me these days, or these years, and I have found no fault in him since he fell unto me unto this day"?*

The spiral downward of a backslider is sure. David finds himself in a most embarrassing situation. The princes of the Philistines have discovered Achish's armor bearer is none other than the famous warrior of Israel who destroyed Goliath, their champion from Gath. As the engagement in war is near, the lords of the Philistines do not want David and his men on their side. Achish tries to defend David's loyalty to him but cannot convince the princes to let him continue on the campaign. As he tries, the princes of the Philistines go into a rage and demand that David and his men go back to Ziklag. Even heathens can recognize the backslider and fear the restoration that could come at any moment. They realize that if David comes to his senses during the middle of the battle, he and his six hundred man army could do a great deal of damage to them.

1 Samuel 29:5, *"Is not this David, of whom they sang one to another in dances, saying, Saul slew his thousands, and David his ten thousands?"*

Achish knew the princes of the Philistines were not going to allow David to go with them. How celebrated was this proverb in the whole region that was ascribed to David by the women of Israel? The lords of the Philistines had heard of this saying concerning David, the one that drove Saul mad.

1 Samuel 29:6, *"Then Achish called David, and said unto him, Surely, as the LORD liveth, thou hast been upright, and thy going out and thy coming in with me in the host is good in my sight: for I have not found evil in thee since the day of thy coming unto me unto this day: nevertheless the lords favour thee not."*

As Achish breaks this news to David, he wants to be sure David understands that it is not him that doubts his loyalty or fears his betrayal. Yet, this is another indictment against David. Achish showers David with praises for what a good job he has done for him. Every single lofty word Achish speaks over David should have driven a dart into his soul because David's talent and anointing were not to be used to advance the uncircumcised. Better for David are the words Achish reports from the lords of the Philistines, *"nevertheless the lords favour thee not."* When John Wesley was told that the Free Thinkers were not speaking favorably of him and his brother Charles, he replied, "I thank God they praise me not."

1 Samuel 29:8, *"And David said unto Achish, But what have I done? and what hast thou found in thy servant so long as I have been with thee unto this day, that I may not go fight against the enemies of my lord the king"?*

Now we have arrived at the lowest point of David's backsliding concerning leaving his people and his prophesied position. He is so low that he pleads for the opportunity to go and fight against the very people he is to father. This is far worse than marching in the wrong army. David actually refers to Israel as the *"the enemies of my lord the king,"* meaning Achish. This is equivalent to Peter's standing in front of the enemies of Christ and denying that he knew Him, for David had moved, through prophecies the Lord had given him, into both the Melchesedec realm and the Messianic. David also lived in this state for quite a season, while Peter repented deeply that very night and preached the gospel at Pentecost some fifty days later.

1 Samuel 29:9, *"And Achish answered and said to David, I know that thou art good in my sight, as an angel of God: notwithstanding the princes of the Philistines have said, He shall not go up with us to the battle."*

With another commendation, Achish gives David the final answer; he will not be going with the army of the Philistines. Achish then gives David his departure directions as well as a release of those men with him. He allows the men to stay the night for it must have been far into the day by the time the decision was made.

1 Samuel 29:11, *"So David and his men rose up early to depart in the morning, to return into the land of the Philistines. And the Philistines went up to Jezreel."*

David's men are most likely very angry, and feeling rejected and embarrassed as they start their three day march back to Ziklag. The Philistines went on to engage in the war against Israel, the war that would end the life of Saul and his sons.

I Samuel 30:1, *"And it came to pass, when David and his men were come to Ziklag on the third day, that the Amalekites had invaded the south, and Ziklag, and smitten Ziklag, and burned it with fire";*

Three days out and three days back for this army was not only a most unfruitful trip, but then they came in sight of the smoking Ziklag. Here one should see firsthand what it costs to march in the wrong army. The bounty of compromise, Ziklag, will always go up in smoke. As the men came close to survey the damage, they probably expected to see the charred bodies of their dead family members. Instead they could tell that they were taken hostage because there was no blood and no bodies.

1 Samuel 30:3, *"So David and his men came to the city, and, behold, it was burned with fire; and their wives, and their sons, and their daughters, were taken captives."*

The city of Ziklag was thought to be exclusively for David and his men without any other inhabitants. Therefore the size of the population of the city would have been about two thousand

and five hundred. David's six hundred men, their wives, and a couple of children would probably be a conservative estimate as some of them, including David, had more than one wife. The loss to them was unbelievable, but if they had received what they deserved, they would have no one left alive. These soldiers had been raiding other cities and destroying other people's women and children.

1 Samuel 30:4, *"Then David and the people that were with him lifted up their voice and wept, until they had no more power to weep."*

These men stood in the ashes of judgment and lamented their loss until they were unable to weep more. It is not recorded here if there was any repentance on the part of this army for their own raids. Perhaps David led them in repentance, but there are no signs of it. In fact their grief, at least in some of the men, turned to anger.

1 Samuel 30:5, *"And David's two wives were taken captives, Ahinoam the Jezreelitess, and Abigail the wife of Nabal the Carmelite."*

There is much speculation as to why this verse records again that David's wives were also taken. Perhaps the record is to drive a point as to the Lord's displeasure with polygamy or maybe to accentuate David's loss.

1 Samuel 30:6, *"And David was greatly distressed; for the people spake of stoning him, because the soul of all the people was grieved, every man for his sons and for his daughters: but David encouraged himself in the LORD his God."*

The great distress David felt was not just because his life was in danger from his own men. He was directly confronted with all of his sin since he left Israel. He is looking at the very exact result of backsliding. His Ziklag is burning, as will all Ziklags, for it is the wages of serving Achish. David's distress was overwhelming on every front. Saul turned to the witch in his despair, but David turned to the Lord. Saul was told he would die the next day, but David was told he would recover all. David encourages himself in the Lord.

Here is where a leader must be very wise. David would not have survived had he not been more than a leader. He had become somewhat of a father to his men. Therefore when some suggested that he be stoned, the sons would not allow such a thing. David is going to prove that he had become somewhat of a father to them, although the men thought of stoning him. After David receives encouragement, he calls for the priest and the ephod, for he is now ready to hear from the Lord and obey. David doesn't know what God will tell him at the time he inquires, but he knows in whom he will again trust. This scene at Ziklag is one of the turning points in David's life and a clear harbinger for all who will leave their calling to serve Achish.

1 Samuel 30:8, *"And David enquired at the LORD, saying, Shall I pursue after this troop? shall I overtake them? And he answered him, Pursue: for thou shalt surely overtake them, and without fail recover all."*

These were very welcomed words of mercy. David's broken heart was healed by the glorious promise that he would recover all. After all of the wickedness he had done, after all of the time he had spent serving the Philistines, and after all of his failure, God takes his case and restores him fully. How can this be? Amazing grace is the only answer.

1 Samuel 30:9, *"So David went, he and the six hundred men that were with him, and came to the brook Besor, where those that were left behind stayed."*

Now David and his men are not marching in rebellion to pursue the interest of the Philistines, but they are marching in the will of God to accomplish that which the God of grace has ordained. At the Brook Besor some of the men couldn't go on. The men were probably totally exhausted even though they were seasoned warriors. They had marched with Achish three days out and after they were sent home, three days back and now they are pursuing the Amalekites.

1 Samuel 30:10, *"But David pursued, he and four hundred men: for two hundred abode behind, which were so faint that they could not go over the brook Besor."*

David had a very small number to take on the Amalekites, even before he left the two hundred at the brook Besor. Now with four hundred he presses on with an amazing energy. Watts said, "The freshly restored walk in an amazing energy." Not only is David walking in the energy of his restoration but he is hearing the voice of the Lord again, and God said he would be a victor.

1 Samuel 30:11, *"And they found an Egyptian in the field, and brought him to David, and gave him bread, and he did eat; and they made him drink water"*;

David's men found the abandoned and sick Egyptian slave, and the find not only spared the life of the slave but blessed David to gain all of the information needed to find the Amalekites. God could have supernaturally shown David the whereabouts of the Amalekites through another means, but He chose this means to encourage the value of taking in the stranger. However, I doubt the major interest in nourishing the man to life was true benevolence but for the sake of his possible information. Three days and three nights without food or water would not in itself have taken this toll on the man, but that with sickness left him nearly dead.

1 Samuel 30:13, *"And David said unto him, To whom belongest thou? and whence art thou? And he said, I am a young man of Egypt, servant to an Amalekite; and my master left me, because three days agone I fell sick."*

This Egyptian slave, abandoned by the Amalekites because he was sick, is an example of the ruthlessness of the enemies of David. And yet the whole campaign was halted for the need of nursing a stranger to life. Herein is a great sermon for the church. The programs and successes of the church are often held up for the lack of helping strangers. The money for the work is in the mouth of the fish. The information that begins to come out of the mouth of this revived slave makes David know that this is God's provision for the success of this campaign.

1 Samuel 30:15, *"And David said to him, Canst thou bring me down to this company? And he said, Swear unto me by God, that thou wilt neither kill me, nor deliver me into the hands of my master, and I will bring thee down to this company."*

It is amazing that the Egyptian slave demanded that David swear by God. Either he was familiar with Judaism or was a worshipper of God himself. Most likely it is a testimony to the notoriety of David and his relationship with God. The young man would be assured that David would keep his word if he swore to him by his God. Evidently David did swear to the boy by his God, but the scripture doesn't record it. The Egyptian led him to the Amalekites, for most likely he had heard when he traveled with them just where they intended to camp, or perhaps his master told him where to meet them in case he survived his illness.

The Amalekites were having a great party celebrating all of the spoils they had gained, through not only their raid on Ziklag, but also the other cities they had looted. Ziklag probably netted them the most bounty, as David was very wealthy and had kept accumulating more spoils with each raid. The Amalekites were probably thinking that David was with the Philistines in a prolonged battle and therefore very careless concerning their watch. In their celebration they never considered the wrath of God about to fall on them through His restored servant David.

1 Samuel 30:17, *"And David smote them from the twilight even unto the evening of the next day: and there escaped not a man of them, save four hundred young men, which rode upon camels, and fled."*

The size of the company of Amalekites is not told us but it was surely significant, for the account of four hundred of them getting away on camels indicates the four hundred were but a remnant. Most likely David and his men waited until dark to attack so as not to reveal how little his army was. After the Amalekites started falling to the swords of the men of David, there was no contest. As in the case of Belshazzar, the party was over and death was everywhere. David the mighty warrior was again operating in the supernatural power of God, and it should be noticed that they slew only the men. David was well aware of God's sparing his women and children, and as for the men, they were already reserved for judgment.

1 Samuel 30:18, *"And David recovered all that the Amalekites had carried away: and David rescued his two wives."*

Imagine David looking through the crowd amidst the screams, lamentations, and anguish of the terrified women and children. He rescues his wives and children and no doubt comforts them after such a trauma. Abigail, a former aristocratic wife of an extremely wealthy man (Nabal), could have often wondered what she had gotten herself into. We find no account of her own personal faith in God, but she was a Jew of the tribe of Judah and was most likely a supporter of David's worship and warfare. It is possible that he was with her in some times of worship, and Abigail could hear the songs of the Lord that David wrote before anyone else.

1 Samuel 30:19, *"And there was nothing lacking to them, neither small nor great, neither sons nor daughters, neither spoil, nor any thing that they had taken to them: David recovered all."*

How sweet to hear the Word of the Lord speaking to you of great deliverance in your great time of distress. There is only one thing better, and that is to see it fulfilled in front of your very eyes. Just exactly as was spoken, David recovered all.

1 Samuel 30:20, *"And David took all the flocks and the herds, which they drave before those other cattle, and said, This is David's spoil."*

Everything the Amalekites had taken through their raids on the villages of Judea before they lighted upon Ziklag became the spoil of David. David didn't mean this to be exclusively his alone, but his to divide as he saw fit, which he did in a very generous way. This energy of the restored David was so dynamic that everyone around him was blessed, and so it should be.

1 Samuel 30:21, *"And David came to the two hundred men, which were so faint that they could not follow David, whom they had made also to abide at the brook Besor: and they went forth to meet David, and to meet the people that were with him: and when David came near to the people, he saluted them."*

These who had stayed by the stuff were no doubt watching and waiting for the return of their comrades with a great expectation. David had probably sent a runner to tell them the good news. There was probably a lot of anticipation as to whether any of these people would receive a part of the spoils, and that began to be a vocal controversy as soon as they arrived. Here is another test of leadership for David, but also an opportunity to set a powerful precedent for all of his future campaigns.

1 Samuel 30:22, *"Then answered all the wicked men and men of Belial, of those that went with David, and said, Because they went not with us, we will not give them ought of the spoil that we have recovered, save to every man his wife and his children, that they may lead them away, and depart."*

This is the first proof that some of David's men did not serve David's God. Now we know that it was this same faction of men that tried to get David to kill Saul on two different occasions. Their counsel is just as pitiful here, as they try to persuade David to send a third of their company away with nothing but their own recovered goods.

1 Samuel 30:23, *"Then said David, Ye shall not do so, my brethren, with that which the LORD hath given us, who hath preserved us, and delivered the company that came against us into our hand."*

David was not about to show either selfishness or partiality with that which the Lord provided. He knew the Lord had given him the victory. He defended the ones who were so exhausted they could not make the full journey by saying that they would also receive their share of the spoil. It seems that David had some sort of sharing system for his soldiers. However, by David's declaring that the spoils were his, it appears he was intending to give everyone an equal share all along. The ones who were trying to persuade David the wrong way were not a strong enough voice to get their will accomplished. David therefore made a statute concerning the matter for future dispersing of spoils. A wise leader may utilize the service of men who are not fully with them as long as they have nothing close to a majority. It should be known by every leader that everyone that is close to you is not necessarily connected to you.

1 Samuel 30:26, *"And when David came to Ziklag, he sent of the spoil unto the elders of Judah, even to his friends, saying, Behold a present for you of the spoil of the enemies of the LORD"*;

David wanted to not only bless his tribe but also to help them recover some of their property, as God had blessed him to do. Some theologians consider David to have another motive by giving the spoils, but offer no solid proof of such except to say that he advanced quickly afterwards. It should be quite evident that the favor of God was upon him, and in that favor he was advancing, instead of using strategic manipulation. We have no reason to believe his careful distribution was anything more than disinterested benevolence.

1 Samuel 30:31, *"And to them which were in Hebron, and to all the places where David himself and his men were wont to haunt."*

It seems that David's distribution was certainly connected to those of his tribe that had helped him while in exile. Again, this is no mark against his benevolence but rather the attribute of rewarding good deeds. It is a major point of a good king to be generous to the people, and David made it clear that the bounty was a result of the destruction of the Lord's enemies. The kingly order is getting well established since David's experience at Ziklag, and necessarily so, for Saul is either dead or dying by the time the bounty was received in Judah, by the hand of the Philistines and his own sword. Had David continued marching in the Philistine army, he would have most likely been killed with Saul and Jonathan.

2 Samuel

2 Samuel 1:1, *"Now it came to pass after the death of Saul, when David was returned from the slaughter of the Amalekites, and David had abode two days in Ziklag";*

Chapter 31 of 1 Samuel does not have a verse that mentions David. It is the account of the pitiful death of Saul. Horribly wounded by the Philistines, afraid of their torture and abuse, he falls on his own sword and dies. David is in Ziklag recuperating from the strenuous journey and intense battle with the Amalekites. He has not yet heard how the battle went between the Philistines and the Israelis because it was far away. So David remains in Ziklag, making do with the accommodations that were not completely destroyed by the fire.

2 Samuel 1:2, *"It came even to pass on the third day, that, behold, a man came out of the camp from Saul with his clothes rent, and earth upon his head: and so it was, when he came to David, that he fell to the earth, and did obeisance."*

An Amalekite youth runs to Ziklag with the horrible report of Israel's horrendous defeat, as well as the death of Saul and Jonathan. He has his clothes rent as a sign of total aspiration and earth on his head. Whether the grief of this young Amalekite is real or feigned is a controversy, for it seems by his further actions that he is an opportunist. Nevertheless, he shows by doing obeisance that he considers David to be the king.

2 Samuel 1:3, *"And David said unto him, From whence comest thou? And he said unto him, Out of the camp of Israel am I escaped."*

David inquires of the young man and discovers that he has escaped out of the camp of Israel. This would not mean he is an escaped slave although we find him later to be an Amalekite. Rather, it would mean that he escaped death in the battle and came to David.

2 Samuel 1:4, *"And David said unto him, How went the matter? I pray thee, tell me. And he answered, That the people are fled from the battle, and many of the people also are fallen and dead; and Saul and Jonathan his son are dead also."*

David hears the sad news of Saul and Jonathan. If David expresses any gladness for Saul's death, it is not detected here or anywhere else in the scripture. In the song he writes concerning Saul and Jonathan, we find nothing but praises for both Jonathan and Saul. David, no doubt, is very deeply moved at the hearing of the passing of his covenant friend Jonathan. It is of note that even though Jonathan certainly never approved of Saul's erratic and bizarre behavior, he died beside him in the battle.

2 Samuel 1:5, *"And David said unto the young man that told him, How knowest thou that Saul and Jonathan his son be dead"?*

David seeks to verify the story of the young man and begins to hear from the young man's lips an incredible and horrific account. The young man was no doubt escaping for his life when the army scattered in defeat, and he then runs across Saul. It is mostly believed that this young man fabricates the story of killing Saul, saying he did so at Saul's own request, for the purpose of making himself look like the one that killed David's main enemy. He may have expected a reward, but instead he got far from it. He tells David that he made sure Saul could not live before he killed him. This remark probably was the point in which David's countenance changed for the worse toward the young man. How often do evil men misunderstand a righteous warrior in this manner? It may be noted that it was an Amalekite that lifted Saul's helmet and bracelet, one of the very tribe Saul had disobeyed God in allowing to live.

2 Samuel 1:11, *"Then David took hold on his clothes, and rent them; and likewise all the men that were with him":*

David expresses the totality of grief and anguish by ripping his clothes and thus setting off a chain reaction as his men did likewise. Surely those "sons of Belial" that were in David's camp were not grieved, for they had twice advised David to kill Saul himself. However they dare not show their gladness, for David was truly and deeply grieved over the death of Saul and Jonathan. This is amazing to many because most any man having been treated like David was by Saul would not have been so grieved at his death, much less have mourned and called a fast. Some scholars say it was only because of Jonathan that he was so grieved, but they have yet to find one trace of anything but love for Saul in David's life.

2 Samuel 1:13, *"And David said unto the young man that told him, Whence art thou? And he answered, I am the son of a stranger, an Amalekite."*

After the fast and the display of grief in honor of Saul and Jonathan, David reexamines the Amalekite that brought him the word of their death. In the young man's report, he had already mentioned that he was an Amalekite, so here we must find David's inquiring more into his lineage, rather than asking him to repeat that he is an Amalekite.

Some Jewish scholars have purported that this young man was a son of Doeg the Edomite. They do so without any real proof. It is true that the Amalekites are from Edom of Esau, for Amalek was the grandson of Esau (Genesis 36:15-16). The young man is careful here to say he is a stranger and an Amalekite. While an Amalekite could be of Doeg, he could not have been the son of Doeg and yet a stranger in Israel, for Doeg was a high ranking official in Saul's cabinet.

2 Samuel 1:14, *"And David said unto him, How wast thou not afraid to stretch forth thine hand to destroy the LORD'S anointed"?*

David asks a very good question, *"How wast thou not afraid to stretch forth thine hand to destroy the LORD'S anointed?"* The lie the young man told about killing Saul at Saul's request will now cost him his own life. David had no reason to doubt the account the young man gave concerning Saul's death. It seems the promotion the young man sought to receive by his story was based on his appraisal of human nature, but David's love for Saul was supernatural.

2 Samuel 1:15, *"And David called one of the young men, and said, Go near, and fall upon him. And he smote him that he died."*

Consider these things: 1) This self-indicted uncircumcised heathen was already judged to die by a former mandate from the Lord (1 Samuel 15:1-3) even though he lied about killing Saul. 2) This public execution, coupled with the corporate fast and mourning, would further state to all parties that David had done nothing to wish for or orchestrate the death of Saul. 3) David knew that the matter of the helmet and bracelet could easily become an issue later, so he wanted to be sure that these items were not something he wanted or had asked for.

2 Samuel 1:16, *"And David said unto him, Thy blood be upon thy head; for thy mouth hath testified against thee, saying, I have slain the LORD'S anointed."*

Here David gives the Amalekite the final sentence of his guilt for taking the life of one of God's anointed. He decrees that in fact he has caused his own death. Some take an issue with David, and they list this as one of his failures. This should not be listed among David's failures or accomplishments, but rather a stern warning for all who stretch their hand against the Lord's anointed.

2 Samuel 1:17, *"And David lamented with this lamentation over Saul and over Jonathan his son"*:

This lamentation is quite a masterpiece of prophetic commendation to the leader of Israel and his people. Here we can see more into the heart of David and his disinterested benevolent love for Saul, as well as for Jonathan. It is also evident that David's heart has been totally reunited with his people, for he does not want the death of Saul to be published in Gath (Verse 20, *"Tell it not in Gath"*) which is the city David had fled to twice. Between Saul, Jonathan, and David, the Philistines suffered a lot of defeats, and David didn't want the daughters of the Philistines to rejoice over the death of Saul and Jonathan.

In his lamentation, David again refers to the anointing oil that was on Saul. David also said, *"Saul and Jonathan were lovely and pleasant in their lives, and in their death they were not divided: they were swifter than eagles, they were stronger than lions."* These gracious words again prove David's true admiration for these fallen men. But David finally moves his lamentation into the heartfelt grief for his covenant friend Jonathan. True love like this never seeks its own. Jonathan never had an ounce of competition with David for the throne of Israel; he knew that David would become king of Israel. Actually, the last words spoken to David by both Jonathan and Saul were prophetic words acknowledging David's destiny to be king.

2 Samuel 2:1, *"And it came to pass after this, that David inquired of the LORD, saying, Shall I go up into any of the cities of Judah? And the LORD said unto him, Go up. And David said, Whither shall I go up? And he said, Unto Hebron."*

David had learned his lesson it seems. He doesn't want to go anywhere that he is not supposed to go. David would have normally just gone home to his people in Judah after the death of Saul, but now he doesn't even take that for granted. He inquired of the Lord whether he should go to Judah. Then he inquired as to what area of Judah, and the Lord told him Hebron. Jerusalem and Hebron are close together and the area had been quite friendly unto David all of the time he was in exile from Saul. One of the reasons David would have questioned the Lord about going to Judah was probably a result of his past failures. He wasn't sure as to whether the Lord would still allow him the joy of living with his people, and he did not know who of Saul's tribe might try to be installed as king of Israel. At this point David would have gone wherever the Lord would have sent him, but he wanted to be sure that he had a clear word of direction.

2 Samuel 2:2, "So *David went up thither, and his two wives also, Ahinoam the Jezreelitess, and Abigail Nabal's wife the Carmelite."*

David returns to Hebron with his family. It is not mentioned here how many children David now has, but we know from other verses that children were born to him from both wives all throughout his exile and his sixteen months stay at Ziklag. These wives had endured the hard days of exile and the despair of being taken hostage from Ziklag. No doubt they were very eager to settle down. Poverty had never been their plight, but being a fugitive was a difficult matter for the health and benefit of their domestic lives.

2 Samuel 2:3, *"And his men that were with him did David bring up, every man with his household: and they dwelt in the cities of Hebron."*

David's men and their families were probably too many for the city of Hebron itself but the adjoining cities and hamlets are here mentioned. David was always sure that those who were with him in adversity were rewarded with him in prosperity. This is a biblical principle that the Apostle Paul alluded to in 2 Timothy 2:12, *"If we suffer, we shall also reign with him: if we deny him, he also will deny us":* Those who suffered with David reigned with him, but those who denied David suffered greatly.

2 Samuel 2:4, *"And the men of Judah came, and there they anointed David king over the house of Judah. And they told David, saying, That the men of Jabesh-gilead were they that buried Saul."*

These men of Judah are the tribal leaders, and their action here is quite bold at a very vulnerable time for Israel, for the following reasons: They anointed David king of Judah 1) Without waiting to see who would take the place of Saul on the throne; 2) Without the approval of any other tribe; 3) In the face of the friction already existing between the tribes over the maltreatment of David by Saul; and 4) Without a recorded input by the priesthood, although they knew that Abiathar, the only surviving priest of Nob, was with David and that Samuel had already anointed David privately.

This seems to be the first David had heard of the heroic deeds of the men of Jabesh-gilead and how they had greatly risked their lives to rescue the bodies of Saul and Jonathan, then burned them and buried their bones.

2 Samuel 2:5, *"And David sent messengers unto the men of Jabesh-gilead, and said unto them, Blessed be ye of the LORD, that ye have shewed this kindness unto your lord, even unto Saul, and have buried him."*

David promises to protect the men of Jabesh-gilead for their act of kindness toward the family of Saul. This was a wise and strategic move for David politically, but he was probably not politically motivated. This act would not only help assure that David was not pleased about the death of Saul, but that there was not great aspiration to be king of the whole nation. David does let them know that the house of Judah had already anointed him king.

2 Samuel 2:10, *"Ishbosheth Saul's son was forty years old when he began to reign over Israel, and reigned two years. But the house of Judah followed David."*

The captain of the host of Israel was Abner, Saul's cousin. Abner took it upon himself to take Ishbosheth, Saul's son, and make him king. This he did most likely to protect his position. Totally unable was Abner to be the actual king, and his ears had heard at least twice from Saul himself that David was going to be king of Israel. Therefore in fear and haste, Abner tried to avert David's taking over the whole nation as king. Abner was successful in a roundabout way for seven years. Ishbosheth himself reigned two years of that time before the war broke out between him and David. However, Judah never again wavered from the house of David, even in the matter of Absalom's coup.

2 Samuel 2:11, *"And the time that David was king in Hebron over the house of Judah was seven years and six months."*

One can observe that the friction between the tribe of David and Saul's dynasty finally became a full blown war which lasted approximately five years of the seven years David was in Hebron. Calmuet states that the war was not continuous, but more seasonal. The following is one of the scenes denoting the nature and character of the war. Abner, who is the captain of the host of Israel, moves into the land of the tribe of Benjamin to engage in battle with Judah and tries to bring them under the submission of Saul's dynasty.

2 Samuel 2:13, *"And Joab the son of Zeruiah, and the servants of David, went out, and met together by the pool of Gibeon: and they sat down, the one on the one side of the pool, and the other on the other side of the pool."*

These two armies meet in Gibeon in the land of Benjamin, (Saul's tribe), and only the pool separated them. Joab the captain of the host of Judah, and Abner the captain of the host of Israel, were there. Abner begins the conflict, and the word "play" in Verse 14 does not mean they were going to play or entertain each other. They were actually going to use weapons among a chosen lot of each group. Joab consents to the engagement by Abner but was most likely eager to fight with his enemy of years. However, it should be noted that had not Abner initiated the battle, Joab would have gone home, because David had promised not to cut off the seed of Saul and probably told Joab not to start the battle but only defend himself (1 Samuel 24:21-22). This promise of David to Saul and his seed was probably a constant thorn in Joab's spirit. It is likely the reason for this strange military procedure and possibly the cause of the longevity of the whole war.

2 Samuel 2:15, *"Then there arose and went over by number twelve of Benjamin, which pertained to Ishbosheth the son of Saul, and twelve of the servants of David."*

This action was to allow the champions of both sides to decide the battle instead of the whole army getting into a bloody battle. Thus there were twelve from Benjamin, Saul's tribe, and twelve from Judah, David's men in particular. Evidently Joab's idea of protecting themselves was by grabbing the beards of their opponents and thrusting a sword in them immediately. This action is totally Joab, for the men had to have been instructed to do so by signal, for it happened in order. If Joab disobeyed David here it would not be the first time or the last time. Nevertheless the battle raged that day.

2 Samuel 2:17, *"And there was a very sore battle that day; and Abner was beaten, and the men of Israel, before the servants of David."*

This was a battle that included two small armies settled around the captains of hosts, Joab and Abner. There has not been much speculation as to the size of the armies, but by the description of the battle and the toll of the dead, it is reasonable to conclude that the armies were quite small. David's nephews, Joab, Abishai, and Asahel seemed to go after Abner, but because Asahel was must faster on his feet, he was able to run down Abner. Their goal was probably to secure a quick and decisive victory, but also to attain Abner's armor which is the grand and great trophy.

As Asahel gained on Abner, he was encouraged two times by Abner to stop pursuing him. It seems Abner didn't want to kill Asahel but finally did so after Asahel got close enough to kill him. Joab and Abishai followed all day, now eager for Abner to die because he had killed their younger brother. Abner escaped to a place of reinforcement, and standing in a safe place he pleads with Joab to stop this dreadful war and loss of life. It seems Abner was realizing that the conflict between the house of Saul and the house of David was going to result in a full blown civil war, by tribes taking sides with either of them. Joab heeds the word of Abner and blows the trumpet and stops the pursuit. Abner goes home.

2 Samuel 2:30, *"And Joab returned from following Abner: and when he had gathered all the people together, there lacked of David's servants nineteen men and Asahel."*

When Joab counted the casualties, he found only twenty missing, including Asahel his brother. Some insert here that twelve of the 360 dead who followed Abner were at the pool, for they interpret that portion of scripture in 2 Samuel 2:16, *"so they fell down together"* to mean that twelve from each side died at once.

2 Samuel 2:31, *"But the servants of David had smitten of Benjamin, and of Abner's men, so that three hundred and threescore men died."*

The loss of life in the camp of Abner under Ishbosheth was eighteen times more than Joab and the men of David. This disproportionate tally reveals the blessing of God that was continuously resting on David's military career.

2 Samuel 3:1, *"Now there was long war between the house of Saul and the house of David: but David waxed stronger and stronger, and the house of Saul waxed weaker and weaker."*

It seems that David and war could never part with each other. As David's dynasty is a type of the church age, Solomon's dynasty is a part of the millennium. Solomon had no war, and his enemies were his servants. David begins to gain more and more strength as the house of Saul begins to diminish. This is good typology for the truth about the church age, for many expect the church to get weaker and weaker before the millennium comes, whereas the opposite is true. There is a remnant that will know their God and do exploits.

2 Samuel 3:2, *"And unto David were sons born in Hebron: and his firstborn was Amnon, of Ahinoam the Jezreelitess"*;

As we see at this time David has many wives. The sons here are six, and each from a different wife. This was a fault in David's life that cost him greatly. Michal, whom Saul took away from David, might have born a child to him before he ran in exile, and most likely he had sons and daughters before arriving at Hebron. That is probably why the scripture makes it clear that these are his offspring while in Hebron. It seems that in his success is where he began to fail. True of many warriors, they can handle adversity better than success. Out of these six sons, none of them became well known for good, but three of them were well known for being extremely unprofitable.

2 Samuel 3:5, *"And the sixth, Ithream, by Eglah David's wife. These were born to David in Hebron."*

Some believe Eglah to be Michal under another name but herein lies the problem: 1) We find no strong relation between the two names. 2) Michal did not come to David in Hebron until Abner brought her to David as part of a peace deal which was toward the end of David's time in Hebron.

2 Samuel 3:6, *"And it came to pass, while there was war between the house of Saul and the house of David, that Abner made himself strong for the house of Saul."*

There is ample proof that Abner actually ran the kingdom of Israel although Ishbosheth was in the office of the king. This is well noted in 2 Samuel 3:11, *"And he could not answer Abner a word again, because he feared him."* Abner makes an attempt to revive the diminishing army of the house of Saul and actually seizes the government. This is also shown by the act of going in to Saul's concubine. Concubines were looked upon as the express property of the king. By going that far with his forwardness, Abner could have been indicted for treason. Ishbosheth confronts Abner for his promiscuity with his father's concubine even though he probably did so trembling.

2 Samuel 3:8, *"Then was Abner very wroth for the words of Ishbosheth, and said, Am I a dog's head, which against Judah do shew kindness this day unto the house of Saul thy father, to his brethren, and to his friends, and have not delivered thee into the hand of David, that thou chargest me to day with a fault concerning this woman"?*

Abner was very angry and asked Ishbosheth if he only considered him a keeper of dogs. Abner then reminds Ishbosheth that it is him who is holding together his wavering and faltering kingdom and being in such a position, "You charge me with a fault concerning a woman?" Abner didn't say he was innocent but that the charge was inconsiderate of his high ranking position. So it is with so many who are in authority by desire for power. When they get such power, they profess themselves able to have that which they want regardless of its morality. When David fell with Bathsheba it was of the same manner!

2 Samuel 3:9, *"So do God to Abner, and more also, except, as the LORD hath sworn to David, even so I do to him";*

Abner is tired of working for a loser, and he either becomes persuaded or reminded by this incident that the kingdom of Israel has been given to David. Abner seems to be saying he is going to help God fulfill this thing of getting David to be king of all of the people of Israel. About the same time as this occurs, David is becoming increasingly uncomfortable with his general, Joab.

2 Samuel 3:10, *"To translate the kingdom from the house of Saul, and to set up the throne of David over Israel and over Judah, from Dan even to Beersheba."*

It is amazing that Abner, who was trying just one day earlier to build enough military might to overtake Judah and bring it into submission, now begins his campaign to bring all of Israel under David's dynasty. This seems to be more calculated than it first appears. Abner could feel the decline of Saul and the rise of David. He knew his only job security would be to try such a feat that would insure him a major role in David's dynasty. At least Abner is very upfront with Ishbosheth. He probably thought he had made this king, and he could take him down as he pleased. Evidently these words of Abner brought silence to Ishbosheth because he was afraid to answer him back. Neither Abner nor Ishbosheth knew their lives would be very short lived from this point.

2 Samuel 3:12, *"And Abner sent messengers to David on his behalf, saying, Whose is the land? saying also, Make thy league with me, and, behold, my hand shall be with thee, to bring about all Israel unto thee."*

Abner begins his work quickly by sending messengers on his behalf to David for a peace treaty, with the condition that Abner would use his vast influence to bring all the rest of the tribes of Israel under David. To this David agreed with one major condition of his own. David told him the peace treaty would move no further unless he delivered Michal, his wife, back to him. David had every right to demand just that. However, Michal now belonged to another, to which David seemed to give not the least consideration. Is this a fault here for David, or is this the correcting of Saul's sin of taking Michal from David and giving her to another?

2 Samuel 3:14, *"And David sent messengers to Ishbosheth Saul's son, saying, Deliver me my wife Michal, which I espoused to me for an hundred foreskins of the Philistines."*

There seems to be no precise explanation as to why David, who is dealing with Abner, sends the message to Ishbosheth demanding he deliver Michal to him. Perhaps 1) David was trying to avert some violence that Abner might have used to bring him Michal.) 2) Michal is the sister of Ishbosheth, and their father is dead. 3) Abner told David without it being recorded that he did not have the power himself to carry out this assignment.

Nevertheless, he commands Ishbosheth to bring back his wife, and he does so at the great distress and grief of Phaltiel, her present husband.

2 Samuel 3:17, *"And Abner had communication with the elders of Israel, saying, Ye sought for David in times past to be king over you"*:

Abner goes right to work on the matter of getting the people of Israel over to the side of David. Abner figures he has nothing to lose, for Ishbosheth is afraid of him and David has treated him kindly. And by now David has his wife Michal. However, it is clear that Abner is moving his agenda more out of a disdain for Ishbosheth than of a love for David. Because of this, we find a great flaw in the entire effort. Abner starts his pitch by reminding them that at one time, the people wanted David to be their king.

2 Samuel 3:18, *"Now then do it: for the LORD hath spoken of David, saying, By the hand of my servant David I will save my people Israel out of the hand of the Philistines, and out of the hand of all their enemies."*

Abner implores the elders of Israel to move fast to endorse David and move him in to power, referring to Ishbosheth's weak position. Abner's very effort in helping David reveals to all of the elders that he believes Ishbosheth is going down. It seems Abner then begins to appeal to the benefit spiritually of having David as king. He cites the prophecy he had heard himself from Saul's lips concerning David's delivering them from the Philistines.

2 Samuel 3:19, *"And Abner also spake in the ears of Benjamin: and Abner went also to speak in the ears of David in Hebron all that seemed good to Israel, and that seemed good to the whole house of Benjamin."*

Abner was very energetic in his efforts and moving fast, he converses with the tribe of Benjamin. It is notable that before he consults with the tribe of Benjamin, he first gets the people of Israel on board for making David king over the entire nation of Israel. Then he comes to the tribe of Benjamin. This is so he will be able to tell them that the other tribes are for it, helping to influence Benjamin, which was the tribe of Saul and the fiercest against David. After completing this, Abner then goes to David with assurance that he can deliver all of Israel to him.

2 Samuel 3:20, *"So Abner came to David to Hebron, and twenty men with him. And David made Abner and the men that were with him a feast."*

Abner had done his groundwork, and he then comes to David. Though the scripture doesn't record it, it is most likely Abner had already sent messages to ensure how he would be accepted because he only took twenty men with him. David made a feast for him which was in itself a message to all that David was at least considering a league with Abner.

This is amazing on two fronts. 1) David had railed strongly on Abner the day he went to Saul's camp and got Saul's spear and bolster. 1 Sam 26:15-17, *"And David said to Abner, Art not thou a valiant man? and who is like to thee in Israel? wherefore then hast thou not kept thy lord the king? for there came one of the people in to destroy the king thy lord. This thing is not good that thou hast done. As the LORD liveth, ye are worthy to die, because ye have not kept your master, the LORD'S anointed. And now see where the king's spear is, and the cruse of water that was at his bolster."* Abner would have had to let go of one of the most degrading and humiliating days of his military career to come to David. 2) David would have to believe that Abner could be loyal to him after he had railed on him that day and be willing to put Abner in some sort of office that would prove that trust.

Some scholars report that Jonathan was a friend to Abner and therefore David was inclined to forgive him.

2 Samuel 3:21, *"And Abner said unto David, I will arise and go, and will gather all Israel unto my lord the king, that they may make a league with thee, and that thou mayest reign over all that thine heart desireth. And David sent Abner away; and he went in peace."*

This could very possibly have been deception on Abner's part, for he had already had those meetings with Benjamin and the other tribes. Yet he makes an announcement to David that he will go and do what he has already done. Some scholars just simply say that Abner was performing part two in telling the other tribes that David is willing to make league with them. However, Abner didn't live long enough for us to find out his motive. David did evidently sanction his mission, for he sent him away in peace.

2 Samuel 3:22, *"And, behold, the servants of David and Joab came from pursuing a troop, and brought in a great spoil with them: but Abner was not with David in Hebron; for he had sent him away, and he was gone in peace."*

The troop Joab and his men were pursuing was most likely one of the Philistine raiding bands who were constantly taking advantage of the conflict between the house of David and the house of Saul. The league with Abner, the feast for him, and the sending away of him in peace was all done while Joab was gone. However, from the information in the following verses we know that Joab and Abner didn't miss each other by much.

The news of Abner's visit was most disturbing to Joab on several fronts. 1) He had no doubt been waiting to kill Abner because Abner had killed his younger brother Asahel. 2) He realized because he both came and went, that David was serious about a long lasting relationship with Abner. 3) His own status with David could be in jeopardy because he didn't carry near the weight and influence over David that Abner had over Ishbosheth. Joab feared the ability of Abner to manipulate David when he was not able to. The difference is that David was a real king and Ishbosheth was a man made leader.

Joab was furious and said to David in 2 Samuel 3:24, *"What hast thou done? behold, Abner came unto thee; why is it that thou hast sent him away, and he is quite gone?"*

Though it is clear that David didn't really fear Joab and kept him in check somewhat, it is also clear that Joab was angry enough to confront the king by asking him why he let Abner get away. When one is so consumed with a personal grudge as Joab, they often wonder why others don't take their case. David had no interest in either killing Abner or rejecting his offer. Always behind every single event in David's life is the key prophetic word that, in fact, he will be the king of Israel of the tribe of Judah that will have a perpetual dynasty. It seems that when David is in harmony with God, he is able to rest in that prophecy and therefore showed no effort in trying to make it come to pass. This is one of the most intriguing of all of David's characteristics -- his ability to rest in God's prophetic Word.

Though Joab accused Abner of being a spy, it is not likely that Joab actually believed it. Joab was a seasoned warrior and knew if it were for the purpose of spying, Abner would have sent others to do such. Joab was probably building his own case for the time David would hear of his assassination of Abner. In fact Joab had probably already devised the diabolical plan to destroy Abner without David's knowledge or approval.

2 Samuel 3:26, *"And when Joab was come out from David, he sent messengers after Abner, which brought him again from the well of Sirah: but David knew it not."*

It appears that Joab was both anxious and angry when he left David. He didn't wait for David to answer, for he was anxious to set in motion his wicked plan of vengeance and anger for David's earlier acceptance of Abner. Joab's plan included sending messengers in David's behalf, bidding Abner to come to the well of Sirah, which was fairly close to Hebron. David didn't know of such a plan, and as we see by his reaction to Abner's execution, he would never have sanctioned the plan had he known of it.

Abner probably returned, either thinking David had further instructions for him or Joab himself wanted to make amends with him. To the latter Joab probably pretended to have a desire, until he had Abner alone privately. Having achieved his goal of having him alone, he killed Abner in cold blood. Joab's men were probably holding Abner's twenty men at bay without knowing Joab's intention. Some hold no fault to Joab for killing him who had killed his brother Asahel. This they do because 1) Abner had pleaded with Asahel to turn back from following him. 2) They were in war that day and both sides had soldiers killed. In spite of the pleading by some for Joab's innocence, David's open condemnation of Joab's deed proves that Joab took vengeance in his own hands and was guilty of a crime outside of war.

2 Samuel 3:28, *"And afterward when David heard it, he said, I and my kingdom are guiltless before the LORD for ever from the blood of Abner the son of Ner"*:

David was greatly disturbed at the slaying of Abner. The actions that follow make some of the case that Jonathan was very fond of Abner. Abner and Jonathan certainly spent plenty of time together, and there was no hint of friction between them. David wanted everyone to know that he had not ordered Joab or anyone else to kill Abner. This was very important, not just for the clearing of himself from such an action as Joab took, but also to assure those soldiers who had remained loyal to Abner that this was not sanctioned by King David but condemned by him. It was completely possible that Abner's death, because he was close kin to Saul, could have sparked an attack against David by the army of Israel.

David then pronounces a curse on the house of Joab for his killing of Abner. Many fault David on this count by treating this matter like Eli's treatment of his sons. Those who fault David here are correct, like Eli who condemned the activity of his sons but never punished them, David condemned the activity of Joab and made sure the nation understood that he was not a part of Abner's death, but he never offered to punish him. Perhaps it was because Joab was David's nephew, but more likely it was a faulty pattern in David's life, for he did the same with his own sons. He condemned the wrong of Absalom but never really punished him. Had David punished Joab like he should have, perhaps Absalom would not have been killed later by Joab that day Absalom hung his head in the tree.

2 Samuel 3:31, *"And David said to Joab, and to all the people that were with him, Rend your clothes, and gird you with sackcloth, and mourn before Abner. And king David himself followed the bier."*

David did not exclude Joab from the required fasting and mourning for the death of Abner. Is this a punishment to Joab for his wicked murder, as some suppose? No it is not. Everyone had to fast and mourn. David's grief seems to be deep and honest. He himself attended the funeral, and he wept and lifted up his voice to cry at Abner's grave. David then delivered a type of anthem of sort describing the murder of Abner, no doubt with Joab listening in some sort of discomfort. Perhaps, Joab was angry or maybe embarrassed, but it is certain he had to be in an emotional discomfort.

2 Samuel 3:35, *"And when all the people came to cause David to eat meat while it was yet day, David sware, saying, So do God to me, and more also, if I taste bread, or ought else, till the sun be down."*

The people most likely figured that David would eat after the funeral, but David very adamantly said he would not eat the rest of the day. David had now totally convinced the people that it was not his will that Abner be killed. David was insistent that Abner was a great warrior and should be honored as a fellow Israeli.

Perhaps David was in some sort of anguish over his lack of disciplining Joab. He seems to understand his weakness in the matter of dealing with Joab and his brother in the slaying of Abner, for he says in Verse *39, "And I am this day weak, though anointed king; and these men the sons of Zeruiah be too hard for me"*: Yet he does nothing to discipline Joab. Joab could also have been turned around here instead of proceeding on to be a hardened killer.

When Ishbosheth hears of Abner's death, he realizes that Israel is falling apart and David is going to be king over the entire twelve tribes. Yet Israel (meaning in this case the eleven tribes) is confused and unstable. Lightfoot comments here on this verse, "Anything could have happened in Israel at this moment were it not for the prophetic word on one King David."

Ishbosheth's half brothers thought to do themselves good and help deliver Israel to David by executing Ishbosheth, Saul's son. These brothers were the only possible heirs to the throne from Saul's family except for Mephibosheth, the son of Jonathan, and he was crippled. Evidently these devised a plan that would insure David's success. Their plan brought about their own penalty of death instead of a promotion in a Davidic dynasty.

2 Samuel 4:8, *"And they brought the head of Ishbosheth unto David to Hebron, and said to the king, Behold the head of Ishbosheth the son of Saul thine enemy, which sought thy life; and the LORD hath avenged my lord the king this day of Saul, and of his seed."*

How foolish of these two sons of Saul to do these things: 1) To ignore the sixth commandment, *"Thou shalt not kill;"* 2) To think they could promote themselves in David's eyes with a wicked murder of the son of someone David loved; 3) To cut off Ishbosheth's head while he slept and bring it to David as though it would be some sort of trophy to David; 4) To think David would be pleased with them for their murder after he has just had to deal with his own general's ruthlessly killing Abner; 5) To think that David needed them to avenge David of his enemies.

2 Samuel 4:9, *"And David answered Rechab and Baanah his brother, the sons of Rimmon the Beerothite, and said unto them, As the LORD liveth, who hath redeemed my soul out of all adversity,"*

David begins his indictment of these two brothers by making it plain to them that their following execution will be carried out in the name of the Lord. Some doctors of theology consider that David felt guilty for not dealing with Joab correctly, and when this same thing comes up again, he is making sure that he avenges innocent blood. David relates to them what they should have already known, being Benjamites, that David slew the man that said he performed a mercy killing on Saul, which he thought would please David. These two are read their rights and proven absolutely guilty.

2 Samuel 4:12, *"And David commanded his young men, and they slew them, and cut off their hands and their feet, and hanged them up over the pool in Hebron. But they took the head of Ishbosheth, and buried it in the sepulchre of Abner in Hebron."*

David's extraordinary execution should confirm David's total exasperation with the shedding of innocent blood and the dying of so many of his former friends and people he shared the king's court with at one time.

2 Samuel 5:1, *"Then came all the tribes of Israel to David unto Hebron, and spake, saying, Behold, we are thy bone and thy flesh."*

These representatives of the tribes of Israel are perhaps a little fickle in their speech. The words are accurate in their substance, but they are quite late in being expressed. However, David again seems to have absolutely no vengeance against those who had formerly opposed him. His pattern was to punish those who presumptuously punished his enemies and to totally forgive and restore those who showed true repentance.

2 Samuel 5:3, *"So all the elders of Israel came to the king to Hebron; and king David made a league with them in Hebron before the LORD: and they anointed David king over Israel."*

The elders of Israel seemed quite eager to make the league with David which Abner began. What Abner began for personal and selfish reasons, the Lord accomplished to fulfill His promise to David and Israel. *So all the elders of Israel anointed David king of Israel.* Now the twelve tribes are once again united, and David the king of the tribe of Judah is now their rightful king. Though all of hell tried to stop this from happening, yet the Word of the Lord prevailed, and David takes his place as king.

2 Samuel 5:4, *"David was thirty years old when he began to reign, and he reigned forty years."*

The significant thing here is that David comes into the fullness of his dynasty at the third anointing, which is important to the extreme thematical thought pattern of the Jews. Three is the number both of confirmation and release. The record of David's age of thirty is meaning at the beginning of David's reign in Hebron of the tribe of Judah only. Then for 33 years he reigned over all of Israel.

The age of thirty is also significant in that the high priest order allows the beginning of the fullness of the priesthood at that age, thirty, and to continue until fifty. Both John the Baptist and Jesus began the fullness of their ministry at age thirty! The Lord was careful for John the Baptist to begin his ministry at thirty because he was the bona fide high priest of Israel. John transferred the Aaronic Priesthood (temporal) to Jesus (perpetual) six months later when Jesus became thirty years of age.

David operated successfully three times in his life as a priest and was allowed to do so through the Melchizedek order (King and Priest), which David's mighty pen gave us. Psalms 110:4 says, *"The LORD hath sworn, and will not repent, Thou art a priest for ever after the order of Melchizedek."* David is a type of the Messiah Jesus, who is also both King and Priest and in fact the Melchizedek order.

2 Samuel 5:6, *"And the king and his men went to Jerusalem unto the Jebusites, the inhabitants of the land: which spake unto David, saying, Except thou take away the blind and the lame, thou shalt not come in hither: thinking, David cannot come in hither."*

These Jebusites had stubbornly held on to a portion of Zion, in particular Jerusalem, the very city where David took the head of Goliath (1 Samuel 17:54). The Jebusites had already survived the attack of the tribe of Judah as well as the tribe of Benjamin (Joshua 15:63 and Judges 1:21). They gave credit to their idols which the Jews called the blind and lame because idols can neither see nor walk. This verse has caused quite a lot of study and controversy as to whether or not David hated the blind people and the lame. Such an indictment would certainly be inaccurate for the Sweet Psalmist of Israel, who penned Psalms 41, Psalms 68, Psalms 69, and others which lovingly deal with the poor and needy.

These Jebusites had become quite steeped in the false security of their idols, so they taunted David because they thought their idols would protect them. David did not hate people who were blind or crippled, but he did hate false gods with a perfect hatred. He was the only king in the history of both Judah and Israel who neither helped nor had a false god.

2 Samuel 5:7, *"Nevertheless David took the strong hold of Zion: the same is the city of David."*

In spite of the taunting from the Jebusites, David took Zion. It might be noted that this is the very first military action David performed as king of the entire nation of Israel. It seems that David knew that the city of Jerusalem and Zion would be a special place on the earth. David proclaimed many prophetic utterances and most likely understood in the Spirit that the same God who prophesied his kingship also had special plans for the city that will now be called the city of David.

2 Samuel 5:8, *"And David said on that day, Whosoever getteth up to the gutter, and smiteth the Jebusites, and the lame and the blind, that are hated of David's soul, he shall be chief and captain. Wherefore they said, The blind and the lame shall not come into the house."*

Verse 7 tells us that David took the city, and this verse tells us how David took Zion and the city of Jerusalem from the Jebusites. It should be noted that David believed he was commissioned of the Lord to drive out the idolaters, according to Exodus 23:23. David believed the Lord would go before him and help him to execute the will of the Lord against the Lord's enemies. This actual mindset is easily seen throughout David's military life.

David offered a reward to the warrior who would get up to the gutter, or water system, and smite the Jebusites and their wicked idols that could neither see nor walk. David hated these idols and desired to make sure they would never come back into Jerusalem again, and in fact they did not as long as King David was alive.

In the account of this very battle in 1 Chronicles we find the description of the reward and the winner of the prize. I Chronicles 11:6, *"And David said, Whosoever smiteth the Jebusites first shall be chief and captain. So Joab the son of Zeruiah went first up, and was chief."* Joab was already captain but on very shaky ground after his ruthlessness in the case of Abner. Some believe that David was desiring to replace Joab in this offer, hoping someone else would win the prize. But Joab, being the warrior he was, secured his own place again by taking the city.

2 Samuel 5:9, *"So David dwelt in the fort, and called it the city of David. And David built round about from Millo and inward."*

This fort was well suited for the new king of Israel except for its size. The Jebusites were never known for expansion efforts. Lightfoot called them an incestuous society. However, that which they did occupy was well built. David extended the fort to contain his growing court and guard. He reached out to Millo which was across the valley, and then built inward. The account in 1 Chronicles 11:8 tells us David concentrated on his house while Joab rebuilt the city.

2 Samuel 5:10, *"And David went on, and grew great, and the LORD God of hosts was with him."*

The scripture makes it clear that David's increase came because of his relationship with the Lord. Many have increased in other ways and means, the Lord allowing it to be so for a season. Not so with David. His increase in every way came as a result of the mighty hand of God's favor upon him. This should speak volumes to those who have an aspiration for greatness and fame. David lovingly passed this wisdom to Solomon when he wrote this psalm for him: Psalms 127:1 A Song of degrees for Solomon. *"Except the LORD build the house, they labour in vain that build it":* David was careful to give the Lord all of the glory for any and all of his accomplishments.

2 Samuel 5:11, *"And Hiram king of Tire sent messengers to David, and cedar trees, and carpenters, and masons: and they built David an house."*

It was not uncommon for neighboring kings to help with the rebuilding of a nation, but many people consider Hiram as a proselyte. We know he later helped Solomon as well. He was a lover of David and seemed quite glad to furnish all of the workers necessary for the construction of David's house. The long years of wars with the Philistines, as well as the civil war, had most likely reduced the skilled labor in Israel. Therefore, Hiram sent them. It should be noted that the term "David's house" should not be taken to mean one building but all that pertained to his family and court.

2 Samuel 5:12, *"And David perceived that the LORD had established him king over Israel, and that he had exalted his kingdom for his people Israel's sake."*

The word "perceived" in this verse is from the Hebrew word "Yada" which is often used in a broad sense for revelatory understanding. However one must consider the strong prophetic confirmation David had received for the very thing that he now sees happening before him. He is hereby stating that he could see what the Lord meant, and he agreed with what he saw prophetically. The power of this perception is qualified by David's understanding that the Lord loved Israel, and His sovereignty had performed the establishing of the Davidic kingdom because of it. Scholars are often back and forth as to whether the Lord loved Israel and blessed David or the Lord loved David and blessed Israel. This is a most needless debate for they cannot be separated in such a way.

2 Samuel 5:13, *"And David took him more concubines and wives out of Jerusalem, after he was come from Hebron: and there were yet sons and daughters born to David."*

This is yet another grave mistake to place on David's list of failures. The matter of having concubines and polygamy were both heathen practices, and herein is David acting like a king the other nations had. That was what the people wanted when they got Saul and this was what Samuel had objected to. Samuel was not opposed to Israel's having a king but he was opposed to their having a king like other nations. David had many children from these women, and he paid a great price for his promiscuity and disregard for the express commandment not to multiply wives to himself (Deuteronomy 17:17). Many theologians believe David actually died from sexually transmitted diseases. This they base on David's own medical malady he describes in Psalms 38.

2 Samuel 5:17, *"But when the Philistines heard that they had anointed David king over Israel, all the Philistines came up to seek David; and David heard of it, and went down to the hold."*

It seems that the Philistines had little to worry about concerning Israel as long as the Israeli tribes were fighting each other. As soon as they came together under one leader they felt they must do something before they got too established. This is true of God's church. The enemy of the Church has little to be concerned about as long as the church is infighting. But as soon as the church comes together, the dark world panics.

As soon as David's intelligence department gave him word of the Philistines' coming toward them, he moved to the hold. David was a guerilla warrior, and he knew how to take cities but didn't want to try to defend one. So David goes to them and camps in a place more suitable to his style of warfare. He finds the Philistines spread all over the valley of Rephaim, also known as the valley of the giants.

2 Samuel 5:19, *"And David inquired of the LORD, saying, Shall I go up to the Philistines? wilt thou deliver them into mine hand? And the LORD said unto David, Go up: for I will doubtless deliver the Philistines into thine hand."*

This particular battle is of major significance. The Philistines knew well that if David was not stopped early in his dynasty there would be a great price to pay. Of all the enemies of the Philistines, no one person had caused them as much grief as David. Therefore, they hated him immensely. Calmuet called them God haters because they were unable to separate David from his God. Lightfoot went so far as to call them antichrist because of the messianic prophecies that continued to flow from David's pen. David humbly asks the Lord if he should go up against the Philistines. It should be noted that he is not asking if he should fight them but if he should attack them or just defend himself. The Lord tells him to go up to them.

2 Samuel 5:20, *"And David came to Baalperazim, and David smote them there, and said, The LORD hath broken forth upon mine enemies before me, as the breach of waters. Therefore he called the name of that place Baalperazim."*

The place of the battle was not called Baalperazim until that day, for the battle took place in the valley of Rephaim. The name Baalperazim is not mentioned anywhere else in the Bible except in 1 Chronicles 14, which is another account of the same battle. Therefore, we conclude that David did attack them in Rephaim and called the place Baalperazim which means the plain of breaches. This was to describe the manner in which God gave them the victory. The Lord seemed to go before them Himself, breaking forth on the Philistines with His matchless power.

2 Samuel 5:21, *"And there they left their images, and David and his men burned them."*

It was not uncommon for the heathens to carry their little gods with them into the battle hoping they would protect them. How foolish they were to trust in dead idols, and how indignant was David concerning their idols, for he burned them with perfect hatred. David was perfect all of his life in the matter of idolatry, and the zeal of God ate him up with a holy jealousy for his God. That produced a holy hatred for idolatry. The Philistines were desperate to stop David, for they immediately reorganized and came again to Rephaim to try to defeat David.

2 Samuel 5:23, *"And when David inquired of the LORD, he said, Thou shalt not go up; but fetch a compass behind them, and come upon them over against the mulberry trees."*

David would not proceed again with such a determined enemy without getting the exact instructions from the Lord. David did not expect a victory without an effort of his own, but he did have a great expectation that the Lord would show him exactly what to do. The instructions were the opposite of his last battle, which tells the church that each battle cannot be necessarily approached with the same strategy. The Lord told David not to go straight up but to come around behind them and wait until the Lord made the noise of war in the mulberry trees. That would be his signal to move with zeal and confidence knowing that the Lord was before him in battle.

2 Samuel 5:25, *"And David did so, as the LORD had commanded him; and smote the Philistines from Geba until thou come to Gazer."*

In David's obedience to the Lord, he gained yet another victory. Amazingly, David had not tasted defeat in a single battle throughout his military career. Beginning with the bear and lion in his seminary of solitude until he closed his eyes in death, David never lost a battle. All of his enemies were defeated the very same way, with the power of God on his life and the Lord going before him.

It appears that the sound in the tops of the mulberry trees would make the enemy alarmed and expecting an attack from the front, while at the same time allowing David's army to come up on them from the rear. The Philistines were smitten and driven all of the way to Gazer which is on the border of their own land. Therefore they were driven completely out of Israel.

2 Samuel 6:1, *"Again, David gathered together all the chosen men of Israel, thirty thousand."*

This gathering of the soldiers was not for a major battle but for an escort and protection for the moving of the Ark of the Covenant. David, through the Lord's power, having pushed the Philistines out of the land, now gets about the business of pursuing his heart's desire. David wanted to get the Ark of God to Jerusalem, or at least to the place on Mount Moriah where he would later have the vision of the house of the Lord at Ornan's threshing floor (1 Chronicles 22:1).

2 Samuel 6:2, *"And David arose, and went with all the people that were with him from Baale of Judah, to bring up from thence the ark of God, whose name is called by the name of the LORD of hosts that dwelleth between the cherubims."*

This was a huge operation when you consider all of the people and the thirty thousand troops to guard it all. Certainly it was a big day for Israel. David testified in one psalm that he was not going to sleep or rest until he placed the Ark in its rightful place (Psalm 132:3-8). This moving of the Ark was so important to David, as shown by this great company coming with him to get the job done. They go to Baale, which is a city in Judah also called Kirjath-jearim (Joshua 15:9). The Israeli people believed that the presence of God for them was between the Cherubim on both sides of the mercy seat. This is where the blood of atonement was applied each year at Yom Kippur, which is the shadow and type of the blood of Jesus that would later be applied on the Mercy Seat in Heaven. David's infatuating love for the Ark was no doubt due to the revelatory and prophetic things surrounding it. In the Spirit David could see, not only the Messiah, but the final and complete work of redemption He would do!

2 Samuel 6:5, *"And David and all the house of Israel played before the LORD on all manner of instruments made of fir wood, even on harps, and on psalteries, and on timbrels, and on cornets, and on cymbals."*

The people were expressing themselves before the Lord with great celebration for the moving of the Ark to its prepared place. Their celebration was stopped short when they came to Nachon's threshing floor, for the oxen stumbled and Uzzah, in trying to steady it, died immediately. The account of this in 1 Chronicles 13 gives greater detail, and yet even with more details, the punishment for the crime seems inappropriate. However, God is never wrong, and the severity of Uzzah's deed becomes clearer in the chapters ahead.

Some believe Uzzah was not a Levite and for this reason he was killed, but in fact he was a Levite, being the brother of Eleazar, who was the one chosen to look after the Ark (1 Samuel 7:1). He died most likely because he really was a Levite and knew that the Ark was not to be carried in a cart but on the shoulders of the Levite priests (Numbers 4:15). Steadying the Ark on a cart, when it was to be carried on the shoulders of the Levites, should not have been done by a Levite. The priests were not doing their function, perhaps by David's design, or possibly by their own lack of zeal for the Word. David seems to blame them in 1 Chronicles 15:13, and then includes himself in the blame in the same verse when he said, *"For because ye did it not at the first, the LORD our God made a breach upon us, for that we sought him not after the due order."* Regardless, this event must be added to the list of faults and failures of David.

2 Samuel 6:8, *"And David was displeased, because the LORD had made a breach upon Uzzah: and he called the name of the place Perez-uzzah to this day."*

This whole scene was very distressing for David, not only because he wanted so badly to bring the Ark home, but also because of the great celebration he had planned and had already begun. This day should probably be considered as one of the worst days in the life of David. The embarrassment was probably also a factor. However, some months later David will make another effort and be sure that he is in the right order. God's glory is not to be moved in a cart which is made of boards and big wheels! Selah.

2 Samuel 6:9, *"And David was afraid of the LORD that day, and said, How shall the ark of the LORD come to me"?*

This horrific event caused David to be afraid to go any further with the Ark in a cart. Actually David probably could have corrected the matter and continued. David was so exasperated that he didn't see any way that he could get the Ark home. It seems that David took the rebuke to say that the Lord didn't want David to move the Ark home; but after a period of time, David realized what the problem was and approached the matter more cautiously. Many ministers completely quit their ministries somewhere between the first attempt to move the Ark and the second. It took David three months to recover and make another effort to move the Ark.

2 Samuel 6:10, *"So David would not remove the ark of the LORD unto him into the city of David: but David carried it aside into the house of Obededom the Gittite."*

We do not know that Obededom invited the Ark to be in his house, or if he was assigned to have it because he was a Levite (1 Chronicles 15:21). However, Obededom entertained the Ark for three months while David was praying through the matter and coming to the conclusion that he had been out of order in his attempt to move it the first time. One might notice that they didn't pull the cart, but carried it, to Obededom's house. It is not likely that Obededom had the motive of receiving the Ark for the blessing's sake but blessed he was. Likewise it doesn't seem that David wanted it at his house for the blessing it brought, for David was a true and pure worshipper.

2 Samuel 6:12, *"And it was told king David, saying, The LORD hath blessed the house of Obededom, and all that pertaineth unto him, because of the ark of God. So David went and brought up the ark of God from the house of Obededom into the city of David with gladness."*

The fear in David is gone now, and his heart is filled with joy as he goes to the blessed house of Obededom to get the precious Ark. Three months have passed, and David is completely confident now what to do in transporting the Ark home. His past embarrassment is gone, and he understands the king by himself cannot move the glory, but he must employ the priests as well (Numbers 4:15). It seems as though David made great preparation in the confidence that now because he has incorporated the priests, he will be able to bring home the Ark. As they began to move, after they had gone but six paces, they offered sacrifices. This could not have been done without substantial preparation concerning the altar and such. Some seem to insinuate that they did this ceremony every six paces throughout the entire journey to Jerusalem, but we find nothing to strengthen this view.

2 Samuel 6:14, *"And David danced before the LORD with all his might; and David was girded with a linen ephod."*

Now we see full proof that David had entered into the Melchizedek order of king and priest, for in his celebration he wears the linen ephod, which is the attire of the priest. He is the type of the Messiah which would be also a Priest forever after the order of Melchizedek. It might be noted that Jesus Himself wore a seamless robe which is the attire of a high priest. The soldiers gambled for it at the cross, but when did he begin to wear it? Most likely after his baptism, because there the priesthood of Aaron was transferred to Him by John the Baptist, who was the genuine high priest of Israel. David, the king of the tribe of Judah, wore the attire of the priest to the amazement of the Levites and the Judahites, as well as one particular woman from the tribe of Benjamin, his wife, Michal.

2 Samuel 6:15, *"So David and all the house of Israel brought up the ark of the LORD with shouting, and with the sound of the trumpet."*

As they saw they were able to move the Ark now that they had the king and priest order, their excitement began to increase. The shouting started, and the trumpets began to sound as they moved the glory of the Lord to the place it was supposed to be. Imagine the joy and anointing mixed together as they approach the city of David. Is this not a picture of the great triumphal entry into Jerusalem, the day often called Palm Sunday? Spontaneous praise began to erupt that day as Jesus the King and the Priest came into the city. Perhaps David could see this in the Spirit through his prophetic gift, and perhaps that is why he asked for the linen ephod.

2 Samuel 6:16, *"And as the ark of the LORD came into the city of David, Michal Saul's daughter looked through a window, and saw king David leaping and dancing before the LORD; and she despised him in her heart."*

When the raw power of God is released in spontaneous prophetic worship, and when the Messiah is portrayed in plain exaltation, not everyone likes it. When the presence of the Lord is thick, it will illuminate who is really on the Lord's side. Michal, the daughter of Saul, hated the whole scene. She didn't hate the Ark. She didn't hate the celebration. She despised her own husband's display of worship and the manner in which he chose to do it. She paid a great price for her display of condemnation for her husband's worship.

2 Samuel 6:17, *"And they brought in the ark of the LORD, and set it in his place, in the midst of the tabernacle that David had pitched for it: and David offered burnt offerings and peace offerings before the LORD."*

We have no description of the tent David prepared, called here a tabernacle. Tenny called this tabernacle "God's favorite house." One thing is sure; it was prepared for the Ark by a true lover of the Lord and a true worshipper. We don't know why David did not try to retrieve the Tabernacle of Moses which was at Gibeon (1 Chronicles 16:39, 21:29). Perhaps David felt some awkwardness toward that effort because of the faction in the priesthood at that time. Or perhaps David could prophetically see how the Lord would change the place of offering to Jerusalem, which he did at the time the fire fell when David offered the sacrifice on Ornan's threshing floor. Lightfoot said that in David's messianic mode of thought, he would not have wanted a separation of the Holy Place in his tent because Messiah would rend that curtain with his own body! As usual, Bishop Lightfoot had amazing insight in saying such.

Evidently there was an altar close to the tent, for many offerings were made there. At this time the burnt offerings were still being offered in Shiloh as well. None of the priesthood serving David had any protest to this tent's being made for the Ark, and there didn't seem to be any effort to get the Ark to Shiloh instead of Jerusalem. Oh, Jerusalem!

2 Samuel 6:18, *"And as soon as David had made an end of offering burnt offerings and peace offerings, he blessed the people in the name of the LORD of hosts."*

Twice here we find the absence of sin offerings. Burnt offerings and peace offerings are different. They are not the type of Jesus' sin offering (Hebrews 10:4). The burnt offering and peace offerings are not for sin but for a sweet smelling sacrifice unto the Lord. Romans 12:1-2 is not referring to a sin offering but a burnt offering and a peace offering. We can be a burnt offering, but we cannot be a sin offering. Upon finishing the offerings, David blessed the people. He pronounced the blessing as both king and priest, and then furnished them food and wine, as did Melchizedek for Abraham.

2 Samuel 6:20, *Then David returned to bless his household. And Michal the daughter of Saul came out to meet David, and said, How glorious was the king of Israel to day, who uncovered himself to day in the eyes of the handmaids of his servants, as one of the vain fellows shamelessly uncovereth himself!"*

Upon David's return to his house, he was met with quite a confrontation. Michal met him and began to chide him. Her accusation was that of uncovering himself before the handmaids. At first glance, it seems she is charging her husband with lewdness, but a closer look will reveal that he actually took off the royal attire and put on the priestly robe. There are several instances in the scripture when those who are proclaimed naked are actually called so because they are without the tallit that signifies their tribal and family order. This concept would explain her referring to him as one common or without true lineage.

2 Samuel 6:21, *"And David said unto Michal, It was before the LORD, which chose me before thy father, and before all his house, to appoint me ruler over the people of the LORD, over Israel: therefore will I play before the LORD."*

David adamantly defended his worship before the Lord, citing the goodness and providence of God upon his life as ample reason for his public display. David was a worshipper in private; therefore, it is certainly legitimate for him to worship in public. David let her know that there would be much more of the same worship, and even more radical to come. David also told Michal that her assessment of the handmaidens was inaccurate, that in fact the handmaidens were not despising him as she did, but honored him for his exuberant worship.

Michal not only wasted her breath in her condemnation of David's worship but brought upon herself a grave situation. She had no more children. Some take this to mean that she was stricken barren; however, it is more likely that she was still able to have children but David never touched her intimately again from that day.

2 Samuel 7:5, *"Go and tell my servant David, Thus saith the LORD, Shalt thou build me a house for me to dwell in"?*

The Lord had given David peace since the day of the noise in the mulberry trees and the defeat of the Philistines. Therefore David turns his attention to building a Temple. He thinks that because he has a cedar house, the Lord should have more than a tent. David tells the prophet Nathan all that is in his heart, but in the night the Lord gives Nathan a check in his spirit and sent him to ask David this question. God explains to David, through His prophet, that He is a moving God and has never dwelt in a house. The Lord further asked David if there had ever been before and to this day a request from Him to build a house of cedar. David's heart to build the Lord a Temple was born out of a heart of worship.

2 Samuel 7:8, *"Now therefore so shalt thou say unto my servant David, Thus saith the LORD of hosts, I took thee from the sheepcote, from following the sheep, to be ruler over my people, over Israel":*

The Lord now speaks a tremendous messianic prophecy, as He explains to David the difference between a tabernacle for His people and a people for His tabernacle. David seemed to think in the natural realm too much, and the Lord reveals to him through this prophecy that the Messiah would come from his lineage. David received and delivered more messianic prophecies than even Isaiah, the major prophet. Here is one of the most significant of all. The house of David would both produce the Messiah and give Israel the preeminence over all other nations. All of the prophets agree with this in perfect harmony.

Luke writes of this in Acts 13:20-23, *"And after that he gave unto them judges about the space of four hundred and fifty years, until Samuel the prophet. And afterward they desired a king: and God gave unto them Saul the son of Cis, a man of the tribe of Benjamin, by the space of forty years. And when he had removed him, he raised up unto them David to be their king; to whom also he gave testimony, and said, I have found David the son of Jesse, a man after mine own heart, which shall fulfil all my will. Of this man's seed hath God according to his promise raised unto Israel a Saviour, Jesus":* This record of Luke can come from several prophecies concerning David, but the general theme is the same. David heard all of this because of his pure desire to build the Lord a house.

2 Samuel 7:17, *According to all these words, and according to all this vision, so did Nathan speak unto David."*

The entire messianic prophecy is now classified as a vision. Watts calls this "the vision of the Davidic Israel." This is certainly true but perhaps more accurately, "the vision of Israel given to David by the prophet Nathan."

2 Samuel 7:18, *Then went king David in, and sat before the LORD, and he said, Who am I, O Lord GOD? and what is my house, that thou hast brought me hitherto"?*

Now David comes into the tabernacle he built for the Ark, and there he pours out his heart before the Lord. David is overwhelmed at the prophecy and vision God gave him and his own involvement in it. He knows of his own failures and seems quite amazed at the powerful and perpetual blessing spoken over him. Let all who read of David also be overwhelmed at the blessing bestowed upon the undeserving house of David. Let not one look lightly at David's sin but look with wonder at the sure mercies of David. These words that David uttered as his heart was overwhelmed with God's revelation are some of the sweetest words in the scripture. God had made David famous, and David would make the God of Israel famous.

2 Samuel 7:20, *"And what can David say more unto thee? for thou, Lord GOD, knowest thy servant."*

David completely understands that the Lord has done this wonderful work, not because he has been good and righteous but rather because of God's word and sovereign plan. Yet one must notice that there is not the least expression of doubt or unbelief as to whether such a thing could or would happen. David knows the greatness of his God, for he had heard the roar of His voice in battle many times and knew the power of God was able to perform everything He spoke. Then David begins to praise his God and boast of the Lord's unique goodness and power. He then begins to speak to the Lord concerning the nation of Israel and how totally blessed Israel is to be chosen by the Lord God of heaven and earth.

2 Samuel 7:26, *"And let thy name be magnified for ever, saying, The LORD of hosts is the God over Israel: and let the house of thy servant David be established before thee."*

Here the amazing power of David's relationship with the Lord is revealed as he basically says to the Lord, "Amen, my Lord. Your will has been revealed to me and my heart was revealed to you. I want to build you a house, and you have chosen to build me a house. Do that which is in your heart and establish my house and my heritage. I am not worthy, but I am completely sure that you will do what you have said to me. Blessed be thy name."

2 Samuel 8:1, *"And after this it came to pass, that David smote the Philistines, and subdued them: and David took Metheg-ammah out of the hand of the Philistines."*

Although David had driven the Philistines completely out of Israel in the last battle, he wasn't satisfied until he had taken Gath, which is here called *Metheg-ammah,* (1 Chronicles 18:1). Gath was the city that Goliath was connected to and also the place David ran to on two different occasions when fleeing from Saul. Most likely David did not feel fully restored from his floundering until Gath fell to Israel. Also, a true warrior is not satisfied just getting the enemy out of his land but will take his enemy's ground as well. Gath in particular was the right city to take, for it was the chief city of the Philistines and lying in the natural fortress of a mountain in Ammah.

2 Samuel 8:2, *"And he smote Moab, and measured them with a line, casting them down to the ground; even with two lines measured he to put to death, and with one full line to keep alive. And so the Moabites became David's servants, and brought gifts."*

David took Moab. He killed a portion of them and made slaves out of the rest. Some theologians try to clear David of this by stating that the lines he used to differentiate the Moabites in judgment were actually to survey their cities, allowing some of them to continue and others to be destroyed. In that argument they bring forth the fact that David had entrusted his family to the Moabites while in exile. The problem with that argument is the fact that his family was never mentioned after David came out of exile. 1 Samuel 22:3-4,*"And David went thence to Mizpeh of Moab: and he said unto the king of Moab, Let my father and my mother, I pray thee, come forth, and be with you, till I know what God will do for me. And he brought them before the king of Moab: and they dwelt with him all the while that David was in the hold."*

Moab probably helped David because of their hatred for Saul, and many Jewish writers declare that the Moabites slaughtered David's family publicly when the tribe of Judah made him king. If so David could have had vengeance, but such was never factually credited to him. It is most likely that David simply understood the horrifying and recurring prophetic doom that the Moabites lived under. Numbers 24:17, *"I shall see him, but not now: I shall behold him, but not nigh: there shall come a Star out of Jacob, and a Sceptre shall rise out of Israel, and shall smite the corners of Moab, and destroy all the children of Sheth."* And who would understand the Star out of Jacob with the scepter but David himself and the coming Messiah.

Yet one should not charge David with killing the Moabites who were of a certain size by measuring them for their doom. Yes, David measured them upon conquering them; that is, he made an estimate of it and distributed the towns and people into three parts. David conquered them and made slaves of them. The Moabites were perpetual and sworn enemies to the Israelites, who therefore were forbidden to admit them into the congregation of the Lord. And though God commanded the children of Israel to spare the Moabites in their march to Canaan, yet afterwards they proved fierce enemies to God and His people, and thereby provoked God to alter His countenance towards them. And now that prophecy in Numbers 24:17 was accomplished. The ones of the Moabites David spared were his servants and they brought him gifts.

2 Samuel 8:3, *"David smote also Hadadezer, the son of Rehob, king of Zobah, as he went to recover his border at the river Euphrates."*

David was in love with the Word. He often referred to the prophetic words of Moses. He seemed to see himself like a Joshua, and therefore it stands to reason that he would invade the Syrian nation to re-establish the boundaries that God had given to Israel in Genesis 15:18, *"In the same day the LORD made a covenant with Abram, saying, Unto thy seed have I given this land, from the river of Egypt unto the great river, the river Euphrates"*: David is following the Word he loved so much. A close look at the pattern of military campaigns David engaged in will reveal that he saw himself finishing what Joshua started, and that for his Lord.

2 Samuel 8:4, *"And David took from him a thousand chariots, and seven hundred horsemen, and twenty thousand footmen: and David houghed all the chariot horses, but reserved of them for an hundred chariots."*

David takes a thousand chariots and seven hundred horsemen. In 1 Chronicles 18:4 the number ascribed to the account of these same events is seven thousand. The account in Chronicles is more detailed and thus speaks of the seven hundred companies, there being ten in each company, with each ten having a ruler or captain, making seven thousand and making both accounts agreeable. David also followed the Word of the Lord by not multiplying to himself horses. Deuteronomy 17:16, *"But he shall not multiply horses to himself."*

David didn't multiply horses but rather subtracted them from his spoil by sparing for service only enough for his guard or his post. Again David is following the Word of the Lord in cutting the sinew of the horses so they cannot be used for chariots of war. Joshua 11:9, *"And Joshua did unto them as the LORD bade him: he houghed their horses, and burnt their chariots with fire."* It is important that since the Lord had shown David so much about how He would establish his house, he moves in prophetic order against the enemies of the Lord.

2 Samuel 8:5, *"And when the Syrians of Damascus came to succour Hadadezer king of Zobah, David slew of the Syrians two and twenty thousand men."*

David utterly defeated the Syrians of Hadadezer who cried for help from their fellow Syrians of Damascus. These made haste to come to help them. However, they were also slain before King David of Israel who was fighting in the anointing of his God. It is this turn of events that seems to have brought a great escalation to David's fame. When both of these factions of

Syrians were so utterly defeated by David, it caused all of the surrounding kings to realize they were helpless before King David and The God of Abraham, Isaac, and Jacob.

2 Samuel 8:6, *"Then David put garrisons in Syria of Damascus: and the Syrians became servants to David, and brought gifts. And the LORD preserved David whithersoever he went."*

David is unwilling to just remove the heathen idol worshippers from Israel but is compelled to take the ground ordained of God to belong to Israel. This is holy zeal in action. David defeats the Syrians of Hadadezer, and then he defeats Syrians of Damascus who came to help them, which means now he can set up his garrisons in the land of the Syrians. This is building and battling together, which is exactly what the Lord desires from us. It is no wonder that the parable about the builder is followed by the parable about the battler in Luke 14:28-32.

The Syrians began bringing gifts to David, which meant they recognized him as their king.

2 Samuel 8:7, *"And David took the shields of gold that were on the servants of Hadadezer, and brought them to Jerusalem."*

David was not taking these gold shields from the servants of Hadadezer just to gain wealth. He had a plan for this gold, even though he would not be building the Temple himself. David knew from the prophecy Nathan delivered to him that his son would build it (2 Samuel 7:12-13).

2 Samuel 8:8, *"And from Betah, and from Berothai, cities of Hadadezer, king David took exceeding much brass."*

Again David is gaining building material for the new Temple. Later we will see how this brass is used in the construction. When Solomon gets ready to build it, everything will be ready and prepared even to the point that some use the word *prefabricated*.

2 Samuel 8:9, *"When Toi king of Hamath heard that David had smitten all the host of Hadadezer,"*

Hamath was a city in the North of Judea but was also a part of Syria, However, these Syrians were in somewhat of a civil war with Hadadezer. Therefore they would have been quite happy to hear of David's victory.

2 Samuel 8:10, *"Then Toi sent Joram his son unto king David, to salute him, and to bless him, because he had fought against Hadadezer, and smitten him: for Hadadezer had wars with Toi. And Joram brought with him vessels of silver, and vessels of gold, and vessels of brass"*:

This Syrian king most likely felt as though he had been delivered from the wrath of Hadadezer, though history declares him stronger than his fellow Syrian enemy. He sends his son with a lot of valuable gifts to congratulate David's victory. This was a very wise move for Toi because he perceived there might be an opening here for him to have a relationship with David. The land that Toi dwelt in would have certainly been in the crosshairs of his conquering campaign as David was seeking for the covenant scriptural boundaries to be restored.

2 Samuel 8:11, *"Which also king David did dedicate unto the LORD, with the silver and gold that he had dedicated of all nations which he subdued"*;

David dedicated the gold, silver, and brass that Toi sent him as a gift to the Lord, just as he had dedicated the spoils he took from his enemies. This is of significance in revealing David's zeal in preparing material for the Temple. Usually the spoils would be separated from the gifts. The Jews basically believe there are only four ways to receive money or wealth: work, trade, gifts and inheritance.

Spoils of war were included in inheritance, for they were not to attack anyone that was not considered the enemy of the Lord. David had been guilty of attacking innocent people when in Ziklag, but since the burning of Ziklag and throughout the rest of his life, he was guiltless in this respect. David is gathering all he can while he can and none of it for himself. There has not been found in David one ounce of greed by any honest theologian on the earth!

2 Samuel 8:13, *"And David gat him a name when he returned from smiting of the Syrians in the valley of salt, being eighteen thousand men."*

Both 1 Chronicles 18:12 and Psalm 60:1 declare those smitten in this battle to be Edomites instead of Syrians. There are at least two possibilities here. 1) These were Edomites fighting for the Syrians. 2) The general name of their enemies was the Syrians, meaning they called all their enemies from that particular region Syrians, as is common in war. David's nephews, Abishai and Joab, smote eighteen thousand Edomites in this valley of salt. In the preface of Psalm 60 it speaks of twelve thousand being slain by Joab, therefore six thousand were slain by Abishai. These two both commanded great armies at this time, but Joab was the captain of the entire host.

Again, we see David's operating according to the ancient prophecies assigned to his enemies. The Edomites were certainly prophetically due to fall under the hand of Israel (Genesis

25:22-23, 27:27-29, 39-40, Psalm 60:6-12). Through this and all of the other military miracles, David who was already famous, became a phenomenal military wonder to the known world.

2 Samuel 8:14, *"And he put garrisons in Edom; throughout all Edom put he garrisons, and all they of Edom became David's servants. And the LORD preserved David whithersoever he went."*

As in verse 8 David is building and battling. He battles for the land and then builds something upon it. David is now in full force, defeating his enemies and taking their wealth to build the national Temple, which will be known as Solomon's Temple. David will also levy taxes on those countries he conquers, and will also use some of the population as servants to advance the kingdom of God. All of this mindset is proper for the church in typology as long as we equate the conquering of the enemies to the gospel to evangelism. The key to all of the success of David is fully known and understood by him. That key is the final statement of this verse, *"And the LORD preserved David whithersoever he went."* This is even so called the key of David by Isaiah in chapter 22 and verse 22 of his prophecy.

2 Samuel 8:15, *"And David reigned over all Israel; and David executed judgment and justice unto all his people."*

David fathered Israel and saw his position as one of servitude more than authority. This attribute was commonly manifesting throughout David's dynasty and got him the great compliment found in Acts 13:36a, *"For David, after he had served his own generation by the will of God, fell on sleep."* He executed authority like a father and a mentor, not a ruler and a manager. Joab was in his special place due to an irrevocable promise David had made to him recorded in 2 Samuel 5:8, though it is clear David was weary with him most of the time, even though Joab was his nephew.

Zadok and Ahimelech shared the office of the high priest for the following reasons: 1) Zadok, being the more pure Aaronic, was in the more obvious and correct order of the priest and king. 2) David knew the faithful priest prophesied in 1 Samuel 2:35, *"And I will raise me up a faithful priest, that shall do according to that which is in mine heart and in my mind: and I will build him a sure house; and he shall walk before mine anointed forever"* was not Abiathar who is here called Ahimelech after his father. 3) David knew by revelation the Zadok priesthood would be the preserved priesthood to introduce the Messiah. This was none other than John the Baptist. 4) David understood the perpetual order of the Zadok priesthood and the exclusiveness of his future office. This the prophet and priest Ezekiel confirms even to the millennium in Ezekiel 44:15-16. Only the Aaronic Levites of the seed of Zadok were allowed around the altar. 5) David knew he had appointed Abiathar out of guilt over the matter of Doeg the Edomite and not because he was told by the Lord to do so.

Fourteen verses show Zadok and Abiathar in the same verse, and that they shared the office is indisputable; but the anointed and the appointed would both prove themselves to be what they were toward end of the Davidic reign. Solomon would finish and complete the matter by putting Zadok in the room of Abiathar (1 Kings 2:35).

2 Samuel 8:18, *"And Benaiah the son of Jehoiada was over both the Cherethites and the Pelethites; and David's sons were chief rulers."*

The Cherethites and the Pelethites are two bands of people who were slingers and archers. They were possibly proselytes to the Jewish faith by Saul and then followed David when he fled from Saul. These Cherethites and Pelethites are actual family names, but because of their great ability with the weaponry of that day, the family names became descriptive of precision use of the sling and bow. Some theologians declare these simply to be archers and slingers and not necessarily family names. A close look at 1 Chronicles 12:2 will prove both cases to be true. *"They were armed with bows, and could use both the right hand and the left in hurling stones and shooting arrows out of a bow, even of Saul's brethren of Benjamin."* They were definitely King David's close guard and are mentioned several times in conjunction with David's immediate cabinet. David's sons were, of course, princes in their own right and chief rulers of the people.

2 Samuel 9:1, *"And David said, Is there yet any that is left of the house of Saul, that I may shew him kindness for Jonathan's sake"?*

It appears that the Lord reminded David not only of his covenant with Jonathan, but the prophecy Jonathan had given about being king over Israel. Jonathan had made a request for David to bless his house when (not if) he became king. 1 Samuel 20:15, *"But also thou shalt not cut off thy kindness from my house for ever: no, not when the LORD hath cut off the enemies of David everyone from the face of the earth."* Therefore, David desired to do something for the good of Jonathan's seed. He begins to make inquiry for finding any of Jonathan's posterity. This reveals the heart of David toward his friends, and especially his covenant friend Jonathan. Saul's tribe had given him much grief; Jonathan was gone, and David could have easily chosen to exempt himself from such a promise. Yet, David honored his covenant to Jonathan and his seed!

2 Samuel 9:2, *"And there was of the house of Saul a servant whose name was Ziba. And when they had called him unto David, the king said unto him, Art thou Ziba? And he said, Thy servant is he."*

David made his wishes known to his closest servants about finding someone of the house of Jonathan to bless. One of Saul's servants named Ziba was a servant of David, and they brought him to David. History tells us that David had servants from every tribe of Israel and many who were not Jews. David seemed to have a unique ability to work easily with people from every creed and color. However, he never allowed idolatry in his dynasty. If the people who came to David were not willing to crush their idols, they would be David's enemies and not his servants.

Most likely someone who knew that Ziba was once a servant of Saul told him what the king wanted. Ziba told David about Mephibosheth, the son of Jonathan who was crippled and living in Lodebar. The fact that David brought Mephibosheth back to sit at his table again proves that David's hatred for the blind and lame (2 Samuel 5:8) was toward idols and not people. Mephibosheth was 5 years old when he was injured, and his injury was related to the death of Saul and Jonathan (2 Samuel 4:4). David therefore would feel even more compassion for him and be more determined to bless him and care for him. Ziba was able to tell David exactly where Mephibosheth lived.

2 Samuel 9:5, *"Then king David sent, and fet him out of the house of Machir, the son of Ammiel, from Lodebar."*

Without hesitation David sent for Mephibosheth. Evidently Machir had taken Mephibosheth into his house out of the goodness of his heart, without political reason. We know he had no ill will for David, as is shown when he helps David during the rebellion of Absalom (2 Samuel 17:27-29). Lodebar was known as the city of no pasture. History tells us it was a very poor city, full of struggling, depressed, and hungry souls. The picture here is that the King (Jesus) sent His servant (the Holy Spirit) to a dark and barren land (the earth) to pick up an undeserving cripple (a sinner) and bring him back in the King's chariot (the Gospel) to sit at the King's table forever (eternal life). This glorious picture has been the basis for many a gospel message.

2 Samuel 9:6, *"Now when Mephibosheth, the son of Jonathan, the son of Saul, was come unto David, he fell on his face, and did reverence. And David said, Mephibosheth. And he answered, Behold thy servant."*

As soon as Mephibosheth arrived, he fell on his face, which was customary for coming before a king. Some say he was most likely fearful for his life, but this would not be likely if in fact Ziba had been the one sent to get him, for Ziba probably knew of the king's good intention toward Mephibosheth. Mephibosheth came humbly, instead of fearfully, for his being five when Jonathan was killed would have been old enough to remember the great love his daddy had for David. The only hint we have that he actually feared for his life is David's salutation to him, "Fear not" which could have been to comfort his overwhelming feeling of unworthiness.

2 Samuel 9:7, *"And David said unto him, Fear not: for I will surely shew thee kindness for Jonathan thy father's sake, and will restore thee all the land of Saul thy father; and thou shalt eat bread at my table continually."*

David reveals his good intention toward Mephibosheth, and no doubt it was more than Mephibosheth could have ever dreamed. All of the land Saul, his grandfather, had acquired would be his. Also, he is now an honored soul and an important part of the royal household. This truly is a picture of amazing grace and the Gospel. The king sent for us to bestow upon us mercy unmerited. He then invites us to sit at His table and under His watchful care forever.

Ziba's response to David's benevolence looked admirable even though it was at his own expense. He seemed to gladly become the servant of Mephibosheth and seemed happy to submit his whole family and servants to the same order. However, he later lied on Mephibosheth to get the land back, proving that he had (or had developed) ill feelings in his heart. Some fault David twice in the matter of helping Mephibosheth. 1) For taking the land from Ziba and giving it all to Mephibosheth, with no apparent recompense; 2) For listening to Ziba's lie and taking the land back from the innocent Mephibosheth in a hasty and ill advised decision (2 Samuel 16:1-4).

2 Samuel 10:2, *"Then said David, I will shew kindness unto Hanun the son of Nahash, as his father shewed kindness unto me. And David sent to comfort him by the hand of his servants for his father. And David's servants came into the land of the children of Ammon."*

David actually wanted to show respect to Hanun because Hanun's father had been so good to him while he was in exile from Saul, most likely while he had placed his family at Moab. History relates that many of the neighbors of Israel were anxious to help David because of their hatred for Saul. David never seemed to forget those who had befriended him in those days, so he sends his servant with words of comfort.

2 Samuel 10:3, *"And the princes of the children of Ammon said unto Hanun their lord, Thinkest thou that David doth honour thy father, that he hath sent comforters unto thee? hath not David rather sent his servants unto thee, to search the city, and to spy it out, and to overthrow it"?*

Hanun, like Rehoboam, took some bad counsel from those around him. These counselors assured Hanun that these servants of David were not there to comfort him, but to spy out the land for a future invasion. Hanun might have been more willing to believe that to be the case because of all of the different cities and countries David had already conquered. Hanun could not have been more foolish. Like Nabal, he highly offended the one who was friendly to him. And of all the people on the earth to offend, he chose the worst one.

2 Samuel 10:4, *"Wherefore Hanun took David's servants, and shaved off the one half of their beards, and cut off their garments in the middle, even to their buttocks, and sent them away."*

Hanun's severe and gross insult was unnecessary. He should have incarcerated them until he could have searched out the truth. Because the Ammonites had done a lot of damage to Israel in times past, Hanun should not be faulted for suspicion of motive here. However, he is faulted for 1) His hasty judgment of David, his father's friend; 2) His scandalous method of insult against the Jews religion, for they were not to cut their beards or hair unless they were mourning or were in a religious ritual involving a shaven head (Leviticus 19:27); 3) Failing to considering the ramifications of humiliating David's men, which in fact humiliated David himself; 4) Sending a signal through his actions that he was prepared for a bloody war; 5) Failing to understand that David's men were not just servants to him, but unlike other kings, they were his sons and converts!

2 Samuel 10:5, *"When they told it unto David, he sent to meet them, because the men were greatly ashamed: and the king said, Tarry at Jericho until your beards be grown, and then return."*

David was greatly concerned for these men and the way they were treated. You will find David as a rule very thoughtful of his men. His terrible treatment of Uriah the Hittite over the matter of Bathsheba is shocking to the students of David's life. Yet even in that instance, David seemed to be trying to cover his sin without mistreating Uriah any further, although he ultimately gave in to the shameful sin he committed. In almost every other case, David placed the feelings of his men above his own desires. In this case of these humbled soldiers, he allowed the men to remain in Jericho until their beards grew out. The whole nation heard of the matter, but David helped the men by not letting the whole nation see them in this condition of having half a beard.

2 Samuel 10:6, *"And when the children of Ammon saw that they stank before David, the children of Ammon sent and hired the Syrians of Beth-rehob, and the Syrians of Zoba, twenty thousand footmen, and of king Maacah a thousand men, and of Ishtob twelve thousand men."*

The Ammonites found out how offended David and his army were with their wicked reaction to David's act of mercy, and they knew David would attack. Therefore, they hired what is called Syrians here to protect them. Upon a close study of these mercenaries and their locations, one will find these are actually Canaanites instead of Syrians. As in the case of the Edomites in 2 Samuel 8:13, it seems the general enemies of Israel were often called Syrians without being so by bloodline.

The Syrians had been defeated and subdued by David already, and these Canaanites were in limbo and felt that they had more to gain by helping to defeat David, so they hired themselves out for that purpose. They probably picked up several footmen that had been defeated by David in the

Syrian war, who would be anxious to deal David a defeat. The Ammonites and their hirelings together made an immense army.

2 Samuel 10:7, *"And when David heard of it, he sent Joab, and all the host of the mighty men."*

David didn't go himself but sent Joab, the captain of the host of Israel. It is likely that only the professional soldiers went to this battle even though that number would equal or surpass the number of the enemy. When the Ammonites realized that Joab was going to attack, they came out of the city toward Joab's army. They were likely trusting in their vast army of mercenaries out in the field being prepared for war. After Joab realized the Ammonites were in front and the so called Syrians in the rear, he wisely divided his army as well.

Joab picked the choice warriors to fight the mercenaries and put the rest of the Israeli army under Abishai, his brother, who was a great general himself. Abishai would fight the Ammonites while Joab would fight the mercenaries. Joab's plan was that if either of their armies were overcome, then the other would come to their rescue. Joab then gave a great speech of encouragement recorded in verse 12, *"Be of good courage, and let us play the men for our people, and for the cities of our God: and the LORD do that which seemeth him good."* Joab also knew the power of God was necessary for them to be victorious, so he ended his words with a full resignation to the will of the Lord.

Joab advanced and his enemies fled. Abishai's adversaries saw it and did the same, giving the Israeli army a great victory. Here we do not find a count of casualties; perhaps there were few. However, this battle caused an uprising of the defeated Syrians, for they could see while this host was gathered it was the opportunity to defeat David. The problem for David's enemies was the fact that though David had Joab and Abishai as his captains, the real Captian of the Host of the Israeli army was the same one Joshua bowed before and took off his shoe.

2 Samuel 10:17, *"And when it was told David, he gathered all Israel together, and passed over Jordan, and came to Helam. And the Syrians set themselves in array against David, and fought with him."*

David, perceiving the undoing of all his victory over the Syrians in danger, gathers all of Israel and leads them himself to the battle field. He felt that this level of combat required his presence on the field. This proves David to have the great quality good leaders must have. He didn't ask others to do something he was not willing to do. David led the campaign to the enemy, although the Syrians engaged in the actual fight first.

2 Samuel 10:18, *"And the Syrians fled before Israel; and David slew the men of seven hundred chariots of the Syrians, and forty thousand horsemen, and smote Shobach the captain of their host, who died there."*

The Lord gave David another great victory. David slew the men of seven hundred chariots. That is seven thousand men because there were ten men to a chariot unit, as it is explained in 1 Chronicles 19:18. This was a decisive victory that accomplished three things: 1) It crushed the uprising of the Syrians and brought the whole of Syria under Israeli rule. 2) It drove back the Ammonites who had submitted to Hadarezer for the purpose of this particular battle. 3) It cited fear in the Canaanites to ever help the Ammonites again.

And yet the Ammonites were not completely punished by the Israelis for their treatment of David's men. But that was soon to come!

2 Samuel 11:1, *"And it came to pass, after the year was expired, at the time when kings go forth to battle, that David sent Joab, and his servants with him, and all Israel; and they destroyed the children of Ammon, and besieged Rabbah. But David tarried still at Jerusalem."*

David sent Joab to battle, and this time Joab destroyed the land of the Ammonites and besieged the capital city of their nation. This was the first campaign of the fighting season, and that started with the Ammonites' receiving full retaliation and punishment for their deeds to David's men.

David no doubt felt quite at ease in his position of power and decided he need not go to war this season. This in itself was not a bad decision, for he had already done the same thing when he sent Joab and Abishai to fight the Ammonites and the Canaanites (2 Samuel 10:7). Most theologians surmise that had he been on the battlefield, he would have been out of the way of temptation concerning Bathsheba. However, temptation can come to us on the battlefield as well as in the home. There is a lesson here, as well as other places in the scripture -- at the time in ministry when it becomes apparent that a leader must begin to delegate his duties, it is a most vulnerable moment for that ministry.

2 Samuel 11:2, *"And it came to pass in an eveningtide, that David arose from off his bed, and walked upon the roof of the king's house: and from the roof he saw a woman washing herself; and the woman was very beautiful to look upon."*

David rose from a late afternoon nap, evidently before sunset, and walked on the roof of his house. He most likely never would have believed what would transpire before the night was ended. There has been much controversy as to Bathsheba's guilt or innocence in this matter. The following observations are among those most mentioned by theologians: 1) How could it be that she did not realize she was in view of the king's roof top? 2) Was there no motive here on Bathsheba's part? 3) Was it simply normal on her part to do as she did? In many countries it is not odd to this day to see women bathing openly in pools or streams. 4) Because it was a ceremonial cleansing (Verse 4) it would not have been supposed to be provocative at all. History relates to us that there was a period of time in church history when converts were baptized in the nude.

Although Bathsheba's guilt or innocence is a constant polemical question, it is sure that David's guilt is clear.

2 Samuel 11:3, *"And David sent and inquired after the woman. And one said, Is not this Bathsheba, the daughter of Eliam, the wife of Uriah the Hittite"*?

Instead of suppressing his aroused emotion and taking the way of escape for every temptation that comes our way (1 Corinthians 10:13), he acts upon it by inquiring about her. A step toward fulfilling an aroused desire is a step of death and destruction, as stated in James 1:14-15 *"But every man is tempted, when he is drawn away of his own lust, and enticed. Then when lust hath conceived, it bringeth forth sin: and sin, when it is finished, bringeth forth death."* David's lust and carnal desire had already taken hold on him so that when he inquired and found out she was married to one of his royal guard, he didn't hesitate to carry out his efforts in fulfilling his wicked and adulterous action. He had already given in to the works of the flesh, and her marital status meant nothing!

When David's sin is mentioned later in 1 Kings 15:5 it is referred to "in the matter of Uriah." Uriah was not only a member of the royal guard (which explains why he lived so close to the king's court), but evidently a proselyte to the Jewish faith which strictly forbids adultery. David, who led him to trust the God who wrote the Ten Commandments with his own finger, now breaks most of them against him.

Bathsheba was the daughter of Eliam called Ammiel in 1 Chronicles 3:5 both of which have the same meaning.

2 Samuel 11:4, *"And David sent messengers, and took her; and she came in unto him, and he lay with her; for she was purified from her uncleanness: and she returned unto her house."*

These men he sent had to know that their leader was at fault. Loyalty should never create blindness, but we see no protest by these messengers concerning the thing that David is doing. This is the paramount sin of David's life. 1) He disregarded the seventh commandment concerning adultery. 2) He had no regard for such a faithful, worthy soldier as Uriah. 3) He had no regard for the soul of Bathsheba. 4) He had no regard for his people Israel in bringing reproach upon the nation. 5) He had no regard for his own family. 6) He had no regard for the coming judgment on the whole matter. 7) He had no regard for the men under him who served him in his sin. 8) He had no regard for the likelihood of fathering a child from another man's wife. This is seen because even if Bathsheba had no seductive agenda, her ceremonial cleansing would have signaled to David that her cycle had just finished and she was most likely to get pregnant.

2 Samuel 11:5, *"And the woman conceived, and sent and told David, and said, I am with child."*

David hears the dreaded news from Bathsheba that she is with child. Bathsheba knew that under the law, Uriah could have her stoned to death (Leviticus 20:10) because he and his immediate family and friends would have known Uriah was not there to get her pregnant. What a horrible place sin brings us to. Will the king of Israel father a child from an adulterous affair? David had wives and concubines from other nations, which is a practice and tradition in Israel. These wives were his, and these concubines were not someone else's wives. But Bathsheba belonged to one of his own court guards and faithful soldiers, Uriah. David felt he must never let this be known. Perhaps he even thought it best for those he had earlier shown no regard for when he committed the wicked act. David begins to devise a plan to hide his sin and save Bathsheba's life.

It should be noted that from the time of his sin with Bathsheba, neither historians nor doctors of theology can find a shred of evidence indicating that the Sweet Psalmist of Israel would pen one psalm, no, not until the psalm of deep contrition and repentance, Psalm 51.

2 Samuel 11:6, *"And David sent to Joab, saying, Send me Uriah the Hittite. And Joab sent Uriah to David."*

David sent a message for Joab to send Uriah home from the battlefield. This in itself would cause no real alarm as Uriah's home was close to David and he was a part of his guard. David's evident plan was for Uriah to come home, and because he would be sleeping with his wife, he would think the baby was his. Because it was very early in the pregnancy, had Uriah done so he would have thought so.

2 Samuel 11:7, *"And when Uriah was come unto him, David demanded of him how Joab did, and how the people did, and how the war prospered."*

David's meeting with Uriah is most pitiful in every way. 1) David pretends to confide in Uriah as a check on Joab's behavior. 2) He pretends to desire a report as to the welfare of the people in the war zone. 3) He pretends to desire a report on how the war is going. 4) He pretends to be concerned for others, and he may have been, but it is clear his main concern is to get his sin hidden.

Uriah could have possibly wondered why David would ask him these questions, when in fact there is ample proof that there were messengers coming to and from the battle front. One characteristic of guilt ridden men is that they form plans to hide what they don't want others to know.

2 Samuel 11:8, "*And David said to Uriah, Go down to thy house, and wash thy feet. And Uriah departed out of the king's house, and there followed him a mess of meat from the king.*"

The abrupt call from the battle field, the unreasonable questions, David's strong desire for him to stay at his own house, and now this quite unusual kindness surely would have compounded to Uriah any suspicion he may have had as to what had brought about this action. Meat from the king's court to a personal home was the highest compliment one could be paid. Uriah refused the good favor he had found with the king and evidently did not eat the food nor go to his house, but stayed at the door of the king and slept there. We can find no hint from Uriah that he actually did suspect there to be unholy action between his wife and David. This was due to his loyalty to David, for David's bizarre action gave him reason to think just that. Uriah was noble, regardless, and yet that was the last thing David wanted, as it spoiled his plan to cover up his sin.

2 Samuel 11:10, "*And when they had told David, saying, Uriah went not down unto his house, David said unto Uriah, Camest thou not from thy journey? why then didst thou not go down unto thine house?*"

Perhaps David displayed his urgency when they told him Uriah stayed all night at the king's door in that he spoke with him immediately. David asked Uriah why he didn't rest after such a journey, and why did he reject such an opportune relief from the war. David could have scolded him for not letting someone else keep the watch for the king. However, his true aggravation was not for the loss of blessing for Uriah but for his own foiled plan.

2 Samuel 11:11, "*And Uriah said unto David, The ark, and Israel, and Judah, abide in tents; and my lord Joab, and the servants of my lord, are encamped in the open fields; shall I then go into mine house, to eat and to drink, and to lie with my wife? as thou livest, and as thy soul liveth, I will not do this thing.*"

When Uriah gave his answer to David concerning why he didn't go down to his wife, it should have brought David to repentance. Uriah said if the Ark is in a tent and all of the soldiers are in tents, I would not feel right going to my house and sleeping with my wife. David should have melted right then before the Lord because 1) Through his sin he had lost his own zeal to build the house for the Ark; 2) His evil plan was met with righteous action from the very one he had sinned against; 3) This was a wakeup call for him to come to his senses; 4) Even the wicked Saul, when he received such a turn from David wept and confessed that David was more righteous than he; 5) Uriah is the one human he had affronted the most in this matter according to 1 Kings 15:5, *"Because David did that which was right in the eyes of the LORD, and turned not aside from any thing that he commanded him all the days of his life, save only in the matter of Uriah the Hittite."*

David should have fallen on his knees before Uriah and confessed to him the whole rotten account of his sin. It is likely that Uriah would have forgiven him and restored him. However that was not the case by far.

2 Samuel 11:12, *"And David said to Uriah, Tarry here to day also, and to morrow I will let thee depart. So Uriah abode in Jerusalem that day, and the morrow."*

David's plan was so devastated that in order to continue his deviant path, he no doubt had to reconsider everything. Therefore he detains Uriah for a couple of days, still hoping Uriah will sleep with his wife. David knew at this point that when Bathsheba's pregnancy was discovered, Uriah would put it all together concerning the sudden attention paid to him by the king.

2 Samuel 11:13, *"And when David had called him, he did eat and drink before him; and he made him drunk: and at even he went out to lie on his bed with the servants of his lord, but went not down to his house."*

David called Uriah to a feast and like the wicked daughters of Lot, (Genesis 19:33-35), tried to get Uriah drunk so he would forget about his loyal commitment of self denial and go home to sleep with his wife. This is an unbelievable and degenerating failure in the life of David. Even in his condition Uriah slept with the other soldiers instead of going home to his wife. David should have seen that the hand of the Lord was against him here and repented. Instead he does the unthinkable.

2 Samuel 11:14, *"And it came to pass in the morning, that David wrote a letter to Joab, and sent it by the hand of Uriah."*

David, having abandoned his efforts to get Uriah to sleep with his wife Bathsheba, now proceeds to his next level of a decadent slide. Even as the wicked woman Jezebel used a letter to send the righteous Naboth to a sure grave (1 Kings 21:8-9), so David sends a letter to Joab, sending the loyal and innocent Uriah to a sure death. What is this? David sins, and it costs Uriah his life! Just think, Uriah was more than willing to die in protecting his king, and now he must die by the hand of his king!

Oh the audacity of the guilt ridden soul; there is no moral limit to such a one! How could the man God used to write such wonderful psalms possibly stoop to such a low level as to send the innocent and unknowing Uriah away with his own death sentence in his hand? The letter instructed Joab to set Uriah in a place in the battle where he would be sure to get killed. One would wonder if David thought of his own words concerning Joab and Abishai in 2 Samuel 3:39, *"the sons of Zeruiah be too hard for me:"* In that same verse, David unknowingly speaks of his own judgment, *"the LORD shall reward the doer of evil according to his wickedness."* At that time David never could have believed that he would do something worse than these who had killed Abner.

2 Samuel 11:17, *"And the men of the city went out, and fought with Joab: and there fell some of the people of the servants of David; and Uriah the Hittite died also."*

It should be noted that Uriah was not the only one to die from this diabolical plan of David. Lightfoot is correct in charging David with many more than one death that day. Even though the Ammonite archers killed Uriah, it was David that was charged with his murder according to the word of the Lord delivered by the prophet Nathan. 2 Samuel 12:9, *"Wherefore hast thou despised the commandment of the LORD, to do evil in his sight? thou hast killed Uriah the Hittite with the sword, and hast taken his wife to be thy wife, and hast slain him with the sword of the children of Ammon."*

2 Samuel 11:18, *"Then Joab sent and told David all the things concerning the war"*;

Joab sends David the full report of the death of Uriah. It is amazing how ready Joab seems to be to aid David in the cover up of the death of Uriah, not even knowing the reason David wanted him killed. Joab protested When David took the census (1 Chronicles 21:3), but he made no protest in helping David kill Uriah. Had David and Joab worked together before in this manner? It is possible, but not probable. However, many observe that by this time Joab had become somewhat of a killing machine, ruthless, and cold hearted. Joab certainly seems very clever in covering for himself and David. He instructed the messengers to be prepared to answer for the absurdity of charging a fortified wall with archers shooting at them, even after Joab told them to do so at the king's command. Joab told the messengers to tell of the death of Abimelech the son of Jerubbesheth who was also so close to the wall that a woman cast a millstone on his head. This should prove Joab is involved in securing his own innocence as well as David's.

2 Samuel 11:22, *"So the messenger went, and came and shewed David all that Joab had sent him for."*

Even as Joab requested, the message was delivered. It now seemed that the plan was successful in concealing the matter of the adultery with Bathsheba. But from the eyes of the Lord there is nothing hidden, and who should know that more than David himself?

2 Samuel 11:23, *"And the messenger said unto David, Surely the men prevailed against us, and came out unto us into the field, and we were upon them even unto the entering of the gate."*

David probably pretends to be hearing this as though he didn't already know the story. After all he is the one that gave the instructions as to how it would all happen. One would wonder if David felt any remorse at all for the report of the death of the innocent and loyal Hittite. Had he grown so cold by now that his heart was glad he could soon go get Bathsheba? How cold and calculated was David? Watts declared he probably wept at night over his sin, but we see no sign of it. Neither do we find any writing of David that matched this time in his life. At least David could not play the hypocrite. It is not believed that David wrote one psalm after his adulterous affair up until Psalm 51, the model of repentance.

2 Samuel 11:25, *"Then David said unto the messenger, Thus shalt thou say unto Joab, Let not this thing displease thee, for the sword devoureth one as well as another: make thy battle more strong against the city, and overthrow it: and encourage thou him."*

David told the messenger to go tell Joab in so many words, not to worry because people get killed in war all the time. It could be that his heart was breaking over his sin all the time he is telling the messenger what to tell Joab. However, again we can't find a hint of remorse. David told the messenger to encourage Joab to go ahead now and take the city. This is pure audacity for one that loves and knows the Word and the history of his people. Did he not consider Ai, that little city that the hordes of Israeli soldiers fell in front of because there was sin in the camp? And that sin was not even in Joshua their leader (Joshua 7). What presumption on David's part!

2 Samuel 11:27, *"And when the mourning was past, David sent and fet her to his house, and she became his wife, and bare him a son. But the thing that David had done displeased the LORD."*

Many theologians doubt the seriousness of Bathsheba's mourning. Clark quotes an ancient scholar, "She shed reluctant tears, and forced out groans from a joyful heart." However the scriptures do not tell us whether or not David confided in her as to his wicked plan. If David did not tell her of his plot to kill Uriah, it is likely that she really mourned the loss of her husband. Yet, it is not likely that David went the entire seven days required for the customary time of mourning (Genesis 50:10), without letting Bathsheba know what his intentions were after the period of mourning. The hastiness for the marriage was to make sure they were married as close to the needed nine month gestation as possible in order to hide David's sin. The whole matter displeased the Lord. Therefore the Lord chastened David, and the very thing he committed such atrocious sins to hide, became known to countless millions from that day to this.

2 Samuel 12:1, *"And the LORD sent Nathan unto David. And he came unto him, and said unto him, There were two men in one city; the one rich, and the other poor."*

Nathan's assignment to rebuke David was not a pleasant one, to say the least, but a necessary one. The Lord has Nathan to use a parable to bring David to sentence his own self to righteous judgment. This in itself is amazing, for nearly two years had passed since that night on the rooftop when he conceded to his own lust for Bathsheba. Some count the time between David's sin with Bathsheba and murder of Uriah and the time of Nathan's rebuke to be less than one year - nine months for the gestation period and a few days that the child was sick. However, most scholars agree that the language concerning the child is that of a weanling. The Hebrew women weaned their children at one year. If in fact the child was weaned, it would make the time almost two years.

Nathan's parable was engaging and orchestrated by the Lord to bring David to repentance. Until Nathan told David, he failed to see the parable was about him.

2 Samuel 12:5, *"And David's anger was greatly kindled against the man; and he said to Nathan, As the LORD liveth, the man that hath done this thing shall surely die"*:

This is the sentence David passed upon his own self, *"the man that hath done this thing shall surely die:"* Then David proceeded to sure up his own guilt even more by requiring the man in the parable to pay back four times what he had taken. David then declared such a person as he had heard of in the parable to be deemed worthy of death without mercy. One would wonder had he known at that time he was the man in the parable, would he have been so harsh?

2 Samuel 12:7, *"And Nathan said to David, Thou art the man. Thus saith the LORD God of Israel, I anointed thee king over Israel, and I delivered thee out of the hand of Saul"*;

This is the climax of the message indicting David of his wicked sin that he had never repented of. Nathan had absolutely left no place for David to stand! Nathan said, *"Thou art the man."* After the indictment comes the prelude to the sentencing. The Lord uses his prophet to remind David of these things: 1) That He had brought him from the sheep fields to be the king of Israel; 2) How good He had been to David; 3) David's disregard for the commandments of the Lord, referring to the sixth, seventh, eighth, ninth, and tenth commandments; 6th *"thou shalt not kill,"* 7th *"thou shalt not commit adultery,"* 8th *"thou shalt not steal,"* (for he stole Uriah's wife) 9th *"thou shall not bear false witness against your neighbor,"* (for he deceived Uriah and purported him guilty to Joab) 10th *"thou shalt not covet."*

David's sentence for punishment now comes to him fourfold, being spoken from his own mouth (verse 6). 1) The sword or conflict will always be in David's house. In this case it appears He is speaking of his immediate family, for after David's death Solomon enjoyed a forty year span of peace. 2) Evil or rebellion will come against David's house from within, again speaking of his immediate family, for it is clear this is referring to Absalom. 3) His wives will be lain with publicly just as David lay with Bathsheba (another man's wife) privately. This did Absalom in 2 Samuel 16:22, *"So they spread Absalom a tent upon the top of the house; and Absalom went in unto his father's concubines in the sight of all Israel."* 4) The child that is born of this wickedness will die!

And yet there are some who declare that there are no repercussions for sin after the cross, citing this was before Jesus took our judgment. Jesus paid the complete price for our sins and gave us the gift of salvation though his unmerited grace toward man. Using the glorious and complete atonement of Jesus' blood to dismiss oneself from the repercussion of sin is most erroneous. The theologians that teach such should get a testimony from the church at Corinth, and in particular from those who ate the Lord's Supper unworthily (1 Corinthians 11:30) or from Ananias and Sapphira (Acts 5)!

2 Samuel 12:13, *"And David said unto Nathan, I have sinned against the LORD. And Nathan said unto David, The LORD also hath put away thy sin; thou shalt not die."*

David confesses his sin. He is caught. He didn't know a soul on earth knew of his sin. His running and hiding is over. He is exposed. His confession and true repentance now begins. There can be no true repentance without confession, and there can be no true confession without true contrition or Godly sorrow (2 Corinthians 7:10). Just as David had pronounced a fourfold punishment on the man in the parable Nathan delivered, he also pronounced the death sentence. Of course the man in the parable turned out to be him. However, Nathan tells David he will not die as a result of his sin, and yet the child will. This last and fourth part of the punishment was delivered after David confessed his sin.

Many believe that confession stops punishment, but how is that so when the scripture clearly teaches us that we will reap what we sow? Galatians 6:7, *"Be not deceived; God is not mocked: for whatsoever a man soweth, that shall he also reap."* The child's death is horrible, as well as all the other parts of David's punishment. But worse than the punishment is the one final mentioned repercussion of David's sin, *"Howbeit, because by this deed thou hast given great occasion to the enemies of the LORD to blaspheme,"* (Verse 14*)*. This is what struck David's heart deeper than any other result of his sin. He had opened the door for the idolaters to blaspheme the Lord he loved.

There was a man who went deep into contrition and repentance for his failure and sin against God. He thought he could go no deeper into Godly sorrow until this was revealed! He began to realize his sin had opened the door for the enemies of the cross to mock. When he heard that in his spirit, it shook his very soul with terror at the thought of the cost of his sin. He was exasperated, for he realized he had advanced the very kingdom of darkness he had spent so much of his life trying to deliver people from. At this, he went so deep into remorse that he could not live had the voice of the Lord not spoken to him saying, "Take my mercy and arise."

Yes, the sins of David and his punishment will be read by multitudes throughout the ages. Yet they will also read of his glorious restoration, and will see him sitting as king of Israel throughout the millennium right beside Jesus the King of Kings.

2 Samuel 12:15, "*And Nathan departed unto his house. And the LORD struck the child that Uriah's wife bare unto David, and it was very sick.*"

After the delivery of David's indictment and the pronouncement of his sentence of punishment, Nathan retired to his house. It seems that Nathan is a personal and trusted prophet to the king. He evidently was living close, if not in the king's court. He had risked his life in delivering that truth to David. Had David been a Saul, Nathan would have died for sure. But David heard the word of the Lord through Nathan, even though it was the saddest news he had ever received. We do not see a slightest indication that David accused God of harshness or injustice in his punishment.

2 Samuel 12:16, "*David therefore besought God for the child; and David fasted, and went in, and lay all night upon the earth.*"

David explains this action to his immediate family and cabinet later in Verse 22, "*And he said, While the child was yet alive, I fasted and wept: for I said, Who can tell whether GOD will be gracious to me, that the child may live*"? Even though the death sentence was given, David knew of the mercies of God, and had read of Moses and father Abraham who had succeeded in getting the Lord to reverse His sentence, so he makes an effort with all of his heart.

By this and his response to the report of the death of Absalom, it appears that David loved his children very much. He went into deep intercession for the child, not sparing himself in any way, to the degree that those around him tried to get him to get up off the ground and eat. David would not. As long as there was breath in the child, he would stay in intercession, no doubt telling the Lord how innocent the child was and how guilty he was, pleading over and over for the child's life.

2 Samuel 12:18, *"And it came to pass on the seventh day, that the child died. And the servants of David feared to tell him that the child was dead: for they said, Behold, while the child was yet alive, we spake unto him, and he would not hearken unto our voice: how will he then vex himself, if we tell him that the child is dead"?*

David's intercession for their child was rejected. The child died after seven days. During those painful days of intercession, David never ate or washed himself, but remained on the earth seeking the Lord. During this process all of his staff and family kept close watch as to his welfare. That is why they feared to tell him when the child died. The intercessional behavior was evidently so deep it caused them to wonder if he would try to destroy himself upon the news of the death of the child. What they didn't know is that David had also been in deep contrition and repentance during that time. The baby was the tool the Lord used to bring David to full repentance, resulting in full restoration.

Many throughout history have foolishly charged God with murder of this child. Antichrists have often used this death to promote their claims that Christians serve a bully god and have a slaughterhouse religion. How foolish! The baby is a martyr whose death brought the light of Israel back.

2 Samuel 12:19, *"But when David saw that his servants whispered, David perceived that the child was dead: therefore David said unto his servants, Is the child dead? And they said, He is dead."*

David could tell by their action that the baby had died, and they would soon see by David's action that he was a changed man.

2 Samuel 12:20, *"Then David arose from the earth, and washed, and anointed himself, and changed his apparel, and came into the house of the LORD, and worshipped: then he came to his own house; and when he required, they set bread before him, and he did eat."*

His family and servants were amazed that David arose with no apparent anger or display of negative emotion. During that time on his face, David evidently had an amazing visitation from the Lord. God met him there and he was shown 1) That the baby was safe in the arms of the Lord; 2) That he was also going to heaven (Verse 23) *"I shall go to him"* 3) That his first duty upon rising up was to go into the house of the Lord and worship; 4) To accept the sovereignty of God in punishment, for there is always mercy in judgment.

2 Samuel 12:24, *"And David comforted Bathsheba his wife, and went in unto her, and lay with her: and she bare a son, and he called his name Solomon: and the LORD loved him."*

Bathsheba was not mentioned in Nathan's scathing indictment and sentence of sin that the Lord sent through him to David. She suffered greatly for her part in the adultery. She lost her husband; she lost a child; and she lost her honor. Yet, we find no word here or elsewhere in the Bible of her guilt. David, as a restored man, comforted her. She would not be stoned. She would be David's wife, for he would not divorce her, and again she conceived and bore a son.

The son which came was the one spoken of in the prophetic word of 1 Chronicles 22:9-10; *"Behold, a son shall be born to thee, who shall be a man of rest; and I will give him rest from all his enemies round about: for his name shall be Solomon, and I will give peace and quietness unto Israel in his days. He shall build a house for my name; and he shall be my son, and I will be his father; and I will establish the throne of his kingdom over Israel for ever."* Solomon would be his name even though the prophet Nathan named him Jedidiah, which means "beloved of the Lord." Amazing love and favor was shown by the hand of the Lord to Solomon. This son was the apple of the Lord's eye and the very one to take the dynasty of David on to new heights.

During the time of Bethsheba's pregnancy is when Joab continued his assault on the city of Rabbah. Remember David had told Joab to fortify himself and overthrow the city after the death of Uriah (2 Samuel 11:25). Some believe the entire siege performed against that city may have taken a full year, for as he approached the completion of the conquest, he notifies David to come. Joab took the city in two parts, first that part known as the royal city.

2 Samuel 12:27, *"And Joab sent messengers to David, and said, I have fought against Rabbah, and have taken the city of waters."*

The part of the city of Rabbah known as the royal city was the part that furnished the water, as it was situated on the river Jabbok. Joab knew that the city would not be able to withstand his siege without the life giving water necessary for their survival. Therefore, Joab sends a message to David, letting him know the thing is coming to an end, for he has shut off their water supply. Joab knows that this victory will be so renown that he should be sure the king is involved, even though Joab and his men did all of the work and sacrifice. So he instructs David to gather all of the rest of the army and come on down for the great finale.

2 Samuel 12:29, *"And David gathered all the people together, and went to Rabbah, and fought against it, and took it."*

With David's bringing all of the rest of the people of Israel fit for war, they no longer needed to starve the city out. They stormed the city and took it. This was the pattern of David in all of his military campaigns. Having now a right relationship with the Lord and a restoration of the joy of God's salvation in his soul, David would once again feel the surge of God's Spirit helping him in war again.

2 Samuel 12:30, *"And he took their king's crown from off his head, the weight whereof was a talent of gold with the precious stones: and it was set on David's head. And he brought forth the spoil of the city in great abundance."*

This crown was a great prize of this victory. It was a phenomenal piece of wealth, although the word "weight" is the same word translated "value" in other places. A talent of gold would be above one hundred pounds. Though David was evidently a very strong man, it is not likely that either he or the king of Ammon could stand such a weight on their heads. Actually, the gold and all of the precious jewels were valued at the amount of a talent of gold. The abundant spoil of the Ammonites' royal city made David much wealthier than he already was. Yet again there is nothing said here, or anywhere in writings by David or about him, that offer any proof that he was set upon his wealth.

2 Samuel 12:31, *"And he brought forth the people that were therein, and put them under saws, and under harrows of iron, and under axes of iron, and made them pass through the brickkiln: and thus did he unto all the cities of the children of Ammon. So David and all the people returned unto Jerusalem."*

Much controversy exists as to whether or not this verse is actually meaning that David tortured the people of Ammon, beginning with Rabbah. Many, including Clark, say that this verse simply means David made slaves of them, making them to use the tools mentioned to work. A short study of the barbaric cruelties the Ammonites practiced would certainly justify the Lord's using David to avenge the deaths of the innocent they murdered. Their wicked practice of sacrificing human babies would by itself bring the wrath of God upon them.

Those who believe David tortured the people also place the event before his repentance at his baby's death. These scholars cite the fact that once before, when David was in a backslidden state at Ziklag, he murdered women and children (1 Samuel 27:9). However at the time of Ziklag, David led a guerilla army and had no social justice to answer to. David also made sure he attacked cities that were already judged of God, though he had no instruction from God to attack them in the state he was in.

Here, even though the Ammonites were wicked, it is not likely that the elders or the priests would have sanctioned such barbaric action that this verse seems to indicate. It is more likely that the people were made slaves and the barbaric murderers of that society were cruelly and justly executed, and the event took place as it was recorded after David's repentance. Therefore, the next verse begins with the account of the rape of David's beautiful daughter Tamar.

2 Samuel 13:1, *"And it came to pass after this, that Absalom the son of David had a fair sister, whose name was Tamar; and Amnon the son of David loved her."*

After the war with the Ammonites, the gathering of the spoils, and their distribution, this bizarre account begins to unfold just as Nathan the prophet had predicted. Absalom's full sister Tamar, (2 Samuel 3:3) became prey to Absalom's half brother Amnon. Amnon got so sick with lust for Tamar, his half sister, that his physical body was affected. He just could not figure out a way of carrying out a plan to satisfy his lust. It seems the sinful actions were much more emulated by David's children than his repentance and worship.

Amnon was David's eldest son from his marriage to Ahinoam the Jezreelitess (2 Samuel 3:2). The matter of polygamy in the Old Testament is and has been of great controversy for the church. David's situation was also unique in that he acquired his wives through his military victories. He was actually carrying out Deuteronomy 21:10-14, *"When thou goest forth to war against thine enemies, and the LORD thy God hath delivered them into thine hands, and thou hast taken them captive, And seest among the captives a beautiful woman, and hast a desire unto her, that thou wouldest have her to thy wife; Then thou shalt bring her home to thine house; and she shall shave her head, and pare her nails; And she shall put the raiment of her captivity from off her, and shall remain in thine house, and bewail her father and her mother a full month: and after that thou shalt go in unto her, and be her husband, and she shall be thy wife. And it shall be, if thou have no delight in her, then thou shalt let her go whither she will; but thou shalt not sell her at all for money, thou shalt not make merchandise of her, because thou hast humbled her."*

Every one of David's wives, before Bathsheba, came that way. Even Abigail was considered the spoils of war to David because Nabal was destroyed by the Lord Himself. Commentators usually do not deal with this issue, but a close study will reveal that David was not condemned for his many wives. However it is apparent that there was a great number of negative happenings as a result of his polygamy. It is clear that under the New Covenant, both polygamy and celibacy are condemned with one stroke (1 Timothy 3:2).

2 Samuel 13:3, *"But Amnon had a friend, whose name was Jonadab, the son of Shimeah David's brother: and Jonadab was a very subtil man."*

Here we again can see more of the dark side of the family life involved in polygamy. Amnon couldn't figure how to get alone with Tamar to take advantage of her. But just as the Lord will send someone to the aid of those who are seeking Him, the enemy of our soul will send someone to help the one who seeks evil. In this case it was Jonadab. The scripture says Amnon had a friend, which is highly satirical for in fact he had a cousin, David's brother's son, who would assist him in his diabolical effort. Jonadab instructs Amnon how to proceed to get Tamar alone. Pretending to be sick which in fact he was, with lust, he made sure his father David came to see him. As David's compassion was moved toward his son, Amnon then requested that he send Tamar to his bedside with nourishment.

2 Samuel 13:7, *"Then David sent home to Tamar, saying, Go now to thy brother Amnon's house, and dress him meat."*

One cannot but think this is another part of the punishment Nathan had predicted. For it was David himself that sent Tamar to her worst nightmare, even though he was tricked by Jonadab's wicked plan. Tamar, not knowing her danger, came and prepared the food as the lustful Amnon watched and burned with his lust. After she was ready to serve the food, Amnon ordered all of the men to leave the room and then as Tamar brought the food to him, he grabbed her arm. Tamar pleaded for him to refrain and even told Amnon to ask the king for her hand, assuring him that the king would let them marry. This seems a strange thing, but Tamar was saying this out of desperation in trying to get Amnon to stop. After her attempts to talk Amnon out of this hideous crime, Amnon overpowered her and raped her. As soon as the rape was accomplished, Amnon hated her and asked for his servant to take her away. She protested by saying this was even more evil than what he had already done. Amnon wouldn't listen.

Tamar left wailing with ashes upon her head and Absalom saw her and asked her if Amnon had been with her. Evidently Absalom was aware of the lust in Amnon's heart. Tamar told Absalom not to pursue the matter, and she remained desolate. Think of the condition of the royal family. Watts asked the compelling question, "Does this not equate to David's being a poor father"? It does appear so, but we must also remember the prophecy of Nathan.

2 Samuel 13:21, *"But when king David heard of all these things, he was very wroth."*

Here is reason for the criticism of David's fathering by Watts. He was very angry about his daughter's rape and the horrible incest, but did nothing to punish Amnon. This was his oldest son, and he no doubt hated to inflict upon him the punishment the law required in Leviticus 20:17, *"And if a man shall take his sister, his father's daughter, or his mother's daughter, and see her nakedness, and she see his nakedness; it is a wicked thing; and they shall be cut off in the sight of their people: he hath uncovered his sister's nakedness; he shall bear his iniquity."*

David also knew that the Lord had pardoned him from the death sentence in the matter of Bathsheba. But David should have remembered that he did receive punishment, and here it seems that Amnon received no correction at all. This could have been the very thing that turned the heart of Absalom against his father, although the rebellion was prophesied by Nathan the prophet (2 Samuel 12:11).

Absalom burned with hatred for Amnon, not jealous hatred, but the hatred of vengeance. David should have punished his son and instructed him concerning his own punishment, thereby teaching all of Israel that no matter your status, there is repercussion and punishment for sin. Though the punishment did not come from David, it did come. Amnon was killed at the command of Absalom when the sheepshearers were in Baalhazor.

Absalom had no doubt been waiting for the opportunity to kill Amnon. He pressed David to send Amnon to the sheep shearing although David thought it not best. After the day's work, when Amnon was merry with wine, Absalom gave the order to his servants to kill Amnon. As soon as everyone saw that Amnon was killed, all of the king's sons fled.

2 Samuel 13:30, *"And it came to pass, while they were in the way, that tidings came to David, saying, Absalom hath slain all the king's sons, and there is not one of them left."*

The first message David received of Amnon's death was inaccurate in that the messenger told him all of his sons were killed by Absalom. David had no reason to doubt this, so he reacted by tearing his clothes and falling on the earth before the Lord. His servants also tore their own clothing to signify their grief as well. David must have known of the deep seated hatred Absalom had for Amnon and of the possibility of Absalom's rebellion. Therefore he believed the day had come that Nathan had prophesied. We do not know the length of time between the inaccurate message and the message from Jonadab correcting the account of the matter. However long it was, it was certainly a time of overwhelming grief for David.

2 Samuel 13:32, *"And Jonadab, the son of Shimeah David's brother, answered and said, Let not my lord suppose that they have slain all the young men the king's sons; for Amnon only is dead: for by the appointment of Absalom this hath been determined from the day that he forced his sister Tamar."*

And who is it that brings David the correct message, none other than his subtle nephew Jonadab. He of all people! Jonadab, who was the master planner enabling Amnon to achieve his wicked sin of rape and incest with Tamar, Absalom's full sister. Now Jonadab reports to the king but he is very careful to take no blame himself. This he does by telling the king that Absalom had planned the death of Amnon since the day Amnon raped Tamar. How convenient for this deceiver to report the story leaving out the part which would condemn himself. Jonadab assures David that only Amnon is dead and Absalom has fled.

As Jonadab finishes speaking, the king's sons come in to the court. All of them began to weep over the death of Amnon and the departure of Absalom from the royal family. Perhaps David was also weeping, and maybe some of his sons, with contrition and repentance over the pitiful and sad spiritual state of the royal family.

2 Samuel 13:37, *"But Absalom fled, and went to Talmai, the son of Ammihud, king of Geshur. And David mourned for his son every day."*

Absalom fled to the home of his own grandfather on his mother's side (2 Samuel 3:3). His premeditated murder of Amnon would have given him no access to the cities of refuge in his own country (Numbers 35:21). He also knew that his grandfather would receive him without concern for his deeds, due to the vengeance he would probably have for David, who took his daughter away. David now has a daughter raped by one of his sons; another one of his sons has killed the son that raped his daughter. The son that killed the other son has now fled and is living in the heathen land of Geshur. Here is David, whose sin is completely forgiven and cancelled, yet he is still reaping the result of his own sin. Yet there are those who insist on believing that the atonement for sin will also take away the repercussion of sin.

2 Samuel 13:39, *"And the soul of king David longed to go forth unto Absalom: for he was comforted concerning Amnon, seeing he was dead."*

David's love for the rebellious Absalom was very evident and perhaps to a fault. David didn't do a thing to punish Amnon who had raped his daughter Tamar. Now he grieves over Absalom who murdered Amnon and even desires to go to him. He resigns from the grief of Amnon's death, realizing he cannot bring him back, and focuses his grief on the fugitive Absalom.

2 Samuel 14

Though the name David is not mentioned in 2 Samuel 14, the title "king" is mentioned twenty-three times. This chapter continues the contentious saga of the royal family. David's horrible dilemma was 1) He could not see his son he loved so well. 2) He could not bring Absalom back to Jerusalem in full restoration, being guilty of murder. 3) He had already foregone punishment on Amnon, whom he has already lost. 4) If he tried to bring Absalom back to Jerusalem, the people and the priesthood would then consider him guilty of the same sin of that of Eli, who preferred his sons above the law of God. 5) Absalom was now in line for the throne. Chileab, who was his eldest brother (2 Samuel 3:3), must have either been deceased or ill equipped to be the king. David's love for Absalom would cause David to desire that Absalom be the next king in Israel, even though the prophecy was that Solomon would be the next king. 6) David knew that it was his own failure to deal with Amnon that most likely caused the murder. 7) As we see later, not all of Israel blamed Absalom for taking matters in his own hand and having his servants kill Amnon.

Joab saw the whole picture and devised an extensive plan to get David to agree to bring Absalom home. What David's conscience would not allow him to do, Joab's plan provided the reason. But David, knowing all of the ramifications, only allowed Absalom to come to Jerusalem, but not to the king's court. This seemed even worse to Absalom than his exile, and it angered him. He no doubt blamed Joab for his pitiful position of being in Jerusalem but not seeing the king's face, which means he was not fully restored, and not in line for the throne. He sends for Joab twice to escort him in to David, and when Joab refused to come, Absalom had his servants set his barley field on fire.

When Joab comes to confront Absalom for burning his barley field, then Absalom explains how horrible his state is, and if this was the way it was going to be, why hadn't he left him in Geshur? At this Joab agrees to assist his royal cousin and escort him into the presence of the king. Joab does so, and as soon as Absalom comes before David he bows himself to the ground and David kisses his son. One cannot but fault David in this, for he is now blessing an unrepentant son. Had Absalom shown any signs of Godly sorrow or repentance, it would have been a completely different matter.

This fault will also cost David greatly, for just as one cannot reason with religion, neither can one restore the unrepentant. Immediately Absalom begins his orchestrated attempt to take the throne away from his father.

2 Samuel 15:12, *"And Absalom sent for Ahithophel the Gilonite, David's counsellor, from his city, even from Giloh, while he offered sacrifices. And the conspiracy was strong; for the people increased continually with Absalom."*

The next thing we read about Absalom after David kissed him and received him into the king's court is his organizing a small army. How this rebellion and anger took over his soul we are not sure, but possibly when Tamar his sister was raped and his father did nothing about it. Nonetheless, the rebellion in him and his unrepentant heart will ultimately cost him both his life and most likely his soul. God's mercy could have been extended to him while he hung in the oak tree by his hair until he was killed. Perhaps in that time he repented and called on the Lord like the thief on the cross.

Absalom's plan was to undermine his father by winning the hearts of the people to himself. He did this by rising early and meeting the people at the gate, telling them what all he would do for them if he were king. Here is an unrepentant rebel turned loose to do all the undermining he possibly can to his father's dynasty. David had left him outside the court hoping that would bring him to repentance, but instead he only grew angrier.

Surely David must have realized that this is the one Nathan had prophesied about in 2 Samuel 12:11, *"Thus saith the LORD, Behold, I will raise up evil against thee out of thine own house."* David did not restrain him at all, and when Absalom felt as though he was ready for his revolt, we read in 2 Samuel 15:7, *"And it came to pass after forty years, that Absalom said unto the king, I pray thee, let me go and pay my vow, which I have vowed unto the LORD, in Hebron."*

Of course this could not mean forty years from the time Absalom began to undermine his father's authority, for the entire dynasty of David was only forty years. A Biblicist does not look for error like Mr. Clark is apt to do, but a Biblicist will look for clarification, which Mr. Wesley is apt to do. Wesley writes, "After forty years-From the change of the government, into a monarchy, which was about ten years before David began to reign. So this fell out about the thirtieth year of his reign."

Absalom does not care to deceive his father by declaring himself to be on spiritual business when he asks for leave from the court. This is all to send out those loyal to him throughout the land to blow a trumpet as he declares himself the new king. Only two hundred men from Jerusalem went with Absalom and they didn't realize why. However that two hundred started a flow of men to Absalom's side, as he offered sacrifices. What a hypocrite to actually offer sacrifices just to get a crowd. Why didn't David's one time loyal friend Ahithophel see through this wicked plot? But when Absalom sent for him, he came, which added great political weight to the uprising but unto his own destruction later (2 Samuel 17:23).

The rebellious coup gained strength in numbers, but they did not have God's blessing because 1) There was no oil ever placed on Absalom's head. Absalom was unauthorized, even though he was used of God to fulfill the prophetic word. This is why Watts said of Absalom, "as guilty as Judas." 2) His followers were gained by manipulation, not integrity. 3) His heart was full of anger and rebellion, while his father's heart was full of love and repentance.

2 Samuel 15:13, "*And there came a messenger to David, saying, The hearts of the men of Israel are after Absalom.*"

This message to David was not unexpected, for in fact he was a prophet himself and a believer in prophesy. He now knew without a doubt that God was going to allow Absalom to drive him from his house and take his wives, in fulfillment of Nathan's prophecy. 2 Samuel 12:11, "*Thus saith the LORD, Behold, I will raise up evil against thee out of thine own house, and I will take thy wives before thine eyes, and give them unto thy neighbour, and he shall lie with thy wives in the sight of this sun.*"

David was very wise when he decided not to fight against this prophesy. He was a warrior that had never lost a fight. He knew that without the blessing of God upon him, he would fail. Therefore David rested in the hope that nothing would happen to the young man Absalom. There was nothing in the prophecy concerning the uprising in his own house that suggested that the rebellious one would die. David would accept his punishment and submit to the Word of God!

2 Samuel 15:14, "*And David said unto all his servants that were with him at Jerusalem, Arise, and let us flee; for we shall not else escape from Absalom: make speed to depart, lest he overtake us suddenly, and bring evil upon us, and smite the city with the edge of the sword.*"

This decision no doubt surprised his servants for they probably didn't expect David to flee. However David had listened closely to the prophetic word of Nathan (2 Samuel 12:11) and knew

Absalom would take the city, but he himself would not be killed. Fleeing his beloved city was the wisest and most benevolent thing he could have done. He did it to spare his servants, his household, and the beloved city itself that he had dedicated to God. All of David's servants indicated they were willing to go or to stay, so David took his immediate family and left ten concubines there. David knew according to Nathan's prophecy in 2 Samuel 12:11 what would happen to these women, and yet he knew that their gender would also save their lives.

As the king began this march of humility and disgrace, many of the people were moved to come with him. Also came the Cherethites, Pelethites, and the Gittites, which were his special guards who were now Jewish proselytes. Also there came with David the six hundred men which were with him in Gath. It seems as though David didn't expect the non-military people to leave their homes, and even tried to talk Ittai the Gittite to go back to serve Absalom.

This seems strange for David to try to persuade what is the chief man of the Gittites to stay and serve Absalom. Yet, we must remember that David loved Absalom very much, and there was no jealousy or competition in his soul for him. Many theologians believe one of his reasons for leaving the city was in simple concern that one of his warriors would kill Absalom. This reason bears weight in the fact that when Absalom was killed in his uprising, David bewailed him to the degree that he discouraged the very ones that defeated the coup. David's people knew his heart was toward Absalom, and neither were they blind to his fault of allowing the unrepentant rebel access to his court.

2 Samuel 15:22, "*And David said to Ittai, Go and pass over. And Ittai the Gittite passed over, and all his men, and all the little ones that were with him.*"

David's attempt to persuade Ittai and his people to return was in vain. David made sure Ittai understood that he did not expect him and his family to be uprooted. He also made it plain to Ittai that he did not know what the days ahead would have in store for them. Yet Ittai insisted on going, so David finally allowed this, and Ittai and all of his men and family members went as well. This is the picture of the love and loyalty David was able to extract from people. And the words of Ittai in Verse 21 express it quite well, "*And Ittai answered the king, and said, As the LORD liveth, and as my lord the king liveth, surely in what place my lord the king shall be, whether in death or life, even there also will thy servant be.*"

This caravan of contrition begins to move with a loud voice of weeping as they go. This is one of the saddest scenes in the scripture, the mighty king of Israel being driven from his own home by his own son. Disgraced by his own moral failures, and prosecuted by his own paternal failure, David marches with his head covered and all of his men with their heads covered, weeping, as they move out of the city of David.

Zadok, that faithful priest, and the Levites brought the Ark of the Covenant and set it at the brook Kidron until all of the people passed over. Zadok was probably making a spiritual and prophetic statement by doing this with the Ark in the same manner the children of Israel crossed the Jordan. The high priest Zadok was also a seer, or prophet, as David acknowledged in Verse 27. Therefore Zadok knew the Lord would restore David.

After the crossing, David told the priests, Zadok and Abiathar, to take the Ark back to Jerusalem along with their sons, and wait to see how the Lord would move. David was resting in the good will of the Lord for his own welfare, for he knew the mercy of God and how the Lord had told him he would build him a house and his son would perform it.

David's sending the priests back to Jerusalem with the Ark has drawn a lot of criticism, suggesting that he could have easily caused their deaths because of their apparent loyalty to David. However, David knew that Absalom would not dare kill these priests like Saul did and this, more than any other thing, proves that David believed he would return restored to Jerusalem. David told the priests to stay in Jerusalem and he would come when he was confirmed by the Lord! Actually, sending the Ark back could have been one of the hardest things David ever did. He loved the Ark of God. He loved the city of God. He loved that tent he had made for the Ark and the wonderful times he had there in worship. He would horribly miss the Ark. The whole caravan was weeping out loud, but David's weeping was probably greatly connected to that Ark.

2 Samuel 15:30, *"And David went up by the ascent of mount Olivet, and wept as he went up, and had his head covered, and he went barefoot: and all the people that was with him covered every man his head, and they went up, weeping as they went up."*

David, in his disgrace, seems to be going the exact same route backwards as Jesus did coming from the garden of Gethsemane after his arrest. David leaves Jerusalem as a result of his sin and Jesus enters the same route to pay for it in full. The people not only had their heads covered but they were barefoot. This is another sign of great distress, as with the renting of the garments. But true to the tradition of that day, traveling grievers would often take their shoes off instead of renting their clothes.

David is facing repercussion for his sin by the very sins of his own child. His attitude in the whole matter is an admirable example of Godly sorrow. True Godly sorrow will be accompanied by a seed of hope and faith. This David expressed in the matter of the Ark and his instructions for the priests in Verse 28, *"See, I will tarry in the plain of the wilderness, until there come word from you to certify me."* Often in David's writings he would spell out his despair and problem but end the psalm with a great word of recovery and restoration. One who has an intimacy with God is never, and never can be really defeated, for his strength is not in himself but in the Lord.

2 Samuel 15:31, *"And one told David, saying, Ahithophel is among the conspirators with Absalom. And David said, O LORD, I pray thee, turn the counsel of Ahithophel into foolishness."*

Now David discovers the defection of one of his top counselors, Ahithophel. He is called here a conspirator. David knew very well that everyone close to him was not necessarily connected to him. Every leader must find this out sooner or later. It is in these times like David is in now, when we find out who is really with us. David asks the Lord to turn the counsel of Ahithophel into nonsense. The Lord granted exactly that to David, which resulted in a horrible and calculated act of suicide for the defector Ahithophel.

2 Samuel 15:32, "*And it came to pass, that when David was come to the top of the mount, where he worshipped God, behold, Hushai the Archite came to meet him with his coat rent, and earth upon his head*":

David stopped on the Mount of Olives to worship; perhaps the very spot that would later become the Garden of Gethsemane, for it has full view of the city of Jerusalem. David worshipped facing Jerusalem, but this would be the last time he would do so with Jerusalem in view, at least until the day he was restored. His grief was overwhelming as he went along the way, and then Hushai the Archite came with the symbols of grief upon his head. Hushai was no doubt from the city of Archi (Joshua 16:2). Like a lot of David's army and close cabinet, he was a proselyte. David was not only the greatest worshipper in the history of Israel, the greatest warrior, and the greatest deliverer of the Word, but he was also the greatest evangelist for the Jewish faith. It is said that he made more proselytes to the Jewish faith than any other worshipper of the true and living God at any time. Hushai was one of the counselors sharing the office with Ahithophel. However, Hushai was faithful.

2 Samuel 15:33, "*Unto whom David said, If thou passest on with me, then thou shalt be a burden unto me*":

While Hushai was a great benefit to David in the court, he would not be in the field. David's honest but blunt assessment was that Hushai would be a burden in exile and a blessing in Jerusalem. Certainly it proved to be so, for the Lord used Hushai to confuse the counsel of Ahithophel. David is faulted by Wesley for telling Hushai to deceive Absalom by telling him he would serve him like he did David, in order to achieve the place of interfering with Ahithophel's counsel. Watts praises David for the same thing and declares him a wise General in doing so.

Why should David be faulted for instructing Hushai in the art of being a spy? David told Hushai that when he gets in the desired position to simply report what he hears from Absalom's cabinet to the high priests. For those who wondered why David was insistent that Abiathar and Zadok keep their grown sons with them in Jerusalem, now we see why. David told Hushai to tell the high priests to send their information to him by their sons. Was Watts not right and Wesley wrong in this thing? This was brilliant military strategy. David knew that neither the priests nor their grown sons would be hindered in coming and going. Here is also again another biblical example of the power of the priest and the king working together to preserve the remnant.

2 Samuel 15:37, *"So Hushai David's friend came into the city, and Absalom came into Jerusalem."*

Hushai has accepted his assignment now and goes back to Jerusalem to carry it out. One must not forget the extremely emotional ordeal this was for everyone. The love for David that most of the people had didn't start when he came to Jerusalem as king. David had been a national hero since the time of his tremendous defeat of Goliath. His exile from Saul was carefully followed by the common folk of Israel. The people knew him, faults and all, but they still loved him greatly. Even so it is with those who study David's life today. In spite of all of his failures he is loved greatly.

2 Samuel 16:1, *"And when David was a little past the top of the hill, behold, Ziba the servant of Mephibosheth met him, with a couple of asses saddled, and upon them two hundred loaves of bread, and an hundred bunches of raisins, and an hundred of summer fruits, and a bottle of wine."*

Leaving sight of his beloved city, David was met by Ziba the servant of Mephibosheth with a tremendous amount of supplies. It seems that Ziba might be operating in another agenda, for he boldly lies concerning his new master Mephibosheth. Ziba seemed to think of everything in his benevolence toward David and his family. However he forgot to consider the fact that the Lord causes us to reap what we sow. David asks the whereabouts of Mephibosheth, and there Ziba lies as to the loyalty of Mephibosheth. By doing so it seems that Ziba is taking this opportunity to advance himself at Mephibosheth's expense. David hastily (far too hastily) tells Ziba he can have back what he took from him to give to Mephibosheth. This hasty act will later cost David.

2Sa 16:5, *"And when king David came to Bahurim, behold, thence came out a man of the family of the house of Saul, whose name was Shimei, the son of Gera: he came forth, and cursed still as he came."*

As David comes to the city of Bahurim, which is a city of Benjamin, the tribe of Saul, Shimei comes out and begins to curse David. We have not heard from this Shimei of Saul's family before now. He makes the foolish mistake of cursing and trying to punish one who is beloved of God, forgiven, yet suffering for his sins. Many a religious person makes the same grave mistake by jumping aboard this kind of action toward the Davids that are reaping the harvest of past sins. God hates to punish one of his repentant children, and woe is the one who thinks they will help God's justice by chiding, exploiting, or helping Him punish. Oh my, God will not even allow one to rejoice over his chastisement to his children much less curse them (Ezekiel 25:3).

2 Samuel 16:6, *"And he cast stones at David, and at all the servants of king David: and all the people and all the mighty men were on his right hand and on his left."*

When Shimei came out like this, David realized that only an absolute idiot or someone trying to commit suicide would try such a feat unless the Lord was allowing it. These soldiers on each side of David were the elite fighting men of the whole earth. Shimei was kicking someone while he was down, and his sin would not go forever unpunished, but there was more to it. Because of his deep and honest humility, David realized what was going on. David knew this sad departure from Jerusalem was a result of his sin of adultery and murder, both of which is punishable by stoning (Leviticus 20:10, Numbers 35:17). For this cause David refused to allow Abishai to cut Shimei's head off. David's spiritual restoration and true repentance now is abundantly manifested, for every wicked thing Shimei could say was said, yet David opened not his mouth.

2 Samuel 16:10, *"And the king said, What have I to do with you, ye sons of Zeruiah? so let him curse, because the LORD hath said unto him, Curse David. Who shall then say, Wherefore hast thou done so"?*

Some have great trouble with David's statement to Abishai, *"so let him curse, because the LORD hath said unto him, Curse David."* This does not mean that the Lord has told Shimei to do evil, but instead Shimei is allowed to do evil. David states it this way because he is humbling himself to the rod of God. David's intimacy with the Lord in repentance allowed him the wisdom to perceive this matter correctly and thereby react properly. David loved Saul and was a part of Saul's family. He realized that through the conflict with Saul, there were many that hated him. He also knew that passing through borders of Benjamin, he would probably encounter some of the ones who despised him. But once again, David showed no vengeance to the late Saul or his tribe, Benjamin. David knew very well what was happening, yet the men around him once again were not discerning of the matter, for they knew not the depth of David's heart with his God.

2 Samuel 16:11, *"And David said to Abishai, and to all his servants, Behold, my son, which came forth of my bowels, seeketh my life: how much more now may this Benjamite do it? let him alone, and let him curse; for the LORD hath bidden him."*

David explained to his servants his ability to withstand the mouth of Shimei in terms they could understand by saying, *"Behold, my son, which came forth of my bowels, seeketh my life: how much more now may this Benjamite do it'?* This they could understand. David's grief over his son's rebellion was cutting at him two ways: 1) The punishment for his sins and the constant prophetic voice of Nathan going off in his mind, *"Behold, I will raise up evil against thee out of thine own house"* 2) It is far harder to face punishment for your sins than to be punished by your children's sins. Every Godly parent of a wayward child suffers with grief for the sins of their children. Yet there is double grief if you know you have caused it. We might say that when one is forgiven, he is ever free of condemnation, the minute he is forgiven. This is true, yet true Godly sorrow for the deed or deeds will manifest every time he thinks of it. This is not morbidity but rather the state of true repentance from Godly sorrow. One might again say, "How then can one be happy?" Read the psalms of David, for they will declare it to you.

2 Samuel 16:13, "*And as David and his men went by the way, Shimei went along on the hill's side over against him, and cursed as he went, and threw stones at him, and cast dust.*"

David assured his men that the Lord would take up his case concerning the wild ranting of Shimei. This assurance David shows is a testimony to his abiding knowledge of forgiveness.

After a distance David and the people stopped to rest and refresh themselves, even as Absalom enters the city of Jerusalem, expecting to find David. It has been speculated by many that David would have been killed and/or his men would have killed Absalom, had he stayed in Jerusalem. It is the latter David feared, not the former, for David knew his work in Jerusalem was not fulfilled. David was not even concerned for the hardship of the life of a fugitive. He was a seasoned guerilla warrior who had spent years in the outdoors. David was concerned with yielding to the Word of the Lord from the prophet Nathan. He knew that yielding to the Word of the Lord is always a safe place.

2 Samuel 16:16, "*And it came to pass, when Hushai the Archite, David's friend, was come unto Absalom, that Hushai said unto Absalom, God save the king, God save the king.*"

As David had requested, Hushai set himself in position to confound the counsel of Ahithophel by feigning allegiance to Absalom. Most likely Absalom was eager to employ Hushai, for Absalom, finding the royal family gone, would certainly need to seek out the best counselors and advisers. He was not the warrior his daddy was and he knew full well that his father had never lost a war. Therefore, he would welcome his father's skilled advisors. Absalom had hoped to make a quick work of his overthrow, but now he is perplexed as to what to do. He immediately asks counsel of Ahithophel first. The counsel was not about military details but of overthrowing an establishment. Ahithophel advised Absalom to go in to his father's concubines, knowing full well that this would completely sever the possibility of reconciliation between David and Absalom. This tent that was spread on the roof top for Absalom to lie with these concubines of David was in the very same place where David looked upon Bathsheba that horrible night (2 Samuel 11:2). Thus the prophecy of Nathan was fulfilled.

2 Samuel 16:23, *"And the counsel of Ahithophel, which he counselled in those days, was as if a man had enquired at the oracle of God: so was all the counsel of Ahithophel both with David and with Absalom."*

Now Ahithophel was famous with the people for giving wise counsel, and Absalom foolishly concluded that the same would continue. However wicked Ahithophel's words were in this case, there is no question as to their wisdom in accomplishing what he desired. Counselors were not considered to be prophets necessarily, and this verse is not implying so when stating his words were as the oracles of God. This is simply a description of the accurateness of his counsel. Even Jesus commended the wisdom of the world in one instance, saying in Luke 16:8, *"The children of this world are in their generation wiser than the children of light."* The reason for magnifying the ability of Ahithophel was to illuminate from what great heights he would fall!

2 Samuel 17:1, *"Moreover Ahithophel said unto Absalom, Let me now choose out twelve thousand men, and I will arise and pursue after David this night"*:

Again, the counsel of Ahithophel is good counsel as far as military strategy goes, but it is not good for the welfare of David. He thinks the twelve thousand men he is requesting could gain the victory over a small, tired, and weary traveling band. Ahithophel offers to Absalom such a plan as to spare the people and kill David. This would be appealing to Absalom, who is hungry for power. He felt that the people could be united to him if David was dead but never if he wasn't.

As Ahithophel's counsel was well received and completed, they now ask for the counsel of Hushai, David's spy. Absalom and the elders of Israel with him told Hushai what Ahithophel had counseled them, and just as David had instructed him, Hushai destroys the counsel of Ahithophel. Hushai reminds Absalom and the elders how disturbed David and his men are over this rebellion, as well as how mighty in war they are. Hushai goes on to remind them David is an expert at guerrilla warfare and will not just be sitting there with the people, waiting for Ahithophel and his men. Hushai explains what will really happen is that David and some of his mighty men will be in hiding, and ambush Ahithophel and kill a lot of his men, which will cause even the bravest of the men with Ahithophel to run.

Hushai, in his effort to make some time for David to get across the Jordan River and gather more soldiers, tells Absalom and his elders to hold up their plan until Absalom can gather an army from across Israel. Hushai had a much better understanding of the loyalty of the people of Israel to David, and he knew that while Absalom was recruiting the army of rebels, the fighting valiant men of Israel would come to David's side. Hushai did an excellent job for his king. He even described vividly Absalom's conquering battle. He then topped it off with placing a question mark on Ahithophel's character, suggesting he might have a personal agenda in wanting to take all of those soldiers himself to go get David.

The elders of Israel and Absalom agreed that the Counsel of Hushai was better than the counsel of Ahithophel. The Lord had answered David's request to confuse the counsel of Ahithophel. When Hushai saw his counsel was heeded, he immediately went to report the whole thing to Zadok and Abiathar as David had instructed him.

2 Samuel 17:16, *"Now therefore send quickly, and tell David, saying, Lodge not this night in the plains of the wilderness, but speedily pass over; lest the king be swallowed up, and all the people that are with him."*

Hushai now not only reports the matter to the high priests but adds his good military counsel to the information that the priests' sons will deliver to David. Hushai counsels David to pass quickly over the Jordan River for his life. All of this time, the news of Absalom's rebellion is moving across Israel from village to village. The nation is in an uproar, and people are seeing a civil war coming, as many of the men begin to choose sides. Absalom has entered into Jerusalem and has taken his father's concubines. David has fled; the priests have stayed, and no one knows what will happen to Israel. The news of some of David's top men defecting most likely stirred the most unrest in Israel.

Lightfoot declared that the eyes of the nation were on the priesthood during this vulnerable time. However, Abiathar and Zadok, the two who shared the office of the high priest, probably appeared to be neutral. Had David allowed them to bring the Ark and follow him, it could have helped his cause as people began to align themselves with either Absalom or David. Yet, the Lord was leading David, and the priests and their sons were aiding him greatly by being in Jerusalem.

2 Samuel 17:17, *"Now Jonathan and Ahimaaz stayed by Enrogel; for they might not be seen to come into the city: and a wench went and told them; and they went and told king David."*

It appears that Zadok and Abiathar had wisely positioned their sons who were to take the message to David outside of the city at Enrogel, which is on the southeast side of Jerusalem. This was so they would not be seen leaving the city from a position where their fathers were stationed. This would have caused onlookers to connect the sons of the priests leaving with access of the counsel given to the king.

The priests employed a young woman slave to bring the information to their sons, probably under the disguise of leaving the city for some practical purpose. As soon as she transferred the information, the sons of the priests were on their way to inform David. They must have left in some sort of an unusual behavior for a lad told Absalom about it. The sons of the priests, Jonathan and Ahimaaz, went as far as Bahurim and stopped at an unidentified house. Evidently Jonathan and Ahimaaz knew they were being followed by Absalom's men, so they incorporated help from this household in getting the pursuers off their trail. The plan they utilized was not unlike that of Rahab's protecting the spies.

Perhaps this unidentified Jewish family had been inspired by reading their own history in the book of Joshua. We see from this scene that there were people who were on David's side in this matter and willing to aid their king any way they could. There is no argument from even one apt theologian to the fact that David had blessed Israel, and that Israel loved David.

2 Samuel 17:21, "*And it came to pass, after they were departed, that they came up out of the well, and went and told king David, and said unto David, Arise, and pass quickly over the water: for thus hath Ahithophel counselled against you.*"

As soon as Jonathan and Ahimaaz were rid of their pursuers, they went on with their mission to give David their report. Their urgent report included the fact that the counsel of Ahithophel was urging them on. They didn't report the wise counsel of Hushai and how he had performed such a great work. Perhaps there was some concern that the counsel of Hushai to wait might be overturned to accept the counsel of Ahithophel, which was to charge speedily.

David's military abilities were more than human wisdom. Those who were clearly under David's authority enjoyed those benefits immensely. These young men, Jonathan and Ahimaaz, were sons of the high priests of Israel. That is why there were watched so closely and that is why David had employed them. David had learned his lesson in his first attempt to move the Ark to Jerusalem - the king can't get the job done without the priests.

2 Samuel 17:22, "*Then David arose, and all the people that were with him, and they passed over Jordan: by the morning light there lacked not one of them that was not gone over Jordan.*"

Upon hearing the report, David immediately gathered the people and went across the Jordan. This crossing was completed by morning, indicating that by this time there was a great gathering with David. From David's pen comes the third Psalm, which indicates that he is still well outnumbered, but his total trust is in His God. This Psalm is headed, "*A Psalm of David, when he fled from Absalom his son.*" Psalm 3:1-3, "*LORD, how are they increased that trouble me! many are they that rise up against me. Many there be which say of my soul, There is no help for him in God. Selah. But thou, O LORD, art a shield for me; my glory, and the lifter up of mine head.*"

Back in Jerusalem, Ahithophel realized his counsel was rejected. Knowing he had no future in the cabinet of Absalom after his counsel had been rejected at such a crucial time, he got his house in order and hung himself. No writers show mercy to the unrepentant traitor, even though his life ended so tragically.

2 Samuel 17:24, "*Then David came to Mahanaim. And Absalom passed over Jordan, he and all the men of Israel with him.*"

David made his way to Mahanaim, a place in the high country in eastern Gilead. This was a calculated maneuver, for David knew how to make the terrain work in his favor. David also knew the fighting mountain men of Gilead were with him. From this move, David gained both the favor of terrain suitable for a guerrilla fighter like himself and also the support of the fierce fighting men of Gilead.

This is the position from which David will fight the forces of Absalom, who is now crossing the Jordan with a huge army he has amassed from all of Israel. Hushai had counseled Absalom to gather such an army in order to give David time to get where he now is, in the highlands of Gilead. Absalom now has made his cousin Amasa his captain, who was also a cousin to Joab. Joab was born of David's sister Zeruiah and Amasa's mother was Abigail (not the former wife of Nabal), which was the daughter of Nahash who was another of Jesse's wives. This means Abigail and Zeruiah were half sisters. Therefore Joab and Amasa were cousins and both of them nephews of David. So it is with civil war - Absalom, David's son, pursuing his father and his cousins, with another one of his cousins in command of his father's army. One can only imagine the emotional disarray the whole nation is in at this point. An inevitable war is now looming, and it is clear that Absalom is the aggressor.

2 Samuel 17:27, "*And it came to pass, when David was come to Mahanaim, that Shobi the son of Nahash of Rabbah of the children of Ammon, and Machir the son of Ammiel of Lodebar, and Barzillai the Gileadite of Rogelim,*"

When David arrived at Mahanaim, he began to see the benevolence of his neighboring countries and their statesmen's heart toward him. It should be noted that some of the people coming to the aid of David are people from the very areas he had conquered and set governors over. They quickly sided with David, and many had enjoyed the security of David's powerful position as well as many had become proselytes to the Jewish religion. The supplies they brought to David and his family showed their extreme thoughtfulness to David's wilderness congregation.

2 Samuel 17:29, "*And honey, and butter, and sheep, and cheese of kine, for David, and for the people that were with him, to eat: for they said, The people is hungry, and weary, and thirsty, in the wilderness.*"

One must remember that there were many with David who were not military. Joab and his men were not in need of beds. They were seasoned warriors. They were neither weary nor struggling in the wilderness, but the non-military had made a long pilgrimage in hard conditions, and the climb to their present elevation would have been hard for many of them. Through the generosity of their neighbors and the fighting men who came to David's aid, he is now comforted and resting in a much better position.

2 Samuel 18:1, *"And David numbered the people that were with him, and set captains of thousands and captains of hundreds over them."*

David prepares for the battle, with his heart aching the whole time for his rebel son Absalom. Even as he sets his troops in order, as he has done so many times before, he is grieving over the life of his son. By this time David has a considerable army, though we are not told the tally. Josephus declares it to be four thousand, but no proof of resource has been found. We can assume the number is at least three thousand for there are three captains named. It is said by others that the number is more than ten thousand, for they told David he was worth ten thousand men when they persuaded him to stay out of the battle field (Verse 3). The army size was never really an issue with David, and once again he will win a decisive victory. The casualties of Absalom's army will total twenty thousand.

2 Samuel 18:2, *"And David sent forth a third part of the people under the hand of Joab, and a third part under the hand of Abishai the son of Zeruiah, Joab's brother, and a third part under the hand of Ittai the Gittite. And the king said unto the people, I will surely go forth with you myself also."*

This powerful army is now going to advance to the battlefield under the direction of the king, but this doesn't mean that David has become the aggressor. He simply sent them out to the battlefield in preparation for the fight, by setting the army in array. David intended to lead one of the bands, which is where Josephus perhaps gets the number four thousand. However, David set captains over thousands and we are not given their names, but when the scripture records the sending forth of Joab, it always mentions his name. Most likely Joab had a third of the captains over thousands directing the thousands under him, and likewise did Abishai and Ittai. The people would not allow David to go out to this battle, not just because of their affection for him, but also for the stability of their nation. The people knew the disarray of their country would turn to total bedlam if David were killed.

Even as the army leaves the city of Mahanaim, David tells his generals to deal gently with Absalom. This again reveals David's heart for his son, but it also reveals the assurance in his heart of a victory in the battle. The psalms David wrote during this time also reveal the assurance he got from the Lord that his enemies would be defeated. David evidently positioned a portion of his army in the thick wooded area to draw the army in to the woods, so his army would have the advantage, while others met the battle in the open field. Perhaps David's army did get the battle going first, but they remain innocent for being the aggressor, because it is Absalom who chased them to this spot.

2 Samuel 18:7, *"Where the people of Israel were slain before the servants of David, and there was there a great slaughter that day of twenty thousand men."*

Just as David had planned with his strategic positioning of his army in the highlands and the thick wooded area, his warriors defeated the much less seasoned warriors of Absalom. What a horrible price to pay for following a rebel; twenty thousand died. More died in the woods than in the field, for the woods was of help to David's men, but a snare to the men of Absalom. This horrific and needless loss of life is forever a lesson to those who rebel against the Lord's set leader.

Some of the lords of England and some of the leaders of the Church of England cite this battle as reason for believing that the American Revolution would fail. Ironically, some of the revolutionaries used the same battle for a plan to use the cover of the woods to fight instead of fighting the British on the field. While Wesley condemned the Revolutionary War in general, he readily admitted that the king of England was of little resemblance to the Sweet Psalmist of Israel.

2 Samuel 18:9, *"And Absalom met the servants of David. And Absalom rode upon a mule, and the mule went under the thick boughs of a great oak, and his head caught hold of the oak, and he was taken up between the heaven and the earth; and the mule that was under him went away."*

Many have believed that Absalom got his hair hung in the huge oak tree, but we find no proof of such in the scripture. Even though he had an unusual head of hair (2 Samuel 14:26), had he been hanging by his hair, his scalp would have given way. His head was hung in the forks of the oak tree most likely, which left him helpless as the mule left him.

One of David's men reported to Joab that he saw Absalom hanging by his head. Joab asked why he didn't kill him and told him he would have paid him well if he had. However, the soldier had heard David tell his generals to go easy on the young man and quickly told Joab that he would not kill Absalom for any amount of money. He even told Joab that he feared that he would have been disciplined for killing Absalom. The soldier couldn't understand Joab's lack of heed to the king's will. Then he saw firsthand Joab's own rebellion as Joab, unwilling to allow Absalom to die from his own quandary, stabbed him in the heart with three darts.

Joab could have brought upon himself great trouble here. If he had let Absalom die, he would have been in line with the king's words. Realizing this, Joab ordered the young men to slay Absalom, even though he was probably already dead; therefore, no one person could be held responsible for taking his life.

After Absalom's death, Joab blew the trumpet, calling David's soldiers to stop the slaughter. Then they buried Absalom in a great pit and laid a huge pile of stones upon his body. The law requires a rebellious son to be stoned (Deuteronomy 21:20-21). Perhaps the providence of God allowed him to be stoned even after he died. It seemed in Absalom's twisted mind he had wanted to be some kind of historical figure in the minds of the people, because some time before his attempted coup, he had made some sort of memorial for himself. This is a very sad end for a very potential laden young man and a child of the king.

There seemed to be controversy as to who will go and tell David that Absalom is dead. They wanted to tell the good news of the great victory over the armies of Absalom, but they knew also that David would be very upset over the death of his son. Ahimaaz, the son of Zadok, asked permission to go and tell David. Joab, realizing the bitter sweet situation, wanted to wait until another day to tell David. Knowing that wouldn't work, he then dispatches Cushi to go and tell the news. This again shows us that Joab really understood his uncle the king. He seemed to want to make it as easy for David as possible even though he was the one who killed Absalom. He knew that the loss of a son for David would be of greater sadness to him than the victory in battle could relieve. Joab finally released Ahimaaz to go as well.

2 Samuel 18:24, "*And David sat between the two gates: and the watchman went up to the roof over the gate unto the wall, and lift up his eyes, and looked, and behold a man running alone.*"

David was waiting with a great mixture of emotion and anxiety as to the outcome of the battle. His bowels of compassion were going out for Absalom and yet his nation's future was at stake. David is sitting at the gate in the city of Mahanaim where he can receive the first news report from the battle. Ahimaaz got to David first but didn't know the particulars. He represents those who run fast but have no message. However, the watchman recognized him and he was allowed to come before David to give the report.

David's first question reveals the anxious heart of a father, "*Is the young man Absalom safe?*" Ahimaaz gave the king a vague answer, not to evade the question, but because he was not briefed properly, which Joab had alluded to when Ahimaaz begged to go. David had him turn aside as Cushi arrived with the news of victory in the battle and the death of Absalom.

Upon Cushi's arrival, he hailed the king and informed him of the victory over the rebels. Then the dreaded news came as David asked Cushi the same question, "*Is the young man Absalom safe?*" Cushi's answer revealed that he would not expect from David anything but rejoicing over the victory. Cushi told David that Absalom was dead, and he would have all of the enemies of David be also. David took no issue with Cushi's answer but was so moved that he went into the chamber and wept. He wailed and moaned for his son's death, wishing that he could have died instead of Absalom. David's broken heart conflicted with the victory celebration. The people desired to mourn with David over Absalom so to identify with his sorrow, but no one deserved a just and untimely death more than Absalom.

The city was emotionally in disarray, for the celebration could not be noised lest the king would be offended. But everybody except David was glad Absalom was defeated. When Joab arrived and heard how the king had withdrawn himself in mourning, he went in to speak to him. Joab found him still mourning with his voice saying, "Oh my son Absalom!" Joab began to rebuke him for causing the very people that saved his life to be ashamed for doing it. Joab told him in so many words: "You are acting as though you would be glad if all of us had died and Absalom was alive." Of course, Joab conveniently left out the fact that it was he who put three darts into Absalom's heart.

Joab told David to go out before the people, if he expected to keep them as his people. Joab told him if he was not willing to go out and comfort the people, it would be worse for him than any trial he had ever been through. Finally David did heed the advice of Joab. The relationship David had with his nephew Joab was often strained and hard to discern, but in this case Joab had wise counsel. David's grief for a rebel became a grief to the faithful who delivered him from the rebel.

Joab knew the state of confusion the nation was in, but it seemed David wasn't thinking properly because of the grief for his son and the knowledge that it was his own sin that caused it. The people who had followed Absalom or were trying to be neutral found themselves in great conflict. They had anointed themselves a king in Absalom; now they had no king. It seems they were coming to their senses by remembering how David had delivered them through the hand of the Lord from all of their enemies. Absalom, the picture of all rebellion, had done nothing but get them into this national debacle.

2 Samuel 19:11, *"And king David sent to Zadok and to Abiathar the priests, saying, Speak unto the elders of Judah, saying, Why are ye the last to bring the king back to his house? seeing the speech of all Israel is come to the king, even to his house."*

David knew that the unifying factor in the nation of Israel was the priesthood. We don't find proof of any of the priesthood's having followed Absalom. So he sends a message back to the high priests in Jerusalem telling them to ask the elders of Judah why they are slow about bringing him back to Jerusalem. This was a very brilliant move on David's part. The tribe of Judah was without a doubt the strongest tribe and leading in governmental affairs. In the short time David was at Jerusalem, it was seen as the capital of all of Israel. David reminds the elders of Israel that they are of his bloodline, and they have the responsibility to restore him in Jerusalem.

Then David does a very interesting thing. He promises to promote Absalom's captain Amasa, to be the captain of the host in Joab's place. Amasa was also a nephew from David's half sister. This announcement caused those in Judah who were afraid to bring David back because of their participation in the coup, to see that David would not be coming back in vengeance. Joab had become increasingly cold blooded and so was Joab's brother, Abishai. David had been vocal about their hardness in times past and it was known in Israel that David was displeased with them. The elders of Judah, after hearing these words concerning the demotion of Joab, sent for David. David then came back as far as the Jordan, and there the tribe of Judah met him to bring him over.

2 Samuel 19:16, *"And Shimei the son of Gera, a Benjamite, which was of Bahurim, hasted and came down with the men of Judah to meet king David."*

It seems that Shimei was one of the first to come to the river to meet David, and it should be noted that he is traveling with the men of Judah, even though he was of the house of Saul. He knew this would make him more presentable to David and make him more apt to accept him when he asked for forgiveness. Ziba also knowing that his lie about his master Mephibosheth was about to be exposed, brings with him one thousand men of the house of Saul, not to do battle, for David's army was with him, but to impress the king that he had that kind of a following among his tribal family.

The tribe of Judah had prepared a ferry boat for David and the royal family to cross the Jordan, and as soon as he crosses, Shimei falls on his face before David, requesting David's forgiveness for cursing him and throwing rocks at him. He actually asked the king not to take it serious even though he admitted he had sinned. Shimei is the case of those who curse the man whom God is punishing while he is in deep repentance. Shimei should have known that though David went over that river leaving Jerusalem in disgrace, he would come back in the power of restoration. Shimeis beware! Don't touch God's anointed during the time of their chastisement! After seeing such a foolish display out of Shimei, Abishai asked if David was now ready to put him to death. It seems to be a constant problem with Joab and Abishai, like the sons of thunder with Jesus, they just didn't understand mercy.

2 Samuel 19:22, *"And David said, What have I to do with you, ye sons of Zeruiah, that ye should this day be adversaries unto me? shall there any man be put to death this day in Israel? for do not I know that I am this day king over Israel"?*

David again refuses to allow the execution of Shimei, citing the goodness of God to him by establishing his dynasty. It is those who have been deep in Godly sorrow and repentance who are the more willing to forgive such atrocious crimes as Shimei committed. David surely was thinking, If God in his mercy could forgive and restore me who is more guilty than this Shimei, surely I can forgive him as he pleads for mercy." Although I don't believe it to be his first incentive, David also knew that it was best for the kingdom not to see an act of severity that the tribe of Benjamin might find offensive. David releases Shimei of his affront to him.

Mephibosheth comes down to meet David now. Here he is called the son of Saul, but actually he is Saul's grandson, a son of Jonathan. Herein is a touching scene as David returns to

Jerusalem. Ziba had told David that Mephibosheth had aligned with the house of Saul and Absalom, and without checking the facts, David gave Ziba back what he had taken from him to give Mephibosheth. Now David learns of Ziba's treachery from the mouth of Mephibosheth, as he stands before David, still in his mode of mourning for the struggling dynasty of his king, David, the one who had delivered him from Lodebar and given him a seat at the king's table. When David found out the truth as to why Mephibosheth didn't come to him, he reversed his decision, and told Mephibosheth to split the property in question with Ziba.

This is listed also among some theologians as a fault of David, for not taking all the property away from Ziba because of his deceit. It is most likely that David realized the matter was in need of correction from the beginning of the transaction. He should not have taken everything away from Ziba to give it to Mephibosheth to begin with, and he should not have taken everything away from Mephibosheth to give it back to Ziba. To correct both hasty acts, he tells them to divide the land. Mephibosheth makes it clear that he is not concerned about money and land but about the prophetic messianic ministry of the Davidic dynasty. This he did by telling David to let Ziba keep it all.

Now Barzillai, an aged wealthy man from Gilead who had helped sustain David in Mahanaim (2 Samuel 17:27), comes to help conduct David across the Jordan River. He was a genuine lover of David, and likewise David loved him. David showed this by inviting Barzillai to come to Jerusalem with him and sit at his table. Barzillai tells David in so many words, "I am too old to move and too old to enjoy such a blessing, and also I might be a burden to you. So I will just go a little farther with you and then return." Lightfoot rightly calls Barzillai, "a sweet soul" and declares him to be a proselyte to Judaism.

Barzillai recommends his servant Chimham to go with David, which David gladly accepts and vows to take care of him in the place of Barzillai. David never forgot Barzillai, for this servant Chimham, whom many suppose to be his son, was rewarded in David's will. David told Solomon in 1 Kings 2:7, "*But shew kindness unto the sons of Barzillai the Gileadite, and let them be of those that eat at thy table: for so they came to me when I fled because of Absalom thy brother.*" After they crossed the Jordan, David blessed Barzillai, and he returned to Gilead as the people continued on to Jerusalem, escorted by the people of Judah and half of Israel. This seems to be a mistake by the king, not waiting for all of the tribes to unite, but instead marching forward with Judah. This could have added to the already fractured relationship between the tribe of Judah and the other tribes.

2 Samuel 19:41, "*And, behold, all the men of Israel came to the king, and said unto the king, Why have our brethren the men of Judah stolen thee away, and have brought the king, and his household, and all David's men with him, over Jordan*"?

When the other tribal leaders arrived, they quickly accused the tribe of Judah of stealing the king. They knew that neither of the tribes was any less guilty of rebellion than the other. The men of Judah defended their action by saying that David is closer kin, meaning of our tribe. The men of Judah told the other tribal leaders that they should not be shocked or angry by their affection for their king and that they received nothing in return for this show of their loyalty.

2 Samuel 19:43, "*And the men of Israel answered the men of Judah, and said, We have ten parts in the king, and we have also more right in David than ye: why then did ye despise us, that our advice should not be first had in bringing back our king? And the words of the men of Judah were fiercer than the words of the men of Israel.*"

The men of Israel bring a good point to the argument by stating that they have ten parts in David and not just one. It is likely that this count is considering Joseph as only one tribe and Simeon to be included in Judah, for at that time their boundaries were interwoven. The men of Israel were speaking a message for the whole of Israel and trying to bring light on the exclusive attitude projected by the tribe of Judah by not even consulting them for the celebration of bringing the king back home.

It should be noted that there is no record of David's getting involved in this dispute. One theologian suggested that David enjoyed the people's contending over him. If that was the case, his enjoyment was short lived, for the dispute escalated sharply as the men of Judah reacted with fierce words to their brethren of Israel.

2 Samuel 20:1, "*And there happened to be there a man of Belial, whose name was Sheba, the son of Bichri, a Benjamite: and he blew a trumpet, and said, We have no part in David, neither have we inheritance in the son of Jesse: every man to his tents, O Israel.*"

This Sheba was loyal to Saul and had never been with or for David. He was probably in support of Saul from those days Saul was hunting David down. Sheba takes Absalom's death and David's weakness as an excellent opportunity for the tribe of Benjamin to make a comeback. Of course, this was futile because the Lord had ordained both that Judah would be the tribe of the Kingdom and that the next king would be Solomon. Nevertheless, Sheba blows the trumpet and calls the people to revolt against David. Did David open this door by marching to Jerusalem in the escort of the tribe of Judah without waiting for the men of the other tribes? That is very possible. The long time friction had already became a faction. The fact that Shimei had those one thousand men with him from the house of Saul to meet David when he begged for his life should not be considered in this revolt. It was not the purpose of those one thousand men to revolt but to strengthen Shimei's plea.

Here is Sheba, much differently, appealing to those who were not of the tribe of Judah to come after him and let the tribe of Judah have David if they want him. That pleased many of the people of Israel who still were loyal to Saul in their hearts. Sheba told Israel to go to their tents which meant, "Do not follow David nor have anything to do with reinstalling him as king over the entire nation." We must remember that David ruled over the tribe of Judah for seven years before he was sanctioned as king over the entire nation. There were many Israeli people who resented that decision of their government.

2 Samuel 20:2, "*So every man of Israel went up from after David, and followed Sheba the son of Bichri: but the men of Judah clave unto their king, from Jordan even to Jerusalem.*"

The men of Israel went with Sheba instead of going to their tents. This shows the depth of the insult the children of Israel felt concerning the march of the tribe of Judah with David and the fierce words they used to defend it. These men of Israel acted out of their emotional wounds instead of their good senses. In all of this, the men of Judah did not flinch but stayed right with their present aim to escort their king all the way into Jerusalem.

2 Samuel 20:3, "*And David came to his house at Jerusalem; and the king took the ten women his concubines, whom he had left to keep the house, and put them in ward, and fed them, but went not in unto them. So they were shut up unto the day of their death, living in widowhood.*"

Upon David's arrival in Jerusalem, he took the ten concubines that Absalom had defiled and placed them in isolation where they were to be taken care of but remain celibate the rest of their lives. He could not divorce them; there was no need for their punishment for they were innocent, and they could not be given to someone else. Some doctors of theology say David did this so he wouldn't have to be reminded of his sin and the judgment for it. However, this is not consistent with all of his other actions concerning the repercussion of his sin. He knew he lost them and could never have relationship with them again. He also knew he should care for them. These women were not neglected for their physical needs, and that which they endured was a result of two men's sins, a father and a son.

After making this decision, David came to the military matters. He gives Amasa orders to assemble the men of Judah for him in three days. For some unknown reason, Amasa was unable to get this accomplished. Perhaps the men were slow to come to him because he had been the captain of the army of Absalom. Perhaps Joab was already working behind the scenes to make sure Amasa was unsuccessful. For whatever reason Amasa was late in getting the job done, it only aided Joab who had commanded the army for so long that the soldiers were probably loyal to him. This was a very shaky time in the nation of Israel. Everyone was unsettled and waiting to see who would emerge. David tried to make Amasa his captain of the host to gain the hearts of the ones who had followed Absalom, as well as to rid himself of Joab.

2 Samuel 20:6, "*And David said to Abishai, Now shall Sheba the son of Bichri do us more harm than did Absalom: take thou thy lord's servants, and pursue after him, lest he get him fenced cities, and escape us.*"

Instead of tapping Joab for this military campaign, David tells Abishai to go hastily with his special forces and stop Sheba before he fortifies himself. There are numerous hints in the preceding verses as well as the following one that David doesn't trust Joab. First he announces to the people that Amasa will take the place of Joab. He then tells Amasa to get his army together in three days time, and when Amasa fails to deliver, David tells Abishai to head up this military campaign. Joab's men and the Cherethites, and the Pelethites, which are David's special guard, along with all of the mighty men, go with Abishai.

Where is Joab? Joab is a warrior, to say the least. He will not tarry under a shade tree. He goes with them, and because of his status being at stake, he does what he always does. He kills those who stand in his way. He pretends to greet Amasa but instead stabs him with a sword and lets him fall in his own pool of blood dying slowly. Joab then takes command of the army, even though David had given that charge to Abishai. See this ruthless Joab whom we have watched degenerate to this mad killing machine, crazed with power, and killing Amasa, his own cousin. Yes, he was used of the Lord to establish the kingdom in David's hand, but is he guiltless of innocent blood? Is he not the one who killed Abner, Absalom, and now Amasa? Did not David say he and his brother Abishai were both too hard for him? (2 Samuel 3:39)

2 Samuel 20:11, "*And one of Joab's men stood by him, and said, He that favoureth Joab, and he that is for David, let him go after Joab.*"

Joab's man, in this announcement, wisely identifies David's name to this activity and thereby gives the more weight to Joab's leadership. The soldiers had no way of knowing that David had not ordered such an execution of Amasa, even though they would not see it as his normal action. The soldiers were accustomed to Joab's being their leader. They probably thought that David sent Abishai out with them while he sent Joab to deal with Amasa.

None of these soldiers would grieve much over the death of Amasa due to the fact that he was the captain of the opposition just a few days earlier, being Absalom's captain. Yet Amasa's laying in the road bleeding stalled the rest of the army that was not with Joab. Someone finally put a cloth on him and moved him out of the way, and the soldiers then began to follow after Joab to stop Sheba. Maybe all of us should stop and look at this Amasa who followed a rebel into battle.

As Joab pursued Sheba, more and more of the men of Judah and Israel began to follow Joab. This pursuit kept Sheba from being able to amass a very large following, so they finally ran into the city of Abel of Bethmaachah. Joab immediately besieges the city. His army pushes against the very walls, and would have broken in, had a wise old woman not intervened. She knew the city had no heart to resist Joab, of all generals, and so she negotiates with Joab for the deliverance of the city. She speaks through the wall to Joab and charges him with desiring to kill fellow Israelis, which Joab flatly denies, yet with respect for the woman.

2 Samuel 20:21, *"The matter is not so: but a man of mount Ephraim, Sheba the son of Bichri by name, hath lifted up his hand against the king, even against David: deliver him only, and I will depart from the city. And the woman said unto Joab, Behold, his head shall be thrown to thee over the wall."*

Joab explains more clearly his mission, and certainly it is to destroy Sheba. However he is also on another mission, to reassert himself into his position as captain of the host. Joab here can taste the victory and the probability of his securing the position he had proved he would kill for. He told the woman to behead Sheba and throw his head over the wall, and he would then leave. The woman was able to accomplish this quickly. The head that possessed the lips that blew the trumpet of rebellion came over the wall without his body as a lesson for those who rise up against the Lord's anointed. God could and did punish his son David, but woe to those who tried to do so themselves without an order from the Lord.

Joab kept his word and returned to Jerusalem with his army. The news that this little uprising was squelched accomplished just what Joab had planned; he was reestablished as David's captain of the host, even though David was not comfortable with his being so. Joab is mentioned first in the list of David's cabinet members, but payday for his sin will not linger.

2 Samuel 20:26, *"And Ira also the Jairite was a chief ruler about David."*

This man Ira is first mentioned here, and yet he is a great officer. He was of the people of Jair being a son of Manasseh and most likely of those loyal Gileadites. Numbers 32:41, *"And Jair the son of Manasseh went and took the small towns thereof, and called them Havoth-jair."* It seems that David had no prejudice toward any tribe or people. Many worked for him who were not Israelites at all. He was faithful to his own tribe of Judah but not a respecter of persons. He loved every Jew and tried to proselyte every non-Jew and incorporate them into the work of the Kingdom. Ira was one of his top cabinet members.

2 Samuel 21:1, *"Then there was a famine in the days of David three years, year after year; and David enquired of the LORD. And the LORD answered, It is for Saul, and for his bloody house, because he slew the Gibeonites."*

There is quite a controversy as to the chronological setting of this verse. Many say it was long before the rebellion of Absalom, and many say there is no such drought talked of anywhere else in the time of David's dynasty. One must notice the first two words of this verse, *"Then there."* While it is true that Jews are not bound to write chronologically, there is still here a *"Then there."* There is no substantial reason to place this event backward or forward, and there is certainly no need to produce another account of this drought. This account is sufficient.

The droughts of the Bible caused even the hardest of hearts to seek the Lord; how much more this worshipper, David. In such seeking, we allow holy self-examination to determine what is stopping the flow of blessing. This David did and discovered the unpunished sins of Saul had come up before the Lord's remembrance -- the innocent blood Saul shed when he went wild in his anger at the priests of Nob and wiped out the entire city where these Gibeonites lived and served the priesthood (1 Sam 22:18-19). They were a part of those Joshua and the whole nation had solemnly promised to protect (Joshua 9:19).

David very well knew that innocent blood would be paid for at one time or another, and after coming to the full realization of the hindrance of blessing, he is anxious to get the matter behind him. There were probably other factors involved in this punishment of drought, but this is the one revealed to David. Innocent blood will always be revenged one day or another, even up to the end of time. This event was not only to satisfy the shedding of innocent blood but also to bring great caution to the nation of Israel not to do the same. The sovereign God has the full right to punish or pardon whom he will without the obligation to give the least reason to one soul on the earth or one being in heaven. David realizes this and calls for the Gibeonites who have been so misused by the nation of Israel, and Saul in particular, in an effort to make atonement and peace.

2 Samuel 21:3, *"Wherefore David said unto the Gibeonites, What shall I do for you? and wherewith shall I make the atonement, that ye may bless the inheritance of the LORD"?*

David who had conquered the nations around him, including the Ammorites to whom the Gibeonites belonged, now seeks their blessing. Such is the manner of Biblical restitution. We hear no complaint from David over the severity or the bizarreness of this humility he had to show the Gibeonites. He was just anxious to obey the Lord and end the drought for the people of Israel. He most likely did not expect the requirement the Gibeonites made when he asked what he must do to make atonement for the sin against them.

They asked for no monetary settlement, which is what David probably expected, but they asked for seven sons or grandsons of Saul to be delivered unto them and they would hang them in the land where the atrocities were committed. To this David agreed. Some say he did so to get rid of the possible threats to his dynasty, but we find absolutely no reason to support such. David plainly defended Saul and Jonathan in every way he could over and over again. The fact remains, he did turn these seven over to the Gibeonites.

2 Samuel 21:7, *"But the king spared Mephibosheth, the son of Jonathan the son of Saul, because of the LORD'S oath that was between them, between David and Jonathan the son of Saul."*

David did not want to yield up *"Mephibosheth the son of Jonathan the son of Saul"* because he had promised him to sit at the king's table and to be his provider. David was willing to release seven men of the house of Saul to fulfill restitution for something Saul did, but not willing to break an honest oath he made. David took two sons of Rizpah and five sons that Michal, the daughter of Saul, had raised for her sister Merab the wife of Adriel, (1 Samuel 18:19).

Clark again proves that he is not a true Biblicist by charging the Word with error here in trying to prove why Michal was Adriel's wife. I have not found one scholar who says she was. Michal was married to David first, then taken from him by Saul and given to Phalti, also called Phaltiel (1 Samuel 25:44). In Clark's labor on this verse, he steals from Michal the good and benevolent work she has done and ascribes the scripture an error. This is the typical results that Bible doubters produce. David delivers these seven men to the Gibeonites, and they were executed before the Lord.

David delivered them to the Gibeonites, but he didn't execute them. Lightfoot declares he would not have, even had he been told to by the Gibeonites. These seven men were hung at the beginning of the Barley harvest and most likely set on gibbets, both being a heathen practice to satisfy angry gods. The Gibeonites, though proselytes to the Jewish religion, were evidently not free from superstition. Rizpah, the mother of two of these slain, reacted in true repentance and yet grief. She actually erected a tent on a rock near the site of execution and stood watch to make sure the birds or the beasts could not get at the corpses. The twenty four hour per day vigil required help from her servants, but they continued until the rain came. We don't know the length of time she kept the vigil but her selfless example and effort inspired David to honor her dead husband Saul.

2 Samuel 21:11, *"And it was told David what Rizpah the daughter of Aiah, the concubine of Saul, had done."*

David most likely felt great emotion upon hearing the deeds of Rizpah. He seemed not to remember the evil deeds Saul had performed against him, but thought of all the days he had been in the court of Saul. This Rizpah David knew personally. Though she was a concubine of Saul, she is the only one we know of belonging to Saul. She is not the mother of Jonathan but certainly a woman of great character, as we see here displayed. David hated this execution of Saul's seed, and especially the heathen way it was conducted, but he was doing what the Lord had told him to do in restitution. The pain of this moment inspired him to make another step in kindness to the house of Saul which included giving these seven men a royal family burial.

2 Samuel 21:12, *"And David went and took the bones of Saul and the bones of Jonathan his son from the men of Jabeshgilead, which had stolen them from the street of Bethshan, where the Philistines had hanged them, when the Philistines had slain Saul in Gilboa"*:

David, being inspired by Rizpah, decided to dig up the bones of Saul and Jonathan which were in Jabesh-gilead in a common grave and bring them to the royal family graveyard. Though the men of Jabesh-gilead had burned their bodies, they buried their bones (1 Samuel 31:12-13). When David retrieves these bones, he combines them with the remains of these seven men and gives them all a king ordered royal burial of honor. Most likely David was glad to perform this and happy he had been inspired to do so. After the completion of all of this, the Lord again smiled upon the land of Israel.

2 Samuel 21:15, *"Moreover the Philistines had yet war again with Israel; and David went down, and his servants with him, and fought against the Philistines: and David waxed faint."*

This is called by some the war with the giant family, and some indeed try to either discredit this event, as Clark does, or set this conflict before the rebellion of Absalom. The fact that David waxed faint in this conflict and his cabinet forced his military resign is ample proof that this account is in its proper chronological place. The Philistines had all been subdued by David but seemed to be revived by a rally of the giant family.

2 Samuel 21:16, *"And Ishbi-benob, which was of the sons of the giant, the weight of whose spear weighed three hundred shekels of brass in weight, he being girded with a new sword, thought to have slain David."*

Ishbi-benob was either likely the brother of Goliath (verse 19, *"slew the brother of Goliath the Gittite"*) or his son (Verse 22, *"These four were born to the giant in Gath,"*). However, there was a giant race in Anak, (Numbers 13:33). This Ishbi-benob who had new weaponry, saw David's weak behavior and thought to press through the warriors in his great armor and kill David. This giant should have spent more time in the history class concerning the giant versus David battles. Many Philistines in those days had already converted to the God of Israel simply because of the good hand of God upon David. Ishbi-benob, although his spear was only half the weight of Goliath's, ignores all else but the desire to be the one that kills David, and attacks him while he is weak.

2 Samuel 21:17, *"But Abishai the son of Zeruiah succoured him, and smote the Philistine, and killed him. Then the men of David sware unto him, saying, Thou shalt go no more out with us to battle, that thou quench not the light of Israel."*

David's nephew Abishai came to his aid and took care of this giant. The one that David had said was too hard for him (2 Samuel 3:39) was the one that God used to save David's life. How many times had David thought to get rid of Joab and Abishai for their apparent ruthlessness, yet it is the fearlessness and military skill of Abishai that delivers him. After such a close call with death, David's mighty men insisted that David hang up his sword.

We do not know just how old David is at this time, but his days are coming to an end. David's full, exciting, and fast moving life with all of his afflictions and battles no doubt took its toll on him. David had started his giant killing ministry at a very young age, and his last battle is killing giants through those he trained and mentored. Before the giant family was completely subdued, there are three more battles recorded where these giants of Gath were killed by David's men.

2 Samuel 21:21, *"And when he defied Israel, Jonathan the son of Shimea the brother of David slew him."*

This giant's son was evidently even bigger than some of the other giants, as he is described as *"a man of great stature."* His fame was that of his deformity. Instead of the normal total of twenty fingers and toes, he had a total of twenty four. Yet he fell before Shimea. This brother of David is mentioned in 1 Samuel 16:9 where he is called Shammah. However his son Jonathan who is not mentioned otherwise in the scripture, is another nephew with great military abilities, although he is not mentioned in those mighty men or top leaders of David. It seems the whole family of Jesse turned out to be valiant fighters and giant killers.

2 Samuel 21:22, *"These four were born to the giant in Gath, and fell by the hand of David, and by the hand of his servants."*

David seemed to impart into his men the tremendous courage and anointing he possessed. The giants of Gath who were such famous warriors seemed to be finished after this. They are mentioned no more except to confirm this same account in the Chronicles. We find in the history of Israel in the writings of several historians, including the often quoted Josephus, the accounts of the giants' going down. The language used to describe these great feats is amazing, giving full glory to the Lord. Yet in the feats of David's mighty men, we find even greater exploits.

2 Samuel 22:1, *"And David spake unto the LORD the words of this song in the day that the LORD had delivered him out of the hand of all his enemies, and out of the hand of Saul"*:

This appears to be the same song recorded in Psalm eighteen except for a few minor alterations. It seems David pulled out his old songs that he had sung when he was young, and rehearsed them in his worship times in the last days of his life. The key to David's songs is found in this verse. *"And David spake unto the LORD the words of this song..."* David sang unto the Lord. The reason for this song's being revived is because he now recognizes that he will finish his course in victory with full and powerful deliverance from all of his enemies. David understands that he is going to complete a life of battle after battle without losing one battle. It is hard to fathom for any military leader, one hundred percent record of victory. David is getting ready to hand to his successor a utopia of sorts with all of the material gathered and stored for the Temple which will be called Solomon's Temple.

The life of this warrior, however, was overshadowed by his life as a worshipper. David's worship was so full and rich that it earned him the title "The Sweet Psalmist of Israel." This particular song has a key verse in it that reveals the secret of both David's war life and also his worship life. Verse 20, *"He brought me forth also into a large place: he delivered me, because he delighted in me."* David knew of his right standing with God through the salvation God had provided through the coming Messiah. David also knew that one of the very things God liked about him was the fact that he had never allowed an idol in his life or dynasty.

He was a dismal failure in so many ways and as far as historians can prove, he never wrote a psalm while in an unrepentant state. David's heart reveals that he would have considered that to be self idolization had he operated as a hypocrite. His immaculate war life, his immaculate worship life, and his immaculate Word life are amazingly manifested in the results of any serious student of his life. The prophecies of David are so powerful and messianic that Bible haters have had to try to discredit them or diffuse them in order to proceed in their attacks against the Word. David's prophetic pen has stunned the world and inspired the Hebrew prophets to give themselves to the seminary of solitude, enabling them to hear the voice of God and write it down as they were moved by the Holy Ghost.

2 Samuel 22:51, *"He is the tower of salvation for his king: and sheweth mercy to his anointed, unto David, and to his seed for evermore."*

It should be noted that the song of David that fills this entire chapter ends with the full proclamation of his covenant blessing. David lived in the light of this promise of perpetual blessing. Some theologians accuse David of spiritual carelessness because of this eternal security he possessed in his soul. We find no need for such an accusation but would rather say David knew he was walking in this covenant blessing. However, he did not expect his assurance of redemption to exempt him from chastisement. Herein is an amazing thing about David. Because he was free from idolatry, he never once railed on the Lord for the just punishment and correction he received. This is because David loved God's justice as well as His mercy. He also loved God's commandments as much as His promises!

2 Samuel 23:1, *"Now these be the last words of David. David the son of Jesse said, and the man who was raised up on high, the anointed of the God of Jacob, and the sweet psalmist of Israel, said,"*

David's fair description of himself is not that of a braggart, but of one who understands what the Lord has done in his life. He understood the term S*weet Psalmist of Israel* was not by the manufacturing of his own songs and script, but by the divine anointing of the Lord upon him. He understood verbal inspiration of the scripture very well and describes it perfectly to preface that which he was about to utter. It is not meant here that these are David's last words, for we find him speaking again, but this seems to be his last prophetic utterances.

Both David's words and the words that are uttered by the Lord through him are recorded and rightfully canonized. Often these prophetic utterances would be concerning the Davidic covenant of his house or posterity, while those around who are outside of the covenant will ultimately be consumed. He here refers to the *sons of Belial* as being those outside the Davidic covenant.

2 Samuel 23:8, *"These be the names of the mighty men whom David had: The Tachmonite that sat in the seat, chief among the captains; the same was Adino the Eznite: he lift up his spear against eight hundred, whom he slew at one time."*

David gives honor and tribute to his mighty men and rehearses some of their great exploits. These mighty men here mentioned have long been the inspiration of both leaders and followers. Leaders are here inspired to be the type as David who inspired others by his own great courage to do likewise. Followers are inspired to serve their leaders with such great loyalty and strength as these mighty men of David did. It is certain for both leaders and followers that we do not attract what we want, but what we are.

The absolutely amazing feats of such men as Adino and others are actually also humanly impossible, and we must remember the supernatural factor as we read of these feats, for they were certainly helped by the power of God. Many non-Biblicists have cited these verses as reason to accuse the scripture of discrepancies because of the different names found in this list and in 1 Chronicles 11:10-47. However, we should not trouble ourselves over such, for it is quite common for the same person to have more than one name. It is also quite clear that military commanders and leaders are an ever changing list, due to casualties or needful changes of command.

2 Samuel 23:9, "*And after him was Eleazar the son of Dodo the Ahohite, one of the three mighty men with David, when they defied the Philistines that were there gathered together to battle, and the men of Israel were gone away*":

This feat by Eleazar was exceptional in the fact that he simply would not quit fighting, even though he was mostly alone. As Adino exemplifies courage, so does Eleazar exemplify consistency. David's mighty men enjoyed the power of God upon them as they fought, and just as they were trained to do, they gave the glory to the Lord for their victories. These top mighty men were all proselytes to the Jewish religion from heathen nations. This is another reason for the differences in the name identification from this account to the other in 1 Chronicles 11:10-47.

Shammah was the third in the top tier of amazing and unusual mighty men. His famous feat displays extreme commitment to the king's interest. Adino exemplifies courage; Eleazar, consistency; and Shammah, commitment. Should a leader possess these characteristics and successfully transfer them to his followers, he will be a powerful force and leave a legacy for sure. Adino could have said, "I am not afraid of eight hundred uncircumcised Philistines." Eleazar could have said, "I shall fight these Philistines and I will never stop, even though my weary hand will stick to the sword." Shammah could have said, "These lentils belong to my king and I will defend his property with my life." While all three of them had some of the same qualities, they excelled in one particular attribute and became a trio of unique protection for King David.

2 Samuel 23:13, "*And three of the thirty chief went down, and came to David in the harvest time unto the cave of Adullam: and the troop of the Philistines pitched in the valley of Rephaim.*"

This is the beginning of a very moving account of the kind of loyalty David enjoyed of his men. The three were evidently not the three top mighty men, just honored in the immediate preceding verses. David had thirty captains and three of them did the feat described in the following verses. This event did not occur while David was in exile from Saul in Adullam. For the conflict here was not with Saul but with the Philistines. It is a mistake to place every reference to the cave at Adullam as the time of David's exile from Saul. There was in fact a cave there in Adullam, but it seems the place where David fortified himself against the Philistines is also called the cave of Adullam. Verse fourteen mentions a *hold* or *fort* which is called *rock* in 1 Chronicles 11:15.

2 Samuel 23:14, *"And David was then in an hold, and the garrison of the Philistines was then in Bethlehem."*

The point of this verse is to prove the position of the Philistine army and the fact that for David's mighty men to get to the well of Bethlehem from their position, they would have to go through the army of the Philistines. The term *harvest time* in verse thirteen is to let us know why David would be in such desire of that water from the well at Bethlehem, for the harvest time was very hot and dry.

2 Samuel 23:15, *"And David longed, and said, Oh that one would give me drink of the water of the well of Bethlehem, which is by the gate!"*

The whim of the king was the shouting orders in the soul of those so loyal to him. David is simply vocalizing a desire for that water from the well of Bethlehem he loved and missed so much. It appears as though he did not either expect or command these men to actually go and get the water.

2 Samuel 23:16. *"And the three mighty men brake through the host of the Philistines, and drew water out of the well of Bethlehem, that was by the gate, and took it, and brought it to David: nevertheless he would not drink thereof, but poured it out unto the LORD."*

David was unique in that he loved God's commandments as much as he loved His promises. Deep consecration can actually allow you to arrive at a place in God where you require neither commandment nor promise. That place is a place where all one needs to know is that God wants it. That is enough! The motivation of a commandment is not needed! The motivation of a promise is not needed! The consecrated one just needs to know He wants it. Herein is a picture of consecration - these men getting this water for their king. They were neither commanded to get it nor promised anything for doing it. These men were operating solely out of consecration to their king. The mighty men broke through the ranks of the Philistines and got David the water he desired and brought it back him. David was so moved that he refused to drink it.

While some see this as an insult to the men who risked their lives to get it, the men actually were paid the highest respect. The fact that the very water David desired so badly, he denied himself in honor of their heroic deeds revealed to them the value he placed upon their lives. Lightfoot treads even further in this realm by declaring that David here acted as a priest, turning this water into one of the seven offerings of Israel, the pour offering (Leviticus 23:13). Lightfoot is standing on good ground because of this statement *"nevertheless he would not drink thereof, but poured it out unto the LORD."*

The feats of Abishai are listed here without the negatives, for this nephew of David often troubled him. The fact that David did try to rid himself of both him and his brother Joab at times is evident, yet their extraordinary military abilities allowed them to remain in the top ranks of David's mighty army. The same thing also earned these words from David concerning Abishai, *"howbeit he attained not unto the first three."*

Benaiah the son of Jehoiada also is listed as one who could run with the three because of his great exploits.

2 Samuel 23:23, *"He was more honourable than the thirty, but he attained not to the first three. And David set him over his guard."*

It seems that these words of tribute David had for Benaiah are showing a pattern that is important to note. David is naming some of the people who could have been the top three if it weren't for the top three being the top three. He is here showing an abundance of military sons being raised up which were powerful and able to be in high ranks, and his relationship with them was alone the key to their ultimate position. David did not allow for jealousy, and this is a type of the Lord Jesus with His disciples. He also had seventy, and out of the seventy, He had twelve. Out of the twelve, Jesus had His inner circle of three. Out of the three, there was only one who leaned upon His breast that referred to himself as "that disciple Jesus loved." David had thirty seven famous mighty men. All of them are mentioned here except for Joab, who was their obvious leader and the captain of the host.

He likewise had an inner circle, and this was determined by relationary order. Now we finally see the proof that Uriah was one of his personal guards whose loyalty David defiled.

2 Samuel 24:1, *"And again the anger of the LORD was kindled against Israel, and he moved David against them to say, Go, number Israel and Judah."*

This text has troubled those who do not understand the universal purpose of God's judgment. Their question seems legitimate. Why would God judge David for something He moved him to do? Yet, in comparing the accounts of this wicked census as also recorded in 1 Chronicles 21, we discover the whole of the matter. Israel had grown spiritually cold and self sufficient through their recent military victories and abundant wealth. At the same time David develops a certain pride in the size and scope of his dynasty. God simply allows Satan to move toward David in the same area of his prideful thinking and entice him to number the people.

1 Chronicles 21:2 says, *"And Satan stood up against Israel, and provoked David to number Israel."* No need for anyone to charge God with being set out to destroy Israel in bully fashion;

nothing could be further from the truth. God's mercy record speaks for itself throughout the scripture. In the full account in both places in the scripture, we will find David is dealing with a pride problem, and the severity of the matter proves the aforementioned accusation that the whole nation had drifted into a national pride.

God's anger against pride is easily detected by the most elementary Bible student. In His anger, He allowed Satan to move against the nation. Satan well knows that to get at a nation, he must provoke the leaders to sin. Satan enticed David to count all of the people to see how many was under his command. Joab could see through the matter of David's pride and tried to talk him out of this thing. Loyalty does not equate to blindness. Joab's argument was basically to remind David that no matter how many people there are, they are all his people.

Joab knew the spirit of pride and hoped to appease it in David by his argument. When it didn't work, he became a little more confrontational and asked David why he even desired such a thing. Joab could not curtail David's drive to do the census and started on the mission reluctantly. For nine months and twenty days they took the census. The report came back without the tally of Benjamin or Levi. This was due to the massiveness of the project, as well as Joab's lack of heart for it.

The sum of the census was staggering, with Joab's finding a total of one million three hundred thousand valiant men, not counting Benjamin or Levi. The number of soldiers lets us know that this failure of counting the people is definitely toward the end of David's dynasty. The sum of the census is different here than the account in 1 Chronicles 21. The one excludes the standing militia while the other adds them, and vice versa, which produces a unity in the different accounts thus explained well by Wesley in his following notes: "The sum here expressed, is only of such as were not in the settled militia waiting upon the king, which being twenty-four thousand for every month, as is largely related, 1 Chronicles 27:1, amounts to two hundred and eighty-eight thousand, which either with their several commanders, or with the soldiers placed in several garrisons might very well make up three hundred thousand. Five hundred thousand-In 1 Chronicles 21:5, but four hundred seventy thousand. Either 1) they were exactly no more, but are called five hundred thousand in a round sum, as is usual in scripture, and other authors, or, 2. the garrison-soldiers, and such as were employed in other services about the king are here included, who are there excluded."

2 Samuel 24:10, *"And David's heart smote him after that he had numbered the people. And David said unto the LORD, I have sinned greatly in that I have done: and now, I beseech thee, O LORD, take away the iniquity of thy servant; for I have done very foolishly."*

No sooner had the census ended and he found out the numbers, David's heart smote him. David was so consumed with the census, having fully fallen for the devil's enticement, that he totally avoided the one question from Joab that could have saved him the great pain to follow and that was, "David, why do you want to count the people?" With every temptation there is a way of escape, and Joab's confrontational question was it. Now David realizes his sinful pride and confesses his sin before the Lord. David's motive for counting the people wasn't exactly to see how many common people were in his kingdom because he only counted twenty and above. So it seemed to be a pride in the army that had grown so amazingly large.

It is evident this wasn't a population census because David neglected the tax that was to be extracted at such a time that was commanded in Exodus 30:11-13, *"And the LORD spake unto Moses, saying, When thou takest the sum of the children of Israel after their number, then shall they give every man a ransom for his soul unto the LORD, when thou numberest them; that there be no plague among them, when thou numberest them. This they shall give, every one that passeth among them that are numbered, half a shekel after the shekel of the sanctuary: (a shekel is twenty gerahs:) an half shekel shall be the offering of the LORD."*

David wasn't thinking about the Lord, nor His work in this census, but was thinking about his military might. The aversion of the plague spoken of in Exodus 30:12 was correlated to the offering extracted from the people for the work of the Lord. David realized it was no small affront to God in neglecting these dues and yet numbering the people. There are far too many instances of David's following the words of the Torah for one to believe that he was unaware of this commandment. Thus David again fails, even in his latter days. The fact that David was well aware of the mercy of the Lord caused Him to call quickly on the Lord to forgive him. He will not ignore true repentance for a long period of time as he did in the case of Ziklag or in the matter of Bathsheba.

2 Samuel 24:11, *"For when David was up in the morning, the word of the LORD came unto the prophet Gad, David's seer, saying,"*

Oh, how sin severs communication with the Lord! David was still the Lord's, but prideful sin had caused the Lord to bring chastisement on His son David. The first thing was that God didn't speak to David here but sent his seer Gad. David had been speaking to the Lord, but the Lord chose to answer through Gad. Also, Gad seemed to be the prophet or seer that spoke into David's life at strategic times of difficulty (1 Samuel 22:5), and certainly this is one of those times.

2 Samuel 24:12, *"Go and say unto David, Thus saith the LORD, I offer thee three things; choose thee one of them, that I may do it unto thee."*

Here David quickly submits to the fact that though his sin is forgiven, there is most certainly going to be a sentence of punishment. If the man whom the Lord declared to be a man after His own heart is not free from the circumstance and punishment of his sin, how is it that so many believers think such, one of whom so boldly said that God only punished people in the Old Testament; in the New Testament he just speaks to us. Of course, He does both and in both dispensations. We must remember all of the wonderful verses in our Bible from the pen of David that extols the very judgment of God. Though David was guilty and Jesus was not, neither shunned the scourge.

2 Samuel 24:13, *"So Gad came to David, and told him, and said unto him, Shall seven years of famine come unto thee in thy land? or wilt thou flee three months before thine enemies, while they pursue thee? or that there be three days' pestilence in thy land? now advise, and see what answer I shall return to him that sent me."*

Gad the prophet comes with the Word of the Lord. The options David is given for the sentence of punishment are quite varying. The very fact that he is given an option is quite amazing and unique in itself. David is given three options: 1) Seven years of famine; 2) three months of military defeat; 3) three days of pestilence. David is urged by the prophet to carefully consider the matter and give him the message that he should give to the Lord.

2 Samuel 24:14, *"And David said unto Gad, I am in a great strait: let us fall now into the hand of the LORD; for his mercies are great: and let me not fall into the hand of man."*

David confirms to the prophet that he realizes how much trouble he now has found himself in but doesn't take the allowed time to decide which of the three options he will take. David wisely said, *"let us fall now into the hand of the LORD; for his mercies are great:"* David knew full well the extended mercies of the Lord. And he brags on those mercies as he gives himself to the coming judgment. It is interesting that he tells Gad to tell the Lord, *"let us,"* not *"let me,"* who caused the whole problem but *"let us."* David knew that he had occasioned the judgment on all of his people in either choice he made. David had never lost a battle in leading the people with him into war. He had lost some soldiers but never a battle. So he quickly chooses the three days of the plague and pestilence. Upon making the choice, the judgment fell.

Throughout the nation, in the exact pattern as the census was taken, seventy thousand people died. Josephus declares that some died suddenly while others wasted away leaving nothing to bury but bones. This report is not confirmed by the scripture itself as is often the case with Josephus. Sudden yes, for the plague was stayed before the three days were accomplished, leaving no time for Josephus' account except for the cleanup of the carnage. It seems the entire judgment lasted *from the morning until the time appointed.* The term *time appointed* could not mean the end of the three days as some suppose, for the people were in great repentance and so God stopped the plague. The *time appointed,* would most likely be referring to the time of the evening oblation, which would be three o'clock in the afternoon, the exact same time Jesus died and ended the plague of sin and death for all of those who receive Him. It should also be noted that the plague stopped at the threshing floor of Araunah, which is the place where Isaac was offered and the place of Solomon's Temple and the place where Jesus was crucified!

2 Samuel 24:17, *"And David spake unto the LORD when he saw the angel that smote the people, and said, Lo, I have sinned, and I have done wickedly: but these sheep, what have they done? let thine hand, I pray thee, be against me, and against my father's house."*

David pleads with the Lord as the judgment falls. He again confesses his sin, but now he moves into an intercessional order by pleading for the people. David's intercessional life is much deeper than is often first noticed. David actually goes as deep as Moses, who requested in Exodus 32:32, *"Yet now, if thou wilt forgive their sin; and if not, blot me, I pray thee, out of thy book which thou hast written."* The difference, however, is apparent. David's sin had caused the problem, and in Moses' case, the people's sin had caused the problem. However, in similarity, David was willing to release the Lord from His covenant with him and his house if only God would spare these innocent people! This depth of intercession brought immediate results from the Lord!

2 Samuel 24:18, *"And Gad came that day to David, and said unto him, Go up, rear an altar unto the LORD in the threshingfloor of Araunah the Jebusite.*

Gad comes to David with specific instructions for averting the plague. He tells David to erect an altar. Places are very important to God. He wanted this altar erected in the very place on Mount Moriah where Solomon's Temple would be built later, and the city of Jerusalem would someday compass the area. 2 Chronicles 3:1, *"Then Solomon began to build the house of the LORD at Jerusalem in mount Moriah, where the LORD appeared unto David his father, in the place that David had prepared in the threshingfloor of Ornan the Jebusite."* In that same general area is Golgotha. John 19:17, *"And he bearing his cross went forth into a place called the place of a skull, which is called in the Hebrew Golgotha:"* This is the proper place for mercy to be extended.

2 Samuel 24:19, *"And David, according to the saying of Gad, went up as the LORD commanded."*

David saw his window of opportunity for God's mercy to be granted and responded immediately. Oh that convicted sinners would do likewise and respond immediately to the goodness of God that calls them. Araunah saw the king and his servants coming, and no doubt could tell how urgent the king's business was. Mixed with the honor of having the king come to his house and the anticipation of wondering what he wanted, as well as the national crisis they were all facing, Araunah bows on his face upon the ground.

A Samuel 24:21, *"And Araunah said, Wherefore is my lord the king come to his servant? And David said, To buy the threshingfloor of thee, to build an altar unto the LORD, that the plague may be stayed from the people."*

David quickly answers Araunah with his urgent plan 1) To buy the property; 2) To build the altar; 3) Offer a sacrifice to avert the plague. Now even though the Lord had stayed the hand of the angel from destroying the people, David knew the matter was urgent. Araunah also knew the matter was urgent, for the whole of the nation was in mourning and in fear.

2 Samuel 24:22, *"And Araunah said unto David, Let my lord the king take and offer up what seemeth good unto him: behold, here be oxen for burnt sacrifice, and threshing instruments and other instruments of the oxen for wood."*

Araunah did not want to sell his property but was more than willing, even honored, for the king to come to his land and make such a request. Araunah wanted to give the entire substance of the sacrifice, including the threshing instruments for the fire. His entire threshing effort would come to an immediate halt, as his oxen would be offered and his tools to furnish the wood. The account in 1 Chronicles 21 affords us the insight needed to understand the absolute emergency of this matter, for the destroying angel was visible to Araunah from the position of the threshing floor. This must have been a terrifying sight, for the sons of Araunah went and hid themselves. Araunah freely gave it all, but he did not see the need of selling the land when the king had full control of its use in this matter.

2 Samuel 24:24, *"And the king said unto Araunah, Nay; but I will surely buy it of thee at a price: neither will I offer burnt offerings unto the LORD my God of that which doth cost me nothing. So David bought the threshingfloor and the oxen for fifty shekels of silver."*

A man under conviction and in deep repentance doesn't blink at a cost involved in his repentance and restitution, but on the contrary, is quite willing to pay fully. How foolish are those in the doctrine of works for salvation to use this verse for their sacrilegious indulgence. This payment for the threshing floor and threshing instruments has nothing to do with the mercy seat and the Day of Atonement but everything to do with Godly sorrow and repentance. Salvation is a free gift paid for by the precious blood of Jesus. Consecration and obedience is quite expensive. Therein lies the cross and self denial, yes the dying to self and the life of total consecration. The forgiven sinner thought nothing of pouring out her life savings from her alabaster box just to please and honor Him who had forgiven her.

There is an alleged discrepancy in the matter of the amount David gave to Araunah. In 1 Chronicles 21:25 we read, *"So David gave to Ornan for the place six hundred shekels of gold by weight."* However, the account in Chronicles is consistently more minute in detail and lists the entire price of the hill which David bought for the preparation of the building of what is called Solomon's Temple. Fifty shekels of silver would be a fair and full price for the threshing floor and the instruments. Fifty shekels of silver would be an insult to God and Araunah both to give for the whole Temple mound, which likely contained the house of Araunah, who was a wealthy man, and also the houses of his servants. Six hundred shekels of gold would be an appropriate price for that.

The account in 1 Chronicles also records that after David offered the sacrifice and the fire fell from heaven, he called the place *the house of God*. David knew then where the Temple would be built and probably paid Araunah the rest of the money at that time. If David would not pay less than the full price for the spot of the threshing floor for one offering, he certainly would pay no less than the full price where hundreds of thousands of burnt offerings would be offered. The same ground here is also where the supreme sacrifice and the only blood was shed that would not just cover sin but take it away. Jesus was crucified on this property!

2 Samuel 24:25, *"And David built there an altar unto the LORD, and offered burnt offerings and peace offerings. So the LORD was intreated for the land, and the plague was stayed from Israel."*

We do not see a priest involved in the building of the altar or the offering of the sacrifices. This does not mean that they were absent but perhaps just not mentioned. However, there are other cases where David was afforded the liberty to do priestly duties, and in one case even wear the attire of the priest. 2 Samuel 6:14, *"And David danced before the LORD with all his might; and David was girded with a linen ephod."* The offerings were both burnt offerings and peace offerings.

In seeing the true repentance in David's heart and the obedience in the sacrifices, God stayed the hand of the destroying angel. David knew that by the Lord's requiring the sacrifice and giving him the details as to where to offer it, He would surely answer the prayer for mercy. Offering the sacrifice was done in faith and obedience. We will never see one instance in which David tried to use anything to get around obedience. God even answered by fire, which is recorded in the account of this experience in 1 Chronicles. This was already God's favorite hill on planet earth, and now it has become David's.

1 Kings

1 Kings 1:1, "*Now king David was old and stricken in years; and they covered him with clothes, but he gat no heat.*"

David is now at least seventy years old. His dynasty lasted forty years and he started when he was thirty. 2 Samuel 5:4, "*David was thirty years old when he began to reign, and he reigned forty years.*" David died at seventy and probably a few months beyond. This event happened less than a year before he died. David lived out the promise of Psalm 90:10 by achieving seventy years of age, but did not exceed the time because of the extreme difficulties of guerilla warfare, domestic difficulties, heart break and diseases of his own failures. Many ascribe to David a venereal disease in his loins by reading his own words to describe his condition recorded in Psalms 38:6-7, "*I am troubled; I am bowed down greatly; I go mourning all the day long. 7 For my loins are filled with a loathsome disease: and there is no soundness in my flesh.*" David's circulation was very poor, and his physicians went to foolish methods to try to help him. Having the young virgin Abishag lay in his bosom did not help him even after all of the trouble his physicians went to in finding her and choosing her.

Laying in this horrible condition and unable to receive healing opened the door for yet another attempt to take over the Davidic dynasty by one non-ordained to do so, Adonijah. He was the son of Haggith and was Absalom's younger brother and David's fourth son (2 Samuel 3:4). This uprising seemed to come from nowhere, but a closer look will reveal that Adonijah had lived with no fatherly restraint at all. Here is an indictment against David for his poor parenting. It seems that David never questioned the behavior of his sons. It took this rebel to reveal the real Abiathar and Joab. Having the powerful influence of the priests who revered Abiathar and the soldiers who revered Joab, Adonijah made the uprising quite serious. He gathered horsemen and chariots together for the takeover.

1 Kings 1:8, "*But Zadok the priest, and Benaiah the son of Jehoiada, and Nathan the prophet, and Shimei, and Rei, and the mighty men which belonged to David, were not with Adonijah.*"

These are the problems for Adonijah: 1) Zadok the faithful priest knew the real Abiathar and did not follow Adonijah. 2) Benaiah, who was in charge of David's personal bodyguards, (2 Samuel 8:18) did not follow Adonijah. 3) Nathan, the mighty prophet of God, knew the spirit of a rebel and did not follow Adonijah. 4) The mighty men of David knew the real Joab and did not follow Adonijah.

Adonijah called the king's sons and his servants to a great feast and gathering. He did not call Solomon his brother, whom he knew to be the one anointed and in line to be the king. He didn't call those closest to David for the obvious reason: Adonijah knew they were faithful to David his father. This attempted coup should be seen as more than a military effort. Adonijah is being used of the enemy to come against the very revival that is about to occur under the dynasty of Solomon.

1 Kings 1:11, *"Wherefore Nathan spake unto Bathsheba the mother of Solomon, saying, Hast thou not heard that Adonijah the son of Haggith doth reign, and David our lord knoweth it not"?*

God uses the Prophet Nathan to save the dynasty of David from another rebellious coup. The prophet goes to the people in behalf of God, but his mission may vary a great deal. Nathan had to go to David earlier to confront him about his sin. Now he is sent by the Lord to go to Bathsheba in behalf of David's dynasty and the lives of Bathsheba and Solomon. Nathan tells Bathsheba of the wicked rebellion of Adonijah and the fact that David is not aware of it.

1 Kings 1:13, *"Go and get thee in unto king David, and say unto him, Didst not thou, my lord, O king, swear unto thine handmaid, saying, Assuredly Solomon thy son shall reign after me, and he shall sit upon my throne? why then doth Adonijah reign"?*

Nathan gives counsel to Bathsheba and reveals a plan to arouse David to take action against the coup and confirm Solomon as his successor. Nathan sends Bathsheba to go before David and assures her that he will also come before David as soon as she has had time to make her speech to him. Bathsheba goes before David, who receives her warmly. She reminds David of his oath before the Lord to install Solomon as king of Israel. She was also very aware of the prophetic word given over her and David's son recorded in 1 Chronicles 22:9 *"Behold, a son shall be born to thee who shall be a man of rest; and I will give him rest from all his enemies round about: for his name shall be Solomon, and I will give peace and quietness unto Israel in his days."* In the light of all of this covenant prophecy, Bathsheba then tells David of Adonijah's uprising and how all of Israel is waiting to hear from him on the matter. She further reminds David that if Adonijah succeeds, both she and Solomon would be considered as traitors.

As Bathsheba finishes her intercession, Nathan comes in as planned and rehearses the whole matter in David's ears. Nathan goes a little deeper in his effort to arouse David to action by asking David a question that he already knows the answer to. He asks if David sanctioned Adonijah's proclamation as king. Then Nathan tells the king how far the matter has gone by including the news that both Joab and Abiathar are giving their full support to Adonijah. Nathan tells David that he, Solomon, and Zadok were not invited to the uprising feast and concludes his speaking by again asking if David if he had sanctioned Adonijah as king without telling him.

Between the intercession of Bathsheba and the address to the king by Nathan, David is fully motivated to restrain a son whom he has never restrained before and to finally deal with Joab which he had never really done before.

1 Kings 1:28, *"Then king David answered and said, Call me Bathsheba. And she came into the king's presence, and stood before the king."*

David immediately calls Bathsheba back in and begins to assure both her and Nathan that he will not fail to keep his vow that he vowed before God. David then assures them that it is Solomon who will be the next king of Israel, and that he will not wait another day to make it so. Adonijah probably thought 1) That David would not be up to doing such a bold thing 2) That Joab and Abiathar would quench by fear any possible restraint of his coup 3) That a quick and strong revolt would accomplish the change in the dynasty.

It is evident that Adonijah didn't consider that the One who gave David the strength to build the kingdom was also the One who gave him the strength to prolong the kingdom and deliver it to the hands of Solomon. How foolish to fight against God and His sovereign will!

It is evident from this account, and also in Chronicles and Proverbs that David had been mentoring Solomon and preparing him for his death. Now he is going to transfer his crown before he dies. We can leave David no slack by saying, "A father who has raised his offspring right can trust them to do right when he dies. One who does not must see to his affairs before he dies." Solomon shall be king this day.

1 Kings 1:31, *"Then Bathsheba bowed with her face to the earth, and did reverence to the king, and said, Let my lord king David live for ever."*

Bathsheba showed both reverence and gratitude to her king and her husband. The blessing she pronounced was especially affectionate as David is at the point of death. Bathsheba wanted David to know that she was not in favor of his dying quickly for her son to be established as king of Israel. Bathsheba would enjoy much more kingdom authority as the mother of the king instead of being just one of the king's wives. It appears David had a special relationship with Bathsheba, though we find no actual verse declaring such.

1 Kings 1:32, *"And king David said, Call me Zadok the priest, and Nathan the prophet, and Benaiah the son of Jehoiada. And they came before the king."*

David begins his task of establishing Solomon as king immediately and in perfect order. The king calls for the priest first, then the prophet and then the military leader. Then David commands his servants to prepare his own mule for Solomon to ride upon and bring him down to Gihon which was a fountain near Jerusalem (2 Chronicles 32:30). This seemed to be a popular gathering place suitable for this occasion.

David made every effort to emphasize the importance of this event. 1) He had the very top officials of his kingdom carry out the coronation. 2) He had Solomon to ride upon his own mule, which Josephus declares to be quite decked out. 3) He uses the sacred anointing oil out of the sanctuary, which signifies the unified effort of the king and the priest. 4) David assures that the transfer of kingship will be in the very most visible place, with room enough to accommodate a large gathering which the public march would cause. 5) David had the servants to blow the trumpet and shout, "God save King Solomon." 6) He had Benaiah the son of Jehoiada shout "Amen" and proclaim a blessing of extended greatness on Solomon's dynasty, even surpassing David's. This would bring the military together with the prophet and the priest who anointed Solomon. 7) They were to bring Solomon back to David's throne and have him sit there.

1 Kings 1:37, *"As the LORD hath been with my lord the king, even so be he with Solomon, and make his throne greater than the throne of my lord king David."*

The blessing here pronounced is worthy of much study in the fact of such greatness that rested upon David. This proclaimed blessing was quite a bit more commonly placed upon a mediocre king, and more often proclaimed by those subjects that would be in need of a greater king. However these are the words David instructed them to say, and many scholars believe them to be as prophetic as Jacob's last words to his sons. As the priest's son reports this event to Adonijah and his followers in verse 47, he is careful to include these prophetic words over Solomon.

1 Kings 1:38, *"So Zadok the priest, and Nathan the prophet, and Benaiah the son of Jehoiada, and the Cherethites, and the Pelethites, went down, and caused Solomon to ride upon king David's mule, and brought him to Gihon."*

This must have been a powerful scene as the high priest, the main prophet, the general, and the king's royal guard *(the Cherethites, and the Pelethites),* march toward the city fountain, escorting Solomon on the king's mule. Everyone told someone else and a multitude gathered quickly. Zadok anointed Solomon with oil, and they blew the trumpet just as they were commanded by the king to do. Then all the people said in unison, "God save King Solomon." The people got out their musical instruments and a spontaneous shout erupted from the people. This is the picture of the remnant triumphant church rallying around the King of Kings and our High Priest, Jesus of Nazareth.

All of this powerful praise was so loud that the rebel and his allies could hear it all the way to Enrogel, where they had just finished the feast of rebellion. The true celebration of the true King will certainly interrupt the feast of sin and rebellion. Joab heard the noise and was in wonderment until the rebel priest's son Jonathan came and told them why the multitude was shouting.

1 Kings 1:43, *"And Jonathan answered and said to Adonijah, Verily our lord king David hath made Solomon king."*

Jonathan told them that David had installed Solomon as King of Israel and how the high priest, the highest prophet, the general, and the royal guard had placed Solomon on the king's mule. Jonathan explains to them how Zadok and Nathan anointed Solomon at the fountain and then escorted him back to the throne of David. He told them this was the reason for the noise they had heard. The more Jonathan told them, the worse it became to them. But yet Jonathan continues.

1 Kings 1:47, *"And moreover the king's servants came to bless our lord king David, saying, God make the name of Solomon better than thy name, and make his throne greater than thy throne. And the king bowed himself upon the bed."*

Jonathan now tells them of the power of the prophetic blessing concerning the power of Solomon's dynasty. He then tops off his report with the most dreaded news the rebels could hear. The king himself has blessed the Lord that he had lived to see the proper transfer to the proper king. The rebels had underestimated the power of God that still rested upon David and the anointing that would now rest upon Solomon.

Adonijah's party ended abruptly as do all of the wicked gatherings of rebels. The guests ran away from Adonijah when they heard this news, and Adonijah ran into Jerusalem and went into the tabernacle David had built for the Ark and grabbed hold of the horns of the altar to plead for mercy. He knew that it was against the Levitical law to slay someone at the altar. Exodus 21:14, *"But if a man come presumptuously upon his neighbour, to slay him with guile; thou shalt take him from mine altar, that he may die."* Adonijah knew he was guilty of death but he also knew where the best place would be to plead for mercy. Solomon granted him mercy but placed a condition upon it. This was his half brother who was worthy of death, but was pardoned with strict condition and ordered to go home.

1 Kings 2:1, *"Now the days of David drew nigh that he should die; and he charged Solomon his son, saying,"*

These last words of David are quite revealing of his heart toward the Lord and the advancement of the kingdom that the Lord had given him watch care over. David was a very special person, and the Lord was careful not to let David get by with even the least amount of self glory or pride. This is true with those so close to the Lord. He is quite severe at times with his chosen vessels by allowing them to fail, only to pick them up again to show them His immaculate mercy. It is time for David to die the death that all must face. Even the one after God's own heart must go this way (Hebrews 9:27).

It is evident from the timeline of David's death that from the time David transferred the kingship to Solomon until the time of his death there were about six months. During this time David no doubt gave Solomon special attention and instruction. We have a summary of these instructions, beginning with David's charge to be a strong man and put God and His commandments first. He reminds Solomon that there is no way that he can expect to prosper if he does not obey the commandments of God. David wanted Solomon to know that even though he would be walking in a continued blessed state of covenant promise, it was conditional based upon his obedience. David warned him as true love warrants.

David then begins to give Solomon his last governmental instructions, which indicate that he had a very sharp mind even until the last breath. David gives these details to help his son to begin to reign with a good balance of grace and truth. David tells Solomon not to allow Joab to go down to his grave as though he had not murdered Abner and Amasa. David told him to use the wisdom he had because dealing with Joab would not be so easy, as he was widely feared by the people and was able to lead a sizable rebellion.

David told Solomon to show kindness to the sons of Barzillai because he had come to him during the rebellion of Absalom and sustained him. David gave Solomon instructions concerning the treacherous Shimei by basically telling him to execute him if he so chose to do so. Wesley charges David with this being David's worst sin, second only to the matter of Uriah, because he had formerly granted Shimei amnesty. Here Wesley is hasty, for when David made the oath not to kill Shimei he was speaking of that particular day. Abishai was requesting to kill Shimei and David would not allow it and he swore such to him in 2 Samuel 19:23, *"Therefore the king said unto Shimei, Thou shalt not die. And the king sware unto him."* It should also be noted that Shimei had one thousand men with him of the house of Saul. This vow should not have been taken as a full pardon, but rather that David would not allow his men to execute Shimei for his wicked and most insidious sin.

1 Kings 2:10, *"So David slept with his fathers, and was buried in the city of David."*

David dies. The mightiest warrior ever in Israel! David wrote the song, "How are the mighty fallen" when Saul and Jonathan died, for they were killed in battle. What shall be written in honor of one who never lost a battle and conquered every enemy of Israel? There has been plenty written about David, but the greatest part of David's legacy is yet before us. David will be raised up during the millennium to reign over Israel beside the King of Kings Jesus, who will reign over all of the earth from the city of Jerusalem. Jeremiah 30:9, *"But they shall serve the LORD their God, and David their king, whom I will raise up unto them."* David was buried in Jerusalem, and of all of the sites in the Holy Land that are disputed for accuracy, this one is perhaps the least disputed - the tomb of King David. One of the reasons for the ability to accurately locate his sepulcher is because sepulchers were not allowed within the precincts of the city of Jerusalem. Jerusalem, however, made an historical exception for David and his royal family.

1 Kings 2:11, *"And the days that David reigned over Israel were forty years: seven years reigned he in Hebron, and thirty and three years reigned he in Jerusalem."*

When we compare this verse with 2 Samuel 5:5, *"In Hebron he reigned over Judah seven years and six months: and in Jerusalem he reigned thirty and three years over all Israel and Judah,"* we find six months unaccounted for except we recognize the time after the coronation of Solomon. So David died between his seventieth and his seventy-first year, for we know he was thirty when he began to reign. 2 Samuel 5:4 *"David was thirty years old when he began to reign, and he reigned forty years."*

A student of the military history of the nation of Israel will stand amazed at these forty years of dynasty. Likewise, a student of the history of the Hebrew prophets will stand amazed at the messianic prophecy that flowed from David. Also a student of Hebrew songs and worship will stand amazed at the "Sweet Psalmist of Israel." If you view David chiefly as a worshipper, it is easy not to count him as a prophet. If you see him chiefly as a prophet, you may not see him as the greatest military general in the history of Israel. If you see him as all three carefully laid out before us in the scriptures with all of his good points and bad, you will see him a man after God's heart!

1 Kings 2:12, *"Then sat Solomon upon the throne of David his father; and his kingdom was established greatly."*

Solomon is King! David has gone to heaven, but most see Solomon as an extension of the Davidic dynasty, and rightfully so. What true father would not want his son to do better than he has? What true son would dare to steal the honor or legacy of his father? Solomon, as a faithful son, sets about to do what his father had instructed him. He first must deal with the treacherous Adonijah. David was a great man but not a great father. Sometimes the faithful sons inherit the problems caused by their father's mistakes. David had never disciplined Adonijah (1 Kings 1:6) and Solomon was given no instructions concerning him. However, like all unrepentant rebels, their true colors show.

Adonijah comes to Bathsheba and asks for Abishag to become his wife. He makes his plea by telling Bathsheba that he almost had the kingdom but now that he lost that to her son and his half brother Solomon, could he at least have Abishag the young virgin they had found for David. Bathsheba was compassionate toward Adonijah, and as he had asked, goes to speak to Solomon for him. Solomon considered the request for David's concubine an act of treason and full proof that there was no repentance in the heart of Adinojah, even though he had told Bathsheba that is was God's will that Solomon was king. It appears that Solomon considered Adonijah to be in league with Joab and Abiathar in requesting Abishag. Therefore Solomon sentences Adonijah to death.

1 Kings 2:24, "*Now therefore, as the LORD liveth, which hath established me, and set me on the throne of David my father, and who hath made me an house, as he promised, Adonijah shall be put to death this day.*"

In putting Adonijah to death, Solomon is not only ridding the nation of a cancerous rebel that actually led the latest coup attempt against him and his father, but he is making a strong statement for all others who walked with him or was tempted to. Directly after the coup attempt, Solomon spared Adonijah and commanded him to go home. Had he done so and not made such a foolish move, he would have been allowed to live. Watts declares Adonijah an unrepentant fool. In Adonijah's execution, Solomon is basically saying to the nation, "If you were a part of any effort to undermine the dynasty of my father David, you had better lie extremely low, for such will not be tolerated by me, even from my own royal family. Thus Solomon had his elder brother executed by Benaiah the son of Jehoiada, the captain of his host.

1 Kings 2:26, "*And unto Abiathar the priest said the king, Get thee to Anathoth, unto thine own fields; for thou art worthy of death: but I will not at this time put thee to death, because thou barest the ark of the Lord GOD before David my father, and because thou hast been afflicted in all wherein my father was afflicted.*"

Solomon now deals with Abiathar, another one of David's mistakes. Abiathar was never a bona fide high priest, but rather appointed so by David out of guilt. Guilt because that day at Nob when Doeg the Edolmite saw Ahimelech give David Goliath's sword, he knew Doeg would tell Saul. When Doeg did tell Saul, he went into a rage and killed all of the posterity of Eli. The only one who escaped was Abiathar, and David appointed him high priest with Zadok. All of this was clearly prophesied in 1 Samuel 2 by an unnamed prophet. The prophecy went on to say that the one that escaped would bring disgrace to Israel.

We have no recorded instructions from David on how to deal with this mess, and when Abiathar followed Joab and Adonijah in the attempted coup, he showed his true colors. Solomon wisely decided not to execute Abiathar but rather stripped him of his office and sent him home to his fields, which means he would till the ground and not even report for a priestly course. Solomon's action in this matter is both wise and just, wrapped in reluctant mercy!

As soon as Joab hears of Solomon's dealing with Adonijah and Abiathar, he flees to the tabernacle to catch hold of the horns of the altar. He is hoping to receive the same mercy which was at first shown to Adonijah. Solomon hears of it and realizes it is the time to take Joab out, for his father had told him he would know the right time to execute him. He sent Benaiah, his captain, to go execute him. When Benaiah came to the Tabernacle of the LORD he tried to get Joab to come out, but Joab refused and said *"Nay; but I will die here."* Now Exodus 21:14 teaches against performing an execution at the altar, so Benaiah went and told Solomon Joab's position. Surprisingly, Solomon told Benaiah to execute him there.

Some scholars fault the young king for this, while others applaud him. It was a difficult decision, just as Joab had intended it to be. Yet many interpret Exodus 21:14 to mean that the murderer cannot approach the altar instead of cannot be executed there. We must concede that in fact Solomon did right because of the words David spoke to him concerning the wisdom he would have for this assignment of ridding Israel of an unrepentant officer who had shed so much innocent blood.

1 Kings 2:32, *"And the LORD shall return his blood upon his own head, who fell upon two men more righteous and better than he, and slew them with the sword, my father David not knowing thereof, to wit, Abner the son of Ner, captain of the host of Israel, and Amasa the son of Jether, captain of the host of Judah."*

It is clear that Solomon knew the exact details of the crimes of Joab. He gave the complete indictment to Benaiah and to all present in his court. Some may have heard of these horrific crimes for the first time at this point, but Solomon was wise to take advantage of the moment and present the clear case of the need to use capital punishment on Joab. Over the years of warfare, Joab had become a killing machine, and it seems there is such a man in every dynasty. David did not order such executions, as Solomon is stating in the case of his cousins Abner and Amasa. Not only did David not order it, he was shocked at the brutality Joab manifested. There is always a payday someday, and this is Joab's.

1 Kings 2:33, *"Their blood shall therefore return upon the head of Joab, and upon the head of his seed for ever: but upon David, and upon his seed, and upon his house, and upon his throne, shall there be peace for ever from the LORD."*

Solomon concludes his verdict for Joab by what Lightfoot calls reversing any curses or spiritual entanglements that may have come on David or his house, because of his allowing Joab to continue in his office after these crimes were committed. It seems Solomon loved his father very much but was also aware of the problem he had in disciplining his sons and his nephews alike. Solomon declared that the shedding of innocent blood would rest upon Joab and his own house, while the house of David would be completely free.

So Benaiah went back to the tabernacle and executed Joab and buried him on his own land. Then Solomon publicly inserted Benaiah as the captain of the host in the place of Joab. Solomon continues cleaning house by installing Zadok as the single high priest, which was a long needed corrective work. Every revival is preceded by the correcting of the priesthood, and the Zadok priesthood had been promised a perpetual priesthood connected with David. Zadok is the faithful priest mentioned in 1 Samuel 2:35, *"And I will raise me up a faithful priest, that shall do according to that which is in mine heart and in my mind: and I will build him a sure house; and he shall walk before mine anointed forever."* This is the reason you will see the sons of Zadok to be the only priests allowed to work at the altar in the millennium (Ezekiel 40:46).

Now Solomon calls for the perfidious Shimei and gives him more time to live, with specific instructions to not leave the city of Jerusalem. It seems that Solomon wanted to allow Shimei to live because of the oath David had made to him. Possibly he considers Shimei as a matter of house arrest by not allowing him to leave the city and was in need of time to consider the matter more. It is not clear, but this is why Wesley considers David's instruction to kill Shimei a sin, and Solomon is willing to disobey David. Nevertheless, Solomon made it clear that if Shimei left the city, he would be put to death. Shimei followed Solomon's instructions for many days but finally left the city for a domestic matter, and when he was caught he was brought before Solomon.

1 Kings 2:44, *"The king said moreover to Shimei, Thou knowest all the wickedness which thine heart is privy to, that thou didst to David my father: therefore the LORD shall return thy wickedness upon thine own head";*

Solomon makes it clear to Shimei that he was all along worthy of death because of the wickedness of his own heart. Solomon is referring to the fact that in all of the time he had allotted Shimei the space to repent, he had not done so. This verse is one that teaches us how David had taught the royal family the power of repentance before the God of heaven who was ever willing to show His hand of mercy. Solomon would keep his word to Shimei and execute him.

1 Kings 2:45, *"And king Solomon shall be blessed, and the throne of David shall be established before the LORD for ever."*

Just as he did in the execution of Joab, Solomon proclaims a blessing on the house of David before executing Shimei. This seems to be a very important declaration for Solomon who is making these types of decisions for the first time in his life. In this case Solomon had told Shimei exactly what would happen if he left Jerusalem. This was well known by the house of Saul. However in both the case of Shimei and in the case of Joab, there was a possibility of repercussion. With Joab, Solomon ran the risk of inciting a military uprising; but with Shimei, he ran the risk of a major problem with the house of Saul. The Benjamites were still somewhat unsettled by the Judahites and their cool treatment of their interests. These two executions being done with such wisdom really fortified Solomon's kingship and thus David's dynasty.

1 Kings 3:1, *"And Solomon made affinity with Pharaoh king of Egypt, and took Pharaoh's daughter, and brought her into the city of David, until he had made an end of building his own house, and the house of the LORD, and the wall of Jerusalem round about."*

Now before Solomon asks for the divine wisdom, he shows how greatly he is in need of it. He makes two monumental mistakes in the first two verses of this chapter. 1) He marries Pharoah's daughter and brings her into the city of David. David would take a wife only in accordance with Deuteronomy 21:10-13, *"When thou goest forth to war against thine enemies, and the LORD thy God hath delivered them into thine hands, and thou hast taken them captive, And seest among the captives a beautiful woman, and hast a desire unto her, that thou wouldest have her to thy wife; Then thou shalt bring her home to thine house; and she shall shave her head, and pare her nails; And she shall put the raiment of her captivity from off her, and shall remain in thine house, and bewail her father and her mother a full month: and after that thou shalt go in unto her, and be her husband, and she shall be thy wife."*

Solomon had no war with Egypt and seemingly only married her to promote his status as a nation. 2) Solomon allows the sacrifices again in the high places. The sacrifices in the high places were not heathen sacrifices or idolatry. They were offered there for convenience because of the situation of the wilderness tabernacle and the Temple not being built yet. This is not listed as a sin of Solomon by most people, but it is definitely a mistake.

1 Kings 3:3, *"And Solomon loved the LORD, walking in the statutes of David his father: only he sacrificed and burnt incense in high places."*

Solomon is accredited with walking in the statutes of David. This very wording seems forward to some, considering the many moral failures of David. We must remember his sins only for our own admonition as to the major price that sin and failure costs. We must not remember David's sins to hold against him. God forgave him; we must not condemn him. David never had an idol. David loved the commandments of God as much as His promises. David went into deep contrition and repentance before God in his worship, as well as his prayers. The statutes here being mentioned are the very tenants of the Levitical law. Solomon loved the sacrificial system just as David did. It is because of his love for the offerings and desire to please the Lord with a sweet smelling savor that God appears to Solomon.

1 Kings 3:6, *"And Solomon said, Thou hast shewed unto thy servant David my father great mercy, according as he walked before thee in truth, and in righteousness, and in uprightness of heart with thee; and thou hast kept for him this great kindness, that thou hast given him a son to sit on his throne, as it is this day."*

Solomon is correlating the dynasty of David his father with the mercy of God. There was more than one occasion in which David's failure called for the death penalty. God, however, heard David's cry for mercy, saw his deep repentance and contrition, and spared him. Solomon is not saying that David was granted blessing because he walked in integrity. He is saying that David's heart was an open book before the Lord, and that David was a man after God's heart by allowing the Lord to break his heart. David loved the Lord, and Solomon knew that, as well as all of his mighty men.

Josephus submits a historical account of one of those mighty men writing about the influence David's prayer life and worship life had upon all his soldiers. He said when they fought with David it was as though they fought in a cloud of blessing. Solomon is here realizing that he has that mantle, and those under him would experience what those under David experienced. Solomon knew it was the grace and kindness of God that had done this work.

1 Kings 3:7, *"And now, O LORD my God, thou hast made thy servant king instead of David my father: and I am but a little child: I know not how to go out or come in."*

Solomon continues his prayer and petition by fully acknowledging that he is king in the place of and representing his father David. This in itself is more than humility, although Solomon is also displaying humility by telling the Lord he doesn't know how to do this. Solomon is actually confessing the awesomeness of his position, being the one God chose to continue the dynasty of David. Solomon knew the prophetic word to David was that the house of David would be perpetual. Therefore he wisely connected himself to the perpetual blessing.

Solomon then begins to acknowledge God's love for his people Israel and asks for wisdom to properly guide them. This pleases the Lord because Solomon, like his father, tapped into the very things dear to God's heart. God granted Solomon's request for wisdom and also gave Solomon all of the things he could have asked for but didn't.

1 Kings 3:14, *"And if thou wilt walk in my ways, to keep my statutes and my commandments, as thy father David did walk, then I will lengthen thy days."*

The Lord also gave Solomon a warning and an incentive wrapped in one. He admonished Solomon to continue in the path of David's walk before Him and He would grant him a long life. After this experience Solomon awoke from his dream, or trance as some call it, and began to worship the Lord and offer sacrifices. Solomon called a feast and the people were blessed. The wisdom that God gave Solomon begins to manifest to the people in such a way that the people feared or reverenced Solomon because they knew the anointing of God was upon him.

1 Kings 5:1, *"And Hiram king of Tyre sent his servants unto Solomon; for he had heard that they had anointed him king in the room of his father: for Hiram was ever a lover of David."*

It seems that Hiram of Tyre was more or less sending his servants to congratulate Solomon, the new king of Israel, and especially because of the fact Solomon was so faithful to his father David, for whom Hiram had such love and respect. This is the same Hiram that built the palace for David (2 Samuel 5:11). It has been widely believed by most that Hiram was not only a lover of David but a strong proselyte to Judaism. He rejoiced for the opportunity to invest in the furtherance of the Kingdom of the God of Israel by building David a palace. Solomon was well aware of Hiram's heart and sent him a message through his servants. David loved his friends well and was very loyal to them; therefore, Solomon reaped the benefit of the reciprocal friendship of his father's friends.

1 Kings 5:3, *"Thou knowest how that David my father could not build an house unto the name of the LORD his God for the wars which were about him on every side, until the LORD put them under the soles of his feet."*

In Solomon's message to Hiram, he explains how his Father David couldn't build the Temple because of the many wars. But actually Solomon is being gracious in explaining it in this manner. The account in 1 Chronicles 22:8 is a bit more revealing, *"But the word of the LORD came to me, saying, Thou hast shed blood abundantly, and hast made great wars: thou shalt not build an house unto my name, because thou hast shed much blood upon the earth in my sight."*

Many believe this is referring to the many raids David made on the neighbors of Israel while he was in Ziklag under the authority of King Achish for those fourteen months (1 Samuel 27:7). These raids were against the enemies of Israel, but there was no war at the time and there was no direction from the Lord for such raids. Solomon acknowledges that there is now peace in the land as Hiram is so full aware of.

1 Kings 5:5. *"And, behold, I purpose to build an house unto the name of the LORD my God, as the LORD spake unto David my father, saying, Thy son, whom I will set upon thy throne in thy room, he shall build an house unto my name."*

Solomon tells Hiram of his plan and purpose to build the Temple. Wisely, Solomon makes sure that Hiram understands that this assignment is the will and last desire of his father and Hiram's friend David. Solomon also wanted Hiram to know that the prophetic word of the Lord had appointed him to build this Temple. After making his case so well, Solomon makes his bold request for the help of Hiram although he promises to pay them their named price. He then commends them for their great skills.

1 Kings 5:7, *"And it came to pass, when Hiram heard the words of Solomon, that he rejoiced greatly, and said, Blessed be the LORD this day, which hath given unto David a wise son over this great people."*

Hiram sent Solomon back a message that reveals the power and anointing that David carried will be evident in the dynasty of Solomon. Hiram rejoiced that he was asked to participate in the building program and cordially committed to the assignment. He told Solomon just how and where he would deliver the cedar and fir trees. Hiram asked for food in return, which Solomon gave to him abundantly each year. This was the beginning of a long term covenant between Solomon and Hiram that was grounded on the merits of David. Solomon is now building his labor force and getting the timber and stones ready to erect the Temple. David had prepared all of the brass, silver, and gold needed, but his preparation for the timber and labor was done through his relationship with others.

Solomon, through the wisdom God gave to him, was a master organizer and organized his great work force with amazing gravity needed for the huge task of building the Temple. For four years Solomon gathered and prepared materials, and in the fourth year his servants and the servants of Hiram began to build what would be the most extravagant Temple in the world at that time in history

1 Kings 6:12, *"Concerning this house which thou art in building, if thou wilt walk in my statutes, and execute my judgments, and keep all my commandments to walk in them; then will I perform my word with thee, which I spake unto David thy father":*

The Lord speaks to Solomon concerning the conditions of His blessing. Whether through a prophet or to him directly, we do not know, but God made it clear to Solomon that no matter how strong the building is, it could be destroyed through immorality. This warning seemed to come after the foundation was built but right before a lot of the structure was raised. The key to this warning from the Lord is the fact that the conditional order was tied to a former word that was given to David. This proves that the very promise that God gave David concerning Solomon was certainly conditional. This was to caution Solomon to build with the fear of God in his heart and with great caution to keep the motive of his father. He did build the Temple in that manner.

The scripture abundantly proves that David lived and died to finish the Temple. Even though he was not able to do it himself, he did everything he possible could. When a leader shows as much devotion for the Lord's work as David did, those around him and following him will reverence the vision as well. 1 Kings 6:14, *"So Solomon built the house, and finished it."* This took seven years, and six more years to build Solomon's house. Then he built a house for Pharaoh's daughter, all of which are aptly described.

1 Kings 7:51, *"So was ended all the work that king Solomon made for the house of the LORD. And Solomon brought in the things which David his father had dedicated; even the silver, and the gold, and the vessels, did he put among the treasures of the house of the LORD."*

Solomon has finished the construction and now is ready to bring in the things David had dedicated to the Lord. These are the spoils of war for the most part. Every time David conquered a nation, he took their gold silver and brass and dedicated it to the Lord. No one has ever estimated the wealth David had and there is not much talk about it. David's writings never indicate that he had any affection in his heart for wealth. Solomon's wealth is spoken of in several places, but that wealth came from David mostly, and then the taxation of the people of the nations that were under the Jewish rule. The important thing here is that the precious jewels and metals were dedicated to the Lord by the man after God's heart, and Solomon reverenced it.

1 Kings 8:1, *"Then Solomon assembled the elders of Israel, and all the heads of the tribes, the chief of the fathers of the children of Israel, unto king Solomon in Jerusalem, that they might bring up the ark of the covenant of the LORD out of the city of David, which is Zion."*

The Ark had been resting in the tabernacle David had built on Zion in the south-west part of Jerusalem, an elevation in the east part of the city. It now was ready to be moved to the new Temple setting in what is now the east part of the city on Mount Moriah. David was not there to behold this great event, but he did see it in the Spirit and much of his life had been poured into the preparation of it. Solomon was well aware of that and called all of the leaders of Israel together for this great event. There has never been an event in any other nation to top this happening. Yet Israel has had an event even greater, and that was the triumphant entry of Christ to Jerusalem on the Sunday called Palm Sunday, the week of His crucifixion. Yet that shall be overshadowed when Jesus returns and his foot touches the Mount of Olives and He once again enters the City of David.

Solomon carefully moved the Ark in priestly order, not making the mistake his father had made the first time he attempted to move it to Jerusalem. The priests sacrificed an innumerable number of animals as they moved the Ark. The priest took the Ark into the Holy Place and set it there in the place so carefully prepared for it. When the priests came out of the Holy Place, a cloud of tangible glory from God filled the whole Temple. Even the priests, who were required to stand, could not do so because of the glory. This supernatural event brought a holy hush on all that was present, and all of the people realized that God had taken his abode in the Temple that was built for Him. If it is truly built for Him, He will certainly fill it. Solomon broke the silence with deep reverent and stirring words then blessed the congregation again before he continued speaking by acknowledging the Word of the Lord to his father David. The congregation stood!

1 Kings 8:15, "*And he said, Blessed be the LORD God of Israel, which spake with his mouth unto David my father, and hath with his hand fulfilled it, saying,*"

Solomon wisely and completely connects his address before the people of Israel to the Davidic covenant. He blesses God and acknowledges Him as the Lord God and confirms what God had spoken by His own mouth to David. Solomon's message here is one of the most anointed ever to come from a leader to his people. His knowledge of the scripture and his proper application of the Word of God to David is utterly amazing.

1 Kings 8:16, "*Since the day that I brought forth my people Israel out of Egypt, I chose no city out of all the tribes of Israel to build an house, that my name might be therein; but I chose David to be over my people Israel.*"

Solomon is explaining the unique relationship David had with the Lord concerning the building of the Temple and how it was that he was allowed to build it in Jerusalem. Solomon is saying that God never chose a city for the Temple to be built in until he chose David to be King. This is very important in the matter of the Davidic covenant. Samuel knew that the people wanted a king like other nations, and he knew that the Lord was not against their having a king, but God would not bless a king that was like the other nations had. Samuel, by protest, anointed Saul of the tribe of Benjamin, but he knew there was no kingly order in Benjamin. Samuel lived long enough to have the privilege to anoint the right king, David.

So it is with the temple of God. God is more interested in building a royal priesthood and peculiar people than a temple. But when David built that tent tabernacle for the Ark and constituted twenty four/seven worship and sacrifice, God saw that it was good and blessed David to gather goods and prepare for the building of the Temple. David was certainly not a king like the kings of other nations, and he did not want to build the Temple like the temples of other nations, who built extravagant buildings in order to advance the status of their nation on the earth. David did not want the Temple to be built for the same reasons kings of other nations wanted to build. David wanted to advance extravagant worship to the true and living God. The dedication of this Temple is about a man honoring God, and God honoring the desires of a man whom He called a man after His own heart.

1 Kings 8:17, *"And it was in the heart of David my father to build an house for the name of the LORD God of Israel."*

Whatever is in the heart of a leader will sooner or later be manifest to his people. Solomon is rehearsing in the ears of all of the people what they already know, that David had it in his heart to build the Temple. He diligently prepared for it. He prayed for it. He had shared his vision concerning it. Yet the Lord still would not let him build it himself. This David submitted to and we can find not one word of complaint about it from David's pen.

1 Kings 8:18, *"And the LORD said unto David my father, Whereas it was in thine heart to build an house unto my name, thou didst well that it was in thine heart."*

Solomon is telling the congregation of Israel something David must have told him during those six months of mentoring Solomon before he died. We don't find the account of this word being given him by a prophet. The Lord must have spoken to David in his prayer time and told him even though he would not be permitted to build the Temple, it is good that he has a desire to do so. This is a hidden jewel in the life of David and a display of that special affection David had for his God and his God had for him. This point of Solomon's address was especially moving to his hearers because David had taught them to love the Lord.

1 Kings 8:20, *"And the LORD hath performed his word that he spake, and I am risen up in the room of David my father, and sit on the throne of Israel, as the LORD promised, and have built an house for the name of the LORD God of Israel."*

Solomon was making it clear that this dedication of the Temple was a result of what David had in his heart to do, and that he, Solomon, was simply raised up in his place to perform it. This is a display of humility and great respect for the Lord's love for David. Great leaders are wise to tap into the Lord's affection for someone belonging to that great cloud of witnesses. Solomon built the Temple for God in the name of (or the room of) David. David, being the type of Jesus, lived on through those he trained and raised up.

The finishing of the Temple and the dedication of it on this day is also a beautiful picture of the father-son order. A father in the faith knows that what he cannot accomplish for one reason or the other, his sons can. Solomon continues his speech to the people and prayer to the God of Abraham, Isaac, and Jacob. Lightfoot calls Solomon an intercessor when he proceeds to remind the Lord of his covenant with David and spreads out his hand before the Lord at the altar. Intercessor, yes, for he dedicates the mercy seat and sees that it is set in place by the priests.

1 Kings 8:24, "*Who hast kept with thy servant David my father that thou promisedst him: thou spakest also with thy mouth, and hast fulfilled it with thine hand, as it is this day.*"

Reminding the Lord of a promise he made to your father in behalf of the congregation is also intercessional. Solomon did this with the utmost faith and assurance, because he knew how the Lord loved David. Solomon is referring to the physical Temple before them that had just been completed, but he is also tapping into the house David saw in the Spirit at the threshing floor of Ornan (1 Chronicles 22:1). This is beginning to move into the messianic realm, and Solomon himself will soon see the fire come down from heaven.

1 Kings 8:25, "*Therefore now, LORD God of Israel, keep with thy servant David my father that thou promisedst him, saying, There shall not fail thee a man in my sight to sit on the throne of Israel; so that thy children take heed to their way, that they walk before me as thou hast walked before me.*"

Whitby charges Solomon with self-projection in this verse, but how could this be when Solomon simply acknowledges that he is the one sitting on the throne of his father, and that only by condition. Solomon is more or less preaching to himself and the children of Israel instead of projecting himself before them. At this point in the life of Solomon, he is very humble and quite overwhelmed at his position entrusted to him by the Lord and his father David. He is looking at his position more as responsibility than authority. This was also the way David beheld his office of king.

1 Kings 8:26, "*And now, O God of Israel, let thy word, I pray thee, be verified, which thou spakest unto thy servant David my father.*"

This is a pivotal point in Solomon prayer. He asks the Lord to now verify his promise to David but yet is overwhelmed and anxiously expectant what might happen next. There is evidence that the more Solomon prayed, the deeper he got into the will and ways of God. Lightfoot declared that the longer Solomon stayed on his knees at the altar, the more there became an ever increasing knowledge that a great manifestation was very eminent. Solomon prays and acknowledges the great benefit and responsibility of having the manifest presence of God in the Temple they have built.

David probably told Solomon over and over again about entertaining the presence of God. Some theologians seem to say that this great mature prayer of Solomon was a result of the divine wisdom that was given to him from the Lord. While this is true, we must not forget the six months David poured into him the things of God concerning worship. This prayer is filled with proof that David had properly transferred to Solomon the great attribute of not only loving God's commandments as much as his promises, but also the great work of contrite repentance from the heart.

Solomon concludes his prayer by acknowledging the glory of God which had been ordained of old and was present when they, as a nation, were brought out of Israel. This was especially pleasing to the Lord, for Solomon was now getting very close to seeing the fire fall from heaven to consume the sacrifice, which indicated God's total pleasure with his supplication.

Solomon finishes his prayer and rises up from his knees on which he had been positioned with his hands spread before the Lord. Solomon then stands up and blesses the congregation with a loud voice by declaring that there has not failed one word of everything God had ever promised to Israel. He declares that this goodness and greatness of God to His people ought to be an adequate incentive to serve Him with all of their hearts. He wisely calls on the congregation to remember this day for the rest of their lives so that all of the world would know that the Lord God was the God of Israel. Like David, Solomon wanted to see the Lord get glory from Israel, and all of the nations of the earth through Israel.

Solomon and all of Israel then began fourteen days of sacrificing thousands and thousands of burnt offerings and having a great feast unto the Lord.

1 Kings 8:66, "*On the eighth day he sent the people away: and they blessed the king, and went unto their tents joyful and glad of heart for all the goodness that the LORD had done for David his servant, and for Israel his people.*"

We can see clearly from this verse how the people, as well as Solomon, connected the supreme bliss of the whole dedication ceremony and feast to the covenant the Lord made with David. They went away so very fulfilled, knowing what the Lord had done for David. That would be almost a strange way of perceiving the blessing of God except for the established prophetic word concerning the house of David. The blessing of God on one man can pass from generation to generation just as a curse can also pass from generation to generation.

After the completion of the dedication and the feast, Solomon has yet another visitation from the Lord who establishes again the conditions of the Davidic Covenant.

1 Kings 9:4, *"And if thou wilt walk before me, as David thy father walked, in integrity of heart, and in uprightness, to do according to all that I have commanded thee, and wilt keep my statutes and my judgments"*:

Now one must remember that this is the Lord's description of David as He speaks to Solomon. *David thy father walked, in integrity of heart, and in uprightness.* How could the Lord speak those words over one who had so much moral failure in his life? Religions of men have no answer for such. Neither shall they ever have. This is the pure mercy of God and the absolute forgiveness of sin, as well as proof that God will not remember their sins. Hebrews 8:12, *"For I will be merciful to their unrighteousness, and their sins and their iniquities will I remember no more."*

This also is ample proof that David walked in the New Covenant while living in the Old Testament, just as Abraham did. How foolish would it be to use this verse to excuse the sin of David as though it did not happen? David suffered greatly from the repercussions of his sins, but it is the mercy of God that forgave them and forgot them. Solomon understands exactly what the Lord is saying to him in this visitation. He knows he is to keep His statutes and commandments. Solomon knows that if he fails to do so, he will suffer for his sin just like David his father did.

1 Kings 9:5, *"Then I will establish the throne of thy kingdom upon Israel for ever, as I promised to David thy father, saying, There shall not fail thee a man upon the throne of Israel."*

The Lord continues to give Solomon conditional warnings tied to the covenant He had made with David. Lightfoot declares that this is so with any nation, and that the longevity of a nation founded by the hand and will of God is directly dependent upon the obedience that nation has to God. The Lord plainly tells Solomon that the promise is good and valid, but if he turns from following the Lord to serve other gods, he will be severely judged.

1 Kings 9:24, *"But Pharaoh's daughter came up out of the city of David unto her house which Solomon had built for her: then did he build Millo."*

Solomon had married the daughter of Pharaoh after the custom of the heathen, which was a terrible mistake. He knew better, and according to the account in Chronicles, he understood the mistake and related it to the house of David and David's love for the Ark of God. 2 Chronicles

8:11, *"And Solomon brought up the daughter of Pharaoh out of the city of David unto the house that he had built for her: for he said, My wife shall not dwell in the house of David king of Israel, because the places are holy, whereunto the ark of the LORD hath come."*

Many scholars consider this verse to be the early clue of Solomon's willing and knowledgeable backsliding. Solomon must have had a great deal of conviction on the matter of Pharaoh's daughter, for he moved her to the city of David, but his heart wouldn't let her stay there. She was no doubt an idolater. Solomon later married the daughters of many other wicked kings and his backsliding continued.

I Kings 11:4, *"For it came to pass, when Solomon was old, that his wives turned away his heart after other gods: and his heart was not perfect with the LORD his God, as was the heart of David his father."*

This verse will reveal to us that in most cases when David is referred to as being perfect, it is in the matter of idolatry. David never had an idol nor did he tolerate idolatry in any form. No other king of Israel or Judah passed that test completely. Solomon started out that way, but his love for women caused him to tolerate and finally embrace the idolatry they brought with them into the marriage. Calumet tells us that David made a Jewish proselyte out of every relationship he maintained. This would have included his wives and concubines.

1 Kings 11:6, *"And Solomon did evil in the sight of the LORD, and went not fully after the LORD, as did David his father."*

So finally Solomon begins the practice of idolatry. He did not quit being a Jew, but he added the worship of idols to his Judaism to please his wives. This David did not do, as the scripture clearly records the purity of David from idolatry. But the partaking of idolatry by the chosen son, chosen to extend the dynasty of David, is also clear in the scripture. But how could he extend the perfect with the imperfect? Just as God blessed Solomon for his father David's sake, He will now blast him for his father David's sake. Solomon would have no doubt been destroyed immediately except for the tender mercies of David!

1 Kings 11:12, *"Notwithstanding in thy days I will not do it for David thy father's sake: but I will rend it out of the hand of thy son."*

The Lord stopped short of ripping the kingdom out of Solomon's hand for the sake of David. We see from this that the blessing on Solomon's life was connected to the Davidic covenant, and the responsibility to walk out the covenant was also connected. When Solomon gave himself to idolatry and refused to take correction, God judged him, but prolonged the sentence until after he died. Solomon knew then that David's freedom from all idolatry brought the blessing on his house, and his engagement in idolatry brought destruction on his son's house.

1 Kings 11:13, *"Howbeit I will not rend away all the kingdom; but will give one tribe to thy son for David my servant's sake, and for Jerusalem's sake which I have chosen."*

The Lord continues to reveal His path of punishment on the house of Solomon, but declares to Solomon that He will allow one tribe in the dynasty of David to remain in Jerusalem. Of course this is the tribe of Judah. The power of the promise God made to David is seen through the restraint the Lord shows in ripping the kingdom out of Solomon's hand. The Lord will allow a descendant of David to remain on the throne in Jerusalem as long as there is one ounce of compliance in the heart of that king.

We must remember that each time the Lord gave the promise to David, there was a conditional order spelled out. Each time David rehearsed the promise in the ears of people, he included the conditional order. Solomon himself was surely warned that the promise he inherited was also conditional upon his remaining free from idolatry. Now Solomon will begin to see his adversaries being stirred up by the Lord Himself. We read in verse 14, *"And the LORD stirred up an adversary unto Solomon, Hadad the Edomite"*: This was just the beginning!

1 Kings 11:15, *"For it came to pass, when David was in Edom, and Joab the captain of the host was gone up to bury the slain, after he had smitten every male in Edom"*;

The Lord began the process of ripping the kingdom away from the son of Solomon even while Solomon was yet alive. From the time he received the sentence and indictment, the Lord began to lift His hand of protection off of the dynasty of Solomon. He began by stirring up an adversary still smarting from the sound defeat of the Davidic dynasty, Hadad the Edomite who was of the king's seed in Edom. Hadad began to ponder on the time when David conquered the land and Joab, his bloody captain, executed the male population, turning it into a matriarchal society. Hadad began to remember his exile from his own people and all of the things he had suffered under David's men. It should be noted that this is a form of judgment often found in the Bible. When God's covenant people begin to serve other gods, God will stir up their enemies against them to chastise them.

1 Kings 11:21, "*And when Hadad heard in Egypt that David slept with his fathers, and that Joab the captain of the host was dead, Hadad said to Pharaoh, Let me depart, that I may go to mine own country.*"

Hadad is stirred up against Solomon, and then he finds out that David is dead, as well as Joab. So Hadad asks permission of Pharaoh to depart from Egypt, where he had been in exile, and return to the land of the Edomites. Reluctantly Pharaoh grants him leave, and Hadad goes to his land to form an enemy to Israel. Then the Lord stirs up another former enemy through one Rezon, a Syrian.

One might notice the tender way the scripture speaks of David's death compared to the wicked and unrepentant Joab. David slept with his fathers but Joab is dead!

1 Kings 11:24, "*And he gathered men unto him, and became captain over a band, when David slew them of Zobah: and they went to Damascus, and dwelt therein, and reigned in Damascus.*"

This verse is part of the report explaining how Rezon connected his vengeance for David to Solomon. David had conquered these Syrians led by Hadadezer king of Zobah, and Rezon was not subdued in the matter but seemed to be waiting for the opportunity to come against Israel. Solomon's sin afforded that opportunity. It is plain to see that the Lord is allowing these kings who are full of vengeance to come against Israel but not allowing everything to transpire until Solomon's death. This is for David's sake!

1 Kings 11:27, "*And this was the cause that he lifted up his hand against the king: Solomon built Millo, and repaired the breaches of the city of David his father.*"

Now even Jeroboam is rising up against Solomon. This wicked man will be the very vessel that is allowed of God to aggravate Solomon, split Israel, lead a civil war, and inspire the worship of the golden calf. Solomon had seen the powerful ability of Jeroboam to recruit and motivate, and tried to make him a leader under him but to no avail. Even in this, Solomon is seen as beginning to diminish. This is all because of the wicked idolatry of Solomon who was often warned by the Lord and his father David.

1 Kings 11:32, "*(But he shall have one tribe for my servant David's sake, and for Jerusalem's sake, the city which I have chosen out of all the tribes of Israel):*"

The prophet Ahijah illustrated to Jeroboam how many tribes of Israel he would rule by tearing his outer clothing into pieces and giving Jeroboam ten pieces. Solomon must have known of this and still didn't repent of his wholesale idolatry. The prophecy was that for David's sake He would leave one tribe in the hands of Solomon and his son after him. However, there are twelve tribes, and Ahijah declares that Jeroboam will rule ten tribes. Some scholars interpret this verse to mean there is one tribe spared for David's sake and one for Jerusalem's sake, which would make two tribes with Rehoboam the son of Solomon and ten tribes with Jeroboam.

When the split finally did occur there, were actually nine and one half tribes with Jeroboam and two and one half with Rehoboam which fulfills all of the prophetic words concerning this matter. Verse 36 of this chapter confirms that one tribe is given for God's name in Jerusalem. Lightfoot declares one tribe for God's name and one tribe for David's name. In fact in Jerusalem there will be a throne in the millennium for the Lord Jesus who is God in the flesh and the King of Kings. There will also be a throne for David, raised from the dead as king of Israel (Jeremiah 30:9).

1 Kings 11:33," *Because that they have forsaken me, and have worshipped Ashtoreth the goddess of the Zidonians, Chemosh the god of the Moabites, and Milcom the god of the children of Ammon, and have not walked in my ways, to do that which is right in mine eyes, and to keep my statutes and my judgments, as did David his father."*

Again the word condemns the idolatry of Solomon and commends the sterling record of David in that realm. David was such a lover of the law of God that even though he failed in the six commandments concerning men, he was perfect in the first four commandments which concern God. One theologian reported David's perfection in this manner, "He broke the last six commandments and was forgiven leaving him perfect in the sight of God and a perfect record concerning the first four."

1 Kings 11:34, *"Howbeit I will not take the whole kingdom out of his hand: but I will make him prince all the days of his life for David my servant's sake, whom I chose, because he kept my commandments and my statutes":*

This shows God's love again for David by not taking the whole kingdom from Solomon. This also shows exactly why every one of the enemies of Israel that had been stirred up against Solomon could only position themselves against Israel, but not really attack Israel until Solomon had passed away.

1 Kings 11:36, *"And unto his son will I give one tribe, that David my servant may have a light alway before me in Jerusalem, the city which I have chosen me to put my name there."*

Once again this is a reference to the coming Messiah and the tribe of Judah. Psalm 132:17 says, *"There will I make the horn of David to bud: I have ordained a lamp for mine anointed."* The prophets and the law demanded the tribe of Judah to produce the Messiah and the Lord is protecting His word by sustaining this tribe. Even though Solomon deserved to be utterly destroyed, God was looking at His promise. One must not confuse God's mercy with His sovereign protection of His spoken word. Mercy is connected with repentance, for Jesus said in Luke 13:3, *"I tell you, Nay: but, except ye repent, ye shall all likewise perish."*

Solomon showed no sign of genuine repentance. The mercy God showed was for David, and the giving of one tribe to his son was for the protection of His prophetic word concerning the Messiah. The following verse should be added to all of the other messianic verses in the scripture, 1 Kings 11:37, *"And I will take thee, and thou shalt reign according to all that thy soul desireth, and shalt be king over Israel."* For it is sure the phrase *And I will take thee* is not referring to Solomon but his posterity which includes the Messiah but does not exclude all of the lineage until He comes.

1 Kings 11:38, *"And it shall be, if thou wilt hearken unto all that I command thee, and wilt walk in my ways, and do that is right in my sight, to keep my statutes and my commandments, as David my servant did; that I will be with thee, and build thee a sure house, as I built for David, and will give Israel unto thee."*

It is true that Jeroboam is receiving the prophetic word to permit him to take ten tribes of Israel. But we must not conclude here that Jeroboam is receiving the warning given to the seed of the tribe of Judah, for he is not of the tribe of Judah, and he is not of a royal family. Jeroboam is the vessel God has raised up to judge the nation of Israel. Yet, the protected tribe of Judah will continue to have condition to the promise. David well understood this concept and taught it to the nation of Israel. The Word of the Lord confirms again and again that the promise to the house of David is conditional. This fact is a great disappointment to those who present promise without condition and use God's grace to frustrate His righteousness and His justice.

1 Kings 11:39, *"And I will for this afflict the seed of David, but not for ever."*

Now the Lord is again allowing Jeroboam to understand that even the affliction on Rehoboam the son of Solomon will not continue through generation after generation. We find full proof of this later when Abijah and the people with Judah defeat the armies of the nine and one half tribes following Jeroboam, with the largest slaughter of humanity that has ever occurred in one day, even until this very day. Five hundred thousand men died in one day of the men of Jeroboam, and not one of the people of Judah. The record is clear in 2 Chronicles 13.

1 Kings 11:43, *"And Solomon slept with his fathers, and was buried in the city of David his father: and Rehoboam his son reigned in his stead."*

Solomon is now dead and buried in the city of David. Now the rending of the kingdom will begin in full. Rehoboam sends for the people to come and make him king in Shechem, but some of the people sent for Jeroboam, who had run to Egypt after Solomon tried to kill him. Jeroboam and many from Israel approach Rehoboam and request relief from the heavy burdens that Solomon had laid upon them. Before Solomon backslid, he held no Jews to heavy taxation or slavery, but his backsliding caused him to not only worship idols but also to lose compassion for the people he was supposed to serve.

Rehoboam asks advice, and instead of listening to the old people, he listens to the young people and basically fell right into the open jaws of Jeroboam, who was waiting to swallow up the tribes. Rehoboam, upon the advice of the young people, promised to make the burden upon the people much harder than they already endured. This was the working out of the prophetic word of the Lord concerning Solomon's son and the judgment.

1 King 12:16, *"So when all Israel saw that the king hearkened not unto them, the people answered the king, saying, What portion have we in David? neither have we inheritance in the son of Jesse: to your tents, O Israel: now see to thine own house, David. So Israel departed unto their tents."*

When Rehoboam, Solomon's son, delivered his drastic news of even more taxation and slavery, the people of Israel rebelled and killed the tax officer Adorom. The people of Israel made it clear that they had no part in David the son of Jesse. It should be noted here that in the elders of Israel's final words, they did not mention either Rehoboam or Solomon but David and Jesse. This is an indicator of 1) The deep divide between Judah and the other tribes. 2) The anointing on David as a father in Israel to hold together the tribes. 3) The destruction of idolatry.

Rehoboam had to flee for his life in his chariot back to Jerusalem. David's dynasty he had built by the power of the Lord's anointing is now split by the power of the Lord's judgment.

1 Kings 12:19, *"So Israel rebelled against the house of David unto this day."*

The defection of Israel from the house of David is rightly called rebellion here even though it is a judgment for Solomon's sin. The people had forgotten so quickly how the tribe of Judah had fought and gained the freedom from wars they had enjoyed for over forty years. It is never right to do wrong. We can no more justify these rebels than we can justify Pilate for crucifying Jesus. The crucifixion was prophesied in Psalm twenty two by David himself, yet Pilate is guilty of high treason against the son of God!

1 Kings 12:20, *"And it came to pass, when all Israel heard that Jeroboam was come again, that they sent and called him unto the congregation, and made him king over all Israel: there was none that followed the house of David, but the tribe of Judah only."*

The children of Israel have proven they were driven by a rebellious spirit. They had absolutely no right to make a king out of Jeroboam and they had no respect to the Word of the Lord which declared that the scepter would not depart from Judah (Genesis 49:10). Had they forgotten so soon the results of having a king from another tribe? Ten tribes here departed from Rehoboam, and no doubt many of those from Benjamin; however, there is sufficient proof that many of those of Benjamin sided with the tribe of Judah. 2 Chronicles 11:12, *"And in every several city he put shields and spears, and made them exceeding strong, having Judah and Benjamin on his side."*

While it is true that only one tribe fully followed Judah, Benjamin and large parts of the half tribes followed Rehoboam as well. The scripture here says no other tribe followed Judah, which is to be interpreted as no entire tribe. However the scripture makes it clear here that these who are following Rehoboam are really following the house of David. Lightfoot declares them to be a remnant with the revelation that the house of the Messiah is coming through the posterity of David!

Rehoboam utilizes the men of Benjamin and organizes an army to fight against Israel. He would no doubt have engaged in a civil war right then but the Lord sent the prophet to tell Rehoboam not to fight against Israel because this whole thing was the judgment of God.

1 Kings 12:26, *"And Jeroboam said in his heart, Now shall the kingdom return to the house of David":*

We can see the pride and wickedness in the heart of Jeroboam manifest here. He paid no regard to the clear word of the Lord delivered unto him concerning the people of Israel and the people of Judah in 1 Kings 11:38, *"And it shall be, if thou wilt hearken unto all that I command thee, and wilt walk in my ways, and do that is right in my sight, to keep my statutes and my commandments, as David my servant did; that I will be with thee, and build thee a sure house, as I built for David, and will give Israel unto thee."*

The Lord never told Jeroboam He would give him Judah or the house of David but Israel. There is a big difference, and Jeroboam had already been told that he would not have all of the tribes. It was the turn of events that Jeroboam thought was indicating that he would have all David had at one time. This is pure presumption on the part of Jeroboam, which will cause him national embarrassment and the loss of five hundred thousand soldiers in 2 Chronicles 13.

Jeroboam realizes the strong pull on the hearts of the people toward Jerusalem and David, so he devises a plan to keep them from coming to the Jewish worship. He made golden calves in Bethel and Dan for them to worship, as well as having a big feast, including sacrifices to Baal. Jeroboam built his own altars and turned the hearts of the people away from God.

1 Kings 13:2, *"And he cried against the altar in the word of the LORD, and said, O altar, altar, thus saith the LORD; Behold, a child shall be born unto the house of David, Josiah by name; and upon thee shall he offer the priests of the high places that burn incense upon thee, and men's bones shall be burnt upon thee."*

It is important to know that the man of God that came to cry out against the altar of Jeroboam at Bethel was from Judah, the only full tribe that Jeroboam didn't control. The man of God prophesies not only the destruction of Jeroboam's wicked idolatrous altar but also that the bones of his false prophets will be burnt upon it. This is a powerful prophecy, but an important key to the prophecy is the fact that the one God will raise up to perform this work of judgment will be of the house of David.

All throughout the history of Israel, following the life of David, we can find this prophetic confirmation that the Lord is not through with the house of David. Josiah will be born in the lineage of David to deal with this idolatry. Jeroboam was infuriated with the prophecy and stretched his hand out against the prophet, only to watch his hand wither up. Then he changed his mind and asked for prayer from the very one he was going to kill.

This demonstrates the power of the Davidic covenant in the messianic order that will always operate in the supernatural. The prophetic word here of the lineage of David has more to say than that a young man by the name of Josiah is coming along. One named Jesus, the Lion of the tribe of Judah, is coming, and He will put all of the enemies of God under His feet just like David did.

1 Kings 14:8, *"And rent the kingdom away from the house of David, and gave it thee: and yet thou hast not been as my servant David, who kept my commandments, and who followed me with all his heart, to do that only which was right in mine eyes";*

Here is a word from the Lord to the wife of Jeroboam who was sent by her husband to Ahijah because their son was sick. She disguised herself, but the prophet knew her and began to prophesy that Jeroboam was given a chance to walk before the Lord and rule ten tribes of Israel but the condition was that he had to walk before the Lord like David. Because he didn't, the prophet is telling the wife of Jeroboam that not only is the child going to die, but he will be the only one of Jeroboam's seed that will die without someone killing him. The prophet goes on to say that

Jeroboam will be judged severely for all of his idolatry. The key here is that not only did the Lord restore David, but He now uses him and his life for a measuring stick for all other kings. This is in itself truly amazing.

1 Kings 14:31, *"And Rehoboam slept with his fathers, and was buried with his fathers in the city of David. And his mother's name was Naamah an Ammonitess. And Abijam his son reigned in his stead."*

Rehoboam the son of Solomon, the son of David, didn't leave the legacy that either his father or his grandfather left. David's legacy now suffers greatly, as his offspring commits wholesale idolatry and allows sodomites to run free in the land. Rehoboam had a perpetual conflict with Jeroboam and was never able to defeat his enemies. Solomon had no war during his forty years, but because of his idolatry, his enemies were constantly positioning themselves against him, and he only escaped destruction because of mercy from God for David's sake.

David had sin and great failure, but repented in deep contrition and was forgiven and restored. He then was able to conquer every one of his enemies. How shall any man deny the biblical fact that an idolater who knows the truth but won't walk in it is unable to stand before his enemies?

1 Kings 15:3, *"And he walked in all the sins of his father, which he had done before him: and his heart was not perfect with the LORD his God, as the heart of David his father."*

Here is David's great grandson Abijam. He follows the path of his father instead of his great grandfather and walks in all of the sins that Rehoboam did. Over and over again we find God crying out for another David, one who will walk in His ways and stay free from idolatry. This is what the Lord is still seeking. He longs for one who will make the Lord the center of his life and devotion like David did. The Lord is longing for another Sweet Psalmist of Israel.

1 Kings 15:4, *"Nevertheless for David's sake did the LORD his God give him a lamp in Jerusalem, to set up his son after him, and to establish Jerusalem"*:

The Lord is allowing this wicked Abijam to remain on the throne for the sake of His promise to David. But he reigned only three years. The thing that is so important is that the lineage of David is protected and preserved for the seed of Jesse that is to come. There were several good kings in the lineage of David that honored the Lord, but none like David, until the Lion of the tribe of Judah appears again to fulfill all that was promised to David and to Israel. Therefore the spiritual warfare was heavy over this lineage to block and stop any righteous seed coming out of David's loins.

1 Kings 15:5, "Because *David did that which was right in the eyes of the LORD, and turned not aside from any thing that he commanded him all the days of his life, save only in the matter of Uriah the Hittite.*"

Again we have a confirmation of David's faithful following of the Lord in the law as well as what he was told of the Lord to do. The exception is mentioned here concerning the matter of Uriah the Hittite. In the matter of Uriah, David broke all six of the commandments that pertain to our service to the Lord. 1) He coveted Uriah's wife. 2) He stole her. 3) He lied to cover his sin with Bathsheba. 4) He had Uriah murdered. 5) He committed adultery with Bathsheba. 6) He dishonored his father and his mother with his wickedness.

All of David's other failures were directly connected to his battle with pride, but in the matter of Bathsheba he broke the commandments. This is an amazing verse concerning the life of David, and there is a warning as well as a confirmation in these words. The warning is that even the greatest of God's men can stumble and fall into the snares of their own lust. The confirmation is that God is faithful to those who are faithful to Him and will honor those who honor Him.

1 Kings 15:8, "*And Abijam slept with his fathers; and they buried him in the city of David: and Asa his son reigned in his stead.*"

Abijam was a miserable failure but was still granted the privilege of being buried in the royal graveyard of the royal lineage of King David. Now it is Asa's turn to reign on the throne of David. Sometimes very pious and holy parents produce very wicked children. Yet in this case, a very wicked father produces a very pious man. Asa's dynasty was a zealously righteous one. Maachah was actually his grandmother (1 Kings 15:2) who had probably reared him. Yet, even she was not exempt from being removed from her high position because of her idolatry. 1 Kings 15:13, "*And also Maachah his mother, even her he removed from being queen, because she had made an idol in a grove; and Asa destroyed her idol, and burnt it by the brook Kidron.*" Asa's zeal reminded the Lord of his servant in the matter of idolatry and he gained the following testimony recorded in 1 Kings 15:11.

1 Kings 15:11, "*And Asa did that which was right in the eyes of the LORD, as did David his father.*"

This is the testimony in summary of Asa. It is a powerful demonstration that there can certainly come one after David who would walk in righteousness before the Lord. The only flaw to what would be otherwise an impeccable character is that Asa did not remove the high places. Such places were erected for the Lord God of Israel, but when the Ark was brought to the tent David erected, worship in the high places ceased. However the idolatry of Solomon, Rehoboam and Abijam had all together desecrated the places and by not prohibiting the use of the high places, Asa stopped short of a thorough cleansing.

Jehoshaphat, the son of Asa, later struggled with the same issue concerning the high places. One must remember that only David was completely free from idolatry, and the next one totally free from idolatry will be the Messiah, Jesus Christ. These two will reign together in the millennium (Jeremiah 30:9).

1 Kings 15:24, *"And Asa slept with his fathers, and was buried with his fathers in the city of David his father: and Jehoshaphat his son reigned in his stead."*

Asa was an industrious man like David and was a great success altogether as a king of Judah. Without a doubt, he was the best example for Israel and the most like his great great grandfather David. Asa passed the dynasty to Jehoshaphat, who was also for the most part a great success as a king. However, unlike David his great, great, great grandfather, Jehoshaphat made more than one affinity with those who were not serving God. After David learned his lesson with his stint with Achish and the burning of Ziklag, we do not find David engaging in an unequal yoke again. Jehoshaphat was not so fast to learn. Finally Jehoshaphat got the message. 1 Kings 22:49, *"Then said Ahaziah the son of Ahab unto Jehoshaphat, Let my servants go with thy servants in the ships. But Jehoshaphat would not."*

Jehoshaphat continued to do foolish things until his death, but he was much more like David than Rehoboam. However, he was still reaping the results of the good revival his father Asa wrought in Israel. Jehoshaphat was surrounded by the good people Asa had placed in office, and there was a zeal for truth planted in him by his father and the prophets of that day. He did finish getting the sodomites out of the land that his father Asa started to do.

1 Kings 22:50, *"And Jehoshaphat slept with his fathers, and was buried with his fathers in the city of David his father: and Jehoram his son reigned in his stead."*

The summary of the dynasty of Jehoshaphat is found in 1 Kings 22:43-44, *"And he walked in all the ways of Asa his father; he turned not aside from it, doing that which was right in the eyes of the LORD: nevertheless the high places were not taken away; for the people offered and burnt incense yet in the high places. And Jehoshaphat made peace with the king of Israel."* Jehoshaphat is buried in the city of David and now Jehoram is on the throne of Judah. The peace Jehoshaphat achieved with Israel was not in the same manner David made peace with people. Wesley said, "I fear Jehoshaphat's peace was born in compromise." This seemed to be a pattern with Jehoshaphat even though he had a good heart toward God and man. What one compromises to gain, he will someday lose, as we see clearly in Jehoshaphat's life.

2 Kings

2 Kings 8:19, "*Yet the LORD would not destroy Judah for David his servant's sake, as he promised him to give him alway a light, and to his children.*"

From time to time in the history of all of the kings of Judah, we have a welcomed reminder of the Lord's affection and also a confirmation of His promise to David. Here again is the promise of a perpetual dynasty for David. Even when a dynasty in Judah is wicked, the prophets will assure both Judah and Israel that the promise is still there. The unrighteous will not embrace it, and to their very own destruction, but the promise is there. This verse is rightly listed with the host of messianic prophetic utterances.

2 Kings 8:24, "*And Joram slept with his fathers, and was buried with his fathers in the city of David: and Ahaziah his son reigned in his stead.*"

Joram the compromiser and imitator of his father-in-law Ahab brought disgrace to the Davidic order but still he was buried in royal fashion. Ahaziah reigned after him, but for a short and pitiful year of copying the character of none other than Ahab his grandfather.

2 Kings 9:28, "*And his servants carried him in a chariot to Jerusalem, and buried him in his sepulchre with his fathers in the city of David.*"

Ahaziah was killed by the direct order of Jehu, the one the Lord raised up to give the assignment of cleansing the nation of Israel from the posterity of Ahab. Ahaziah a king of Judah was killed while in affinity with Israel, even though he well knew Jehoshaphat was nearly killed in his own alignment with Ahab. In spite of this, Ahaziah was buried in the royal graveyard with David.

2 Kings 11:10, *"And to the captains over hundreds did the priest give king David's spears and shields, that were in the temple of the LORD."*

Athaliah, the mother of Ahaziah, but the daughter of the king of Israel, went on a rampage to destroy all of the seed of David as soon as she found out her son was dead. This was none other than a diabolical plot to destroy the seed from which the Messiah would come in trying to snuff out the seed of David. The dark world has always been well aware of God's promise to David that the Messiah would come from his lineage. Athaliah thought this to be her express opportunity to gain control of the nation, but God's promise to David was right in her way.

Jehosheba, Ahaziah's sister, took Joash, one of the sons of Ahaziah, and hid him away in the Temple with the priests to preserve the line of David in the tribe of Judah. The little king was hidden away, and the priests passed out the weapons to the people who were assigned to protect this one and only royal seed of David remaining! The priests then rose up and in the authority of this little king, smashed down all of the altars of Baal and executed the murderous Athaliah.

Joash begin to reign at the age of seven and reigned forty years in a very successful dynasty being connected with the priesthood. One should note that in every single instance when the right king (tribe of Judah) and the right priest (Levi, Aaron, and Zadok) are in covenant, there is always a move of God. This is the Melchizedek order of the king and the priest.

2 Kings 12:21, *"For Jozachar the son of Shimeath, and Jehozabad the son of Shomer, his servants, smote him, and he died; and they buried him with his fathers in the city of David: and Amaziah his son reigned in his stead."*

At the end of the dynasty of Joash, he was threatened by the king of Syria and gave all the valuable things of Judah and of the house of the Lord to pay the Syrians not to attack them. This was evidently not the will of God, and Joash was later assassinated, leaving his country in disarray. The end of this life of Joash does not accurately portray his successful dynasty. However in the case Joash, his dynasty was driven by a holy and powerful priesthood, whereas the revival of Hezekiah was driven by a righteous and powerful kingship. Whether it is the king the driver and the priesthood the trailer or the priesthood the driver and the kingship the trailer, any time these two operate in covenant, there is a revival. Joash went down as a very successful and godly king of Judah, walking in the pattern of David.

2 Kings 14:3, *"And he did that which was right in the sight of the LORD, yet not like David his father: he did according to all things as Joash his father did."*

Amaziah began to reign at twenty-five years old and reigned for twenty-nine years. His dynasty again is measured by the perfect standard of David, who had no idols and allowed no idolatry during his dynasty. This is what this verse is referring to. Amaziah like his father, but not like David, left the high places and allowed the unscriptural burning of incense to continue. He had a troublesome dynasty in his internal as well as external affairs. He eventually completely backslid (2 Chronicles 25:27), and lost all of the gold and treasures that David had left after the building of the Temple. Israel defeated him in an extension of the civil war between the two. The dynasty of David has weakened a great deal by now, but the light has not gone out, and the Lord will not forget His covenant with His servant David.

2 Kings 14:20, *"And they brought him on horses: and he was buried at Jerusalem with his fathers in the city of David."*

In spite of Amaziah's sin and failure, he was carried back from the city he was slain in (Lachish) to the royal graveyard. The term *brought him on horses,* most likely refers to a chariot though it is not mentioned here. The plurality of horses would not be necessary to transport a body, and a chariot was the customary way of transportation of a king. If in fact this is referring to a chariot it would indicate the sentiment of the people relating back to David himself! These same ones who carried this loyalty for David got for their next king the son of Amaziah. 2 Kings 14:21, *"And all the people of Judah took Azariah, which was sixteen years old, and made him king instead of his father Amaziah."* Azariah began to build Judah back with some success.

2 Kings 15:7, *"So Azariah slept with his fathers; and they buried him with his fathers in the city of David: and Jotham his son reigned in his stead."*

Azariah (also known as Uzziah) had one of the longest dynasties, fifty two years. But like his father he would not remove the high places. Israel had gone into wholesale idolatry long ago but Judah had now had several kings in a sequence that had served the Lord but would not pull down the high places. However, Azariah was stricken with leprosy and later died from the disease. He was not actually buried in the royal cemetery because of his disease. 2 Chronicles 26:23, *"So Uzziah slept with his fathers, and they buried him with his father's in the field of the burial which belonged to the kings; for they said, He is a leper: and Jotham his son reigned in his stead."* The place he was buried was owned by the kings but was not the actual royal burial grounds. This is an indicator of a protective type loyalty the people had for David. David was the first king to be buried inside of Jerusalem as cemeteries were forbidden inside of cities.

2 Kings 15:38, "*And Jotham slept with his fathers, and was buried with his fathers in the city of David his father: and Ahaz his son reigned in his stead.*"

Jotham started his reign at twenty-five years old and reigned for sixteen years. His story was pretty much the same as his father. 2 Kings 15:34-35 "*And he did that which was right in the sight of the LORD: he did according to all that his father Uzziah had done. Howbeit the high places were not removed: the people sacrificed and burned incense still in the high places. He built the higher gate of the house of the LORD.*" He was buried with the lineage of David. His son Ahaz would be the next king but not a follower David's God.

2 Kings 16:2, "*Twenty years old was Ahaz when he began to reign, and reigned sixteen years in Jerusalem, and did not that which was right in the sight of the LORD his God, like David his father.*"

Ahaz became an avid worshipper of idols and certainly departed from the teachings of his fathers. The king of Syria teamed up with the king of Israel and tried to snuff out Judah. They laid a siege on Jerusalem but could not take it. The prophet Isaiah was sent to prophesy to Ahaz and a most strange thing happened. Ahaz, though backslidden from the example of David, was not only protected from the siege by the Lord but given the famous messianic prophesy. Isaiah 7:10-14, "*Moreover the LORD spake again unto Ahaz, saying, Ask thee a sign of the LORD thy God; ask it either in the depth, or in the height above. But Ahaz said, I will not ask, neither will I tempt the LORD. And he said, Hear ye now, O house of David; Is it a small thing for you to weary men, but will ye weary my God also? Therefore the Lord himself shall give you a sign; Behold, a virgin shall conceive, and bear a son, and shall call his name Immanuel.*"

This should reveal to all just how strong this covenant God made with David really is. Notice the prophecy was to the house of David, and that with a divine complaint of their ways. Then the Lord dropped this powerful prophecy to again establish the fact that the Messiah is coming through the house of David no matter what, and that a virgin will bear him. One would think this powerful revelation would be given to Asa or Joash, but this iniquitous Ahaz was given this word.

2 Kings 16:20, "*And Ahaz slept with his fathers, and was buried with his father's in the city of David: and Hezekiah his son reigned in his stead.*"

Ahaz received the most powerful prophecy that had been given in decades by one of the most powerful prophets that ever served Israel, Isaiah. However nothing changed his wicked course. He had no regard for the God of Israel. He commanded the priests to comply with his idolatry. He desecrated the Temple furniture to adorn his own palace. He shut down the worship to the true and living God. What an iniquitous wretch, and yet he fathered a godly son.

2 Kings 17:21, *"For he rent Israel from the house of David; and they made Jeroboam the son of Nebat king: and Jeroboam drave Israel from following the LORD, and made them sin a great sin."*

This verse is the Lord's summary for the reasons for His judgment on the nation of Israel. It also reveals His heart toward the house of David. David was totally innocent of each of the points the Lord is citing in His indictment. 1) The children of Israel were delivered from the bondage of Egypt but didn't appreciate it enough to serve the Lord that delivered them. 2) Israel walked in the statutes of heathens. 3) Israel secretly participated in idolatry all over the land. 4) The children of Israel burned incense to images they had made. 5) They ignored the prophets the Lord sent them. 6) They hardened their hearts against the Lord. 7) They caused their sons to pass through the fire by divination and enchantments. 8) They worshipped the two national gods Jeroboam made.

David did none of these things, neither did he allow them or condone them. Therefore the life of David sets the standard in being totally idol free. Israel's greatest worshipper of God was David!

2 Kings 18:3, *"And he did that which was right in the sight of the LORD, according to all that David his father did."*

This is the summation of the life of Hezekiah. He was right in the sight of the Lord. Hezekiah was twenty-five years old when he began to reign. Judah had a great revival in the days of Hezekiah. He wisely began his dynasty by repairing the Temple and demanding the sanctification of the priesthood. He was the son of a wicked father, and the father of a wicked son. Yet, he was the most like David, even more so than Asa and Joash. He even pulled down the high places. 2 Kings 18:4, *"He removed the high places, and brake the images, and cut down the groves, and brake in pieces the brasen serpent that Moses had made: for unto those days the children of Israel did burn incense to it: and he called it Nehushtan."*

In his zeal Hezekiah even destroyed the brazen serpent that Moses had erected as a symbol of Christ. The children of Israel had made it an object of worship instead of a symbol of redemption. Hezekiah did not seem to have the same kind of moral failure that David had and therefore the following statement exists: 2 Kings 18:5, *"He trusted in the LORD God of Israel; so that after him was none like him among all the kings of Judah, nor any that were before him."*

Some doctors of theology cite this verse to argue that in fact David was not the greatest king in all of Israel. However a polemical study will prove that this verse does not include either

David or Solomon. This verse is referring to the kings of Judah after the split under Rehoboam and to the remaining kings of Judah until the time of the Messiah Himself. It is true, and to their credit, David was for seven years the king of Judah. Yet from his very first anointing as king it was as the king of Israel. The other tribes of Israel would not accept him until the posterity of Saul was totally subdued.

We should use this verse to rather argue that the Lord proclaimed David to be the king of Israel, and he was, even though the other tribes rejected him! Even so Jesus is the King of Kings regardless of who accepts Him or rejects Him. It seems that the Lord could see his servant David in Hezekiah and the King of Kings through them both. The Lord's love for David is abundantly clear, even though he laid upon him severe judgment at times. Hezekiah enjoyed the favor of David on his life. 2 Kings 18:7, *"And the LORD was with him; and he prospered whithersoever he went forth: and he rebelled against the king of Assyria, and served him not."* Hezekiah was wise enough to tap into the sure mercies of David!

2 Kings 19:34, *"For I will defend this city, to save it, for mine own sake, and for my servant David's sake."*

The enemies of Israel had thought they would surely destroy Judah and Hezekiah. They even mocked the faith Hezekiah had in his God. Hezekiah was strengthened in his God and by the hand of the good prophet Isaiah. Lightfoot mentions the heart of David in Hezekiah and the voice of the prophetic in Isaiah as resulting in the great deliverance of little Judah before the Assyrian giant. One should study closely the powerful prayer of Hezekiah when he was surrounded and find that he could pray like David. At the conclusion of Hezekiah's powerful prayer, the Lord sent the prophet Isaiah to assure him that the Lord would surely deliver him for His own sake and David's sake!

2 Kings 20:5, *"Turn again, and tell Hezekiah the captain of my people, Thus saith the LORD, the God of David thy father, I have heard thy prayer, I have seen thy tears: behold, I will heal thee: on the third day thou shalt go up unto the house of the LORD."*

Isaiah had been sent of the Lord earlier to tell Hezekiah that he was going to die from his sickness and to get his house in order. Hezekiah prayed another powerful prayer for help and Isaiah was told to go back and deliver Hezekiah a word from the Lord concerning the sickness he was dying from. In this verse, the Lord told Isaiah to come with this salutation: *"Thus saith the LORD, the God of David thy father."* God wanted Hezekiah to understand that his pronounced healing was connected to the Davidic covenant! It is verses like this one that constantly confirm the power of both God's covenant and His relationship with David!

2 Kings 20:6, "*And I will add unto thy days fifteen years; and I will deliver thee and this city out of the hand of the king of Assyria; and I will defend this city for mine own sake, and for my servant David's sake.*"

The prophet proceeds to tell Hezekiah that he will certainly be delivered from the hand of the king of Assyria, in addition to being healed. Both the deliverance from his enemies and healing were a result of God's relationship with David. Calmuet asks the question concerning this verse and those like it, "Is it possible that God would bless one in honor of another, but isn't Hezekiah himself David like?" He and many other theologians have approached such an idea carefully as not to tread on the ground of dual mediatorship, which is solidly condemned in 1 Timothy 2:5, "*For there is one God, and one mediator between God and men, the man Christ Jesus.*" However, we have the clear proof that God Himself connects some of His manifold blessing to His relationship with His saints.

Many verses imply that God gives mercy or blessing for David's sake. The six verses that plainly state this are 1 Kings 11:32, 1 Kings 15:4, 2 Kings 19:34, 2 Kings 20:6, Psalm 132:10, and Isaiah 37:35. In Psalm 132:10 there even seems to be an encouragement to remind God of His covenant with David in prayer, "*For thy servant David's sake turn not away the face of thine anointed.*" David is not an intercessor or a mediator for us, and we can never pray in any other name but the name of Jesus. But the tender mercies of David are very dear to the heart of God.

Hezekiah finished his dynasty with a question of his character because he seemingly was too impressed with idolaters, and perhaps through this weakness, he strengthened the hands of those who made the idols. He was rebuked sharply by the Lord, but like Solomon had his judgment delayed until after his death.

2 Kings 21:7, "*And he set a graven image of the grove that he had made in the house, of which the LORD said to David, and to Solomon his son, In this house, and in Jerusalem, which I have chosen out of all tribes of Israel, will I put my name for ever*":

After Hezekiah's death, his son Manasseh reigned in his place. Manasseh was twelve years old when he began to reign, and he reinstated idol worship in the land. The total shift from revival in the days of Hezekiah to wholesale idolatry in the young life of Manasseh seems to be some proof that problems were already developing in the last part of Hezekiah's dynasty. Idol worshippers in high positions of authority were quite ready to guide the young Manasseh in their direction.

This did not happen in David's case. It began in the latter days of Solomon, and there were years of slow change before Israel went back to idolatry. Therefore when Manasseh is being exposed, part of his exposure was the fact that Manasseh placed idols in the very place the Lord had shown both David and Solomon He had chosen for His Name. It is the place where both David and Solomon had prayed down fire!

2 Kings 22:2, *"And he did that which was right in the sight of the LORD, and walked in all the way of David his father, and turned not aside to the right hand or to the left."*

This is King Josiah who is walking in the ways of David, but before the reign of Josiah, Amon reigned for a short and wicked two years. There was a conspiracy against Amon, and he was assassinated by his own servants. Then the people of the land killed all of those who were involved in assassinating him. The people then made Josiah king and buried Amon outside the royal family cemetery.

Josiah was a good king, and he did not partake in idolatry himself. But one must remember to achieve the same standard as David in this matter, they had to not participate in idolatry but also not allow it. This was a struggle for each king after the backsliding of Solomon. When one king would be opposed to idolatry, the people who also opposed it would rally behind that king. This would include the priesthood and most of the tribe of Levi which was in the vicinity of Jerusalem.

Just as there was a preserved seed of David the king in Israel, there was also a preserved priesthood in Levi, and particularly in Zadok. This seed would be preserved until the end, but would be manifest in John the Baptist for the transfer of the Aaronic priesthood to Him who is a Priest forever after the order of Melchizedek! Josiah was a lot like Joash and had similar results. The priests played a big part in the revival under Josiah. They found the law of the Lord in the house of God. There had probably been a stop to the reading of the Word under the reign of the wicked kings. Josephus said it was a decree under Manasseh. He was certainly wicked enough to produce such a decree.

However when the priests found the Torah, they began again to read and honor the Word of God. Josiah was greatly affected, as we read in 2 Kings 22:11, *"And it came to pass, when the king had heard the words of the book of the law, that he rent his clothes."* A holiness revival continued under Josiah. He was a great king, but in all of his goodness, he was not able to avert the coming judgment upon Judah and Israel. The deeds of Manasseh had pretty much sealed the certainty of coming judgment. Yet the covenant of David is preserved!

1 Chronicles

1 Chronicles 2:15, "*Ozem the sixth, David the seventh*":

This verse calls David the seventh son and the account in 1 Samuel 16:10 states that David was the eighth son. They are both correct, however, for one of the sons of Jesse died not long after the account of 1 Samuel 16:10.

1 Chronicles 3:1, "*Now these were the sons of David, which were born unto him in Hebron; the firstborn Amnon, of Ahinoam the Jezreelitess; the second Daniel, of Abigail the Carmelitess*":

Here is the record of the sons of David at Hebron. This record only includes those sons who were born to him while he ruled in Hebron which began seven years before he ruled all of Israel. Here the second son is called Daniel. In 2 Samuel 3:3 he is called Chileab. It is a recurrent thing among the Jews for men to have two names, especially when they lived in more than one country, as we see in the case of Daniel and the three Hebrew children.

The two records, The Chronicles and the Samuels, provide the critics of the Bible much material for their alleged discrepancies. However, close study of the scripture will prove the allegations false. One must not pit the accounts of David in the Chronicles against the record found in the Samuels. It is like the four gospels in this regard. Each gospel brings more clarification to the other, not competition or contradiction.

1 Chronicles 3:9, "*These were all the sons of David, beside the sons of the concubines, and Tamar their sister.*"

Here is a list of David's sons, and as we can see none of them achieved a great deal except Solomon, and he backslid. In fact most of them brought reproach to Israel. David lacked in fathering greatly. The list here and in 2 Samuel 5 has a difference of two and again it is because these two died early, in between the time of the records that are respectively given. The list of David's successors is in itself fascinating. Wesley writes these words concerning it, "How seldom has a crown gone in a direct line, from father to son, as it did here, for seventeen generations! This was the recompense of David's piety."

1 Chronicles 4:31, "*And at Bethmarcaboth, and Hazarsusim, and at Bethbirei, and at Shaaraim. These were their cities unto the reign of David.*"

These are some of the cities that were actually given to the tribe of Simeon by Joshua but they were never conquered by that tribe. The tribe of Simeon never grew like the other tribes. Because of their lack of courage and tenacity, they failed to conquer much of the land inside their designated boundaries. It was David who finally drove out the enemies of Israel and conquered the land.

1 Chronicles 6:31, *"And these are they whom David set over the service of song in the house of the LORD, after that the ark had rest."*

Here is more proof that, in fact, David worked closely with the priesthood and in particular as a type of authority over them. David set them over different activities in the Temple. It appears from reading all of the verses on this subject, that David had three different groups of singers, with a leader over each of them and a sort of head leader over all of the singing people in the Temple. David takes great pains to offer up correct worship. After his failure to get the Ark back to Jerusalem in his first attempt. David never left the priesthood out of his efforts to worship God around the Ark. He had professional singers of the tribe of Judah to insure that the Lord was continually blessed. This is David!

1 Chronicles 7:2, *"And the sons of Tola; Uzzi, and Rephaiah, and Jeriel, and Jahmai, and Jibsam, and Shemuel, heads of their father's house, to wit, of Tola: they were valiant men of might in their generations; whose number was in the days of David two and twenty thousand and six hundred."*

This is most likely referring to the census that David took which angered the Lord greatly. The number of the tribes, in particular in the case of that Census, was not tallied by tribe in the record found in 2 Samuel 24:9. This is revealing that the very history of the nation of Israel was distinguished and measured in era by the amazing dynasty of King David, *"in the days of David!"*

1 Chronicles 9:22, *"All these which were chosen to be porters in the gates were two hundred and twelve. These were reckoned by their genealogy in their villages, whom David and Samuel the seer did ordain in their set office."*

The king and the priest order is a Melchizedek order that can be traced throughout the verses. Melchizedek was both king and priest. David operated three times as a priest and was blessed for it. Saul tried to operate just one time as a priest and was judged for it. Yet when the right king of Judah worked in covenant with the right priest of Aaron, there was always a release of anointing. This is surely a great secret for the blessing of the dynasty of David.

This verse has come under great scrutiny because Samuel's death is recorded in 1 Samuel 26:1 and the Ark was not moved to the temporary tabernacle David erected in Jerusalem until 2

Samuel 6. How was the famous prophet Samuel involved in setting up the priesthood courses before the Ark was in place? It is a credible question, but because David lived with Samuel for a period of time in his exile from Saul (1 Samuel 19:18), David most likely was instructed in the design of the Temple work and as soon as the temporary tabernacle was in place, David executed Samuel's design.

1 Chronicles 10:14, *"And enquired not of the LORD: therefore he slew him, and turned the kingdom unto David the son of Jesse."*

In this verse and the preceding one we have a short record of Saul's rebellion, and a brief reason for the Lord's stripping the kingdom out of his hand and giving it to David!

1 Chronicles 11:1, *"Then all Israel gathered themselves to David unto Hebron, saying, Behold, we are thy bone and thy flesh."*

There are times when the account of David's life in the Chronicles is more explicit than the record in First and Second Samuel. However in this case it is not. The verse here does not mention the struggle with the posterity between the time of 1 Chronicles 10:14 and this verse. The whole of the reign at Hebron is not spoken of as well, for this verse is the account of the elders of all of Israel coming to anoint David king over all of Israel not just Judah.

This happened after David had reigned in Hebron for seven and one half years and had dealt with the efforts of rulers of the other tribes to revive the dynasty of Saul. They had a major problem in doing so because the Word of the Lord had already spoken that David was God's chosen vessel to reign in Israel. David was faithful over Judah for seven and one half years, holding on to the prophetic word of God. In these seven and one half years he wrote a great number of psalms and spiritual songs!

1 Chronicles 11:3, *"Therefore came all the elders of Israel to the king to Hebron; and David made a covenant with them in Hebron before the LORD; and they anointed David king over Israel, according to the word of the LORD by Samuel."*

Neither the account here nor the account in 2 Samuel 5 gives us the details of the covenant or league the elders of Israel made with David. It is most likely that there was not a written agreement but an understanding that would cover at least two concerns for both parties. 1) The people of Judah who were still angry at the other tribes for their rebellion against David would not be able to persuade David to treat those tribes with partiality because David was of their tribe. 2) The leaders of Israel would be able to persuade the people to fully accept and embrace their king to be of the tribe of Judah.

There was no need for a peace treaty because David had fully and completely emerged as the victor in every respect. The people did, however, need assurance from their king. There is not a shred of evidence that David showed any partiality for his own tribe or any vengeance for their mistreatment of him!

1 Chronicles 11:4, *"And David and all Israel went to Jerusalem, which is Jebus; where the Jebusites were, the inhabitants of the land."*

This is the first military campaign for David after he became the king of the whole nation. It seems as soon as he was established as king, he was ready to take the land promised to Israel and conquer what would be the capital of the whole world one day. The Jebusites had stubbornly occupied this land (Joshua 15:63), but David knew there was something about this place!

(See commentary on 2 Samuel 5:6).

1 Chronicles 11:5, *"And the inhabitants of Jebus said to David, Thou shalt not come hither. Nevertheless David took the castle of Zion, which is the city of David."*

This is the account of the conquering of Jerusalem found also in 2 Samuel 5. This account is shorter and doesn't record the taunting Jebusites who were so sure their gods were going to spare them again. David had called their gods blind and lame and in fact they were. David easily took the city and took over the famous castle of Zion and evidently lived there (verse 17).

1 Chronicles 11:6, *"And David said, Whosoever smiteth the Jebusites first shall be chief and captain. So Joab the son of Zeruiah went first up, and was chief."*

This is the account of David hoping someone else would be the winner of his reward, for David was at this time feeling quite uncomfortable with Joab, his nephew and captain. Again 2 Samuel 5 has a more detailed record of this matter.

1 Chronicles 11:7, *"And David dwelt in the castle; therefore they called it the city of David."*

The city was quickly known as the city of David! The enemies of Israel to this day call the Davidic generations by the name of Zionist. Watts is correct by calling the haters of the Zionist to be haters of David as well as His Messiah!

1 Chronicles 11:9, *"So David waxed greater and greater: for the LORD of hosts was with him."*

The whole of David's military success was the fact that the Lord was with him. Yet David was also with the Lord. The greatest worshipper in the history of Israel spent countless hours in the Lord's presence. Prophecies would come to him. Songs would fill his heart. Even when David went to war, it was to him an expression of worship. As far as David was concerned he was waging war on the enemies of the Lord. This is proven in the case of Saul. David knew that Saul was not the enemy of the Lord but was under the Lord's judgment. Therefore, David never attacked Saul, even though he could have done so easily. David waxed greater because he only fought against those who were the enemies of God!

1 Chronicles 11:10, *"These also are the chief of the mighty men whom David had, who strengthened themselves with him in his kingdom, and with all Israel, to make him king, according to the word of the LORD concerning Israel."*

While the foremost reason for the military success was because the Lord was with him, in this verse there is seen also another reason. The mighty men that surrounded David strengthened themselves with him. There are two basic ways this verse is interpreted: 1) The mighty men were in fact the reason for David's amazing military success because they were with him. 2) The mighty men were in fact mighty because they were with David.

It seems both of the reasons are correct. Many have wondered at the great accomplishments of some of the giants of the faith. Yet they were all accompanied by great people. Does the Lord bless a ministry or a man? This is the question that religion has not solved and perhaps doesn't know how. However, when God breathes upon a life and uses them mightily, many are drawn to that anointing and strengthened by it. This is the case of David which produced a compound anointing and became the greatest military sensation the world has ever known!

1 Chronicles 11:11, *"And this is the number of the mighty men whom David had; Jashobeam, an Hachmonite, the chief of the captains: he lifted up his spear against three hundred slain by him at one time."*

The reason for the difference in the names of the mighty men is given on the commentary in 2 Samuel 23:8, but there is also a difference in the number for those slain at one time by this mighty man. This account gives the number three hundred while the account in 2 Samuel gives eight hundred. This most likely is because the three hundred were slain by him alone and five hundred more by those armor bearers assigned to him. Wesley rightly defends the Word by the following statement, "The slaughter of all is justly ascribed to him, because it was the effect of his valor."

1 Chronicles 11:13, *"He was with David at Pasdammim, and there the Philistines were gathered together to battle, where was a parcel of ground full of barley; and the people fled from before the Philistines."*

The record in both Samuel and Chronicles are not only complementary of each other but correctional. In the record of these mighty men of David, we can see this clearly. The record in Samuel is more detailed, but both are careful to document amazing feats so as to confirm the supernatural component involved.

1 Chronicles 11:15-18, *"Now three of the thirty captains went down to the rock to David, into the cave of Adullam; and the host of the Philistines encamped in the valley of Rephaim. And David was then in the hold, and the Philistines' garrison was then at Bethlehem. And David longed, and said, Oh that one would give me drink of the water of the well of Bethlehem, that is at the gate! And the three brake through the host of the Philistines, and drew water out of the well of Bethlehem, that was by the gate, and took it, and brought it to David: but David would not drink of it, but poured it out to the LORD,*

The detailed commentary of this same account is found in 2 Samuel 23:13-17.

1 Chronicles 11:25, *"Behold, he was honourable among the thirty, but attained not to the first three: and David set him over his guard."*

There is something to be said of the amazing ability of David to properly evaluate and appoint those around him for the work of the kingdom. The army David built was the premier fighting force of the known world. The structure David built was evidently divinely inspired, and the pattern he had with his men was not unlike Jesus had with His disciples. David rewarded those who excelled, just like Jesus did and does. An eighteenth century scholar of theology went to great pains to prove that both David and Jesus had favorites. The piece was brought to Wesley who declared, "What a waste of time for an accomplished theologian, both David and Jesus would readily confess themselves guilty of that which they are accused." Of course God is a rewarder of them that diligently seek Him, and David was one of His favorites.

1 Chronicles 12:1, *"Now these are they that came to David to Ziklag, while he yet kept himself close because of Saul the son of Kish: and they were among the mighty men, helpers of the war."*

In the case of this list, the account is more detailed than that of the account in Samuel. There are three lists in this chapter and they account for the men who joined David at different times. The ones who came to him at Ziklag while David was in exile seemed to be the most significant as far as his closest guard and best fighting men. Many of them were not Jews when they first came to David. The amazing thing often overlooked in David's military triumphs is that he didn't just make warriors out of misfits, but he made Jews out of heathens!

1 Chronicles 12:8, *"And of the Gadites there separated themselves unto David into the hold to the wilderness men of might, and men of war fit for the battle, that could handle shield and buckler, whose faces were like the faces of lions, and were as swift as the roes upon the mountains"*;

These of the tribe of Gad are heralded as great warriors, but it should be noticed that the whole tribe is not meant to be seen in this light. Those who were not as fierce and fast either were not accepted of David or did not want to fight beside him. These mentioned in the list of Gadite warriors were some of the top fighting men in David's mighty army. Not much is said of them elsewhere in the scriptures, but here their description is of great caliber. Great warriors attract great warriors. David had some who were close to him but not connected to him. The Gadite warriors were both close and connected!

1 Chronicles 12:16, *"And there came of the children of Benjamin and Judah to the hold unto David."*

These are Saul's kindred coming to David, and they are accompanied by some of the tribe of Judah which had been either insubordinate before or aloof for some reason. It should be noted that there was always some of the tribe of Judah that did not connect with David, and there was always some of the tribe of Benjamin that did. The relationship David of Judah had with Jonathan of the tribe of Benjamin was well known in Israel. The mixed feelings of uncertain loyalty toward either David or Saul were rampant through both tribes.

1 Chronicles 12:17, *"And David went out to meet them, and answered and said unto them, If ye be come peaceably unto me to help me, mine heart shall be knit unto you: but if ye be come to betray me to mine enemies, seeing there is no wrong in mine hands, the God of our fathers look thereon, and rebuke it."*

This is great wisdom and courage manifesting through David. It is evident in his approach toward this meeting that David's security in his walk before God provided both the wisdom and the courage he displayed. David let them know quickly that there would be no toleration for any division or undermining of the work God was doing in his midst. David was not fully trusting of these at the first because of all of the past abuse he had received from the tribe of Benjamin. David points out to them his total innocence of doing Saul or his tribe any damage. He lets them know that the same God who had fought his battles for him would also rebuke them if they had any ideas of vengeance!

1 Chronicles 12:18, *"Then the spirit came upon Amasai, who was chief of the captains, and he said, Thine are we, David, and on thy side, thou son of Jesse: peace, peace be unto thee, and peace be to thine helpers; for thy God helpeth thee. Then David received them, and made them captains of the band."*

It is not known for sure if this is the same Amasai who had been appointed captain over the host of the army of Saul by Ishbosheth. What is known is that this Amasai spoke quickly and with clout to David by the spirit, and thus David recognized and received them without any more doubt. David had warned them by the spirit that they would certainly be found out if they were up to evil, and now he accepts them through the spirit. After he received them, he made them rulers for him, whereas they had been chief men of Saul. This was a bold move and again shows David's great administrational ability which was no doubt a spiritual gift that David operated in!

1 Chronicles 12:19, *"And there fell some of Manasseh to David, when he came with the Philistines against Saul to battle: but they helped them not: for the lords of the Philistines upon advisement sent him away, saying, He will fall to his master Saul to the jeopardy of our heads."*

This is a very short but telling account of David's rejection by the Philistine lords as fully recorded in 1 Samuel 29. It seems these of Manasseh were coming to fight beside David as he went with Achish, but when they were rejected, they followed David back to Ziklag where they discovered the tragedy of their city burned and their families taken captive. This is strange, but there were some bands of Israeli warriors that were very confused as to what to do and where to go when David, a national hero, was in exile from Saul the king. They were professional fighters and developed into little wandering bands that hired themselves to any who would divide with them the spoil.

1 Chronicles 12:21, *"And they helped David against the band of the rovers: for they were all mighty men of valour, and were captains in the host."*

The account in Samuel does not record this help from these mighty men of war from the tribe of Manasseh. Here we see that they were instrumental in helping David retrieve all his family, goods, and even the spoils of the Amalkites. In the case of retrieving property back from the enemy, the property stolen was customarily given back to the owners, and then the spoil taken from the enemy was divided between the soldiers who helped retrieve it. In the account in Samuel there was an exception noted. David declared, *"This is David's spoil"* (1 Samuel 30:20). David no doubt took good care of these warriors in the dividing of the spoil.

1 Chronicles 12:22, *"For at that time day by day there came to David to help him, until it was a great host, like the host of God."*

This was the turnaround for David as far as the numbers in his army goes. After the victory over the Amalkites through the help of the warriors of Manasseh, there came to him more and more warriors every day. The actual turnaround for David was his repentance in the ashes of Ziklag, where he received the encouragement he needed and the Word from God to proceed. Then the recovering of all from the Amalkites, the taking of the spoil of all they had, the distribution to all who helped him, and the knowledge among the tribes that God was with David all began to cause a mighty build up of an army which is described in detail in the following verses.

1 Chronicles 12:23, *"And these are the numbers of the bands that were ready armed to the war, and came to David to Hebron, to turn the kingdom of Saul to him, according to the word of the LORD."*

These numbers listed in the following verses are separate from the other lists that are given, beginning with the southern tribes. This number of soldiers could not have been amassed before the death of Ishbosheth, who was the last hope for the house of Saul to be revived. Israel began to see again that not only was David blessed by the hand of God but was destined by the will of the Lord to be the undisputed king of Israel by the very Word of the Lord.

1 Chronicles 12:31, *"And of the half tribe of Manasseh eighteen thousand, which were expressed by name, to come and make David king."*

We can see from the wording of this verse that the half tribe of Manasseh had a great company of men on this side of the Jordan that were evidently handpicked to represent all of their tribe, including those on the other side of Jordan, as we see in verse 37. These mentioned here evidently were willing to sign some sort of ledger or something confirming there alliance with David. We can also see the importance of this verse in allowing the national love for David to be unabated at this time by the tribal boundaries.

1 Chronicles 12:38, *"All these men of war, that could keep rank, came with a perfect heart to Hebron, to make David king over all Israel: and all the rest also of Israel were of one heart to make David king."*

There are a lot of the men of Israel that did not come to this gathering for reasons that are not given. However, we know from the count of fighting men in 1 Chronicles 21:5-6 there were over one and one half million, not counting Benjamin or Levi. It is not possible for the population to grow to that extent in those few years separating this gathering and that census. Therefore many fighting men did not come. This is why the verse declares that those who did come were of a perfect heart or totally unified with the rest of Israel who did not come.

1 Chronicles 12:39, *"And there they were with David three days, eating and drinking: for their brethren had prepared for them."*

The feast was evidently prepared for by the three tribes who dwelt closely to the place of the gathering. That would be Issachar, Zebulun, and Naphtali. They probably furnished most of the necessities for the feast, which would explain the phrase *for their brethren had prepared for them.* Also the whole of verse 40, *"Moreover they that were nigh them, even unto Issachar and Zebulun and Naphtali, brought bread on asses, and on camels, and on mules, and on oxen, and meat, meal, cakes of figs, and bunches of raisins, and wine, and oil, and oxen, and sheep abundantly: for there was joy in Israel."*

This was one of the most unified and forgiving times in the history of Israel, and it was circled around making David king. There would never be one better. Never will Israel be brought to such a high position on the world scene until He who is the Messiah will come to this earth with nail prints in His hands and feet. Only then will the glory of Israel rise and surpass the level David led them to. Clark describes David in this manner, "a statesman, warrior, hero, poet, and in divine favor he stands unrivalled in the annals of the world: by him alone were the Israelites raised to a pitch of the highest splendour; and their name became a terror to their enemies, and a praise in the earth."

1 Chronicles 13:1, *"And David consulted with the captains of thousands and hundreds, and with every leader."*

The word consulted here does not mean that he asked the leaders permission or that there was a democratic decision as to the direction and purpose ahead of them. David was a theocratic leader who was not a dictator. This is an important and rare balance! Even though David's discourse with his leaders was concerning bringing the Ark home, it is important to see that a theocratic leader need not be afraid to deliberate with those he is called to lead, but in fact should be afraid not to.

1 Chronicles 13:2, *"And David said unto all the congregation of Israel, If it seem good unto you, and that it be of the LORD our God, let us send abroad unto our brethren every where, that are left in all the land of Israel, and with them also to the priests and Levites which are in their cities and suburbs, that they may gather themselves unto us":*

David, being a lover of God and a true worshipper, was very interested in getting the Ark home. The account in 2 Samuel goes into much more detail concerning this effort. However, this account shows something very clear that is of great significance in the story of David's life. The Ark not being in a house or tabernacle bothered David immensely and is rightly counted in many commentaries as an affliction of David. Psalms 132:4-5, *"I will not give sleep to mine eyes, or slumber to mine eyelids, Until I find out a place for the LORD, an habitation for the mighty God of Jacob."*

This psalm is entitled by Watts as the psalm of David's afflictions. The same thought is implied by the introduction of this psalm, commonly found in the Authorized Version. The very passion for the Lord that burned David's heart was considered an affliction for him. When a soul begins to long for God to be honored so deeply that he is in affliction of heart, it proves the heart beat of that individual to be that one God said was after His heart. David proceeds by sharing his heart with all of the people of Israel. He knew this sacred endeavor would bring the healing among the tribes that was greatly needed.

1 Chronicles 13:5, *"So David gathered all Israel together, from Shihor of Egypt even unto the entering of Hemath, to bring the ark of God from Kirjath-jearim."*

It seems from the account in 2 Samuel that there were key people from every tribe throughout the original boundaries Joshua had formed that came to this event. This multitude is numbered at thirty-thousand in 2 Samuel 6:1, but this count could have been exclusive of those just looking on and the non-military people. There is strong unity and support throughout all of Israel for the effort.

1 Chronicles 13:6, *"And David went up, and all Israel, to Baalah, that is, to Kirjath-jearim, which belonged to Judah, to bring up thence the ark of God the LORD, that dwelleth between the cherubims, whose name is called on it."*

This effort is also considered a corrective work concerning the negligence of Saul in leaving the Ark at Kirjath-jearim. Saul was not like David in this matter, for he was not concerned enough in his heart for the Ark to make any attempt to recover it or cover it. Certain men had taken it to the house of Abinadab, according to 1 Samuel 7:1, *"And the men of Kirjath-jearim came, and fetched up the ark of the LORD, and brought it into the house of Abinadab in the hill, and sanctified Eleazar his son to keep the ark of the LORD."*

Saul could live every day with the Ark being there but David couldn't. Saul could go for forty days listening to the giant blaspheme the God of Israel, but David couldn't stand it one day! It is such a shame David put the Ark on the cart instead of the shoulders of the Levite priests.

1 Chronicles 13:8, *"And David and all Israel played before God with all their might, and with singing, and with harps, and with psalteries, and with timbrels, and with cymbals, and with trumpets."*

This verse and the next three verses that mention David's name is the record of the same account as we find in 2 Samuel 6:5-11. The only variation is with the name many consider to be the owner of the threshing floor where Uzza died. In the account of 2 Samuel 6 we see it was *"Nachon's threshing floor."* In this account it is called *"the threshing floor of Chidon."* Actually a close study will reveal it is not the name of a property owner, but a place near the city of David.

For the full commentary of this first attempt to bring the Ark home see commentary of 2 Samuel 6:5-11.

1 Chronicles 13:11, *"And David was displeased, because the LORD had made a breach upon Uzza: wherefore that place is called Perezuzza to this day."*

See commentary of 2 Samuel 6:5-11

1 Chronicles 13:12, *"And David was afraid of God that day, saying, How shall I bring the ark of God home to me?"*

See commentary of 2 Samuel 6:5-11

1 Chronicles 13:13, *"So David brought not the ark home to himself to the city of David, but carried it aside into the house of Obededom the Gittite."*

See commentary of 2 Samuel 6:5-11

The record of the second effort of David to bring the Ark home to Jerusalem is continued immediately in 2 Samuel 6:12. However, in the Chronicles we have record of some of the events that took place during the three months before the second effort was made. These three months must have been very difficult for David. Some tremendous psalms were written during the sleepless nights caused by longing for the Ark to be in Jerusalem and David's first and fatal attempt to get it there.

1 Chronicles 14:1, *"Now Hiram king of Tyre sent messengers to David, and timber of cedars, with masons and carpenters, to build him an house."*

The following verses are almost identical to the account in 2 Samuel 5 of this same event. Therefore we reference the commentary in 2 Samuel 5:11.

1 Chronicles 14:2, *"And David perceived that the LORD had confirmed him king over Israel, for his kingdom was lifted up on high, because of his people Israel."*

See commentary on 2 Samuel 5:12

1 Chronicles 14:3, *"And David took more wives at Jerusalem: and David begat more sons and daughters."*

There is an alleged discrepancy concerning the list of David's children. Eliphalet and Nogah are not listed in the account in 2 Samuel, but Beeliada appears to be the same as Eliada. Most likely one list counts only the living while the other list counts them all.

Otherwise see commentary on 2 Samuel 5:13

1 Chronicles 14:8, *"And when the Philistines heard that David was anointed king over all Israel, all the Philistines went up to seek David. And David heard of it, and went out against them."*

There is a slight variation between this verse and in the verse that contains the account of this development in 2 Samuel 5:17, which states that when David's intelligence learned of the movement of the Philistines, he went to the hold. Here in this verse it does not tell of David's going to a fort or hold but simply states, *"And David heard of it, and went out against them."* This can be easily explained as David most likely went to the hold to organize his men for the battle in which he would fight the Philistines.

Otherwise see the commentary on 2 Samuel 5:17

I Chronicles 14:10, *"And David enquired of God, saying, Shall I go up against the Philistines? and wilt thou deliver them into mine hand? And the LORD said unto him, Go up; for I will deliver them into thine hand."*

See the commentary on 2 Samuel 5:19

1 Chronicles 14:11, *"So they came up to Baalperazim; and David smote them there. Then David said, God hath broken in upon mine enemies by mine hand like the breaking forth of waters: therefore they called the name of that place Baalperazim."*

See the commentary on 2 Samuel 5:20

1 Chronicles 14:12, *"And when they had left their gods there, David gave a commandment, and they were burned with fire."*

See commentary on 2 Samuel 5:21

1 Chronicles 14:14, *"Therefore David enquired again of God; and God said unto him, Go not up after them; turn away from them, and come upon them over against the mulberry trees."*

See commentary on 2 Samuel 5:23

1 Chronicles 14:16, *"David therefore did as God commanded him: and they smote the host of the Philistines from Gibeon even to Gazer."*

See commentary on 2 Samuel 5:25

1 Chronicles 14:17, *"And the fame of David went out into all lands; and the LORD brought the fear of him upon all nations."*

This verse does not have a counterpart in 2 Samuel like many of the verses before it. The fame of David was coupled with great amazement as to the tremendous feats he was able to accomplish. This is like the fame of Jesus which spread over Israel because of the mighty deeds He did. David's name was on the tongue of nearly every Israeli, either for good or for bad. Like Jesus, people either hated him or loved him, but no one could doubt the works that were done through him.

David knew it was the power of God that rested upon him that accomplished the mighty work and was glad that the nations were hearing of the things that the Lord did through him. Even David's enemies were afraid of him and his army. God Himself brought the fear of David down on the nations. Historians have approached David's life very carefully in the same manner. Not much writing can be found that doubts the mighty works David accomplished through the anointing of God upon his life!

1 Chronicles 15:1, *"And David made him houses in the city of David, and prepared a place for the ark of God, and pitched for it a tent."*

David did build his own house, but the term here is *houses,* because he no doubt built each wife and child an apartment or some sort of home. A three month period of time had lapsed since David's first and unsuccessful attempt to move the Ark to Jerusalem (1 Chronicles 13:14). The tent he had pitched was unoccupied for those months, as David each day looked at it and reflected upon why it was empty and how he could get the Ark home.

Some have questioned why the tabernacle of Moses was not brought from Gibeon, citing that perhaps the Gibeonites were unwilling to part with such a sacred historical object. But we must remember that David never intended the Ark to remain for long in the tent. He had spent much of his life preparing for the building of the magnificent Temple. Much gold, silver, brass and precious stone was already lying in store waiting for that time.

1 Chronicles 15:2, *"Then David said, None ought to carry the ark of God but the Levites: for them hath the LORD chosen to carry the ark of God, and to minister unto him for ever."*

David was a student of the Word and realized that the scripture strictly forbids the Ark to be moved on anything but the shoulders of the Levite priests (Deuteronomy 10:8). That is why the staves were placed in the sides of the Ark (Exodus 25:14). David realized what happened and stated it carefully in 1 Chronicles 15:13, *"For because ye did it not at the first, the LORD our God made a breach upon us, for that we sought him not after the due order."*

The account of the second attempt to move the Ark reveals all that David learned from his first attempt. This is one of the amazing things about the life of David, his determination to get it right for the glory of the Lord. He was angry and afraid of the Lord when Uzzah died, but through his relationship with the Lord and his Word, David realized God was God and He was the one who had put it in his heart to move the Ark, and He was the one that wanted it moved a certain way!

1 Chronicles 15:3, *"And David gathered all Israel together to Jerusalem, to bring up the ark of the LORD unto his place, which he had prepared for it."*

The details of the account of the second attempt to bring the Ark to Jerusalem is not covered in 2 Samuel. In verse 10 of chapter six of 2 Samuel, it states that David could not get the Ark home, so he took it to the house of Obededom the Gittite. Then in verse 11 we read of the blessing on the house of Obededom while the Ark was there three months. In verse twelve we read of David's going to get the Ark from the house of Obededom. None of the details are there in 2 Samuel concerning David's very careful placement of the priests on the assignment of moving the Ark. It is believed by some that the revelation of the priesthood of Melchizedek was given to David during these three months that the Ark was in the home of Obededom; therefore, he saw himself leading the priestly duties as a king and a priest!

1 Chronicles 15:4, *"And David assembled the children of Aaron, and the Levites"*:

Here we have the beginning of the very detailed list of eight hundred sixty two incorporated in the moving of the Ark to Jerusalem. Imagine the great amount of confidence in David's heart necessary to put this all together after such a colossal failure three months earlier. The list of these priests in this order has much to say concerning the future order of service and the manner in which they were appointed. The priestly order David set in place for the House of the Lord was still in place in the days of John the Baptist, even though there was a rebuilt Temple!

1 Chronicles 15:11, *"And David called for Zadok and Abiathar the priests, and for the Levites, for Uriel, Asaiah, and Joel, Shemaiah, and Eliel, and Amminadab,"*

After the assembly of the priests is complete, David gathers the leaders of the families of the high priests, Zadok and Abiathar, along with six of the major Levites. These six were elders of the Levitical tribe. David then commands them to be sanctified in order to bring the Ark unto Jerusalem. The verse that follows insinuates that the priests were not sanctified. 1 Chronicles 15:13a *"For because ye did it not at the first, the LORD our God made a breach upon us"* but in the second part of the verse, David acknowledges his own failure for allowing the lack of order that he allowed. Verse13b, *"for that we sought him not after the due order."* David is making every possible effort to please the Lord, bring Him glory, and usher in a national revival!

1 Chronicles 15:16, *"And David spake to the chief of the Levites to appoint their brethren to be the singers with instruments of musick, psalteries and harps and cymbals, sounding, by lifting up the voice with joy."*

Watts laments because David the king is placing the priests in their positions of service, claiming that he is out of his authoritative sphere. It rather should be noted that David actually told the priests to appoint their brethren in the various positions of worship. Lightfoot declares that David is operating in the Melchizedek order and is actually operating in the King and Priest order by ordering the priests to sanctify themselves and to appoint the worshippers in such a fashion as to insure the God of Israel was vividly and loudly worshipped.

Jesus fed the five thousand, yet He did not even tell the people to sit down in groups of fifty. He told the disciples to tell them to sit down in groups of fifty. David is credited with appointing the priests, but he told the leaders of the priests to do it. This can be seen in Solomon's following the set order David commanded as recorded in 2 Chronicles 8:14, *"And he appointed, according to the order of David his father, the courses of the priests to their service, and the Levites to their charges, to praise and minister before the priests, as the duty of every day required: the porters also by their courses at every gate: for so had David the man of God commanded."* Notice this is called *the order of David!*

1 Chronicles 15:25, "*So David, and the elders of Israel, and the captains over thousands, went to bring up the ark of the covenant of the LORD out of the house of Obededom with joy.*"

David knew that order and organization are not enemies of the Holy Spirit but that in fact there is great joy and confirmation in operating in the correct order! What a contrast from the first effort to move the Ark. It may be noted that all this bringing of the Ark back to Jerusalem is strong type for the restorationist who believes the church will finally migrate back to its full apostolic authority and beyond. In this, the type of the moving of the Ark is completely legitimate. The Ark is every ounce Jesus, from the rod that budded inside of it to the very material it is made from. The Ark or Jesus will simply be placed back to His rightful position in the Church. That is restoration!

1 Chronicles 15:27, "*And David was clothed with a robe of fine linen, and all the Levites that bare the ark, and the singers, and Chenaniah the master of the song with the singers: David also had upon him an ephod of linen.*"

This robe of fine linen is the ephod. (See the commentary in 2 Samuel 6:14.) This magnificent multitude carefully gathered for the express purpose of moving the most sacred piece of furniture in all of the history of Israel, was led by none other than the restored man after God's heart, King David!

1 Chronicles 15:29, "*And it came to pass, as the ark of the covenant of the LORD came to the city of David, that Michal the daughter of Saul looking out at a window saw king David dancing and playing: and she despised him in her heart.*"

See commentary in 2 Samuel 6:16

1 Chronicles 16:1, "*So they brought the ark of God, and set it in the midst of the tent that David had pitched for it: and they offered burnt sacrifices and peace offerings before God.*"

See Commentary on 2 Samuel 6:17

1 Chronicles 16:2, "*And when David had made an end of offering the burnt offerings and the peace offerings, he blessed the people in the name of the LORD.*"

See commentary on 2 Samuel 6:18

1 Chronicles 16:7, "*Then on that day David delivered first this psalm to thank the LORD into the hand of Asaph and his brethren.*"

Not only did David plan every minute detail of bringing the Ark from the house of Obededom, he also planned the ceremony for the placing of the Ark in the tent he had prepared for it. This verse shows us that David even picked out the songs that were sung for the ceremony. This song he chose for the first one is taken from two psalms in the book of Psalms: 105:1-15 and Psalms 96:1-11. He had written them earlier, no doubt by the Spirit of the Lord, and knew for what occasion they would be sung or proclaimed.

David then instituted worship twenty-four hours a day, a worship vigil that offered continuous service by the priests as well as the singers and musicians. 1 Chronicles 16:37, "*So he left there before the ark of the covenant of the LORD Asaph and his brethren, to minister before the ark continually, as every day's work required*": This is the only time in the history of Israel where such a thing took place. David was such a worshipper that he desired His God to be worshipped extravagantly at all times even when he was asleep!

1 Chronicles 16:43, "*And all the people departed every man to his house: and David returned to bless his house.*"

David came back to his house but left the priests and worshippers there to do their service in courses that he set up. These courses that David set the Levites to serve were very scriptural, and even until the time of Jesus, they were honored. Luke 1:5, "*There was in the days of Herod, the king of Judaea, a certain priest named Zacharias, of the course of Abia: and his wife was of the daughters of Aaron, and her name was Elisabeth.*" The course of Abia was the eighth course. 1 Chronicles 24:10, "*The seventh to Hakkoz, the eighth to Abijah.*"

The time of the birth of Jesus can be traced by the very course of Abia. After Zacharias finished his course, Elizabeth conceived. Six months later Mary conceived of the Holy Ghost. We suppose that Jesus was in the womb of Mary for nine months. Therefore Jesus was born one year and three months after the eighth course of priestly service! David's influence and anointing is inseparable from the Messiah.

David came home and blessed his house but also dealt with the criticism of Michal.

1 Chronicles 17:1, "*Now it came to pass, as David sat in his house, that David said to Nathan the prophet, Lo, I dwell in an house of cedars, but the ark of the covenant of the LORD remaineth under curtains.*"

See commentary on 2 Samuel 7:1-2

1 Chronicles 17:2, "*Then Nathan said unto David, Do all that is in thine heart; for God is with thee.*"

See commentary on 2 Samuel 7:3

1 Chronicles 17:4, "*Go and tell David my servant, Thus saith the LORD, Thou shalt not build me an house to dwell in*":

See Commentary on 2 Samuel 7:5

1 Chronicles 17:7, "*Now therefore thus shalt thou say unto my servant David, Thus saith the LORD of hosts, I took thee from the sheepcote, even from following the sheep, that thou shouldest be ruler over my people Israel*":

See Commentary on 2 Samuel 7:8

1 Chronicles 17:15, "*According to all these words, and according to all this vision, so did Nathan speak unto David.*"

See commentary on 2 Samuel 7:17

1 Chronicles 17:16, "*And David the king came and sat before the LORD, and said, Who am I, O LORD God, and what is mine house, that thou hast brought me hitherto?*"

See commentary on 2 Samuel 7:18

1 Chronicles 17:18, "*What can David speak more to thee for the honour of thy servant? for thou knowest thy servant.*"

See commentary on 2 Samuel 7:20

1 Chronicles 17:24, "*Let it even be established, that thy name may be magnified for ever, saying, The LORD of hosts is the God of Israel, even a God to Israel: and let the house of David thy servant be established before thee.*"

See commentary on 2 Samuel 7:26

1 Chronicles 18:1, *"Now after this it came to pass, that David smote the Philistines, and subdued them, and took Gath and her towns out of the hand of the Philistines."*

In this same account in 2 Samuel 8:1, Gath is called Methegammah. There is no such town or area that bears that name and for that reason it is variously translated. However it seems clear by comparing the two verses that for some reason or another Gath was called Methegammah. David is now dismantling the Philistine kingdom. However he has strong ties to many in Gath.   (See commentary on 2 Samuel 8:1)

1 Chronicles 18:2, *"And he smote Moab; and the Moabites became David's servants, and brought gifts."*

The account of this in 2 Samuel 8:2 records the controversial brutality of David in his dealing with the Moabites. Here it is not mentioned. (See commentary on 2 Samuel 8:2)

1 Chronicles 18:3, *"And David smote Hadarezer king of Zobah unto Hamath, as he went to stablish his dominion by the river Euphrates."*

See commentary on 2 Samuel 8:3

1 Chronicles 18:4, *"And David took from him a thousand chariots, and seven thousand horsemen, and twenty thousand footmen: David also houghed all the chariot horses, but reserved of them an hundred chariots."*

See commentary 2 Samuel 8:4

1 Chronicles 18:5, *"And when the Syrians of Damascus came to help Hadarezer king of Zobah, David slew of the Syrians two and twenty thousand men."*

See commentary 2 Samuel 8:5

1 Chronicles 18:6, *"Then David put garrisons in Syriadamascus; and the Syrians became David's servants, and brought gifts. Thus the LORD preserved David whithersoever he went."*

See commentary 2 Samuel 8:6

1 Chronicles 18:7, *"And David took the shields of gold that were on the servants of Hadarezer, and brought them to Jerusalem."*

See commentary on 2 Samuel 8:7

1 Chronicles 18:8, *"Likewise from Tibhath, and from Chun, cities of Hadarezer, brought David very much brass, wherewith Solomon made the brasen sea, and the pillars, and the vessels of brass."*

The cities of Tibhath and Chun are called Betah and Berothai in 2 Samuel 8:8. Most likely one account is the name of the city in Hebrew and the other in Syrian. Wesley writes, "Either therefore the same cities were called by several names, as is usual, the one by the Hebrews, the other by the Syrians, or those were two other cities, and so the brass was taken out of these four cities." The significant thing about this note from Wesley is the handling of what would be called by others a discrepancy. Wesley never looked for error but for explanation. May this commentary on the life of David ever follow the splendid example of Wesley, a true Biblicist.

1 Chronicles 18:9, *"Now when Tou king of Hamath heard how David had smitten all the host of Hadarezer king of Zobah"*;

See commentary on 2 Samuel 8:9

1 Chronicles 18:10, *"He sent Hadoram his son to king David, to enquire of his welfare, and to congratulate him, because he had fought against Hadarezer, and smitten him; (for Hadarezer had war with Tou;) and with him all manner of vessels of gold and silver and brass."*

Hadoram is also called Joram in the account of this in 2 Samuel. Otherwise read the commentary of 2 Samuel 8:10.

1 Chronicles 18:11, *"Them also king David dedicated unto the LORD, with the silver and the gold that he brought from all these nations; from Edom, and from Moab, and from the children of Ammon, and from the Philistines, and from Amalek."*

See commentary on 2 Samuel 8:11

1 Chronicles 18:13, *"And he put garrisons in Edom; and all the Edomites became David's servants. Thus the LORD preserved David whithersoever he went."*

See commentary on 2 Samuel 8:14

1 Chronicles 18:14, *"So David reigned over all Israel, and executed judgment and justice among all his people."*

See commentary on 2 Samuel 8:15

1 Chronicles 18:17, *"And Benaiah the son of Jehoiada was over the Cherethites and the Pelethites; and the sons of David were chief about the king."*

See commentary on 2 Samuel 8:18

1 Chronicles 19:2, *"And David said, I will shew kindness unto Hanun the son of Nahash, because his father shewed kindness to me. And David sent messengers to comfort him concerning his father. So the servants of David came into the land of the children of Ammon to Hanun, to comfort him."*

See commentary on 2 Samuel 10:2

1 Chronicles 19:3, *"But the princes of the children of Ammon said to Hanun, Thinkest thou that David doth honour thy father, that he hath sent comforters unto thee? are not his servants come unto thee for to search, and to overthrow, and to spy out the land?"*

See commentary on 2 Samuel 10:3

1 Chronicles 19:4, *"Wherefore Hanun took David's servants, and shaved them, and cut off their garments in the midst hard by their buttocks, and sent them away."*

See commentary on 2 Samuel 10:4

1 Chronicles 19:5, *"Then there went certain, and told David how the men were served. And he sent to meet them: for the men were greatly ashamed. And the king said, Tarry at Jericho until your beards be grown, and then return."*

See commentary on 2 Samuel 10:5

1 Chronicles 19:6, "*And when the children of Ammon saw that they had made themselves odious to David, Hanun and the children of Ammon sent a thousand talents of silver to hire them chariots and horsemen out of Mesopotamia, and out of Syriamaachah, and out of Zobah.*"

The difference in the names and numbers with the account in 2 Samuel 10 is easily explained by both the commentary on 2 Samuel 10:6 and also the fact that some of the soldiers fought in conjunction with the chariots, not necessarily meaning that everyone had their own chariot. Those assigned to chariot warfare were numbered with "the chariots." This explanation is confirmed by the actual ancient manner of warfare of that day.

1 Chronicles 19:8, "*And when David heard of it, he sent Joab, and all the host of the mighty men.*"

See commentary on 2 Samuel 10:7

1 Chronicles 19:17, "*And it was told David; and he gathered all Israel, and passed over Jordan, and came upon them, and set the battle in array against them. So when David had put the battle in array against the Syrians, they fought with him.*"

See commentary on 2 Samuel 10:17

1 Chronicles 19:18, "*But the Syrians fled before Israel; and David slew of the Syrians seven thousand men which fought in chariots, and forty thousand footmen, and killed Shophach the captain of the host.*"

The seven thousand men belonged to seven hundred chariots, and the forty thousand men were the combination of footmen with horsemen. Otherwise, see commentary on 2 Samuel 10:17.

1 Chronicles 19:19, "*And when the servants of Hadarezer saw that they were put to the worse before Israel, they made peace with David, and became his servants: neither would the Syrians help the children of Ammon any more.*"

See commentary on 2 Samuel 10:19

1 Chronicles 20:1, " *And it came to pass, that after the year was expired, at the time that kings go out to battle, Joab led forth the power of the army, and wasted the country of the children of Ammon, and came and besieged Rabbah. But David tarried at Jerusalem. And Joab smote Rabbah, and destroyed it.* "

See commentary on 2 Samuel 11:1

1 Chronicles 20:2, "*And David took the crown of their king from off his head, and found it to weigh a talent of gold, and there were precious stones in it; and it was set upon David's head: and he brought also exceeding much spoil out of the city.*"

See commentary 2 Samuel 12:30

1 Chronicles 20:3, "*And he brought out the people that were in it, and cut them with saws, and with harrows of iron, and with axes. Even so dealt David with all the cities of the children of Ammon. And David and all the people returned to Jerusalem.*"

See commentary on 2 Samuel 12:31

1 Chronicles 20:7, "*But when he defied Israel, Jonathan the son of Shimea David's brother slew him.*"

See commentary on 2 Samuel 21:21

1 Chronicles 20:8, "*These were born unto the giant in Gath; and they fell by the hand of David, and by the hand of his servants.*"

See commentary on 2 Samuel 21:22

1 Chronicles 21:1, "*And Satan stood up against Israel, and provoked David to number Israel.*"

See commentary on 2 Samuel 24:1

1 Chronicles 21:2, "*And David said to Joab and to the rulers of the people, Go, number Israel from Beersheba even to Dan; and bring the number of them to me, that I may know it.*"

See commentary on 2 Samuel 24:2

1 Chronicles 21:5, "*And Joab gave the sum of the number of the people unto David. And all they of Israel were a thousand thousand and an hundred thousand men that drew sword: and Judah was four hundred threescore and ten thousand men that drew sword.*"

The difference in the sum of soldiers resulting in the abominable census recorded here and in 2 Samuel 24:9 is discussed in detail in the commentary on 2 Samuel 24:1.

1 Chronicles 21:8, "*And David said unto God, I have sinned greatly, because I have done this thing: but now, I beseech thee, do away the iniquity of thy servant; for I have done very foolishly.*"

See commentary on 2 Samuel 24:10

1 Chronicles 21:9, "*And the LORD spake unto Gad, David's seer, saying,*"

See commentary on 2 Samuel 24:11

1 Chronicles 21:10, "*Go and tell David, saying, Thus saith the LORD, I offer thee three things: choose thee one of them, that I may do it unto thee.*"

See commentary on 2 Samuel 24:12

1 Chronicles 21:11, "*So Gad came to David, and said unto him, Thus saith the LORD, Choose thee*"

See commentary on 2 Samuel 24:13

1 Chronicles 21:13, "*And David said unto Gad, I am in a great strait: let me fall now into the hand of the LORD; for very great are his mercies: but let me not fall into the hand of man.*"

See commentary on 2 Samuel 24:14

1 Chronicles 21:16, *"And David lifted up his eyes, and saw the angel of the LORD stand between the earth and the heaven, having a drawn sword in his hand stretched out over Jerusalem. Then David and the elders of Israel, who were clothed in sackcloth, fell upon their faces."*

See commentary on 2 Samuel 24:17

1 Chronicles 21:17, *"And David said unto God, Is it not I that commanded the people to be numbered? even I it is that have sinned and done evil indeed; but as for these sheep, what have they done? let thine hand, I pray thee, O LORD my God, be on me, and on my father's house; but not on thy people, that they should be plagued."*

See commentary on 2 Samuel 24:17

1 Chronicles 21:18, *"Then the angel of the LORD commanded Gad to say to David, that David should go up, and set up an altar unto the LORD in the threshingfloor of Ornan the Jebusite."*

See commentary on 2 Samuel 24:18

1 Chronicles 21:19, *"And David went up at the saying of Gad, which he spake in the name of the LORD."*

See commentary on 2 Samuel 24:18

1 Chronicles 21:21, *"And as David came to Ornan, Ornan looked and saw David, and went out of the threshingfloor, and bowed himself to David with his face to the ground."*

The account in 2 Samuel does not record the reaction of Ornan's sons when they saw the destroying angel. They went and hid themselves (Verse 20). The sight of the wrath of God must have been most dreadful. Otherwise see commentary on 2 Samuel 24:18.

1 Chronicles 21:22, *"Then David said to Ornan, Grant me the place of this threshingfloor, that I may build an altar therein unto the LORD: thou shalt grant it me for the full price: that the plague may be stayed from the people."*

See commentary on 2 Samuel 24:21

1 Chronicles 21:23, *"And Ornan said unto David, Take it to thee, and let my lord the king do that which is good in his eyes: lo, I give thee the oxen also for burnt offerings, and the threshing instruments for wood, and the wheat for the meat offering; I give it all."*

See commentary on 2 Samuel 24:22

1 Chronicles 21:24, *"And king David said to Ornan, Nay; but I will verily buy it for the full price: for I will not take that which is thine for the LORD, nor offer burnt offerings without cost."*

See commentary on 2 Samuel 24:24

1 Chronicles 21:25, *"So David gave to Ornan for the place six hundred shekels of gold by weight."*

For the explanation of the alleged discrepancy concerning the threshing floor, see commentary on 2 Samuel 24:22.

1 Chronicles 21:26, *"And David built there an altar unto the LORD, and offered burnt offerings and peace offerings, and called upon the LORD; and he answered him from heaven by fire upon the altar of burnt offering."*

The Account of David's sacrifice and the Lord answering him by fire is not recorded in 2 Samuel, although 2 Samuel 24:25 tells of David's making the sacrifice and the plague stopped. What follows after the fire falling on David's sacrifice is one of the most amazing events in David's life.

1 Chronicles 21:28, *"At that time when David saw that the LORD had answered him in the threshingfloor of Ornan the Jebusite, then he sacrificed there."*

David perceived that when the Lord answered him with fire, God had changed the place of the sacrifice. This change was very significant in the history of Israel. That is why David says in the first verse of the next chapter, 1 Chronicles 22:1, *"This is the house of the LORD God, and this is the altar of the burnt offering for Israel."* This display of God's fire signified to the Jews that God was stopping His judgment on the nation and their leader, but He was also now showing Israel that Jerusalem would be the place for the presence of the Lord to permeate from there to all nations. Solomon was taught this from his father David and was also able to pray down fire in this same place.

Before the time of this plague, the place of sacrifice was in Gibeon where the tabernacle of the LORD, which Moses made in the wilderness, was. It is amazing that God would change the whole sacrificial system at the prayer of David, who at the time was being punished. Yet it was the offering that David made to appease judgment that reminded God of the supreme sacrifice for sin that would be made on this site a millennium later. The judgment for sin would be poured out upon God's own Son there, who is called the Son of David. It is only fitting that David would be involved in the change of the place of the sacrifice.

1 Chronicles 21:30, *"But David could not go before it to enquire of God: for he was afraid because of the sword of the angel of the LORD."*

This means that the direction David would have gone to make a sacrifice would have been toward Gibeon, but that is the direction the destroying angel was blocking. This reveals that David was of a mind to offer sacrifice before he received the instruction from the prophet Gad to offer it on Ornan's threshing floor. It is most likely that David would have proceeded to Gibeon and lay prostrate before the Lord there. However, he was probably relieved to not have to leave the city he loved so much, and when the fire fell, he knew where to build the Temple that he had prepared to build for so many years. This was the go ahead he had sought for a long time. He found it in sackcloth and contrition from his own failure!

1 Chronicles 22:1, *"Then David said, This is the house of the LORD God, and this is the altar of the burnt offering for Israel."*

There was no house there in the natural, yet David saw the house of the Lord. David knew when the fire fell that the house of God would be on that piece of real estate. We must remember David is a prophet as well as a king. The glory of the Lord had brought a witness to David's heart so powerfully that immediately he began to prefab the Temple. He had already gathered a lot of gold, silver, and brass for the project. He wanted the Ark of the Covenant to be in a magnificent edifice.

1 Chronicles 22:2, *"And David commanded to gather together the strangers that were in the land of Israel; and he set masons to hew wrought stones to build the house of God."*

This action confirms that David actually saw the house in the spiritual realm. Like Moses on the mountain who saw the pattern for the Tabernacle in the Wilderness, David evidently saw the pattern for what is called Solomon's Temple right here at this time. How else would he have known what size to make the stones and all of the other parts he was in the process of pre-fabricating? David thought it wise to utilize the gifting found in the proselytes in Israel to work on this project. These would have been practicing Jews that were not born Jews. David didn't just conquer nations; he made Jews out of them.

1 Chronicles 22:3, "*And David prepared iron in abundance for the nails for the doors of the gates, and for the joinings; and brass in abundance without weight*";

The Lord would not allow David to build the Temple but did not restrain him from pre-fabrication. This preparation was massive as illustrated by the terms *iron in abundance,* and *brass in abundance without weight.* The magnitude of precious metals used in Solomon's Temple is a historical wonder. There is an indication of the amount of gold used to overlay the nails found in 2 Chronicles 3:9, "*And the weight of the nails was fifty shekels of gold. And he overlaid the upper chambers with gold.*" The mention of the *joinings* here is speaking of the hardware needed to put the material together.

1 Chronicles 22:4, "*Also cedar trees in abundance: for the Zidonians and they of Tyre brought much cedar wood to David.*"

These were David's friends and very happy to serve him, but Watts reminds us they were well paid for their trouble. Later Solomon hired them for his own efforts and paid them well. The Zidonians themselves declared that there is none better at hewing wood than them (1 Kings 5:6).

1 Chronicles 22:5, "*And David said, Solomon my son is young and tender, and the house that is to be builded for the LORD must be exceeding magnifical, of fame and of glory throughout all countries: I will therefore now make preparation for it. So David prepared abundantly before his death.*"

David considered Solomon to be both young and tender. There must have been quite a contrast between David and his son Solomon. David was called a man of war. Solomon was never referred to as such, and even Rehoboam, the son of Solomon, was described as both young and tender (2 Chronicles 13:7). David did not see Solomon as being up to the task of building the Temple of the Lord without his help. David seemed to want to insure that Solomon would not cut corners and lessen the cost or size of this place of worship.

It seemed that David's heart for the house of worship was of such a powerful degree that many scholars believe he was looking prophetically into that time when Jerusalem would be the capital of the entire world. This does not seem preposterous at all in light of the messianic revelation that constantly flowed from God's heart to David's heart and from David's heart to David's pen.

In that passion, David charges Solomon before he dies to build the house of God. We know of no record of blueprints or building plans. Some demand there had to be some blueprints just because of the natural necessity in building such an edifice that shamed even the temple of Diana in Ephesus. One should not limit the power of God in this respect, however, most likely there was some sort of drawings.

1 Chronicles 22:7, "*And David said to Solomon, My son, as for me, it was in my mind to build an house unto the name of the LORD my God*":

Here is the record of David's delivering to Solomon the prophecy of his being the one to build the house of God. David's words correspond with the prophecy of Nathan in 1 Chronicles 17:7-15. It seems that David is quoting this prophecy to Solomon, but in Nathan's words, Solomon's name is not mentioned. This fact is a key to not only understanding David's prophetic anointing but also his boldness to follow the prophetic voice and extend it by the Spirit of God. Why? Because it was expressly forbidden, both to steal a prophets word, as well as to add to them or take any part of them away! The more one studies the prophetic life of David, the more amazed they are sure to become.

Some of David's instruction to Solomon is here recorded, and the summary of that which he told Solomon is this: 1) I could not build the Temple but I wanted to. 2) I am a man of war and because I was, you can be a man of peace, for I have conquered your enemies for you. 3) I have prepared everything you need for the construction of this most magnificent edifice. 4) Get up and do it, for it is now ready!

1 Chronicles 22:17, "*David also commanded all the princes of Israel to help Solomon his son, saying,*"

David left nothing undone that he could possibly do. This zeal for the house of the Lord describes David's heart and passion. He didn't want Solomon to have a problem with recruits, so he even commanded all of the leaders of Israel to help Solomon. We can see David's heart in his instructions in 1 Chronicles 22:19, "*Now set your heart and your soul to seek the LORD your God; arise therefore, and build ye the sanctuary of the LORD God, to bring the ark of the covenant of the LORD, and the holy vessels of God, into the house that is to be built to the name of the LORD.*" We find the detailed account of David's charge to the princes concerning their support for this project in 1 Chronicles 28:1-6.

1 Chronicles 23:1, "*So when David was old and full of days, he made Solomon his son king over Israel.*"

This is the short summary of David's making Solomon king in his place. The full story is found in 1 Kings 1:33-39. The struggle for the dynasty continued until the very minute Solomon was anointed with oil by Zadok the priest. There is always a struggle from the powers of hell to keep the right king and the right priest from coming into proper order. The dark world knows they will suffer heavy loss when the Melchizedek pattern is complete.

1 Chronicles 23:5, *"Moreover four thousand were porters; and four thousand praised the LORD with the instruments which I made, said David, to praise therewith."*

The sheer mass of porters described here helps one to see the magnitude of the whole assembly of the house of the Lord. Imagine the monumental effort David made in pre-fabricating the Temple and then assigning all of the officers for every single position including the porters, and that being four thousand! Some even ascribe David as the manufacturer of the very instruments of worship. However this verse actually means David had them made through his commandments to his servants, even though 2 Chronicles 29:26 declares them to be David's instruments. *"And the Levites stood with the instruments of David, and the priests with the trumpets."* It is most likely that David made or assisted in making his own harps.

1 Chronicles 23:6, *"And David divided them into courses among the sons of Levi, namely, Gershon, Kohath, and Merari."*

This division and appointment of the priesthood is recorded more precisely in 1 Chronicles 6 and is completely confirmed in 2 Chronicles 8:14. This interaction of the priesthood with David has amazed theologians throughout the ages. How could David take such authority over the priesthood, and yet he himself was not the one who anointed Solomon, but Zadok? Is it not because of the messianic power in David's life and that Judah would ultimately be the tribe of both the king and the high priest, Jesus of Nazareth?

1 Chronicles 23:25, *"For David said, The LORD God of Israel hath given rest unto his people, that they may dwell in Jerusalem for ever"*:

Here David is careful to give glory to the Lord for the defeat of all of his enemies. It is said in several different ways by the students of the life of David that even when David doesn't mention the Lord in his victory speeches, there is ample proof in his writings that he never thought he did anything without the help of the Lord. This is very provable and yet the Lord would not even let him rest in the least bit of false security. David had learned through his failures that the sovereignty of God had chosen him for the victorious king and the city of Jerusalem for His glory to dwell!

1 Chronicles 23:27, *"For by the last words of David the Levites were numbered from twenty years old and above"*:

David lowers the age to twenty for the draft of the Levites, obviously engaging more priests in the service of the Lord by course. The scripture doesn't tell us any other reason for the change in recruiting and thus it is not needed. The population of the people engaging in worship demanded more priests, and the next verse gives support to that need. The key to understanding David's heart is manifested here in this change in recruiting age for the priesthood. 1) David understands the altar and the function of the Aaronic priesthood which begins at thirty years of age instead of twenty or twenty five as stated in Numbers 4:3, *"From thirty years old and upward even until fifty years old, all that enter into the host, to do the work in the tabernacle of the congregation."*

The high priest order is always thirty years of age; therefore both John the Baptist and Jesus began their ministry at age thirty. David also began to reign in Hebron at thirty. 2) David is clearly making sure the priestly order is as accurate scripturally as he can make, it and yet there are not enough Aaronic priests to keep the flow of worship and sacrifice going continually. David would never again disregard the priestly order after his dismal failure of trying to move the Ark to Jerusalem in the first attempt.

1 Chronicles 24:3, *"And David distributed them, both Zadok of the sons of Eleazar, and Ahimelech of the sons of Ithamar, according to their offices in their service."*

David himself made sure the priestly order was accurate. He was very careful to place the Zadok priesthood in an appropriate place, according to the prophecy of the unnamed prophet whose words are recorded beginning at 1 Samuel 2:27. David no doubt knew the prophecy well and leaned his weight upon it through his dark days as a refugee from Saul. David evidently taught Solomon that Zadok was the faithful priesthood. Therefore, Solomon removed Abiathar from sharing the office of the high priest with Zadok.

In the tenth verse of this chapter we see that Abijah is listed as the eighth course. This course was still intact at the time of Jesus' birth. Luke 1:5 *"There was in the days of Herod, the king of Judaea, a certain priest named Zacharias, of the course of Abia: and his wife was of the daughters of Aaron, and her name was Elisabeth."* This is significant in establishing a time of Jesus' birth because he was born one year and three months after the finishing of the eighth course. We count nine months for John to arrive and six months later for the birth of Jesus! All of the courses and the priestly families that served in them are here recorded.

1 Chronicles 24:31, *"These likewise cast lots over against their brethren the sons of Aaron in the presence of David the king, and Zadok, and Ahimelech, and the chief of the fathers of the priests and Levites, even the principal fathers over against their younger brethren."*

This verse clearly justifies Lightfoot's amazing teaching on the difference of meaning between the terms priests, Levites, and the sons of Aaron. No one could approach the altar unless they were sons of Aaron (Exodus 28:43). Yet all of the sons of Aaron were both priests and Levites. All of the Levites were priests, but not all were the sons of Aaron. Inactive priests were called Levites, but in their courses they were called priests, and in the altar work they had to be the sons of Aaron. John the Baptist was the first born son of an Aaronic father, (Zacharias burned incense). Elizabeth, who was barren until John was born, was of the daughters of Aaron (Luke 1:4). All priests, including the sons of Aaron, could have at times been called Levites or priests, but the division was at the altar of consecration, which was only for Aaron and his sons. It should be noted that Zadok can easily be traced as one of the sons of Aaron!

1 Chronicles 25:1, "*Moreover David and the captains of the host separated to the service of the sons of Asaph, and of Heman, and of Jeduthun, who should prophesy with harps, with psalteries, and with cymbals: and the number of the workmen according to their service was*":

Wesley declares this work of separating the singers and musical prophets was done by David mostly through his ability as a prophet. Wesley believed the delegation of tasks to his captains was done in that anointing as well. Wesley's statement should not cause one to stumble, for David's amazing ability to lead and organize was prophetic and supernatural. Since Wesley himself was said to be supernaturally gifted with a supernatural ability to put the right person in the right position, it is fitting that it would be his commentary that would bear this out about David.

One should notice David's recognition of those who could prophesy with harps. Watts declared that the harp section of the worship team in Jerusalem had to be one of the world's wonders at that time. Yet, we find no record of David's playing his harp publicly except for Saul. It seemed his gift was reserved for those intimate moments with the Lord when the Lord poured through him His own heart!

1 Chronicles 26:26, "*Which Shelomith and his brethren were over all the treasures of the dedicated things, which David the king, and the chief fathers, the captains over thousands and hundreds, and the captains of the host, had dedicated.*"

It should only be expected that the greatest worshipper in the history of Israel was also the greatest donor in the project of building the house of worship. David's wealth is not often spoken of. The immense wealth he accumulated was never seen as his own but for the work of the Lord. David placed trusted men over the treasury and seemed to never worry over his money or ask for the account of his wealth. Completely free and disinterested generosity was characteristic of the Sweet Psalmist of Israel!

1 Chronicles 26:31, *"Among the Hebronites was Jerijah the chief, even among the Hebronites, according to the generations of his fathers. In the fortieth year of the reign of David they were sought for, and there were found among them mighty men of valour at Jazer of Gilead."*

This is the last year of David's dynasty. He reigned seven and one-half years in Hebron and thirty-three in Jerusalem, over all of Israel (1 Kings 2:11). This diligence in setting everything in order in its place not only shows David's working in supernatural power, but it also shows us the extent of David's tenacity in seeking out the very best of the best to place over the work. Pastors and leaders ought to learn from this example, for the work of God deserves such diligence!

1 Chronicles 26:32, *"And his brethren, men of valour, were two thousand and seven hundred chief fathers, whom king David made rulers over the Reubenites, the Gadites, and the half tribe of Manasseh, for every matter pertaining to God, and affairs of the king."*

David's care and concern reached all the way to those Jews on the other side of Jordan. He employed them in the work of the Lord and made sure that they were able to do both spiritual and temporal business. Many trust the care of the church to those who are successful in business, but not in spiritual matters, thinking they do well in doing so. God's business is not properly administered without the grace of the Holy Spirit. David well knew this and therefore he chose men who could minister to God and man!

1 Chronicles 27:18, *"Of Judah, Elihu, one of the brethren of David: of Issachar, Omri the son of Michael"*:

This account of one of the brothers of David is quite rare. We don't read much of their activities. Some historical research has been done, but even at that, not much is known of their exploits which were perhaps scarce. There seemed to be a sort of jealousy toward David from his brothers when he came to the battlefield the day of his battle with Goliath, somewhat like that of Joseph's brothers. Eliab was the eldest brother of David, and it was he that spoke against David before the battle with Goliath (1 Samuel 17:28). Shimeah, David's brother, was known for having a son named Jonadab who was "a very subtil man" involved in the rape of David's daughter Tamar (2 Samuel 13:3). But he also had a son named Jonathan who was a great warrior (2 Samuel 21:21). Eliab, Abinadab and Shammah are mentioned in Saul's army (1 Samuel 17:13).

1 Chronicles 27:23, *"But David took not the number of them from twenty years old and under: because the LORD had said he would increase Israel like to the stars of the heavens."*

This is quite a contrast from the root of pride satan found to tempt David to count the people in 1 Chronicles 21. Here David counts only those twenty and above while leaning on the good Word of God who promised innumerable Hebrews to come!

1 Chronicles 27:24, *"Joab the son of Zeruiah began to number, but he finished not, because there fell wrath for it against Israel; neither was the number put in the account of the chronicles of king David."*

Joab knew David was out of the will of God in counting these people, even though he was not a godly man himself. Lightfoot declared Joab to be a Jew only in his mind. Yet it should be noted that all that the wicked say is neither untrue nor unwise. Sometimes even the wicked can be used to reprove the righteous. Joab didn't finish the census, nor did he record the number, although we have the tally as for as Joab went. Someone recorded it.

1Chronicles 27:31, *"And over the flocks was Jaziz the Hagerite. All these were the rulers of the substance which was king David's."*

Here is another indication of the immense wealth of King David that is often pointed out throughout this commentary. This commentary of the life of David often reflects David as a wealthy man and a prophet purposefully. Why? Because many do not consider David as either one. He never called himself a prophet or a wealthy man, and neither does the scripture refer to him as either. However, a deeper study of the verses will reveal that he was both!

1 Chronicles 27:32, *"Also Jonathan David's uncle was a counsellor, a wise man, and a scribe. and Jehiel the son of Hachmoni was with the king's sons":*

Here is yet another Jonathan who is David's uncle, and one greatly esteemed for his scholarly wisdom. David employed the greatest and wisest tutors for his sons as well, which is what is meant by the phrase, *"Jehiel the son of Hachmoni was with the king's sons."* David had many great men around him, and evidently David taught Solomon his son the great importance of having wise counsel, for Solomon spoke of it in two separate places in the Proverbs. Proverbs 11:14 says, *"Where no counsel is, the people fall: but in the multitude of counsellors there is safety."* And Proverbs 24:6 says, *"For by wise counsel thou shalt make thy war: and in multitude of counsellors there is safety."* The delight and respect David had for wise counsel was overshadowed by his love for the Word of the Lord. Psalm 119 is a masterpiece poetically, mathematically, and is also total exaltation of the Word!

1 Chronicles 28:1, *"And David assembled all the princes of Israel, the princes of the tribes, and the captains of the companies that ministered to the king by course, and the captains over the thousands, and captains over the hundreds, and the stewards over all the substance and possession of the king, and of his sons, with the officers, and with the mighty men, and with all the valiant men, unto Jerusalem."*

David now assembles all of those mentioned here for a final word of public instruction. He has many proselytes from many nations employed in his top tiers of leadership. This mixed congregation is now assembled at the king's request. One of the busiest and most productive lives ever lived is coming to an end, and David is sure to end it properly and fully with his vision extending far beyond his days.

1 Chronicles 28:2, *"Then David the king stood up upon his feet, and said, Hear me, my brethren, and my people: As for me, I had in mine heart to build an house of rest for the ark of the covenant of the LORD, and for the footstool of our God, and had made ready for the building"*:

David stands on his feet, which indicates that he is healed or improved from his infirmity recorded in 1 Kings 1:1. He then speaks in a very transparent manner with his people as to the very specific prophecies he had received and given concerning the building of the Temple. The people knew they were listening to a man that loved the Lord with all of his heart and loved the Ark of His Covenant immensely. David delivered a very passionate and emotional discourse to the people, sharing his heart and exhorting the people to stay true to the Lord with all of their hearts. David declared that by the will of God, it is Solomon that will build what he could only provide for! Then he spoke directly to Solomon in the presence of all of the people saying, "Do it."

1 Chronicles 28:11, *"Then David gave to Solomon his son the pattern of the porch, and of the houses thereof, and of the treasuries thereof, and of the upper chambers thereof, and of the inner parlours thereof, and of the place of the mercy seat,"*

How could one give such a strong commandment to build without giving the plan to do it? It is not the way of the Lord to command you to do something without the instructions to do it. Neither is it the way of strong and Godly leaders to do so. God's commandments and patterns in the scripture are explicit. There are a hundred times more verses concerning the building of the Tabernacle and the Temple than on the creation itself. God didn't need instruction on creating the universe and spends very little time on telling us how He did it. Yet He takes great pains in explaining to us what He wants us to do for Him.

1 Chronicles 28:19, *"All this, said David, the LORD made me understand in writing by his hand upon me, even all the works of this pattern."*

Perhaps here is the record of a blueprint, though the parchment itself is not mentioned. Scholars are not in unity as to whether there was an actual blueprint, but this verse seems to indicate that God actually gave him the ability to write out all of the details as to how to build the Temple. Because we do not have the record of that as we do the Tabernacle in the wilderness, it seems to aggravate some, but for no good reason. Solomon's Temple is adequately described, and few doubt David's ability to hear God, first, on how to build it, and second, on how to deliver the instructions to Solomon.

1 Chronicles 28:20, *"And David said to Solomon his son, Be strong and of good courage, and do it: fear not, nor be dismayed: for the LORD God, even my God, will be with thee; he will not fail thee, nor forsake thee, until thou hast finished all the work for the service of the house of the LORD."*

In this powerful verse, David covers every area of concern for young Solomon. 1) He must have strength to not get discouraged. 2) He must have courage to not be afraid. 3) He must have faith that God will not fail him. 4) He must have perseverance to finish the project. 5) He must remember who it is all for.

A preacher lovingly left this verse in a sealed envelope to be presented after his death to his son who was also called to the ministry!

1 Chronicles 29:1, *"Furthermore David the king said unto all the congregation, Solomon my son, whom alone God hath chosen, is yet young and tender, and the work is great: for the palace is not for man, but for the LORD God."*

David again stirs up his people to assist the young Solomon as he did in 1 Chronicles 22:5. The lifelong dream of David will become a reality through his son Solomon, but David seems concerned for the youth of Solomon and the magnitude of the national task. Herein is the heart of David for the work of his God!

David then begins to share with the people what he had given to the Lord's house and why he had given it. 1 Chronicles 29:3, *"Moreover, because I have set my affection to the house of my God, I have of mine own proper good, of gold and silver, which I have given to the house of my God, over and above all that I have prepared for the holy house."*

Again we can see both David's immense wealth and how he considered it to be for the Lord alone!

1 Chronicles 29:9, *"Then the people rejoiced, for that they offered willingly, because with perfect heart they offered willingly to the LORD: and David the king also rejoiced with great joy."*

The vision is transferred! The people received the assignment, and they received the heart to give to the work as David did! It is usually not wise to speak of our own generosity, but sometimes it is needful for the motivation of others. Only those whose hearts are free from covetousness should do so. Paul reluctantly told of his generosity to the church at Corinth. Nehemiah did so to reprove the greed in his company of workers. Wesley did so to reprove the stingy and encourage the givers! David here does so, and both he and the people enter in to great joy.

1 Chronicles 29:10, *"Wherefore David blessed the LORD before all the congregation: and David said, Blessed be thou, LORD God of Israel our father, for ever and ever."*

Praise begets praise. The tremendous amount of joy that was very present at that time was filled with praises unto the Lord. Therefore David praises the Lord and blesses Him in the congregation for giving the people the heart of praise! David gives an excellent discourse of worshipful words unto the Lord in the ears of the people. David was not only a private worshipper but a public worshipper. This is a very high time in the history of the nation of Israel and is picturesque of the coming millennium in which the Christ will lead the nation of Israel into the great glory that will cover the earth!

1 Chronicles 29:20, *"And David said to all the congregation, Now bless the LORD your God. And all the congregation blessed the LORD God of their fathers, and bowed down their heads, and worshipped the LORD, and the king."*

The praise now leads to very solemn worship. After David blesses the Lord, he tells the people to bless the Lord. In so doing, they are moved to bow their heads in reverence to the God of Abraham, Isaac, and Jacob.

The verse seems to be saying that the people are worshipping David. Yet, it is the Lord they are giving glory to, and it is David they extend civil appreciation toward. David never had an idol. He never allowed an idol. He hated idolatry with a perfect hatred. He was leading the congregation in worshipping the Lord. He himself was engaged in worship. To interpret this verse to mean the people were worshipping David would be a polemical travesty. This is a very high time for Israel, and they are giving glory to the Lord and appreciation to David!

The vision is transferred. The people have a heart to give. The people are full of praise. The people have a heart to worship. They have a heart to make sacrifices by the priesthood in the order David set up. Israel is in revival!

1 Chronicles 29:22, "*And did eat and drink before the LORD on that day with great gladness. And they made Solomon the son of David king the second time, and anointed him unto the LORD to be the chief governor, and Zadok to be priest.*"

This revival continues with the second crowning of King Solomon as the king of Israel. The first time was a small and rushed ceremony that required haste to quell the rebellion of Adonijah (1 Kings 1:1-51). This second time was a lot different. The uprising had been aborted. The nation was united. David was feeling much better from his infirmity. The worship was high. The will of the Lord was revealed to the whole congregation.

Like his father David, Solomon was anointed king three times. Zadok, the faithful priest, was also re-sanctioned at this time which is quite significant, for Zadok was like a vice president in the king and priest order. As often borne out in this commentary, when the right king of Judah comes in unity with the right priest of Levi, there will always be a revival!

1 Chronicles 29:23, "*Then Solomon sat on the throne of the LORD as king instead of David his father, and prospered; and all Israel obeyed him.*"

The great transaction was completed. Solomon is now king and the second in authority over the earth. Jews mostly believe that their king is second in command over all of the earth, second only unto God himself. Now this will be proven during the millennium, as David will be raised up as king of Israel while Jesus is king over all nations (Jeremiah 30:9).

1 Chronicles 29:24, "*And all the princes, and the mighty men, and all the sons likewise of king David, submitted themselves unto Solomon the king.*"

The nation of Israel has now accepted the kingship of Solomon without reservation. This is a key to the success of Solomon, as well as the wisdom God gave him. David took care of the whole matter of transferring the loyalty of the people from him to Solomon his son. He did so by sharing with them the private prophecy given to him by Nathan the prophet, as well as the prophecies that he himself had received from the Lord.

There is no record of any more rebellion toward the house of David. When Solomon began to backslide, the Lord allowed trouble to come to his house from within. But at this time the Lord blessed Solomon with the favor of David, and so the people submitted to him or more literally "put their hand under his."

1 Chronicles 29:26, *"Thus David the son of Jesse reigned over all Israel."*

Now the scripture begins another short summary of David's dynasty by concluding the report of his powerful life. Many scholars have tried to claim these last verses are mistakenly put here. However, these words being here not only draw the curtain on the life of David, who ended his days with honor and riches, but bring direct confirmation to every reader that, in fact, David (through his son) was still reigning over Israel. One might easily conclude that other than the Lord Jesus, there has never been a more amazing life than that of the Sweet Psalmist of Israel.

1 Chronicles 29:29, *"Now the acts of David the king, first and last, behold, they are written in the book of Samuel the seer, and in the book of Nathan the prophet, and in the book of Gad the seer,"*

The Chronicles were mostly written by Gad and Nathan. Other prophets were probably involved. Many believe Samuel was also involved in some of the writings of the Chronicles, but they were mostly finished by Gad and Nathan. There certainly is plenty of evidence that the authors of the chronicles had more than just intellectual knowledge of David. Clark declares there were books of Gad and Nathan but they were lost. Wesley believed that when you read the Chronicles you were reading the books they said were lost. After Samuel, the major influence by prophets in the life of David was Gad and Nathan. No one knew him better than these two prophets and Zadok the priest!

2 Chronicles

2Chronicles 1:1, *"And Solomon the son of David was strengthened in his kingdom, and the LORD his God was with him, and magnified him exceedingly."*

Solomon the son of David, this is how he will be known by the people of Israel all throughout the ages. The extreme blessing of God fell upon Solomon. Consider his blessings. 1) His God is Jehovah the God of Abraham, Isaac and Jacob. 2) His father was a man after the Lord's own heart. 3) His father had taught him the ways of the Lord. 4) His father had orchestrated for him the most powerful worship and sacrifice assembly ever put together on earth to honor the living God. 5) His father had commissioned him to build the most magnificent Temple the world has ever known. 6) His father had subdued all of his potential enemies. 7) His father had spent his last 3 months giving him instructions to do the work ahead. 8) His father had given him the most terrific military machine ever assembled. 9) His father had left him with untold riches.

The wonder of the blessing on Solomon, the son of David, would stun the nations and leave the elite of the world speechless!

2 Chronicles 1:4, *"But the ark of God had David brought up from Kirjathjearim to the place which David had prepared for it: for he had pitched a tent for it at Jerusalem."*

Solomon has now led the congregation of Israel to the high place in Gibeon to sacrifice, for that was where the Tabernacle of Moses was. The Ark is in Jerusalem, but the Tabernacle is in Gibeon. Bishop Patrick declares this trip to Gibeon was an unexplainable action on Solomon's part. Loweth declares it to be an inexcusable compromise! However, God blessed Solomon immensely when he got there. It seems to be a compromise, and yet he was blessed, leaving speculation to run in every direction.

We do know 1) David knew by the spirit that Jerusalem was the place to sacrifice after the Lord answered by fire on Ornan's threshing floor. 1 Chronicles 22:1 *"Then David said, This is the house of the LORD God, and this is the altar of the burnt offering for Israel."* 2) David gave no instruction that we can find, implied or otherwise, about going or not going to Gibeon to sacrifice. 3) David was also blessed during his own failure, both at Ziklag and Ornan's threshing floor. 4) Through David, there was a definite shift in the place of offering sacrifice from the high places to Mount Moriah.

However, Solomon's trip to Gibeon to offer sacrifices remains a debate unsettled among theologians. Lightfoot declares this to have occurred in the second year of Solomon's reign, and that the incident shows Solomon is already moving away from the messianic order by going to Gibeon. Those who question Lightfoot often cite the fact that the Lord appeared to Solomon at Gibeon and there imparted to Solomon his request for wisdom. Their legitimate question is that if Solomon was out of the will of God, why would the Lord bless him there? Yet, 1 Kings 3:3 drives a nail in the attempt to release Solomon of any wrong in this matter, even though the Lord blessed him there. *"And Solomon loved the LORD, walking in the statutes of David his father: only he sacrificed and burnt incense in high places."*

It seems that Solomon, young and tender, in his zeal for the Lord, thought he was doing right, and with a pure heart went to great trouble to sacrifice in both places to be sure to please the Lord. Solomon just didn't have the freedom to completely depart from religion in order to follow the revelation of his father. This is the case with religion in general, and is also the very root of reason for the Jews rejecting Jesus!

2 Chronicles 1:8, *"And Solomon said unto God, Thou hast shewed great mercy unto David my father, and hast made me to reign in his stead."*

Solomon's words are pure, pious, and humble. He realizes his anointing is directly connected with his father. See commentary on 1 Kings 3:6.

2 Chronicles 1:9, *"Now, O LORD God, let thy promise unto David my father be established: for thou hast made me king over a people like the dust of the earth in multitude."*

See commentary on 1 Kings 3:7

2 Chronicles 2:3, *"And Solomon sent to Huram the king of Tyre, saying, As thou didst deal with David my father, and didst send him cedars to build him an house to dwell therein, even so deal with me."*

See commentary on 1 Kings 5:1

2 Chronicles 2:7, *"Send me now therefore a man cunning to work in gold, and in silver, and in brass, and in iron, and in purple, and crimson, and blue, and that can skill to grave with the cunning men that are with me in Judah and in Jerusalem, whom David my father did provide."*

Here is proof that Solomon had learned from his father David the value of having the right person leading the right project. Solomon is not looking for men, he has them. He is looking for a man who is capable of leading the men that he has to do the work with the material that David had provided. David not only provided the material but the mentoring Solomon needed to oversee the overseers.

2 Chronicles 2:12, *"Huram said moreover, Blessed be the LORD God of Israel, that made heaven and earth, who hath given to David the king a wise son, endued with prudence and understanding, that might build an house for the LORD, and an house for his kingdom."*

See the commentary on 1 Kings 5:7

2 Chronicles 2:14, *"The son of a woman of the daughters of Dan, and his father was a man of Tyre, skilful to work in gold, and in silver, in brass, in iron, in stone, and in timber, in purple, in blue, and in fine linen, and in crimson; also to grave any manner of graving, and to find out every device*

which shall be put to him, with thy cunning men, and with the cunning men of my lord David thy father."

The man that was needed has been found. A woman of the tribe of Dan married into the tribe of Naphtali, for in 1 Kings 7:14 this man is called *"a widow's son of the tribe of Naphtali."* This would be the man that would connect the cunning men of Solomon with the cunning men of David, and all of them are assisted by the amazing abilities of the Sidonians!

2 Chronicles 2:17, *"And Solomon numbered all the strangers that were in the land of Israel, after the numbering wherewith David his father had numbered them; and they were found an hundred and fifty thousand and three thousand and six hundred."*

David had numbered these strangers or non-Jews as is recorded in 1 Chronicles 22:2 *"And David commanded to gather together the strangers that were in the land of Israel; and he set masons to hew wrought stones to build the house of God."* David did so for their work, and Solomon is following the very same pattern. Some of these were proselytes to the Jewish faith, while others were pure heathens. The ones who became Jews and proved themselves to be so were not bondservants, as the heathens, but actually received wages. Solomon, like his father, was a very generous man. Both believed in hard work. Both believed that it was legitimate to employ heathens to advance the work of Jehovah!

2 Chronicles 3:1, *"Then Solomon began to build the house of the LORD at Jerusalem in mount Moriah, where the LORD appeared unto David his father, in the place that David had prepared in the threshingfloor of Ornan the Jebusite."*

There seemed to be no competition for the building site in Solomon's heart, even though he led the people to the high place in Gibeon to offer sacrifices. Solomon was instructed very carefully, not only how to build the Temple, but where to build it. Probably some of the ancients jockeyed for having it built where the tabernacle of Moses was, or some other sacred place, but David knew when the fire fell that day on the threshing floor of Ornan, that the Temple would be built there!

Solomon began to build the house of the Lord in his fourth year as king. The delay of four years is not explained. It seems the building of the Temple was prepared by David, and David told Solomon to do it. Why the delay? One year was a sabbatical year and it is understood that there would be no workers available. On the surface, it appears that Solomon was slow in carrying out his father's orders.

Solomon built his own house afterward, so that project was started, but the Temple was finished in seven years. 1 Kings 6:38, *"And in the eleventh year, in the month Bul, which is the eighth month, was the house finished throughout all the parts thereof, and according to all the fashion of it. So was he seven years in building it."* The next verse tells of the house for Solomon. 1 Kings 7:1, *"But Solomon was building his own house thirteen years, and he finished all his house."* The strongest possibility is that the servants of Hiram took that long to finish the pre-fabrication. The next thirty seven verses describe the instruction he received from David and the Lord for building the Temple.

2 Chronicles 5:1, *"Thus all the work that Solomon made for the house of the LORD was finished: and Solomon brought in all the things that David his father had dedicated; and the silver, and the gold, and all the instruments, put he among the treasures of the house of God."*

The Temple is finished, and Solomon brings in the sanctified vessels that David had lovingly dedicated to the Lord, along with the royal treasures. It seems that Solomon didn't use all of the gold and silver David had saved for the house of the Lord. David had prepared more than was needed, for now Solomon is placing the gold from David in the treasury of Israel. Otherwise see the commentary on 1 Kings 7:51.

2 Chronicles 5:2, *"Then Solomon assembled the elders of Israel, and all the heads of the tribes, the chief of the fathers of the children of Israel, unto Jerusalem, to bring up the ark of the covenant of the LORD out of the city of David, which is Zion."*

Immediately upon moving in the sacred and dedicated articles, he calls the assembly together for the task of moving the Ark. This same account is nearly word for word in 1 Kings 8:1-9. See the commentary on 1 Kings 8:1.

2 Chronicles 6:4, *"And he said, Blessed be the LORD God of Israel, who hath with his hands fulfilled that which he spake with his mouth to my father David, saying,"*

Here is a display of the wisdom God gave Solomon. He is not saying, "Look what I have done," although in verse two it seems Solomon is headed that way. He says in 2 Chronicles 6:2, *"But I have built an house of habitation for thee, and a place for thy dwelling forever."* Solomon clearly gives the Lord credit for building the Temple. Yet he goes even further; he declares that in the word spoken to David was the latent power to accomplish that which the word spoke. This is very Jewish in the fact that this is the way they looked at the Word of God, especially David. Nearly every one of the heroes of faith mentioned in Hebrews eleven demonstrated this level of faith. If God commanded it or prophesied it to be done, in that Word is the enablement. It is not an emotional matter, but a spiritual principle or precept! David's love for all of the Word of God was transferred to Solomon.

2 Chronicles 6:6, *"But I have chosen Jerusalem, that my name might be there; and have chosen David to be over my people Israel."*

Solomon continues this powerful discourse by rehearsing in the people's ears the Word of the Lord concerning David and Jerusalem. Solomon obeyed the word of the Lord given to David, even though as of yet the Lord had not spoken to him concerning the sacrifice not being made in the high places or in the Tabernacle of Moses in Gibeon. This could be another reason for Solomon's leading the children of Israel to Gibeon and making the great number of sacrifices there in his second year as king. Later Solomon himself received the word on that matter in 2 Chronicles 7:12, *"And the LORD appeared to Solomon by night, and said unto him, I have heard thy prayer, and have chosen this place to myself for an house of sacrifice."* Even after all of that, Solomon eventually turned to idolatry.

2 Chronicles 6:7, *"Now it was in the heart of David my father to build an house for the name of the LORD God of Israel."*

Although in the Hebrew these are very passionate words, Watts calls this an understatement concerning David and his desire to build a house for the Ark of the Covenant to rest in. Wesley said, "David's heart was made quite glad as the Lord revealed to him the instructions to build the House of God because his heart was heavily bent to do it!"

2 Chronicles 6:8, *"But the LORD said to David my father, Forasmuch as it was in thine heart to build an house for my name, thou didst well in that it was in thine heart"*:

This is one of the confirmations that in fact the Lord was pleased with the passion David had for the building of the Temple. In reading all of the words recorded that God said about the matter, it almost seems that the Lord didn't even want the Temple built. In fact the Lord is most interested in the heart we have for pleasing Him and honoring Him. It blessed the Lord that David had such a heart to do this for Him, even though it wasn't something He needed or required. For this reason it blessed the Lord all the more. Solomon is also making the point that the Lord halted David's plans, and told David his son would build it, even Solomon.

2 Chronicles 6:10, *"The LORD therefore hath performed his word that he hath spoken: for I am risen up in the room of David my father, and am set on the throne of Israel, as the LORD promised, and have built the house for the name of the LORD God of Israel."*

The prayer that follows, and the fire that falls, is ample proof that Solomon at this time is humble before the Lord. His discourse is designed to glorify the Lord and to honor his father David. This is the key to great blessing. To glorify God and to honor whom God honors. There are many who suppose that because they glorify God, they have liberty to dishonor the one the Lord has honored. This is a great mistake, and one that David did not make. He was afraid to touch Saul because God had honored him with the anointing oil from the horn of Samuel.

2 Chronicles 6:15, *"Thou which hast kept with thy servant David my father that which thou hast promised him; and spakest with thy mouth, and hast fulfilled it with thine hand, as it is this day."*

Solomon proceeds with the ceremony. Placing the Ark in front of the people and on a huge platform, Solomon kneels before the Lord and proceeds to pray. Solomon first acknowledges the presence and power of the Lord and then reminds the Lord of His great mercy and His covenant with those who walk uprightly before Him. Then Solomon acknowledges David and the promise the Lord made unto him and how it was fulfilled on this memorable day. One could only try to imagine the spiritual electricity in the air in these moments before the fire of God fell!

2 Chronicles 6:16, *"Now therefore, O LORD God of Israel, keep with thy servant David my father that which thou hast promised him, saying, There shall not fail thee a man in my sight to sit upon the throne of Israel; yet so that thy children take heed to their way to walk in my law, as thou hast walked before me."*

Solomon wisely reminds the Lord of His word to David. But Solomon also wisely acknowledges the established conditional order to that promise. It is not wise to remind God of His promises and then ignore the conditions of the promises. This is what the proponents of unconditional security often do, and even try to establish doctrine to excuse themselves of God's conditional order. David did no such thing, nor did Solomon. Even when David failed, he understood the consequences, because he loved the law of the Lord.

In all of David's writings and all that is written about him in the scripture, there is not a hint of him ever presuming on the Lord's mercy to excuse him of consequences! Even in his intercession for the child born from the adulterous affair with Bathsheba, he never sought his own relief from consequences but rather for the innocent child!

2 Chronicles 6:17, *"Now then, O LORD God of Israel, let thy word be verified, which thou hast spoken unto thy servant David."*

Solomon continues to tie his intersession and supplication to the blessing of the Lord on the life of David. Then Solomon has a moment of adoration in which he reflects on the magnitude of the Lord's infiniteness compared to his own finiteness. This is a common form of worship and adoration. David, who without a doubt is the premier worshipper of the Lord of all times, often took this approach. Solomon continues to remind the Lord of what He has said and what He has done. A famous minister was deriding people who prayed by reminding God what He said and telling God who He is. The minister went on to prove his lack of Bible knowledge by his comments, for the greatest Bible prayers are full of the very attributes he was deriding.

2 Chronicles 6:42, *"O LORD God, turn not away the face of thine anointed: remember the mercies of David thy servant."*

Solomon ends his prayer by relating all that he has said to the mercy the Lord has shown and promised David. We must pray in Jesus' name, not David's, but it is still okay to remind the Lord of His relationship with David when making intercession. After all, this is the last phrase Solomon made before the fire of God fell from heaven in the presence of the whole nation of Israel.

2 Chronicles 7:6, *"And the priests waited on their offices: the Levites also with instruments of musick of the LORD, which David the king had made to praise the LORD, because his mercy endureth for ever, when David praised by their ministry; and the priests sounded trumpets before them, and all Israel stood."*

After the fire fell, the priests could not enter because of the glory of the Lord! The raw power and presence of the Lord prohibits even the finest of religious exercises. David of all people knew that very well. Solomon was probably schooled very well in the same area.

After a certain period of time, the priest began to do the work they were assigned to do. Solomon begins to offer sacrifices, and the Davidic order is implemented. The amazing number of burnt offerings proves the extent of extravagance David had commanded for use in their worship. Yet in the preparation of the actual songs and instruments, David had really labored as well.

As stated earlier in this commentary, there are several verses that seem to indicate that David wrote the songs for the dedication of the Temple, and even made the instruments used in praise and worship. It is no wonder we find this verse stating that David is praising the Lord through their ministry! Although he wasn't there, yet he was, because he had written the songs, made the instruments, and set the order for the whole effort!

2 Chronicles 7:10, *"And on the three and twentieth day of the seventh month he sent the people away into their tents, glad and merry in heart for the goodness that the LORD had shewed unto David, and to Solomon, and to Israel his people."*

Notice that the great success of the entire feast and dedication of the Temple was attributed to the goodness of the Lord shown unto David and then to Solomon. The people were glad, and because of the goodness of the Lord to David, the people were blessed. The Lord again appears to Solomon and gives him the famous recipe for revival found in 2 Chronicles 7:14, *"If my people, which are called by my name, shall humble themselves, and pray, and seek my face, and turn from their wicked ways; then will I hear from heaven, and will forgive their sin, and will heal their land."* The Lord is emphasizing the conditional order for the continual blessing from the Lord, *"If my people."*

2 Chronicles 7:17, *"And as for thee, if thou wilt walk before me, as David thy father walked, and do according to all that I have commanded thee, and shalt observe my statutes and my judgments";*

The Lord is letting Solomon know that he is blessed, but the continuation of the blessing that he enjoys because of David is totally dependent and conditional upon his obedience to the ordinances of God. After all that David did wrong, it seems amazing that Solomon would hear from the Lord basically, "If you walk like David did you will be blessed but if you don't, you won't!" David being used by the Lord Himself as a standard of holiness behavior is in itself a picture of amazing grace!

2 Chronicles 7:18, *"Then will I stablish the throne of thy kingdom, according as I have covenanted with David thy father, saying, There shall not fail thee a man to be ruler in Israel."*

It is evident that the Lord desires for Solomon to do right and bestow the Davidic blessing upon him. It is also evident that the covenant blessing between Him and David is conditional. Many theologians who teach unconditional order in the area of salvation have great trouble understanding that God's extreme promise to perpetually have a descendant of David on the throne of Israel could be both messianic and conditional. Yet it is!

2 Chronicles 8:11, *"And Solomon brought up the daughter of Pharaoh out of the city of David unto the house that he had built for her: for he said, My wife shall not dwell in the house of David king of Israel, because the places are holy, whereunto the ark of the LORD hath come."*

After over twenty years into his dynasty, Solomon brings Pharaoh's daughter out of Jerusalem into a house he has built for her outside the holy city. We can see Solomon's reasoning from the text in 1 Kings 3:1, *"And Solomon made affinity with Pharaoh king of Egypt, and took Pharaoh's daughter, and brought her into the city of David, until he had made an end of building his own house, and the house of the LORD, and the wall of Jerusalem round about."*

It seems that Solomon considered it alright for Pharaoh's daughter to be in Jerusalem until the Ark arrived. This verse also shows the total respect Solomon had for the Ark and also for the great love David had for it. His reasoning, however, for marrying Pharaoh's daughter is far from wise. God gave Solomon great wisdom, but He didn't give him unconditional wisdom without the possibility of doing something really stupid!

2 Chronicles 8:14, *"And he appointed, according to the order of David his father, the courses of the priests to their service, and the Levites to their charges, to praise and minister before the priests, as the duty of every day required: the porters also by their courses at every gate: for so had David the man of God commanded."*

Solomon offered the number of sacrifices that Moses required, but for the order of the service, he followed the commandment of David. Here David is called *"the man of God."* This phrase is found two more times in the scripture. In this particular verse, the rendering of the phrase is clearly promoting a good reason for a whole nation to follow his commandments in worship.

2 Chronicles 9:31, *"And Solomon slept with his fathers, and he was buried in the city of David his father: and Rehoboam his son reigned in his stead."*

This verse ends the great account of the amazing son of David, Solomon. He is most certainly buried in the royal cemetery but had nowhere near the legacy of his father David. The difference is easy to prove. It was the idolatry of Solomon that opened the door for the enemies of Israel to prosper. Thus the nation will be divided in the reign of his son Rehoboam.

Solomon's glory is mentioned by the Lord Jesus Himself in the powerful Sermon on the Mount. Jesus was referring more to the wealth and riches Solomon had than the legacy he left. Solomon simply backslid from the place he started with the Lord. He loved many strange women, and allowed their idols in his presence. This his father would have never allowed. The glory of Solomon was inherited from David, not maintained by his own life!

2 Chronicles 10:16, *"And when all Israel saw that the king would not hearken unto them, the people answered the king, saying, What portion have we in David? and we have none inheritance in the son of Jesse: every man to your tents, O Israel: and now, David, see to thine own house. So all Israel went to their tents."*

The great division in the nation of Israel had been festering for a long time. Even in the days of Solomon, the division was growing. David's dynasty was free of idolatry. Unity kept increasing, and separation from those practicing idolatry was the national practice. Under Solomon, idolatry began to gain in Israel. It should be noted that idolatry will separate a people as fast as holiness, for neither can support the other.

The nine and a half tribes that rebelled did so against Rehoboam, the grandson of David, but really it is David they rebelled against. The devilish Jeroboam is called to lead the rebels and so he does, all the way to the hell of wholesale idolatry. They said, "Let David (his descendants and his tribe) take care of their own, but we will go to our tents." Thus was the nation divided, just as the prophet had spoken. Then the rebels killed the head of the taxation, and Rehoboam fled to Jerusalem, proving the fierceness of the divide and setting the stage for the inevitable civil war.

2 Chronicles 10:19, "*And Israel rebelled against the house of David unto this day.*"

Theologians have laid the blame for the horrible bloodshed that came through this rebellion at the feet of Rehobam because of his foolishness. Some lay the blame at the feet of the rebellious tribes and the influence of Jeroboam. The blame should be laid at the feet of every idol worshipper in the land, and everyone who failed to oppose it with vigor, for that is the pattern of David. He never practiced idolatry and never tolerated it! Prophets don't decide what happens. They see it and speak it. The prophet said this would happen, but he certainly didn't decide it or desire it.

2 Chronicles 11:17, "*So they strengthened the kingdom of Judah, and made Rehoboam the son of Solomon strong, three years: for three years they walked in the way of David and Solomon.*"

Here is an extreme example of the power of the right king and the right priest coming together and producing a revival. Jeroboam had taken ten tribes of Israel and driven them into idolatry by building them golden calves and ordaining priests himself which were not even Levites. The Levites then came from all over Israel and began to work with Rehoboam. Their influence changed Rehoboam, and brought the blessing of God to the kingdom of Judah for three years. The Davidic covenant was and is connected to the salt covenant as is plainly stated in 2 Chronicles 13:5 and will be clearly seen in the Zadok priesthood in the millennium. The king of Judah with the Levitical priesthood came together perfectly in David, and Rehoboam enjoyed the same for a season!

2 Chronicles 11:18, "*And Rehoboam took him Mahalath the daughter of Jerimoth the son of David to wife, and Abihail the daughter of Eliab the son of Jesse;*"

Rehoboam married his cousins. This granddaughter of his grandfather David was more than likely the daughter of the son of a concubine. Jerimoth is only here mentioned, and 1 Chronicles 3:9 tells us that in fact they are not counted or named necessarily. "*These were all the sons of David, beside the sons of the concubines, and Tamar their sister.*" Therefore the total of David's offspring is not known by scripture or by history.

2 Chronicles 12:16, "*And Rehoboam slept with his fathers, and was buried in the city of David: and Abijah his son reigned in his stead.*"

Rehoboam's revival lasted only a short three years, after which he backslid and led all of Judah with him. This resulted in the judgment of God by allowing an invasion by their enemies. Then the nation repented, and God spared them. 2 Chronicles 12:12, *"And when he humbled himself, the wrath of the LORD turned from him, that he would not destroy him altogether: and also in Judah things went well."* This allowed Rehoboam to end his dynasty in the strength of the Lord and to be buried in honor beside David.

2 Chronicles 13:5, *"Ought ye not to know that the LORD God of Israel gave the kingdom over Israel to David for ever, even to him and to his sons by a covenant of salt?"*

This is the third mention of the salt covenant, found previously in Leviticus 2:13 and Numbers 18:19. Here is plenty of evidence of three things: 1) The covenant of salt was an established covenant in the minds of Jews, even when they were backslidden. Abijah would have been an absolute idiot to speak this word to an army twice the size of his if he wasn't sure that they knew what the salt covenant was. 2) The covenant of salt was considered the covenant connected to the messianic kingdom of David, or the covenant in which David had received the kingdom. The tens and tens of thousands of animals David had ordered Solomon to sacrifice each had the salt of the covenant on them. It was absolutely forbidden to offer a sacrifice without salt on it (Leviticus 2:13; Mark 9:49). Therefore Jeroboam and his army of rebels and backsliders knew exactly what Abijah was referring to. 3) The covenant had to be considered so powerful by Abijah and his army that they spoke these words to Jeroboam in the perfect peace that God would honor His covenant with David and the coming Messiah.

We can find no evidence that there was an ounce of fear in Abijah or his men. Abijah preached a powerful sermon to his backslidden fellow Jews, with the absolute unction and poise that comes from being right with the Lord and walking in holiness. This is the meaning of the salt covenant, being justified freely by the one and only sin offering (Jesus) and walking in personal holiness, which is the absolute privilege and duty of every true recipient of grace!

2 Chronicles 13:6, *"Yet Jeroboam the son of Nebat, the servant of Solomon the son of David, is risen up, and hath rebelled against his lord."*

This is the premier example of the amazing boldness that comes when one is walking in the Salt Covenant. Abijah has proclaimed that the covenant of salt he is walking in was given to him as a son of David. Now he tells Jeroboam before his eight hundred thousand man army, "You are not even the least in the tribe of Judah." He is actually telling Jeroboam that he is the rebellious son of his father's slave.

Facing an army twice the size of his, Abijah has the boldness of a lion because he knows he is in covenant with the Lord of Hosts! Abijah goes on to insult Jeroboam with a righteous indignation like Elijah had when he asked the worshippers of Baal if their god was hard of hearing.

2 Chronicles 13:8, *"And now ye think to withstand the kingdom of the LORD in the hand of the sons of David; and ye be a great multitude, and there are with you golden calves, which Jeroboam made you for gods."*

This statement is amazingly attached to the connection between the Salt Covenant and the Davidic Covenant. These should never be separated, for the kingdom David received was by the covenant of salt, and the longevity of the blessing on the dynasty of David was absolutely connected by condition to the Levitical sacrificial covenant of salt. Therefore Abijah in the power of God's presence, declares to Jeroboam how foolish it is for him to think he can possibly when this battle, even though he has eight hundred thousand soldiers. *"The righteous are bold as a lion"* (Proverbs 28:1). This is absolute confidence that comes when one is absolutely right with his God and is completely dependent upon His covenants.

Jeroboam played the fool and ignored the powerful warning of Abijah, the Salt Covenant preacher. He attacked Abijah, and lost five hundred thousand men, the largest slaughter of humanity ever to occur in one day in all of history and until this very day.

2 Chronicles 14:1, *"So Abijah slept with his fathers, and they buried him in the city of David: and Asa his son reigned in his stead. In his days the land was quiet ten years."*

Abijah certainly laid the foundation for his son Asa, who was a very godly man. Abijah's amazing victory over Jeroboam set him in a very powerful place, and in that place is where he seems to have finished his course. Abijah had the good sense to attach himself to the legacy of one whom the Lord loved, David!

2 Chronicles 16:14, *"And they buried him in his own sepulchres, which he had made for himself in the city of David, and laid him in the bed which was filled with sweet odours and divers kinds of spices prepared by the apothecaries' art: and they made a very great burning for him."*

Asa's dynasty was an amazing one. He was like his great-great grandfather, David. Asa loved the Word of God, and when it was delivered to him, he did all that he could to fulfill its demands. He even took his own mother out of office in his zeal to clean up idolatry. She had made an idol in a grove.

Asa cleaned up idolatry and even removed the high places in Judah. However, he did not remove the high places from the rest of Israel or the nations he conquered. Josephus declared Asa to be a student of David, and yet David would not have left the high places! Some say Asa ordered the high places removed, and the task wasn't done, but even that would not have happened on David's watch.

All in all, Asa was a powerful man of God and was buried close to David in a sepulcher he himself prepared. However there is a sadness to the end of his dynasty. He died of a disease in his feet. 2 Chronicles 16:12 *"And Asa in the thirty and ninth year of his reign was diseased in his feet, until his disease was exceeding great: yet in his disease he sought not to the LORD, but to the physicians."* There is no record of the type of disease, nor is there any reason given for his failure to go to the Lord for healing.

2 Chronicles 17:3, *"And the LORD was with Jehoshaphat, because he walked in the first ways of his father David, and sought not unto Baalim";*

Jehoshaphat reigned after his father Asa and was careful to walk in the ways of his father David. David was famous for his zero toleration for idols and idolaters. While this great-great-great grandson, Jehoshaphat was intolerant of idols, he was not only tolerant of idolaters but even covenanted with them. His amazing life is speckled with accounts of compromise and connections with those who were not serving the living God. His affinity with Ahab almost cost him his life!

2 Chronicles 21:1, *"Now Jehoshaphat slept with his fathers, and was buried with his fathers in the city of David. And Jehoram his son reigned in his stead."*

See commentary on 1 Kings 22:50

2 Chronicles 21:7, *"Howbeit the LORD would not destroy the house of David, because of the covenant that he had made with David, and as he promised to give a light to him and to his sons for ever."*

This Jehoram, the son of Jehoshaphat, was a wicked tyrant that even killed his own brothers in order to strengthen his power base. He walked in the ways of the backslidden people of Israel and engaged in wholesale idolatry. However, the covenant God made with David was so strong that God chose not to destroy him. Even though the Lord had made it clear to both David and Solomon that the promise was conditional, this verse makes it clear that the Lord is 1) Very longsuffering 2) In love with His own covenant with David.

Truett was wise to say, "When I petition God, I sometimes remind Him of His longsuffering with David and His covenant with David's sons." However, finally God dealt with Jehoram.

2 Chronicles 21:12, *"And there came a writing to him from Elijah the prophet, saying, Thus saith the LORD God of David thy father, Because thou hast not walked in the ways of Jehoshaphat thy father, nor in the ways of Asa king of Judah,"*

There is a great amount of speculation as to how Elijah, who was taken up to heaven in the reign of Jehoshaphat (2 Kings 2:11), could have sent a letter to Jehoram. However, he could have prophetically written a letter before his death to be sent to the king of Judah at a certain time in the future. Prophets have named kings that would reign generations before they appeared on the scene and long after the prophet himself died. This would not be so unbelievable in that light. However, there could have been other prophets named Elijah. One should notice through the prophet's words that blessing is tied to the posterity of David, but so is the indictment of the sins of those who do not walk like David did.

2 Chronicles 21:20, *"Thirty and two years old was he when he began to reign, and he reigned in Jerusalem eight years, and departed without being desired. Howbeit they buried him in the city of David, but not in the sepulchres of the kings."*

So despised by the people was this wicked king that there was no desire for him to live and no regret when he died. The decision to allow him to be buried in the city of Jerusalem, but not in the sepulcher of the kings, was a moral one and a wise one. He showed not the least signs of repentance in all of the record of his dynasty. David is the witness (Isaiah 55:4) to all who call on the Lord for mercy in true repentance. So why should the remains of this unrepentant sinner be allowed to attend the same ground as the very witness of God concerning mercy and repentance, David?

2 Chronicles 23:3, *"And all the congregation made a covenant with the king in the house of God. And he said unto them, Behold, the king's son shall reign, as the LORD hath said of the sons of David."*

This is the account of the crowning of Joash, king in the proper lineage as a son of David. Joash was the only son of the seed royal that was not destroyed by Athaliah in her fit of rage. This is the case of the preservation of the right king being orchestrated by the right priests. The priests saved Joash, of the sons of David, and hid him six years before presenting him as king. The presentation of the right king by the right priests brought about the glory of the Lord again for Israel. These priests had identified with the everlasting covenant of God described by Isaiah as *"the sure mercies of David"* (Isaiah 55:3).

2 Chronicles 23:9, *"Moreover Jehoiada the priest delivered to the captains of hundreds spears, and bucklers, and shields, that had been king David's, which were in the house of God."*

Before the crowning of Joash, the priests actually armed themselves with the spears, bucklers, and shields that David had taken away from his enemies. These priests were armed and ready to protect the entire ceremony of the crowning of Joash from the wicked assault of Athaliah if she tried one. When the people saw Joash, they were so thankful to see what they thought they would never see again, and that is the royal seed of David and rightful heir to his throne! The common people thought all of the seed of David had been destroyed.

Athaliah heard the noise of the inauguration. She was horribly shocked that one of the seed of David was still alive. Even so will the haters of David and his God be shocked to find David raised up and seated beside Jesus, the Lion of the tribe of Judah, throughout the millennium (Jeremiah 30:9). Athaliah tried to accuse the priests of the Lord of treason, hoping to stop the setting of Joash as king, instead of being able to kill Joash like she planned. The people rose up and killed her. The result was the right king, a son of David, was in covenant with the correct priesthood, and of course, revival followed!

2 Chronicles 23:18, *"Also Jehoiada appointed the offices of the house of the LORD by the hand of the priests the Levites, whom David had distributed in the house of the LORD, to offer the burnt*

offerings of the LORD, as it is written in the law of Moses, with rejoicing and with singing, as it was ordained by David."

Jehoiada was a mighty man of the Lord that we seldom hear about. He was the priest that rallied Israel to install the Davidic king, Joash. He didn't stop there. Jehoiada proceeded to reinstall the priestly order that David had set up. Lightfoot declares Jehoiada to be filled with zeal for the king and the priest to come together again in Israel. That is certainly what happened. The revival that followed was extensive, as is always the case in this king and priest order, which is in fact the order of Melchizedek!

2 Chronicles 24:16, *"And they buried him in the city of David among the kings, because he had done good in Israel, both toward God, and toward his house."*

Because Jehoiada had been such an influence in Israel, and because he had been instrumental in preserving the Davidic order, they buried him in the city among the kings. This is another reason that we should concur with Lightfoot that Jehoiada was an unsung hero who served the Lord with all of his heart, and that he was a lover of David! After the death of Jehoiada, the princes of Judah gained permission from Joash to worship again in the high places.

One of the points of the constant pull back to idolatry was the inconvenience for the children of Israel to assemble in Jerusalem. That is why Jeroboam placed the golden calves in Dan and Bethel. He knew the people would be compelled to stay at home and worship rather than make a trip to Jerusalem.

Joash faced both pressure from the idolaters and a stern rebuke from the prophets and the very priest that preserved his life, Jehoiada. Joash caved in to the idolators and did the unthinkable. He commanded Jehoiada's son, the priest, to be executed in the court. This deed caused him to be called an idolater himself by many theologians. Joash did not repay the kindness of Jehoiada but killed his son, thus breaking in pieces the king and priest order that had brought Israel such a revival. Later that year, the Syrians came and took the treasure of Israel and slew the very princes that had talked Joash into allowing the idolatry to return.

2 Chronicles 24:25, *"And when they were departed from him, (for they left him in great diseases,) his own servants conspired against him for the blood of the sons of Jehoiada the priest, and slew him on his bed, and he died: and they buried him in the city of David, but they buried him not in the sepulchres of the kings."*

After the Syrians had left Judah, Joash was sick, and his own servants conspired with the sons of Jehoiada and killed Joash on his bed. He was buried in Jerusalem, but not with the kings, because of his departure from the Lord which allowed the enemies of Israel to conquer them. This ending of Joash is in sharp contrast with his forefather David!

2 Chronicles 27:9, *"And Jotham slept with his fathers, and they buried him in the city of David: and Ahaz his son reigned in his stead."*

See commentary on 2 Kings 15:38

2 Chronicles 28:1, "*Ahaz was twenty years old when he began to reign, and he reigned sixteen years in Jerusalem: but he did not that which was right in the sight of the LORD, like David his father*":

See commentary on 2 Kings 16:2

2 Chronicles 29:2, "*And he did that which was right in the sight of the LORD, according to all that David his father had done.*"

Finally, a righteous king, Hezekiah, has come that will re-establish both the Davidic dynasty and the Melchizedek order. He cleaned up and repaired the Temple and compelled the priests to be sanctified. Then he made a covenant with them. In this case we see the king preserving the priesthood, whereas in the case of Jehoiada, we saw the priests preserving the king (Joash). This is the point of the great battle in the heavenlies. Satan knows he suffers heavy loss every time the right king and the right priest come together in holiness and covenant before the Lord.

2 Chronicles 29:25, "*And he set the Levites in the house of the LORD with cymbals, with psalteries, and with harps, according to the commandment of David, and of Gad the king's seer, and Nathan the prophet: for so was the commandment of the LORD by his prophets.*"

Hezekiah was the son of a wicked father and the father of a wicked son. Yet, he was a very dedicated worshipper of the Lord and clearly a respecter of David's dynasty. He knew very well that the order of the priests and the organization of worship were divinely inspired through David and the prophets who served the Lord with him. Hezekiah very wisely followed with utmost caution these instructions concerning the house of the Lord. David, himself a prophet, received great instruction to maintain the king and priest order. However, we must not leave out the prophet. It is the prophet that breathes on the order of the king and the priest, as we see in the book of Haggai. Both chapters of Haggai prove the necessity of prophetic involvement when setting forth the order of the King and the Priest!

2 Chronicles 29:26, "*And the Levites stood with the instruments of David, and the priests with the trumpets.*"

David was accused of being a narcissist by Bardoni after he learned that David organized the worship for the house of the Lord, appointed the priests to serve in it, wrote the songs they sang in it, provided the instruments they played in it, and picked a son (Solomon) to do it all just the way he planned it. Bardoni made a big mistake in his assessment of the man after God's heart. David was not a narcissist, but a man with an insatiable desire to worship the living God and lead a nation to do so as well!

2 Chronicles 29:27, "*And Hezekiah commanded to offer the burnt offering upon the altar. And when the burnt offering began, the song of the LORD began also with the trumpets, and with the instruments ordained by David king of Israel.*"

Hezekiah is commanding the priesthood in the pattern and order of David. Clark said, "It is said that the millennium Temple will be filled with worship and service according to the order of David." Why not, Mr. Clark? David will be there to lead it! (Jeremiah 30:9)

2 Chronicles 29:30, "*Moreover Hezekiah the king and the princes commanded the Levites to sing praise unto the LORD with the words of David, and of Asaph the seer. And they sang praises with gladness, and they bowed their heads and worshipped.*"

Here is yet again proof that David wrote the lyrics and probably the music for the worship in the house of the Lord. Asaph is here listed as a seer of David's as well as one who helped David write the words for the music. Asaph is also listed as a seer in 2 Chronicles 35:15. There is a question among theologians as to whether this is the same Asaph to which several of the psalms are ascribed. Why not?

2 Chronicles 30:26, "*So there was great joy in Jerusalem: for since the time of Solomon the son of David king of Israel there was not the like in Jerusalem.*"

This great revival and outpouring of the blessing of the Lord reminded Israel of the very days when this order was first established. Yet even this revival will be overshadowed by the New Testament outpouring at Pentecost. And Ravenhill said, "There will be a Pentecost to come that will out Pentecost, Pentecost." Hezekiah's revival is a type of the restoring of the tabernacle of David! (Acts 15:16)

2 Chronicles 32:5, "*Also he strengthened himself, and built up all the wall that was broken, and raised it up to the towers, and another wall without, and repaired Millo in the city of David, and made darts and shields in abundance.*"

Hezekiah is determined to not only re-establish the Davidic order, but to free Israel of the Assyrian tax and control. Hezekiah knew that the enemies of Israel had gained control over them because of the idolatry in the land. He also knew that David had won his victories because he was free from idolatry and honored the living God. He knew that reinstating the sacrificial order and making the covenant he had made with the priests caused the salt to begin to flow again. In that confidence that walking in the Salt Covenant brings, he refused to submit to Assyria. As a result, Sennacherib comes to fight against Judah.

While Hezekiah trusted the Lord, he also carefully inspected his defense and rebuilt the wall in Millo which is the lower portion of the original city of Zion. It is clear that Hezekiah is copying the pattern and mentality of David. God honored Hezekiah. 2 Chronicles 32:22 *"Thus the LORD saved Hezekiah and the inhabitants of Jerusalem from the hand of Sennacherib the king of Assyria, and from the hand of all other, and guided them on every side."* Hezekiah literally fulfilled the prescription for revival that brought the fire of God down to both David and Hezekiah!

2 Chronicles 32:30, *"This same Hezekiah also stopped the upper watercourse of Gihon, and brought it straight down to the west side of the city of David. And Hezekiah prospered in all his works."*

As Hezekiah had already altered the water supply lines in his preparation for the aggression of Assyria, he now takes the opportunity to bring the water straight in to the city of David. This made the water works for the city a lot more efficient and shows us the wisdom and blessing he operated in like his father David. The anointing of the Lord rests upon Hezekiah, not just for war, but also for peace and the building of a nation.

2 Chronicles 32:33, *"And Hezekiah slept with his fathers, and they buried him in the chiefest of the sepulchres of the sons of David: and all Judah and the inhabitants of Jerusalem did him honour at his death. And Manasseh his son reigned in his stead."*

All of the accomplishments of Hezekiah, but mostly his great revival of the Jewish faith, earned him an honorable spot in the grave yard of the kings of Judah. 2 Kings 20:21 gives the record of the death of Hezekiah but fails to speak of his honorable place of rest. Manasseh, his son, reigned in his place and acted as though he had never as much as heard of David.

2 Chronicles 33:7, *"And he set a carved image, the idol which he had made, in the house of God, of which God had said to David and to Solomon his son, In this house, and in Jerusalem, which I have chosen before all the tribes of Israel, will I put my name for ever"*:

This horrible and wicked Manasseh, through his wholesale idolatry, undid everything his Godly father established. He broke covenant with God, and even went so far as to set the idols in the House of the Lord in Jerusalem. It was so hideous that Lightfoot declared it to be no less than an abomination of desolation of sort. For his sin, God punished him through the Assyrian army with thorns and fetters, thus bringing him to humility. In his humility, he cried unto the Lord, who restored him to Jerusalem. This account of his repentance is not included in 2 Kings.

Also see the commentary on 2 Kings 21:7

2 Chronicles 33:14, *"Now after this he built a wall without the city of David, on the west side of Gihon, in the valley, even to the entering in at the fish gate, and compassed about Ophel, and raised it up a very great height, and put captains of war in all the fenced cities of Judah."*

After his repentance, Manasseh came back to Jerusalem and built the wall to fortify Jerusalem. It should be noted that Manasseh's ability to fortify the city of Jerusalem was directly correlated to his removing of the idols from the land. David well established in his prophetic writings that no man can stand before his enemies with golden calves in his Temple!

2 Chronicles 34:2, *"And he did that which was right in the sight of the LORD, and walked in the ways of David his father, and declined neither to the right hand, nor to the left."*

Josiah the son of Amon, the wicked son of Manasseh, was only eight years old when he began to reign. He followed the ways of David and probably like young Joash, he was guided and led by the holy remnant of priests in the lineage of Zadok. The fact that he walked in the ways of David would insure the incorporation of the priesthood, and because of his young age, even the leadership of the priesthood. Josiah will be able to once again put the king and priesthood together to see another tremendous revival in the land!

2 Chronicles 34:3, *"For in the eighth year of his reign, while he was yet young, he began to seek after the God of David his father: and in the twelfth year he began to purge Judah and Jerusalem from the high places, and the groves, and the carved images, and the molten images."*

This revival had its beginning in the early days of Josiah as he began to seek the Lord. There were a few years of strengthening his position, and then Josiah began to tear down all of the idols his grandfather Manasseh and his father Amon had set up. As they were cleaning the house of the Lord of idolatry, they found a book of the law of the Lord. The scribe and the priest brought the law of the Lord to Josiah, and he embraced it like David. David loved the law of the Lord, and so did Josiah.

Josiah then made a covenant with the remnant, the priest, and the prophet. 2 Chronicles 34:29-31, *"Then the king sent and gathered together all the elders of Judah and Jerusalem. And the king went up into the house of the LORD, and all the men of Judah, and the inhabitants of Jerusalem, and the priests, and the Levites, and all the people, great and small: and he read in their ears all the words of the book of the covenant that was found in the house of the LORD. And the king stood in his place, and made a covenant before the LORD, to walk after the LORD, and to keep his commandments, and his testimonies, and his statutes, with all his heart, and with all his soul, to perform the words of the covenant which are written in this book."*

The revival in the land strengthened even more and turned into a movement in the land. The deep repentance and consecration brought holy cleansing to the entire nation. The revival of the keeping of the law was significant in the movement, as the people trembled at the Word of the Lord again!

2 Chronicles 35:3, *"And said unto the Levites that taught all Israel, which were holy unto the LORD, Put the holy ark in the house which Solomon the son of David king of Israel did build; it shall not be a burden upon your shoulders: serve now the LORD your God, and his people Israel,"*

The revival intensifies as they read and apply the law of the Lord they had discovered. Josiah first reinstated the Passover, as is also recorded in 2 Kings 23:21-22. Now he brings back the Ark of the Covenant to the Holy of Holies in the House of the Lord. Evidently it had been taken out by Amon, the son of Manasseh, and the father of Josiah. This is a bold move and the turning point as far as the revolution is concerned. Watts declared that the more Josiah studied the history of David, the more he realized he had his mantle. This is probably a very accurate explanation as to what was going on in Israel!

2 Chronicles 35:4, *"And prepare yourselves by the houses of your fathers, after your courses, according to the writing of David king of Israel, and according to the writing of Solomon his son."*

Josiah is in full command of the priesthood by this time, and is very careful to set everything concerning the service of the Lord in pure Davidic order. There is no question that David set the order of the courses that the priests served, and this he did in the power of the messianic anointing that rested upon him. Now this anointing is upon Josiah.

2 Chronicles 35:15, *"And the singers the sons of Asaph were in their place, according to the commandment of David, and Asaph, and Heman, and Jeduthun the king's seer; and the porters waited at every gate; they might not depart from their service; for their brethren the Levites prepared for them."*

Josiah follows completely the instructions David gave Solomon for the service of the Lord in the Temple, right down to the singers and musicians. It is quite amazing to see this revival that even surpasses the revival in the days of Hezekiah.

The report of this revival is in the continuing verses, 2 Chronicles 35:15-18, *"And the singers the sons of Asaph were in their place, according to the commandment of David, and Asaph, and Heman, and Jeduthun the king's seer; and the porters waited at every gate; they might not depart from their service; for their brethren the Levites prepared for them. So all the service of the LORD was prepared the same day, to keep the passover, and to offer burnt offerings upon the altar of the LORD, according to the commandment of king Josiah. And the children of Israel that were present kept the passover at that time, and the feast of unleavened bread seven days. And there was no passover like to that kept in Israel from the days of Samuel the prophet; neither did all the kings of Israel keep such a passover as Josiah kept, and the priests, and the Levites, and all Judah and Israel that were present, and the inhabitants of Jerusalem."*

After the great outpouring, Josiah made a deadly military mistake when he failed to follow a prophetic word, and it cost him his life. He died at about forty years of age. He was held in high esteem by the people of Israel and was publically lamented over by none other than Jeremiah, the weeping prophet. He was buried in the cemetery of his fathers.

Ezra

Ezra 3:10, *"And when the builders laid the foundation of the temple of the LORD, they set the priests in their apparel with trumpets, and the Levites the sons of Asaph with cymbals, to praise the LORD, after the ordinance of David king of Israel."*

Even in this reconstruction of the Temple many generations after David had lived and died, one can see the colossal effort of the people of Israel to follow the order set forth by David. Burchett writes, "See how David being dead yet speaketh, for the very order for all that is done in this new Temple will be chartered by none other." It is true that Ezra, the priest, knew that every single revival since the fire fell at Onran's threshing floor for David, has been connected with the Salt Covenant, in which God gave the kingdom over Israel to David (2 Chronicles 13:5). In fact, when Ezra returns to begin the work of rebuilding, he came with much salt for the sacrificial offerings. Ezra 7:22b, *"and salt without prescribing how much."* The offering for the new Temple could not be offered without salt (Leviticus 2:13).

Ezra 8:2, "*Of the sons of Phinehas; Gershom: of the sons of Ithamar; Daniel: of the sons of David; Hattush.*"

This son of David is only mentioned here in the rebuilding of the Temple and three times in Nehemiah at the rebuilding of the wall. This simply means Hattush was a decendant of David.

Ezra 8:20, "*Also of the Nethinims, whom David and the princes had appointed for the service of the Levites, two hundred and twenty Nethinims: all of them were expressed by name.*"

These called Nethinims were not Jews, nor were they Gibeonites, but rather slaves of different conquered people groups that David had proselytized and given to the Levites for the service of the Lord. Solomon added to that number which was ever changing as their population and need of service changed. David didn't just conquer nations; he made Jews out of them and put them to the work of the kingdom!

Nehemiah

Nehemiah 3:15, "*But the gate of the fountain repaired Shallun the son of Colhozeh, the ruler of part of Mizpah; he built it, and covered it, and set up the doors thereof, the locks thereof, and the bars thereof, and the wall of the pool of Siloah by the king's garden, and unto the stairs that go down from the city of David.*"

It is noted that from Jerusalem one must always go down, and when traveling to Jerusalem, the term *up to Jerusalem* is mostly used. However, steps and ramps are very common in and around Jerusalem, as there are often steep places within the walls of the city as well as outside. These steps mentioned here are said to be the steps that David went out and came in.

Nehemiah 3:16, "*After him repaired Nehemiah the son of Azbuk, the ruler of the half part of Bethzur, unto the place over against the sepulchres of David, and to the pool that was made, and unto the house of the mighty.*"

Nehemiah was called of God to rebuild the walls that were broken down and the gates that were burned with fire. The progress now brings them to the royal cemetery where David and his sons were buried, and then on to the cliffs where was the lodging of David's famous mighty men.

Nehemiah 12:24, *"And the chief of the Levites: Hashabiah, Sherebiah, and Jeshua the son of Kadmiel, with their brethren over against them, to praise and to give thanks, according to the commandment of David the man of God, ward over against ward."*

Here we see the amazing and continuing influence of David's order of worship. It seems inconceivable in religious thinking that David, with all of his failure, would set the very pattern of worship! Such, however, is the way of the Lord with the redeemed. Other than Judas who betrayed Jesus, Peter was the only disciple to deny Him. Yet it is Peter that was chosen to deliver the Pentecost sermon just fifty days later. David is a trophy of God's redemption!

Nehemiah 12:36, *"And his brethren, Shemaiah, and Azarael, Milalai, Gilalai, Maai, Nethaneel, and Judah, Hanani, with the musical instruments of David the man of God, and Ezra the scribe before them."*

These musical instruments of David were protected and preserved during the holocaust, but neither history nor the scripture gives us the details. Most likely they were carefully protected by the priesthood. Some were taken to Babylon, for the Babylonians who had captured the Jews mocked them by requesting their songs after they had hung their harps in the willow trees (Psalms 137:2). There are three verses that refer to David as *the man of God*: 2 Chronicles 8:14, Nehemiah 12:24, and this verse. In each case, it is a reference to David's worship!

Nehemiah 12:37, *"And at the fountain gate, which was over against them, they went up by the stairs of the city of David, at the going up of the wall, above the house of David, even unto the water gate eastward."*

It seems that after the wall was built, the worshippers and the priests retraced the path in which the wall was completed, giving thanks and offering sacrifices in the manner which David had commanded.

Nehemiah 12:45, *"And both the singers and the porters kept the ward of their God, and the ward of the purification, according to the commandment of David, and of Solomon his son."*

The amazing work and study involved in setting the wards, porters, and singers in the very same fashion that David and Asaph had set them, is a marvel. David's influence was so strong that even after the captivity, there were holy men in Israel that would settle for nothing less than to minutely follow that which David had ordained!

Nehemiah 12:46, *"For in the days of David and Asaph of old there were chief of the singers, and songs of praise and thanksgiving unto God."*

This verse is simply a clarification as to how David and Asaph had set up the order of worship, as well as a report of the diligence of both Ezra and Nehemiah to copy it!

Psalms

Psalms 3:1, A Psalm of David, when he fled from Absalom his son. *"LORD, how are they increased that trouble me! many are they that rise up against me."*

Because the Psalms are not composed in chronological order, it is easy to ascribe this psalm to the time in David's life when he was fleeing from Jerusalem because of Absalom. Clark goes so far as to say the psalm was probably written as David passed the Mount of Olives, weeping with his clothes torn. This could be accurate, but there is no scripture to prove it or deny it. However, the psalm shows David's great anguish and distress and proves that through his prayer of faith, he obtained help form the Lord.

Psalms 4:1, To the chief Musician on Neginoth, A Psalm of David. *"Hear me when I call, O God of my righteousness: thou hast enlarged me when I was in distress; have mercy upon me, and hear my prayer."*

David was masterful at prayer. He would always acknowledge the Lord and say great words of adoration before making his request. Even though this psalm is also ascribed to David as he fled from Absalom, he took time to worship before petitioning. He did so by acknowledging God as the "God of my righteousness." David was referring to God's righteousness imputed to him. David knew that the work God delights in is to impute righteousness to one who dares to believe Him. David asked the Lord to hear his prayer and knew He most certainly would.

Psalms 5:1, To the chief Musician upon Nehiloth, A Psalm of David. *"Give ear to my words, O LORD, consider my meditation."*

This psalm gives us insight as to the vocal content of David's prayer. He was a tenacious prayer warrior as well as a mighty military warrior. David not only saw himself as righteous through redemption, but would be so bold as to contrast his imputed and personal righteousness to the wickedness of his enemies. It is almost as if he would brag on God's righteousness, then look at his imputed righteousness, and then consider his own personal righteousness at that time, then make the contrast into a vocal petition before the Lord! This is an amazing example for any serious intercessor, as well as the newest babe in Christ!

Psalms 6:1, To the chief Musician on Neginoth upon Sheminith, A Psalm of David. *"O LORD, rebuke me not in thine anger, neither chasten me in thy hot displeasure."*

David would often make such statements to the Lord in what Watts called prayer songs. David would often make his prayers songs of praise, petition, and worship, all in the same course. Wesley said, "David's ability to flow from one platform to another in psalms was mathematically supernatural!" It seems apparent that David would assign certain psalms to certain instruments. This psalm, starting in great despair and petition on an eight string instrument, ends in a crescendo of solid faith.

Psalms 7:1 Shiggaion of David, which he sang unto the LORD, concerning the words of Cush the Benjamite. *"O LORD my God, in thee do I put my trust: save me from all them that persecute me, and deliver me"*:

Shiggaion, a word for the lineup of the song and instrument, reveals the great care and effort of David in worship, as well as petition. This psalm is sung unto the Lord, but is concerning one of David's enemies. It is amazing the way David would sing about his troubles and his enemies to the Lord in a way of making his case for his own protection from them. Over and over again we see David presenting his enemies as God's enemies, and God's enemies as his own.

Cush is most likely one of Saul's assigned hunters of David. Cush had most likely made a swelling remark of being the one who killed David in behalf of Saul. So David writes a song about it! David ends the piece with absolute faith in the Lord's help. David wanted these kinds of songs to be sung by the worshippers of the Lord, so he recorded them, and commanded them to be sung by the singers he appointed. He then commanded Solomon to continue them in his dynasty.

Psalms 8:1, To the chief Musician upon Gittith, A Psalm of David. *"O LORD our Lord, how excellent is thy name in all the earth! who hast set thy glory above the heavens."*

This is one of the most quoted and memorized of the Davidic psalms. Gittith is a certain piece of music suited to an instrument assigned to gathering, harvest, abundance, celebration. Other psalms that use this piece are Psalm 81:1 and 84:1. The reason this psalm of David is so popular is because David here brags on God's willingness to condescend to finite man with his love and devotion! There is no doubt that David is filled with awe at God's willingness to look at mere man.

Psalms 9:1, To the chief Musician upon Muthlabben, A Psalm of David. *"I will praise thee, O LORD, with my whole heart; I will shew forth all thy marvellous works."*

Muthlabben is the name of the tune and the instrument or both. David did not wait for anyone else to begin to praise the Lord. He is saying, "I will do it, and I will do so with my whole being!" This psalm is very revealing of the inner motivation of David in worship of the Lord and the agenda free zeal he had for motivating others to also worship the living God!

Psalms 11:1, To the chief Musician, A Psalm of David. *"In the LORD put I my trust: how say ye to my soul, Flee as a bird to your mountain?"*

Here is an example of the pressure David was often under to flee. His entire military life was filled with those around him who often advised him to do so. David is declaring that he has put his trust in the Lord and doesn't need to flee. This psalm is filled with a confidence in the Lord and His provision. David's heart at this point is tightly knit to both the imputed righteousness of the Lord and the personal righteousness he was walking in. It should be noted that later David did cave in to the fear of Saul (1 Samuel 27:1), which started fourteen months of fleeing from his calling only to wind up in the ashes of Ziklag! From those ashes in his deep contrition, the Lord told him that he would recover all (1 Samuel 30:8). He never fled again!

Psalms 12:1, To the chief Musician upon Sheminith, A Psalm of David. *"Help, LORD; for the godly man ceaseth; for the faithful fail from among the children of men."*

David is briefly looking at the sad condition of those who are godly and their seemingly diminished state. In his assessment, he begins to declare the solid truth that the Lord will come to the aid of the needy one who places his trust in the Lord. David also refuses to brag on the wicked. There is not one case in all of David's writings in which David shows any awe or respect for the wicked. He considered the unrepentant soul, no matter their status, to be the enemy of his God.

Psalm 13:1, To the chief Musician, A Psalm of David. *"How long wilt thou forget me, O LORD? for ever? how long wilt thou hide thy face from me?"*

David is known to pour out his total complaint before the Lord when he prayed! This was considered by Spurgeon as an art in his prayer. Lightfoot considered it to be nothing more than the freedom of expression afforded him by his intimacy with God. The desperation he faced at the time of these prayers was more than is often considered. Some have criticized those who tell God what he already knows. Yet, the people who pray with the most recorded success often do just that. David did!

Psalms 14:1, To the chief Musician, A Psalm of David. *"The fool hath said in his heart, There is no God. They are corrupt, they have done abominable works, there is none that doeth good."*

David was very strong in his condemnation of atheism. It is no wonder that the Lord would use him to pen these strong words. David is referring to the absolute degenerate state of an infidel. Not one of them does good, and neither can anything they do be good because of their reprobate status. David goes on into a messianic word in the end of this psalm in looking forward to that day when the Lord will not tolerate atheism on the planet.

Psalms 15:1, A Psalm of David. *"LORD, who shall abide in thy tabernacle? who shall dwell in thy holy hill?"*

This psalm asks a question and answers it as well. David here is not referring to the imputed righteousness that grace affords, but rather is speaking of the personal righteousness necessary for a constant abiding in the courts of the Lord. David well knew that one can come boldly into the throne room of God through the work of redemption, but to hang out there without being conformed to His image is impossible. The depth of this knowledge in David's life is amazing, even though many consider David only qualified to speak of imputed righteousness.

Psalm 16:1, Michtam of David. *"Preserve me, O God: for in thee do I put my trust."*

As so often is the case in David's prayer and praise songs, he moves into the prophetic realm concerning the coming Messiah. In verse six, David speaks of his godly heritage, and then he speaks words that confirm the origin of his knowledge. The psalm continues to gain prophetic power and reaches the climax that distinguishes the subject of his conversation to rest on Him who is to come. One of the most celebrated messianic texts is verse 10, *"For thou wilt not leave my soul in hell; neither wilt thou suffer thine Holy One to see corruption."* Both Acts 2:31 and 13:35 refer to this verse in teaching that no mere man, including David, could fulfill this prophecy.

Psalms 17:1, A Prayer of David. *"Hear the right, O LORD, attend unto my cry, give ear unto my prayer, that goeth not out of feigned lips."*

David is drawing God's attention to his sincerity. This would seem absurd in the natural, to tell God how much you mean the words you are saying to Him. David often did this in the beginning of his psalms. Yet, when one can hear the heart of David, he will be able to see the heart of God concerning what is acceptable to Him in our efforts in prayer. David refers to a cleansing in the night as his grounds for stating his right standing with God. This is not only boldness in prayer but a solid proof that David rested in the mercy of God's grace, knowing that through that grace, he had right standing with the Lord! He boldly states the contrast of the unrepentant heathens who are trying to snuff him out.

Psalms 18:1, To the chief Musician, A Psalm of David, the servant of the LORD, who spake unto the LORD the words of this song in the day that the LORD delivered him from the hand of all his enemies, and from the hand of Saul: And he said, *"I will love thee, O LORD, my strength."*

This psalm is also recorded in 2 Samuel 22:1-51 almost word for word. However, the phrase *I will love thee, O LORD, my strength,* in this verse is not found in that account. Bishop Patrick declares that David wrote this psalm after he was older, while reflecting upon his deliverance from Saul, instead of writing it in the time of his despair. Yet many other students of the Word say he wrote this, and others like it, immediately after he knew the Lord had completed his deliverance from Saul. Also see commentary on 2 Samuel 22:1.

Psalms 18:50, *"Great deliverance giveth he to his king; and sheweth mercy to his anointed, to David, and to his seed for evermore."*

David ends his psalm with a powerful declaration, not only for himself but for his posterity. He declares that the mercy the Lord has given him is for all those who follow Him. This does in no way negate the conditional order to this blessing as some suppose. Some Jewish scholars declare themselves to be blessed solely because they are Jews, and some who have obtained the sure mercies of David have declared themselves blessed solely because they have obtained that mercy, even though they do not walk uprightly before the Lord. David was told several times by the prophets, and the Lord Himself, that the promise was conditional upon his walking in the ways of the Lord.

Psalms 19:1, To the chief Musician, A Psalm of David. *"The heavens declare the glory of God; and the firmament sheweth his handywork."*

One of the most quoted psalms of David ends with one of the most powerful petitions of David in Verse 14, *"Let the words of my mouth, and the meditation of my heart, be acceptable in thy sight, O LORD, my strength, and my redeemer."* David had a holy hatred for sin and failure, whether in others or his own self. David cries out for inner holiness in this psalm. He loved the Lord so much that he hated the thought of grieving Him. David actually felt like God does about sin, even when it was his own. This attribute of David is the reason we cannot find one instance of David's condoning sin or justifying it in any way!

Psalms 20:1, To the chief Musician, A Psalm of David. *"The LORD hear thee in the day of trouble; the name of the God of Jacob defend thee";*

David connects his petition to the covenant the Lord made with Jacob. The covenant God made with Jacob is called by some the covenant of deliverance. David knew the covenant of God with Jacob afforded the promise to the tribe of Judah to provide the king. Genesis 49:10, *"The sceptre shall not depart from Judah."* David knew that promise was his, and as he sang or spoke about it, the power of the promise became more real to him. This is one of the secrets of David's amazing victories. He not only knew the covenants and promises of God, but he spoke them. He sang them, and he lived them. He said as he spoke them in Verse 6, *"Now know I that the LORD saveth his anointed."* In this manner David often encouraged himself in the Lord.

Psalms 21:1, To the chief Musician, A Psalm of David. *"The king shall joy in thy strength, O LORD; and in thy salvation how greatly shall he rejoice!"*

Again as David proceeds in this psalm, it turns from him to the Messiah that is to come. Theologians have asked whether David was aware of the prophetic nature of his words, or did he just write what was given him without understanding that he was speaking of Christ. There is ample evidence that he knew the Christ Himself. If Abraham knew Him, so did David. Jesus plainly spoke of his pre-existent life in John 8. David knew what the Holy Spirit revealed to him concerning the Savior that was to come! The Apostle Peter declared that David spoke by the Holy Ghost (Acts 1:16).

Psalms 22:1, To the chief Musician upon Aijeleth Shahar, A Psalm of David. *"My God, my God, why hast thou forsaken me? why art thou so far from helping me, and from the words of my roaring?"*

Most of the psalms of David that contain messianic prophecies conclude with the strongest messianic language. This psalm begins with the very strongest messianic utterance of the entire verse. Jesus quoted the first of this psalm while dying on the cross (Matthew 27:46). Jesus knew he was fulfilling this verse at His death! The entire psalm completely identifies crucifixion eleven hundred years before Jesus was born and four hundred years before crucifixion was invented as a way of capital punishment. Just as David's arm was strengthened in battle by the power of God, his pen was anointed with the raw prophetic power of God, inflamed by the revelation of the coming Messiah!

Psalms 23:1, A Psalm of David. *"The LORD is my shepherd; I shall not want."*

The favorite psalm of so many! It speaks of the shepherd and the sheep. It is a subject very dear to the heart of David. David graduated from the seminary of solitude as a shepherd. He learned the power of God in protecting the sheep, and he learned the shepherd's heart in caring for them. Though this particular psalm is not listed as a messianic writing from David's pen, it might be noted that David's comparison of a shepherd to the Lord was completely validated by the Master Himself who said in John 10:11, *"I am the good shepherd."*

Ps 24:1, A Psalm of David. *"The earth is the LORD'S, and the fulness thereof; the world, and they that dwell therein."*

David moves into the glorious realm of the king and priest in this psalm. Lightfoot declared that David sang this song as he moved the Ark to Jerusalem. He had tried to move the Ark once before without the priesthood, and had learned a great lesson from the loss of Uzza. Now he not only moves the Ark on the shoulders of the priests, but David himself takes on the attire of the priest. Thus in the spirit, he began to see Jesus coming into Jerusalem as the King of Glory!

Psalms 25:1, A Psalm of David. *"Unto thee, O LORD, do I lift up my soul."*

This is a very tender psalm that was written by David when he was older. He very gratefully contrasts his state with the state of the unrepentant. There is a hint that David is here still feeling guilty for his past sins. However, it is more likely that he is relating to his greatest grief over his failure, and that is described by Nathan the prophet in 2 Samuel 12:14, *"Howbeit, because by this deed thou hast given great occasion to the enemies of the LORD to blaspheme."*

David's greatest grief over his failure is that he considered his sin to have aided the enemy. However, in repentance and justification, he has both the boldness and the faith to ask the Lord not to allow his enemies to triumph over him! In the mentality of a warrior, he could see that his failure had aided his enemies, which were in his mind God's enemies as well!

Psalms 26:1, A Psalm of David. *"Judge me, O LORD; for I have walked in mine integrity: I have trusted also in the LORD; therefore I shall not slide."*

Here is a prophetic picture of the Salt Covenant that David walked in (2 Chronicles 13:5). David trusted in the Lord for his imputed righteousness and walked in personal righteousness. His critics will say, "What a scoundrel, a whoremonger, an adulterer, and even a murderer." David let Shimei curse him and call him names (2 Samuel 16). David knew that the penalty for adultery was stoning, so he allowed Shimei to throw stones at him. He didn't try to justify any failure in his life, but in repentance and God's mercy, he enjoyed the full assurance of total forgiveness. With a heart of thanksgiving, he walks in newness of life and total victory while his critics curse.

David is so overwhelmed with the goodness of God! He is totally in love with the Word. In this verse David writes of his secret in Psalms 25:14, *"The secret of the LORD is with them that fear him; and he will shew them his covenant."* The world will see David raised up from the dead to reign as vice king of the planet, a trophy of grace, and a testimony as to the power of God's covenant.

Psalms 27:1, A Psalm of David. *"The LORD is my light and my salvation; whom shall I fear? the LORD is the strength of my life; of whom shall I be afraid?"*

Written after his fourteen months of fleeing from the presence of Saul, David had finally learned not to be afraid at all. The thing that struck the heart of John Wesley was the fact that the Moravians had the testimony of David. Near shipwreck in the hull of the boat, Wesley found them sitting quietly and calmly. Wesley, in fear, exclaimed to them, "Have you no fear at all?" One of them replied to Wesley, "I thank my God, no." Wesley vowed afterwards that he would have what they had, for what they had was more than he. David's fear of Saul cost him greatly, and the fourteen months in Ziklag turned into ashes and the despair of having his family stolen. Perfect love casts out fear. Through the recovery of all he had lost, David's confidence in God reached the level that this psalm expresses!

Psalms 28:1, A Psalm of David. *"Unto thee will I cry, O LORD my rock; be not silent to me: lest, if thou be silent to me, I become like them that go down into the pit."*

David here shows us yet another secret of his great prayer life. He expresses here total abandonment of hope in his own personal efforts. He acknowledges his situation in honesty and then basically says, "Lord I am calling on you and you alone; if you don't help me, I will not make it." He prays the same way in Psalms 143:7. David knew that it pleases the Lord when we look totally to Him in faith. David is also saying, "I will not do as others who in a desperate place will consult familiar spirits or false gods." David is clearly saying, "I will die before I do that!" This is total abandonment unto the Lord and His ability to deliver those in despair!

Psalms 29:1, A Psalm of David. *"Give unto the LORD, O ye mighty, give unto the LORD glory and strength."*

Just as the writer of Hebrews writes a chapter known as the *faith chapter* (Hebrews 11), just as the Apostle Paul writes a chapter known as the *love chapter* (1 Corinthians 13), so David writes a chapter that should be known as the *voice chapter*. Wesley believed David wrote this psalm in a thunder storm and Psalm 8 on a moon lit night. However, it is most likely more of a revelation of the awesome power of God's voice that he had heard even as he went to battle.

Psalms 30:1, A Psalm and Song at the dedication of the house of David. *"I will extol thee, O LORD; for thou hast lifted me up, and hast not made my foes to rejoice over me."*

This is more proof that David not only prepared the physical material for the Temple, but also wrote the songs for the dedication and the worship vigil that continued for thirty-plus years. This is a personal testimony, but yet it is applicable to the whole of the nation of Israel and spans throughout its history. David testifies of a physical healing here in which many consider the healing of his disease he describes in Psalms 38 and in 1 Kings 1:1, where his cabinet made a carnal attempt to cure him. In this psalm and in Psalms 103:3, David refers to a physical healing that enabled him to finish both his mentoring of Solomon and his songs for the dedication of the Temple.

Psalms 31:1, To the chief Musician, A Psalm of David. *"In thee, O LORD, do I put my trust; let me never be ashamed: deliver me in thy righteousness."*

David assures the Lord that his trust is only in Him, and pleads with him not to allow him to be ashamed or disappointed, because of his dependence on Him. This in itself reveals the supplication that often accompanied David's prayer songs. Supplication has often been seen by some as doubt and weakness. However, the critics of supplication should compare their results in prayer with David's, who was not bashful about pleading for a work to be done that he had already confessed would happen.

Psalms 32:1, A Psalm of David, Maschil. *"Blessed is he whose transgression is forgiven, whose sin is covered."*

As David rejoices in his freedom from sin and condemnation, he delivers revelation as to the four levels of sin and failure. He first speaks of transgression, then sin, then iniquity, then the dreaded guile which hides all of the other three. David knew the depths of sin and failure. He had cried out for cleansing in the inner secret parts of his being, as is recorded in the 51st Psalm.

David probably asked himself a thousand times how could he have had such a capability of evil within him to commit such an offense against God in the matter of Bathsheba. Though David understands God's requirement for personal holiness, he well knows not to put his trust in his own personal righteousness, but in the Lord's imputed righteousness. The freedom he rejoices in throughout this psalm comes from the deep appreciation of being purged completely (Ps 51:5-7). David has a great confidence in the Lord's ability to cleanse.

Psalms 34:1, A Psalm of David, when he changed his behaviour before Abimelech; who drove him away, and he departed. *"I will bless the LORD at all times: his praise shall continually be in my mouth."*

There is little in this psalm to suggest the event to which it is ascribed. David was in great danger when he first came to Achish, and pretended to be crazy, which saved his life (1 Samuel 21:13). It is most unlikely that David was led of the Lord for such action. However, the psalm goes on to declare how the Lord delivers us out of our troubles. Perhaps David was referring to his own folly when he wrote in verse 6, *"This poor man cried, and the LORD heard him, and saved him out of all his troubles."* David teaches us well that the gracious Lord will deliver the contrite from his problems, even if he caused them himself!

Psalms 35:1, A Psalm of David. *"Plead my cause, O LORD, with them that strive with me: fight against them that fight against me."*

Upon reading this psalm, Watts said, "Only a fool would attack a man that had a relationship with God that affords such a prayer." The entire psalm is David's plea for the Lord to preserve his righteous cause. The psalm includes thanksgiving for the deliverance he is praying for. This is true of David, the man of faith. However, many theologians declare that this was easy for David to write because the psalms that bear this were written after the conflict had passed. He did write some psalms in the pattern of reflecting on what the Lord had done for him, but Josephus quotes historians who cite David often finding a solitary place in the evening to worship and pray and write, even on military campaigns! David had a tremendous prayer and worship life in which he constantly poured himself out to his God.

Psalms 36:1, To the chief Musician, A Psalm of David the servant of the LORD. *"The transgression of the wicked saith within my heart, that there is no fear of God before his eyes."*

A strange introduction David gives to this psalm. Clark says, "How can the transgression of the wicked speak within my heart?" Clark spends far too much energy proclaiming alleged error in the Word. No serious student takes this statement to mean that David at this time was speaking of his own state. Wesley solves the mystery best as he speaks for David, "When I consider the manifold transgressions of ungodly men, I conclude within myself, that they have cast off all fear of the Divine majesty." The psalm continues in its order of contrast by comparing the righteous and the righteousness of God with the wicked!

Psalm 37:1, A Psalm of David. *"Fret not thyself because of evildoers, neither be thou envious against the workers of iniquity."*

Verse one of this psalm is considered to be one of David's most profound statements. Scholars accuse Solomon of writing loftier than he lived, but David's worst critics never offered him such criticism. There is no hint of David ever having jealousy at all, much less of the wicked. David continues in this psalm to utterly destroy any reason for anyone to envy the wicked. He concluded by saying in verse 34, *"Wait on the LORD, and keep his way, and he shall exalt thee to inherit the land: when the wicked are cut off, thou shalt see it."* And verse 40, *"And the LORD shall help them, and deliver them: he shall deliver them from the wicked, and save them, because they trust in him."* David assures the reward for serving God is worthy of the wait.

Psalms 38:1, A Psalm of David, to bring to remembrance. *"O LORD, rebuke me not in thy wrath: neither chasten me in thy hot displeasure."*

A close look at this psalm reveals that David is not asking that God not rebuke him or chasten him. David is asking God to not do so in His wrath. David well understood the difference between chastisement and wrath. He knew that wrath was appointed to heathens and infidels. David goes on to describe what appears to be the same disease mentioned in 1 Kings 1:1. He perfectly describes diseases that are sexually transmitted. David also ascribes his disease to his behavior in Verse 18, *"For I will declare mine iniquity; I will be sorry for my sin."*

David complains that while he is enduring this pain and infirmity, his enemies are rejoicing and taking advantage of the occasion. The enemies of David should have considered that he was the man after God's heart. This equates in God's eyes to "I will chasten the apple of my eye but don't you touch him." The enemies of Israel and those who rejoice when Davids fall, to this very day need to understand this very thing!

Psalms 39:1, To the chief Musician, even to Jeduthun, A Psalm of David. *"I said, I will take heed to my ways, that I sin not with my tongue: I will keep my mouth with a bridle, while the wicked is before me."*

David sends this psalm to Jeduthun who is one of the top musicians (1 Chronicles 16:41, 42). In this psalm, we can see how David walked through battles. This psalm is ascribed to the time of his illness. He relates to the wicked around him, but his speech is concerned with infirmities in his body and the hopelessness of an incurable disease. David gets quite melancholy in portions of this psalm, but has a great resolve only to write of it in worship and not open his mouth to complain or blame God. We can surmise from this and other psalms that David poured out his complaint before the Lord and the Lord only. Most men pour out their complaints before men and only men.

Some believe that David is silent here because he knows his infirmity is connected to his behavior (verse 8). While this is possible, it is not probable, for no one more than David knew the Lord's deliverance from trouble, even when he created it. However, David also knew the Lord's chastening and never questioned the Lord's hand of fatherly punishment, even though he would request relief (Verse 10).

Psalms 40:1, To the chief Musician, A Psalm of David. *"I waited patiently for the LORD; and he inclined unto me, and heard my cry."*

This is a psalm of celebration. In the preceding psalm, we saw how David went through the deep battles, and in this psalm, we see how he rejoiced when he was delivered. Just as he held his tongue in trial, he loosed it in triumph. From the application of this example, all of the church could prosper. In the trial he refused to speak, and in the triumph he refused to be quiet!

Psalm 41:1, To the chief Musician, A Psalm of David. *"Blessed is he that considereth the poor: the LORD will deliver him in time of trouble."*

It seems David begins this psalm with a consideration for the poor, but a closer look reveals that David is revealing his posture before the Lord and his faith in God's healing hand of mercy for those who are down. Many ascribe this verse to the help of those in poverty, and certainly no theme of the scriptures would be violated in doing so. However, the more accurate application is that David is speaking of his own condition before the Lord and his own failure being the cause of his condition. While it is easy to see David's benevolence to the poor, it is also easy to see that his poor spirit is that of contrition. Verse 4 says, *"I said, LORD, be merciful unto me: heal my soul; for I have sinned against thee."*

This psalm goes into a messianic revelation of the betrayal by Judas. In fact, Jesus quotes verse 9 of this Davidic psalm at His betrayal! John 13:18, *"I speak not of you all: I know whom I have chosen: but that the scripture may be fulfilled, He that eateth bread with me hath lift up his heel against me."* It is amazing how much of the heart of God must have constantly been flowing in David, for he would be uttering of his own state and then flow into the sufferings of the Messiah!

Psalm 51:1, To the chief Musician, A Psalm of David, when Nathan the prophet came unto him, after he had gone in to Bathsheba. *"Have mercy upon me, O God, according to thy lovingkindness: according unto the multitude of thy tender mercies blot out my transgressions."*

This is the masterpiece example for true repentance. Lightfoot heralded this work as "marvelous, the course for every true repentant." The composition of this psalm gives David first place in yet another category: no one has excelled beyond David in worship to the Lord; no one has excelled beyond David in battle for the Lord; no one has excelled beyond David in prophetic writings about the Lord; and no one has excelled beyond David in repentance before the Lord! This psalm is the manual for repentance. The contrition of David is the fruit of a true worshipper. When one is in constant adoration of the Lord, when he fails the one he adores, Godly sorrow will consume that individual. Not only does David's worship prove his love for the Lord, but his broken contrition over his failure also proves it.

In this psalm we find one of the most controversial things David ever said in verse 4, *"Against thee, thee only, have I sinned, and done this evil in thy sight: that thou mightest be justified when thou speakest, and be clear when thou judgest."* Calmuet said, "What! he killed a innocent man, stole his wife, employed his officers in the cover for his sin! How audacious to say he only sinned against God!" Calmuet should have considered the depth of Godly sorrow David was inflamed with. In the light of his contrition, he could only see God!

Psalm 52:1, To the chief Musician, Maschil, A Psalm of David, when Doeg the Edomite came and told Saul, and said unto him, David is come to the house of Ahimelech. *"Why boastest thou thyself in mischief, O mighty man? the goodness of God endureth continually."*

David felt he made a great mistake by not killing Doeg they day he got the sword of Goliath from Ahimelech as he was fleeing from Saul. 1 Samuel 22:22, *"And David said unto Abiathar, I knew it that day, when Doeg the Edomite was there, that he would surely tell Saul: I have occasioned the death of all the persons of thy father's house."*

This psalm seems to have been written long after the actual happening because of the lack of repentance in the text. The death of all the priests of Nob no doubt weighed heavily on the heart of David. In this psalm, David also makes a comparison between himself and Doeg, which is very unlikely that David would have done at the very time of the event, because of his grief at his failure.

Psalm 53:1, To the chief Musician upon Mahalath, Maschil, A Psalm of David. *"The fool hath said in his heart, There is no God. Corrupt are they, and have done abominable iniquity. there is none that doeth good."*

David started this psalm with almost the same words of Psalm 14:1. This psalm ends with David's passionate desire for Messiah. It is believed that this passion is one of the keys to his constant moving into that spiritual realm of messianic prophetic bliss.

Psalms 54:1, To the chief Musician on Neginoth, Maschil, A Psalm of David, when the Ziphims came and said to Saul, Doth not David hide himself with us? *"Save me, O God, by thy name, and judge me by thy strength."*

This is a time of great despair and disappointment in David's life. Some of David's own tribe had betrayed him. They also revealed his location to Saul who was hunting him down (1 Samuel 23:19). In verse 3 of this psalm, he calls them strangers. It is the most insulting thing that could have been said about anyone of his own people. David's disgust with his betrayers is evident, but he quickly turns it over to the Lord and declares that God will take care of these enemies. and he will employ himself in praising God!

Psalms 55:1, To the chief Musician on Neginoth, Maschil, A Psalm of David. *"Give ear to my prayer, O God; and hide not thyself from my supplication."*

This is a Davidic psalm that is often ascribed to the horrible time of the rebellion of Absalom, his very own son. However, Verse 9 casts a great doubt on that assumption, *"Destroy, O Lord, and divide their tongues":* It is very unlikely that David would have called for the destruction of Absalom. Whatever the occasion is, David is most emotional and overwhelmed by his conflict. His anguish comes pouring out of his innermost spirit! He moves into the realm of the great conflict of the Christ and the antichrist, and prophetically writes that which is sure to come forth at both the First and Second Advent of Christ!

Psalms 56:1, To the chief Musician upon Jonath-elem-rechokim, Michtam of David, when the Philistines took him in Gath. *"Be merciful unto me, O God: for man would swallow me up; he fighting daily oppresseth me."*

The long name here Jonath-elem-rechokim, is the occasion of the psalm. It means "the silent dove of distant lands." The subject of this psalm is evidently the oppression of Saul, David's innocence, and his journey to a distant land. David had connections with Gath, which was one of the five provinces of the Philistines. David must have been quite lonely. He knew he was a giant killer, not a killer of his own king. He felt defenseless as far as retaliation, knowing that even if Saul was unprotected by his army right before him, he would not harm him. Of course, later that is exactly what happened.

David prays with great confidence that the Lord will deliver him and fight his battle for him. Theologians, who ascribe psalms that have vengeance in them as though David is speaking of Saul, should not do so. David did not ask God to kill Saul, nor did he desire it. He prayed earnestly for Saul to have a change of heart. In this case he believed that God would turn him back. Verse 9, *"When I cry unto thee, then shall mine enemies turn back: this I know; for God is for me."* David firmly believed the prophetic words of his covenant friend Jonathan who predicted David would replace Saul!

Psalms 57:1, To the chief Musician, Altaschith, Michtam of David, when he fled from Saul in the cave. *"Be merciful unto me, O God, be merciful unto me: for my soul trusteth in thee: yea, in the shadow of thy wings will I make my refuge, until these calamities be overpast."*

In our trials often come our most prolific words. Two of the most profound utterances from David are found in this chapter. Verse one, *"Be merciful unto me, O God, be merciful unto me: for my soul trusteth in thee: yea, in the shadow of thy wings will I make my refuge, until these calamities be over past,"* and verse 7, *"My heart is fixed, O God, my heart is fixed: I will sing and give praise."* The two of them together deliver a great message to the body. 1) It is God we implore for mercy. 2) It is God we place our trust in. 3) It is God who is our refuge 4) It is God who preserves us through the storm. 5) It is God who fixes our heart. 6) It is God our heart must be fixed on!

Psalms 58:1, To the chief Musician, Altaschith, Michtam of David. *"Do ye indeed speak righteousness, O congregation? do ye judge uprightly, O ye sons of men?"*

There is no recorded words of David that are more stout against the ungodly than we find here in this psalm. David was aflame with jealousy for God. It is sometimes hard to understand that strong condemning words like we find in this psalm actually are born in deep worship. He says in verse 8, *"As a snail which melteth, let every one of them pass away: like the untimely birth of a woman, that they may not see the sun."*

Did David have no mercy for these people at all? David was the staunch enemy of the enemies of God, and the best friend of God's children. His zeal for God was passionate. His worship for the Lord made him jealous. His life mission was to get all of the earth to worship the living God, and to build an amazing place in the center of the earth to do it. Wicked, unregenerate, unrepentant heathen oppose that purpose. These were not like his fellow Jews who were tracking him down. From them he asked to be delivered. But these he calls for their destruction! These were called by Lightfoot "antichrists." When the Lord returns, He will have no mercy on the antichrist and his forces of unrepentant heathen!

Psalms 59:1 To the chief Musician, Altaschith, Michtam of David; when Saul sent, and they watched the house to kill him. *"Deliver me from mine enemies, O my God: defend me from them that rise up against me."*

There was a mixed group of Jews and Gentiles that Saul had employed against David to assassinate him. David asks for deliverance from those who were Jews, and destruction for those who were not. This shows David's absolute fear and awesome respect for the covenant people of God. Of the Jews he says in verse 11, *"Slay them not, lest my people forget: scatter them by thy power; and bring them down, O Lord our shield."* Of the heathen he says in verse 13, *"Consume them in wrath, consume them, that they may not be: and let them know that God ruleth in Jacob unto the ends of the earth. Selah."* It should be noted that the non-Jewish men with David were proselytes to the Jewish faith!

Psalms 60:1, To the chief Musician upon Shushaneduth, Michtam of David, to teach; when he strove with Aramnaharaim and with Aramzobah, when Joab returned, and smote of Edom in the valley of salt twelve thousand. *"O God, thou hast cast us off, thou hast scattered us, thou hast been displeased; O turn thyself to us again."*

This beautiful psalm known as Shushaneduth (lily of a testimony) is also called a "Golden Psalm." However, it doesn't start out so beautifully. It begins by bemoaning the state of Israel before Joab and his brothers slaughter eighteen thousand Edomites. Joab's forces alone are attributed to having slain twelve thousand. It is not unlike Davidic psalms to describe a horrible state before rejoicing over the deliverance from it. Saul and his royal mess had caused the nation of Israel to lose the great battle in which Saul and Jonathan were killed. David is describing their deplorable state. He does not mention that in that particular war, he was serving the Philistines in Ziklag, and was even at one time marching with Achish to fight against Israel.

The displeasure David refers to here could have possibly been a hint of the awful state his nation was in at the time that Saul spent so much of his time and energy tracking David down. He quickly moves from that low time in Israel's recent past to the great victory the Lord has brought them through his mighty men. Clark has no justification in tearing apart either the psalm or the introduction of it.

Psalms 61:1, To the chief Musician upon Neginah, A Psalm of David. *"Hear my cry, O God; attend unto my prayer."*

David's heart is seen in this psalm through the four "I wills" he avows. 1) Verse 2: *"I will cry unto Thee."* 2) Verse 4: *"I will abide in thy tabernacle forever."* 3) Verse 4: *"I will trust in the covert of thy wings."* 4) Verse 8: *"So will I sing praise unto thy name for ever, that I may daily perform my vows."* These four declarations not only show the heart of David, but they should be the sincere goal of every true follower of Christ! These four also prove that when the heart is bent toward the Lord, one can make such a declaration void of pride and self-sufficiency and know it is God that gives him the volition of will to serve his God.

Psalm 62:1, To the chief Musician, to Jeduthun, A Psalm of David. *"Truly my soul waiteth upon God: from him cometh my salvation."*

Jeduthun was a renown musician (1 Chronicles 9:16) that David trusted with his anointed lyrics. This psalm is a declaration of faith, the type of which David constantly affirms, even in his exile from Saul. He proclaims that he will not be moved, probably referring to his prophetic promise to someday rule over all of Israel.

This psalm is attributed to the time frame of David's time in Carmel and his encounter with Nabal and Abigail (1 Samuel 25). It is believed that verse 10, *"Trust not in oppression, and become not vain in robbery: if riches increase, set not your heart upon them"* is a reference to David's honesty while he roamed on Nabal's property, in that David never took a thing from his flock, but instead protected it. Nabal acted a fool and all of Nabal's wealth, as well as his wife Abigail, became David's. David became very wealthy and yet cannot be charged with setting his affection on mammon!

Psalm 63:1, A Psalm of David, when he was in the wilderness of Judah. *"O God, thou art my God; early will I seek thee: my soul thirsteth for thee, my flesh longeth for thee in a dry and thirsty land, where no water is";*

To discredit David's prophetic office is to ensure one's inability to understand this psalm. David sees in the realm of the Spirit in the early hours, as well as the night watches. He sees the sanctuary before it is ever built. He sees the Ark setting there in its place. He sees himself the king of Israel. Finally, he sees his enemies in utter failure and ruin! Rest assured, dear reader, David's morning and evening devotions were filled with revelatory messianic glory!

Psalm 64:1, To the chief Musician. A Psalm of David. *"Hear my voice, O God, in my prayer: preserve my life from fear of the enemy."*

There are many proofs that David believed in vocal prayer and petition. It seems that he was able to open his mouth and see God fill it with wonderful adoration and prophetic declaration. Then David would write it down, and later, either he would put it to music or he would assign it to a musician to do so. In this psalm David does not speak of himself destroying those who come against him, but declares that God will do it in his behalf. This is again proof that this is referring to a time when Saul was his enemy. David was never the enemy of Saul.

Psalm 65:1, To the chief Musician, A Psalm and Song of David. *"Praise waiteth for thee, O God, in Sion: and unto thee shall the vow be performed."*

Some historians strip David's authorship from this psalm, and try to say it was written by Haggai, Jeremiah, or Ezekiel. They claim the psalm does not follow an exact pattern of poetic math as most of David's writings do. However, there are other psalms ascribed to David similar to this one that they do not bother to question. The flow of praise and adoration in this psalm span the annals of time to land in the blissful millennium when all of the nations will come to Zion to worship the true and living God! David will literally be there to see it (Jeremiah 9:30) and once again hear the saints sing this song he wrote.

Psalm 68:1, To the chief Musician, A Psalm or Song of David. *"Let God arise, let his enemies be scattered: let them also that hate him flee before him."*

This psalm was written for the moving of the Ark of the Covenant. David often wrote psalms to sing at certain events, and because of his great love for the Word of God, he knew Moses uttered certain words as he set forth the Ark. Therefore the first words of this psalm agree with Moses' words in Numbers 10:35, *"And it came to pass, when the ark set forward, that Moses said, Rise up, LORD, and let thine enemies be scattered; and let them that hate thee flee before thee."* David begins with these words and moves the psalm in messianic momentum to describe the God to whom the Ark belongs and the church He bought with the blood of Christ.

David had immense revelation of the fact that the Gentiles would also be a part of the universal church and often wrote of it. He himself made more Gentiles into Jews than any other man in history! David knew that all of the enemies of God could not stop the wonderful flow of grace that would build God's church and bring God's glory upon the earth.

Psalm 69:1, To the chief Musician upon Shoshannim, A Psalm of David. *"Save me, O God; for the waters are come in unto my soul."*

This psalm contains much messianic value. David begins to speak of his dismal condition. In and out of that, he moves into the reproaches of Christ. The Jews would often relate activities of their day to the utterances of David, as we see in John 2:17, *"And his disciples remembered that it was written, The zeal of thine house hath eaten me up."* The disciples are relating to verse nine of this psalm.

What seems to many as a verse taken out of text by the disciples should be seen and applauded as good keen discernment of Davidic prophecy! In verse 21 of this psalm we find a prophetic utterance of anguish that is amazing: *"They gave me also gall for my meat; and in my thirst they gave me vinegar to drink."* There is nothing Jesus or any of His disciples did toward fulfilling this prophecy, yet it is fulfilled by the very ones that crucified Jesus. It is true with David's present condition in metaphor but Christ literally was given gall and vinegar. Matthew 27:34, *"They gave him vinegar to drink mingled with gall: and when he had tasted thereof, he would not drink."* As is normally the case, David ends the psalm with the sure declaration of his enemy's judgment and his own sure victory.

Psalm 70:1, To the chief Musician, A Psalm of David, to bring to remembrance. *"Make haste, O God, to deliver me; make haste to help me, O LORD."*

There are four clear instances in which David pleads with God to hurry up, or make haste, not counting Psalm 40 which has some of the very same words as this psalm. David's intimate relationship with the Lord surely afforded him this luxury. The true heart of David is seen in this psalm, interacting with the heart of God. This sort of hurry up prayer and supplication is actually pleasing to the Lord for more than one reason. 1) In such a prayer, there is no doubt of God's ability to deliver. 2) There is no doubt as to whether or not God is going to deliver. 3) There is no doubt as to the ultimate outcome.

Psalm 72:20, *"The prayers of David the son of Jesse are ended."*

David most likely wrote this song close to the end of his life. He wrote it for Solomon, but neither Solomon nor David, nor any other human king that has ever lived could be the subject of several of these utterances. One is in verse 11, *"Yea, all kings shall fall down before him: all nations shall serve him."* Another one is in verse 19, *"And blessed be his glorious name for ever:*

and let the whole earth be filled with his glory; Amen, and Amen." These are definitely messianic verses, and the sweet instruction of a prophetic father to a son of the posterity of Judah!

Psalm 78:70, *"He chose David also his servant, and took him from the sheepfolds":*

This verse is a part of a psalm which is an intense narrative of the nation of Israel The singers and the musicians who composed this psalm have claimed prophetic status as they speak of the glorious God of Israel and His goodness in judgment. Verse 2, *"I will open my mouth in a parable: I will utter dark sayings of old."* In so doing they speak descriptive words of David's humble beginnings.

Psalms 86:1, A Prayer of David. *"Bow down thine ear, O LORD, hear me: for I am poor and needy."*

This psalm is a good example of David's prayers. It is balanced in petition and praise, as most of David's prayers are. Calmuet said of this psalm, "If one could pray like David he could fight like David!"

Psalm 89:3, *"I have made a covenant with my chosen, I have sworn unto David my servant,"*

This psalm is a good example of how the musicians and poets were constantly tapping into the covenant God made with David, even as they write. This is written at a time of spiritual, as well as military, down turn in Israel and Judah. The petition is for the Lord to move in mercy and connection with the Davidic covenant. Part of that covenant is sometimes referred to as the "sure mercies of David" (Isaiah 55:3 and Acts 13:34). Thus the writer of this psalm quotes God's word of promise to David.

Psalm 89:20, *"I have found David my servant; with my holy oil have I anointed him":*

The writer here is speaking of prophetic utterances of Nathan and Gad. The quote here is not a verbatim quote, but truly can be verified as prophetic words given to David on several occasions. The whole of Israel was well aware of the Lord's love for David and what had been spoken to and through the prophets of the Lord. At this time of great despair, the nation of Israel is longing for a David to arise again, someone with the anointing David had. All through the chronicles of the kings of Israel, we find a documented desire for leaders like David to arise. Some of these longings are messianic in value, for the desire these writers are feeling and expressing are not just for a David, but for the Messiah, called the son of David!

Psalm 89:35, *"Once have I sworn by my holiness that I will not lie unto David."*

Preceding this verse are some of the strongest words written on the strength of the Davidic covenant that are found anywhere in the scripture. One is verse 22, *"The enemy shall not exact upon him; nor the son of wickedness afflict him."* Another is verse 23, *"And I will beat down his foes before his face, and plague them that hate him."* However, the prophet ends these words with a complaint of the present condition, which could be taken as an explanation of the need for a David to arise!

Psalm 89:49, *"Lord, where are thy former loving kindnesses, which thou swarest unto David in thy truth?"*

In speculation over who wrote this psalm, Calmuet declares the psalm is "too bold for an unknown writer." Understanding the boldness of the psalm is not hard, but it was common for any intercessor in that day to connect their petition to God's love for David and His covenant with him. This same thing is wise unto this very day. Those who labor hard in prayer with a desperate need should even to this day practice the very same thing. God is a covenant God, and there is much proof in the scripture that God not only allows such petitions that connect with a promise given to others, but enjoys it!

Psalm 101:1, A Psalm of David. *"I will sing of mercy and judgment: unto thee, O LORD, will I sing."*

This psalm is ascribed to David and was written after he received the prophecy that he would become king, but before he actually did. David affectionately describes how he will execute the highly esteemed office of king of Israel in the very type of the coming Messiah. It is believed by the Hebrew ancients that the priest would read this psalm before the inauguration of a new king.

Psalm 103:1, A Psalm of David. *"Bless the LORD, O my soul: and all that is within me, bless his holy name."*

Some of the Hebrew scholars project that this psalm is not Davidic but was written by a psalmist in the time of captivity. Yet the inscription "A psalm of David" is found in all of the versions. There is no reason to doubt that David wrote it, and the people of the captivity sang it. The psalm contains every major component of a Davidic psalm in pattern and construction. It is a sweet psalm and a very formidable work of the Sweet Psalmist of Israel!

Psalm 108:1, A Song or Psalm of David. *"O God, my heart is fixed; I will sing and give praise, even with my glory."*

Because this psalm is an actual compilation of two other songs of David, it gives us ample proof of their often use, and also the fact that the Hebrews would sing them or pray them in difficult times. The first five verses of this psalm can be found in Psalm 57:7-11. Verses six through thirteen are found in Psalm 60:5-12.

David's relationship with the Lord made his songs and prayers most popular. David had written celebratory songs as well as songs of supplication. He wanted his flock to have songs of great expression in the best of times, as well as the very worst of times! David's songs are a picture of David's heart for the people of Israel. Imagine a past great and favorite songwriter in our land also being the greatest general of all times in our military, as well as the favorite president! We have no such leader to reminisce!

Psalm 109:1, To the chief Musician, A Psalm of David. *"Hold not thy peace, O God of my praise"*;

David knew the bitter taste of being betrayed by his own son. Yet, David's words in this psalm do not match his affection for Absalom. These stark words are probably directed to Ahithophel and his wicked counsel. This psalm was written during the height of the betrayal. However, as often is the case, David moves from his own pain of betrayal to prophetically speaking of our Lord's betrayal. Peter taught us to apply a portion of this psalm to the betrayer of all times, Judas Iscariot, when he said, *"For it is written in the book of Psalms, Let his habitation be desolate, and let no man dwell therein: and his bishoprick let another take."* (Acts 1:20)

Psalm 110:1, A Psalm of David. *"The LORD said unto my Lord, Sit thou at my right hand, until I make thine enemies thy footstool."*

David gives to us here a very clear messianic prediction. The Pharisees in the days of Jesus were totally silenced by the Lord Jesus when He used this verse to prove to them that the prophecy was in fact about Him instead of David. We read in Matthew 22:41-46, *"While the Pharisees were gathered together, Jesus asked them, Saying, What think ye of Christ? whose son is he? They say unto him, The Son of David. He saith unto them, How then doth David in spirit call him Lord, saying, The LORD said unto my Lord, Sit thou on my right hand, till I make thine enemies thy footstool? If David then call him Lord, how is he his son? And no man was able to answer him a word, neither durst any man from that day forth ask him any more questions."*

David continues in this psalm describing the Messiah, and the Pharisees well knew the rest of the psalm. This was a pivotal point in the ministry of Jesus, as he finally silenced the pharisaical entourage assigned to trap Him in His words. David knew he wasn't the Messiah, but he knew he was the shadow and type. David did conquer all of his enemies and gain control of all of the land given to Abraham by the Lord. David also spoke of the Christ being of the order of Melchizedek, who was both a perpetual king and a perpetual priest. Yes, Jesus is both our High Priest and the King of Kings! David knew him by the Spirit!

Psalm 122:1, A Song of degrees of David. *"I was glad when they said unto me, Let us go into the house of the LORD."*

Haweis declares that David wrote this psalm for the Israelites to sing as they came to Jerusalem to worship during the time of the feasts. There is no reason to doubt that, even though the Temple was not constructed until after the death of David. It is evident that David saw the Temple in the Spirit, first at the threshing floor of Ornan (I Chronicles 22:1), and then later to the degree that he could instruct Solomon exactly how to build it. In his spirit by the Holy Spirit, David was with the celebrants as they made their pilgrimage to Jerusalem!

Psalm 122:5, *"For there are set thrones of judgment, the thrones of the house of David."*

David could not only see the finished Temple but could also see that the people were properly judged and governed. Righteous judgment was of great importance to David, as his dynasty proves over and over again. This verse was connected with Colossians 2:5 by the great theologian Loweth. Paul declares in Colossians 2:5, *"For though I be absent in the flesh, yet am I with you in the spirit, joying and beholding your order, and the stedfastness of your faith in Christ."* Paul was beholding the order of the church at Colossae by the Spirit of God because of his great passion for the Lord to be pleased with their efforts. In that respect, we can understand David's spiritual presence at the thrones of judgment for Israel generation after generation and then beyond, though the Messiah himself!

Psalm 124:1, A Song of degrees of David. *"If it had not been the LORD who was on our side, now may Israel say"*;

This work of David is not ascribed to any particular deliverance, but could be sung at the occasion of any deliverance! The theme is simple but profound. Where would we be if the Lord had not heard our cry and delivered us by His mighty hand? David knew the anguish of being hunted down, though he was an innocent man. He also knew the power of God's deliverance without his lifting a hand!

Psalm 131:1, A Song of degrees of David. *"LORD, my heart is not haughty, nor mine eyes lofty: neither do I exercise myself in great matters, or in things too high for me."*

David is defending his charge of haughtiness and confirming his humility before the Lord. His own brothers had charged him with arrogance, then later Joab seemed to lay the same charge on him as he tried to persuade him not to number the people (1 Chronicles 21:3). David did seem to battle pride at times, but one instance of his approaching the Lord in that manner cannot be found. No powerful leader can escape such an accusation from either his friends or his enemies, and sometimes both.

Psalm 132:1, *A Song of degrees." LORD, remember David, and all his afflictions:"*

Most theologians agree that this psalm was written by Solomon about David. This is mostly because some of the same words in this psalm occur in the closing of Solomon's prayer in 2 Chronicles 6:41-42. Wathen sums up the controversy of the authorship of this psalm quite well by saying, "If in fact this is not a Davidic psalm in pen, it is quite so in passion." It is not uncommon that Solomon would invoke the passion of David in his prayer or song. It is also most probable that David was successful in transferring his passion for the Ark to Solomon to the degree this psalm sets forth. Nowhere else is this level of passion for the placing of the Ark in its resting place but the heart of David!

Psalm 132:10, *"For thy servant David's sake turn not away the face of thine anointed."*

Some who believe and teach plural mediator ship, such as the Roman church teaches, have cited this verse. They say that Solomon was invoking David's influence in his petition. Nothing could be farther from the truth. 1 Timothy 2:5 plainly states, *"For there is one God, and one mediator between God and men, the man Christ Jesus."* The Roman church prays to Mary and dead saints. Solomon comes nowhere close to doing so. He simply reminds God of his relationship with David and makes a plea connected with a covenant. This is not error on Solomon's part. This is good discernment and displayed wisdom.

Psalm 132:11, *"The LORD hath sworn in truth unto David; he will not turn from it; Of the fruit of thy body will I set upon thy throne."*

Because Solomon is David's posterity, he reminds the Lord of His promise to David for his sons. Solomon clings to the clear prophetic word that David had received. No doubt David had shared the word of the Lord with Solomon concerning his being chosen to be the one to stand in that promise. David said to Solomon in 1 Chronicles 22:8-9, *"But the word of the LORD came to me, saying, Thou hast shed blood abundantly, and hast made great wars: thou shalt not build an house unto my name, because thou hast shed much blood upon the earth in my sight. Behold, a son shall be born to thee, who shall be a man of rest; and I will give him rest from all his enemies round about: for his name shall be Solomon, and I will give peace and quietness unto Israel in his days.*

This leaves no doubt as to why Solomon leans heavily upon the Lord's promise to David as he makes petition.

Psalm 132:17, *"There will I make the horn of David to bud: I have ordained a lamp for mine anointed."*

Before Solomon concludes with his declaration of God's favor for David resting on him, he acknowledges the conditional part for himself and the people of Israel. We find this in Verse 12, *"If thy children will keep my covenant and my testimony that I shall teach them, their children shall also sit upon thy throne for evermore."*

Solomon understands his obligation and duty but also understands he cannot even perform such without the sure mercies of David! Solomon expects God's favor on his life because of the Word delivered unto him.

Psalm 133:1, A Song of degrees of David. *"Behold, how good and how pleasant it is for brethren to dwell together in unity."*

The profundity of this verse is often overlooked because of a zeal for unity. However, there is so much in this little psalm that spans the annals of time, which proves the powerful prophetic anointing that rested upon David. David is not just seeing ecumenical unity. The Hebrew word from which we translate unity is the word *yachad*. This word doesn't just mean we have all come together for a common purpose. It means we are gathered in uniformity or we proceed in united order. Ecumenicalism says, we are all on different paths but we will all end up at the same destiny. *Yachad* says we are all on the same road and as we march forward to the same place we march in uniformity.

David was seeing by the Spirit the future answer to the Lord's Prayer found in John 17. Jesus prays in Verses 11, 22, and 23 that there would be a complete oneness between Him and His. David saw that being established through the priesthood connecting with the king so he mentions the Aaronic order of the flow of anointing that comes down. That is the very flow that is necessary for the kind of unity David is talking about. Then David takes us on a geographic lesson to prove what he is speaking of. Mount Hermon is the tallest of the Zion Mountains. Its base is almost sea level and it rises abruptly approximately nine thousand feet, which causes the dew flow to be most unusual and famous.

At the base of Hermon is the humble beginning of the Jordan River. It flows down to the Sea of Galilee and then on downward to the Dead Sea, which is the saltiest place on earth, the lowest place on earth, and no flesh can live there! This is the real flow that depicts a remnant church that is so dead to self that they overcome the world. Why? Because they love not their life unto death (Revelation 12:11).

Psalm 138:1, A Psalm of David. "*I will praise thee with my whole heart: before the gods will I sing praise unto thee.*"

Dr. Hammond declares this Davidic psalm was utilized by Haggai and Zechariah as they engaged in rebuilding the Temple and as they promoted revival. The Septuagint renders Dr. Hammond great support by entitling this psalm as "A Psalm of or for David, Haggai, and Zechariah." Evidently these two prophets used this psalm to teach the people of Israel concerning gratitude and praise.

The psalm certainly shows David's readiness to worship before his own people as well as heathen kings (gods). Some scholars believe the word *gods* is referring to angels (Psalm 8:5) and some believe the word is referring to idols (Psalm 97:7). Idols should be ruled out by any serious student of David's life. They would certainly know that David would smash the idol to thousands of pieces before he ever began to worship!

Psalm 139:1, To the chief Musician, A Psalm of David. "*O LORD, thou hast searched me, and known me.*"

Wesley agrees with many Jewish doctors of theology that this is the most excellent of all of the Davidic psalms. Clark casts a shadow as to whether David even wrote it, declaring it to be long after David lived and died. There is no need or value in doubting the authorship of David on this fine work. He ends this psalm with a cry for the Lord to try him and search him thoroughly, only after he completely establishes God's ability to know every minute detail about his body, soul, and spirit. One of the secrets of David's amazing relationship with the Lord is his zeal to be transparent before the Lord and welcoming any and every correction from his all-knowing Lord.

Psalm 140:1, To the chief Musician, A Psalm of David. "*Deliver me, O LORD, from the evil man: preserve me from the violent man*";

Most attach this Davidic psalm to David's flight from Saul. It is not likely that David is calling Saul all of these names and calling for him to be burnt with the coals of fire falling on him and then go down to hell itself (Verse 10). Throughout the scripture, there is not a hint of such vengeance in David's heart for Saul. Some say the sum of David's patience with Saul was because of David's covenant with Jonathan, the son of Saul. However, David respected Saul's anointing, even when Saul was hunting him down like an animal.

It should be noted that the Jewish doctors have proven a distinct difference of tone when David is seeking deliverance from Saul and when he is seeking deliverance from heathen. He clearly calls for the death and destruction of idolaters because he considers them to be a total offense to his God. He doesn't pray for Saul's destruction, but that he would be delivered from Saul. David, no doubt, did view Saul as the father of his covenant friend who was a deranged jealous backslider to be pitied and prayed for.

Psalm 141:1, A Psalm of David. *"LORD, I cry unto thee: make haste unto me; give ear unto my voice, when I cry unto thee."*

Here is an intensely sweet psalm that reveals David's love and appreciation for the heavenly Father's chastening hand as well as His hand of blessing. This is a testimony of pure praise. How can our praise be pure without such? A true lover of God will appreciate both works of His hand!

Psalm 142:1, Maschil of David; A Prayer when he was in the cave. *"I cried unto the LORD with my voice; with my voice unto the LORD did I make my supplication."*

This amazing psalm is a prayer David made unto the Lord when he was in the cave. David recorded it, and the children of Israel sang it on certain occasions. Twice David was in a cave. He was in the cave of Adullam when he ran from King Achish (1 Samuel 22:1). Also David was in the cave of Engedi, where he hid from Saul (1 Samuel 24:1-3).

Though the title doesn't tell us which cave this was, it is fairly easy to see that it was the cave of Engedi, for the tenor of the verse matches the experience of the cave in Engedi much better. David had a severe test in this cave, both with his heart and his own men. David had the opportunity here to rid himself of his enemy. Although he was no doubt very weary of the life of a fugitive and under pressure from his men to kill Saul, David refused. David came through this severe test with a severe anointing!

Psalm 143:1, A Psalm of David. *"Hear my prayer, O LORD, give ear to my supplications: in thy faithfulness answer me, and in thy righteousness."*

David reminds God of His supreme faithfulness and righteousness. Dr Hammond is correct when he connects this psalm to a more mature and experienced David. David is looking back at the other times God has delivered him and drawing both faith and boldness from it. The older we get, the more we have to look back on and gain strength from. However, David had this pattern from a very young age. Remember, he did the very same thing when giving Saul the reason he had such a confidence that he could take the giant out. He referenced the lion and the bear. He also was careful to give God all of the glory!

Psalm 144:1, A Psalm of David. *"Blessed be the LORD my strength, which teacheth my hands to war, and my fingers to fight":*

David knew it was an affront to the Lord for him to think he was invincible in himself. David also knew that it was a great compliment to God for him to declare his invincibility based on the power of God within him. This psalm is ascribed to David by the Syriac which states "A Psalm of David when he slew Asaph, the brother of Goliath." It is definitely a victory shout with a deep amazement that the Creator would actually work so mightily through a mortal man!

Psalm 144:10 *"It is he that giveth salvation unto kings: who delivereth David his servant from the hurtful sword."*

By this time in the life of David there was a great legendary effect surrounding his military success and amazing victories. Some historians tell of a constant increase in songs and stories about David from the time the women of Israel sang their first song about him until the very end of his life. The first song was incredible in itself, and Saul's jealousy was inflamed the day they sang it. 1 Samuel 18:7-8, *"And the women answered one another as they played, and said, Saul hath slain his thousands, and David his ten thousands. And Saul was very wroth, and the saying displeased him; and he said, They have ascribed unto David ten thousands, and to me they have ascribed but thousands: and what can he have more but the kingdom?"*

David wants it to be very clear that it is the Lord that trained him; it is the Lord that empowers him; and it is the Lord that gives him divine protection.

Psalm 145:1, David's Psalm of praise. *"I will extol thee, my God, O king; and I will bless thy name for ever and ever."*

This is the last psalm that bears David's name, even though there are five psalms that follow this one. They are called the "Hallelujah Psalms." However, this psalm was strategically placed in the entire book of psalms because it gives every good reason for mankind to give God praise. David, the greatest worshipper who ever lived on the earth, now gives every good reason for every single person to worship and praise the everlasting God of Abraham, Isaac, and Jacob!

Proverbs

Proverbs 1:1, *"The proverbs of Solomon the son of David, king of Israel."*

The book of Proverbs is filled with wisdom and with understanding, much of which first came to David by the Holy Ghost and was then delivered to Solomon and the nation of Israel in general. However, this is the only mention of David in the entire book. There is very little dispute as to whether Solomon wrote many of the proverbs, as well as compiling the entire book. Nor should we doubt Solomon wrote by divine revelation. Yet much was taught him by his father David!

Ecclesiastes

Ecclesiastes 1:1, *"The words of the Preacher, the son of David, king in Jerusalem."*

Like the book of Proverbs, only in the first verse of this book do we find a mention of David. David's influence however, is from the beginning to the end of Ecclesiastes. By the time of this writing, Solomon is already backsliding in the matter of idolatry. Solomon cannot blame any of his propensities for idolatry on his father David. Solomon was well aware of his father's sad and horrific failures. Yet he had seen firsthand the complete and total restoration of his father. One thing Solomon never saw was his father bow down to an idol. He knew his father never allowed idolatry in the coasts of Israel.

David hated idolatry with a perfect hatred. Lightfoot brought attention to the lack of condemning idolatry in Solomon's writings. Although we do not find anger or disrespect for David in any of Solomon's writings, we also cannot find sound condemnation for idolatry. Solomon first married idolaters. He then allowed idolatry in his house. Then he did the unthinkable; he engaged in idolatry. There is no question that his involvement in idolatry was a wholesale disrespect for his father who despised it so much. When Solomon went into idolatry, he displayed and spread disrespect for David's perfect record concerning idolatry.

Song of Solomon

Song of Solomon 4:4, *"Thy neck is like the tower of David builded for an armoury, whereon there hang a thousand bucklers, all shields of mighty men."*

Solomon's adoration of his bride is most definitely the type of Christ's love for his church. The bride's adoration for Solomon is also a type of the church's adoration for Christ. It is in Solomon's description of the neck of the bride that he refers to the tower of David. Solomon is here referring to strength and majesty. The neck is the part of the body that turns and holds the head. Her neck was probably adorned with necklaces and ornaments. This reminded Solomon of some tower David built where hung the beautiful and elaborate bucklers David provided for his fighting men.

Isaiah

Isaiah 7:2, *"And it was told the house of David, saying, Syria is confederate with Ephraim. And his heart was moved, and the heart of his people, as the trees of the wood are moved with the wind."*

It seems that the prophet is mentioning David here to illuminate the strong contrast with what is happening here with Syria and what happened in David's time when he completely subdued the Syrians and made slaves out of them (2 Samuel 8:6-8). The message here is an indictment for the idolatry in Israel, which did not exist in David's dynasty. Essentially Isaiah is stating, "David had no idols and subdued the Syrians, but we have them today, and the Syrians are upon us." However, Isaiah will go on to prophesy the deliverance for Israel because of the house of David!

Isaiah 7:13, *"And he said, Hear ye now, O house of David; Is it a small thing for you to weary men, but will ye weary my God also?"*

This verse hardly seems to fit with the amazingly famous prophecy of the next verse; *"Therefore the Lord himself shall give you a sign; Behold, a virgin shall conceive, and bear a son, and shall call his name Immanuel."* However, in the order of the contrast between David and Ahaz, the Spirit of the Lord expresses great prophetic zeal for the everlasting covenant God has with

David. Therefore, Isaiah is used of God to express the weariness of God with the unbelieving Ahaz and then scales the span of time and tells of the virgin born Messiah from the tribe of Judah!

Isaiah 9:7, "*Of the increase of his government and peace there shall be no end, upon the throne of David, and upon his kingdom, to order it, and to establish it with judgment and with justice from henceforth even for ever. The zeal of the LORD of hosts will perform this.*"

This amazing messianic prophecy becomes even more amazing when consideration is made of its total confirmation of the prophecies given to David by Gad and Nathan, as well as the Davidic prophecies he penned himself. Luke gives great insight to the power of this prophetic word of Isaiah as the angelic prophesy comes forth in chapter one and verses thirty-two and thirty-three: "*He shall be great, and shall be called the Son of the Highest: and the Lord God shall give unto him the throne of his father David: And he shall reign over the house of Jacob for ever; and of his kingdom there shall be no end.*"

The prophet Nathan had told David the same thing in 2 Samuel 7:12-13 "*And when thy days be fulfilled, and thou shalt sleep with thy fathers, I will set up thy seed after thee, which shall proceed out of thy bowels, and I will establish his kingdom. He shall build an house for my name, and I will stablish the throne of his kingdom for ever.*" Therefore, the Davidic order of the Messiah is without question in the mouth of two or three witnesses.

Isaiah 16:5, "*And in mercy shall the throne be established: and he shall sit upon it in truth in the tabernacle of David, judging, and seeking judgment, and hasting righteousness.*"

The tabernacle of David is established in Christ, and therefore the body of Christ, the church, is to be seen as the partial fulfillment of the tabernacle of David. Stopping short of Replacement Theology, we must realize that the tabernacle of David will be literally fulfilled in the millennium. It should also be noted that the deliverance of Israel from the oppression of the nations around them is seen in the work of the coming Messiah by rebuilding the tabernacle of David. Amos 9:11, "*In that day will I raise up the tabernacle of David that is fallen, and close up the breaches thereof; and I will raise up his ruins, and I will build it as in the days of old*":

This is a reference to David's conquer of every enemy in the coasts of the land God gave to Abraham! This is seen again in the Acts of the Apostles 15:16, "*After this I will return, and will build again the tabernacle of David, which is fallen down; and I will build again the ruins thereof, and I will set it up*":

What the Jews failed to see is that first the son of David (Messiah) had to come as a suffering servant. Israel will realize this when they "look on Him whom they have pierced."

Isaiah 22:9, *"Ye have seen also the breaches of the city of David, that they are many: and ye gathered together the waters of the lower pool."*

This city of David is Jerusalem, called so at the time David took it from the Jebusites (2 Samuel 5:7 and 9). There were two lakes that supplied Jerusalem with water, the upper pool and the lower pool. This reference to the lower pool, and the people gathering there, is related to the work Hezekiah did to the city of David (2 Kings 20:20), as well as a deeper spiritual application at the end of the "Age of the Gentiles."

Isaiah 22:22, *"And the key of the house of David will I lay upon his shoulder; so he shall open and none shall shut; and he shall shut, and none shall open."*

This key of David has been often disputed as to its spiritual application in eschatology. Taking it to be so literal as to mean the Messiah's absolute and transferable authority seems to be hard for most theologians. However, there is ample proof that Jesus was referring to this Davidic key when he stated in Matthew 16:19, *"And I will give unto thee the keys of the kingdom of heaven: and whatsoever thou shalt bind on earth shall be bound in heaven: and whatsoever thou shalt loose on earth shall be loosed in heaven."*

This is messianic, and this is Davidic, which Lightfoot declared "cannot be separated." The fact that this key is given to the church of Philadelphia proves it is not given unconditionally. Revelation 3:7, *"And to the angel of the church in Philadelphia write; These things saith he that is holy, he that is true, he that hath the key of David, he that openeth, and no man shutteth; and shutteth, and no man openeth"*; The church in Philadelphia was the only church of the seven in which Jesus found no reason for rebuke.

Isaiah 29:1, *"Woe to Ariel, to Ariel, the city where David dwelt! add ye year to year; let them kill sacrifices."*

Ariel here is a Chaldean word which means "lion of God." This is Jerusalem, and this lamentation of the prophet was not only dealing with the immediate invasion of one Sennacherib, but it is properly ascribed to others, like Titus of Rome, whom God allowed to destroy Jerusalem. It should be noted that even the place where David lived for 33 years was not exempt from judgment. One must carefully remember that every promise of God and every covenant of God contains conditional order. God despised having to judge His beloved city, the city of His beloved David!

Isaiah 37:35, *"For I will defend this city to save it for mine own sake, and for my servant David's sake."*

It seems that more than the intercession of the remnant, it was the affront by Sennacherib as he blasphemed God (Isaiah 37:23) that actually caused the Lord to deal a heavy blow on the Assyrians. The Lord did mention Hezekiah's prayer, and in the next chapter we find, in fact, Hezekiah knew how to pray. But both the present and coming final judgment on Sennacherib are connected to the mockery Sennacherib tried to make of God and the lineage of David. This reveals the strong emotion the Lord has for His servant David, as this verse declares, *"for mine own sake, and for my servant David's sake."* If you were the enemy of God, you were the enemy of David. If you were the enemy of David, you were the enemy of God!

Isaiah 38:5, *"Go, and say to Hezekiah, Thus saith the LORD, the God of David thy father, I have heard thy prayer, I have seen thy tears: behold, I will add unto thy days fifteen years."*

Even in Hezekiah's most fervent cries of supplication, while the very sentence of death is upon Him, God makes it clear that it is the lineage of David that has enhanced his petition and prayer toward God! The Lord looks at Hezekiah and hears though remembrance David's repentance and contrition! This son of David received the sure mercies of David, and the sentence of death was lifted. God gave Hezekiah fifteen more years!

Isaiah 55:3, *"Incline your ear, and come unto me: hear, and your soul shall live; and I will make an everlasting covenant with you, even the sure mercies of David."*

This and the following verse reveal a most powerful revelation of the mindset of God toward David. He encourages the weary, hungry, fainting soul to listen for the Lord's mercy and covenant. God is waiting for that broken vessel that has come to the very end of his rope and hope, to cry out to Him like David did, and to covenant with Him as David did, and to worship Him like David did. He encourages that one defeated by his own failure to look at His covenant with a failing and faltering David.

To the utter grief of all of the religious spirits on the earth, under the earth, and above the earth, it is David that will be raised from the dead to sit beside Him as He rules the earth for a thousand years (Jeremiah 30:9). The sure mercies of David and the covenant God has with David will be a sure display of God's infinite mercy to the repentant for all of the nations to behold. For sitting beside Jesus, who never sinned at all and who furnished the perfect blood for the redemption of mankind, will be David, His restored servant! This is the meaning of the following verse, Isaiah 55:4, *"Behold, I have given him"* (David) *for a witness to the people, a leader and commander to the people."*

Jeremiah

Jeremiah 13:13, *"Then shalt thou say unto them, Thus saith the LORD, Behold, I will fill all the inhabitants of this land, even the kings that sit upon David's throne, and the priests, and the prophets, and all the inhabitants of Jerusalem, with drunkenness."*

God is totally disgusted with the pride of Judah and the pride of Jerusalem (verse 9). Their pride and feeling of invincibility led them to stubborn rebellion, which led them to reject the Word and turn to idols. God's indictment to them by Jeremiah through the visual message of the marred girdle leaves no one out, even the kings that sat on David's throne. This statement is to make them know how angry God is with them, because all of Judah knew what strong feelings God had for David. They were to surmise that God would do a thorough work of Judgment if in fact He touched the throne of David!

Jeremiah 17:25, *"Then shall there enter into the gates of this city kings and princes sitting upon the throne of David, riding in chariots and on horses, they, and their princes, the men of Judah, and the inhabitants of Jerusalem: and this city shall remain for ever."*

This amazing promise is in reference to the Word of the Lord concerning the children of Israel's keeping the Sabbath. It is apparent that the Lord has indicted Judah in the beginning verses of this chapter, and is now showing them what He would do to take away their reproach and give them the sure mercies of David. The connections to the Sabbath in five preceding verses are to show that the nation has rejected the law of God. There is a principle among the Jews well explained by James the Apostle in James 2:10, *"For whosoever shall keep the whole law, and yet offend in one point, he is guilty of all."* David was an avid Sabbath keeper, as well as a keeper of all of the high Sabbaths.

Jeremiah 21:12, *"O house of David, thus saith the LORD; Execute judgment in the morning, and deliver him that is spoiled out of the hand of the oppressor, lest my fury go out like fire, and burn that none can quench it, because of the evil of your doings."*

The warnings have all ceased, and now the woe is here. Judah will be judged and carried away. The prophets were ignored; the Sabbath was violated; the idols were erected; and even the throne of David was desecrated. Jeremiah delivered the word of the Lord that the house of David would be destroyed! Even though judgment can no longer be averted, there will be one more plea for repentance delivered to the people. Through the dismal time of this judgment, God supernaturally preserves the lineage of David.

Jeremiah 22:2, *"And say, Hear the word of the LORD, O king of Judah, that sittest upon the throne of David, thou, and thy servants, and thy people that enter in by these gates":*

"O king of Judah," this is Jehoiakim (Jeremiah 22:18), the direct descendent of David. The prophets rehearse the conditional order of God's promise to David in order to leave them without excuse for their coming judgment (1 Kings 8:25).

Jeremiah 22:4, *"For if ye do this thing indeed, then shall there enter in by the gates of this house kings sitting upon the throne of David, riding in chariots and on horses, he, and his servants, and his people."*

This seems at first to be a repeat of Jeremiah 17:25. However, a closer look will reveal that, in fact, one of the pleas is toward the city, and one is toward the house of David. God was making sure that the indictment and sentence was thorough, and leaving no excuse as to His longsuffering and absolute righteousness in judging them. This word delivered through the weeping prophet is compared by Lightfoot to the Lord Jesus looking over Jerusalem in its horrible wicked condition, and weeping over the city, stating how willing He was to have averted the judgment that was sure to come had they only repented. Even for David's sake, God will not avert judgment where there is no repentance.

Jeremiah 22:30, *"Thus saith the LORD, Write ye this man childless, a man that shall not prosper in his days: for no man of his seed shall prosper, sitting upon the throne of David, and ruling any more in Judah."*

These words are not to be taken as a contradiction to the promise God made to David and to his seed. Rather, it is the Lord's word through the prophet against Coniah. the son of Jehoiakim, king of Judah. It seems the Lord's wrath against Coniah was not all the fault of Coniah. He was evidently idolized by the people themselves. It was common among the heathen to worship their king, and Israel had already slipped into that pit. Now Judah was heading that way. God absolutely declared that neither he nor his seed would sit on David's throne. This is not against David, as some scholars suppose, but rather these are words of great honor for the throne of David which would never allow worship of a man.

Jeremiah 23:5, *"Behold, the days come, saith the LORD, that I will raise unto David a righteous Branch, and a King shall reign and prosper, and shall execute judgment and justice in the earth."*

This is one of many such messianic prophecies concerning the Second Advent of Christ and the millennium reign. These verses are what caused the people who had the revelation that Jesus was the Christ to call Him the son of David. However, because they did not have the revelation of the suffering servant, or the age of the Gentile, they misinterpreted this prophecy to believe He was going to deliver them from the Roman Empire at His first coming.

Jeremiah 29:16, *"Know that thus saith the LORD of the king that sitteth upon the throne of David, and of all the people that dwelleth in this city, and of your brethren that are not gone forth with you into captivity";*

The wonderful promises of the Lord to Israel by the prophet concerning their future deliverance that began in Verse 11 were interrupted by a severe indictment to the wicked Jews in both Judea and Babylon. It appears His mention of David here is to press upon them that even though His covenant with David is sure, it doesn't exempt them from temporary severe judgment.

Jeremiah 30:9, *"But they shall serve the LORD their God, and David their king, whom I will raise up unto them."*

Is there any doubt that David will be the vice king of all of the earth during the millennium? The nation of Israel will be the ruling nation of all the earth and David will be the king of Israel. Jesus is the King of Kings of the whole earth in the capital city of Jerusalem, which is also the capital city of the whole earth. The King of Kings will headquarter in Jerusalem and have national headquarters in every nation, with appointed kings or rulers sitting on thrones of each nation. David's throne will be in the City of David, Jerusalem, the capital of Israel and the capital of the whole earth. Some scholars try to say that David in this verse is referring to Messiah. However, *"the LORD their God"* is Jesus, and *"David"* is David!

Jeremiah 33:15, *"In those days, and at that time, will I cause the Branch of righteousness to grow up unto David; and he shall execute judgment and righteousness in the land."*

This messianic verse is referring to Jesus, who is the Branch of the root of Jesse. This verse is very similar to Jeremiah 23:5-6, *"Behold, the days come, saith the LORD, that I will raise unto David a righteous Branch, and a King shall reign and prosper, and shall execute judgment and justice in the earth. In his days Judah shall be saved, and Israel shall dwell safely: and this is his name whereby he shall be called, THE LORD OUR RIGHTEOUSNESS."*

The Messiah had to be of the lineage of David, and thus both Mary and Joseph were of David, but the blood in Jesus was pure and from God through the virgin birth.

Jeremiah 33:17, *"For thus saith the LORD; David shall never want a man to sit upon the throne of the house of Israel";*

The seed of David was hidden in Christ, and Christ was hidden in the seed of David. The prophetic word quoted by Jeremiah is from the prophet Nathan to David hundreds of years earlier. 2 Samuel 7:16-17, *"And thine house and thy kingdom shall be established for ever before thee: thy throne shall be established for ever. According to all these words, and according to all this vision, so did Nathan speak unto David."*

In the New Testament we find an angel of the Lord, Gabriel, speaking words similar to this to Mary when the throne of David in the physical sense had long since ceased to exist. Luke 1:32-33, *"He shall be great, and shall be called the Son of the Highest: and the Lord God shall give unto him the throne of his father David: And he shall reign over the house of Jacob for ever; and of his kingdom there shall be no end."*

Jeremiah and all of the prophets were aware of these prophecies, yet they were not just repeating them, or necessarily quoting them. The Holy Ghost clearly uttered the same message through different vessels to bring the witness in the mouth of two or three.

Jeremiah 33:21, *"Then may also my covenant be broken with David my servant, that he should not have a son to reign upon his throne; and with the Levites the priests, my ministers."*

This is the most powerful utterance concerning the strength of the Davidic covenant. The preceding verses show us this. We read in verses 19 & 20, *"And the word of the LORD came unto Jeremiah, saying, Thus saith the LORD; If ye can break my covenant of the day, and my covenant of the night, and that there should not be day and night in their season";* In other words, as long as there is day and night, there will be my covenant with David. If you can stop there being day and night, you can stop my covenant with David.

Most believers only view their commitment to God in their estimation to their standing with God. However, much of the relationship David enjoyed with God was because David could see God's commitment to him. This view is not often found in the life of even the most powerful of believers. Yet, in fact, the Dear Lord is committed to us in holy covenant through the royal priesthood of the New Covenant believers!

Jeremiah 33:22, *"As the host of heaven cannot be numbered, neither the sand of the sea measured: so will I multiply the seed of David my servant, and the Levites that minister unto me."*

Lightfoot declares this prophecy to include the host of believers that make up the church of Jesus Christ which is grafted into the Commonwealth of Israel (Ephesians 2:1-19). This is very believable, due to the Davidic lineage producing the Messiah, and the mention of the priesthood, which equates to a royal (king) priesthood (priest), which the New Testament Church is called (1 Peter 2:9). In that sense, we can see not only Jews akin to David in this innumerable throng, but the entire multitude of the redeemed!

Jeremiah 33:26, *"Then will I cast away the seed of Jacob, and David my servant, so that I will not take any of his seed to be rulers over the seed of Abraham, Isaac, and Jacob: for I will cause their captivity to return, and have mercy on them."*

Here the Lord reiterates through His prophet how impossible it is to break His covenant with David. The Lord uses His prophet to scold the scoffers who had written off the tribes of Judah and Levi. Here is another verse that shows God's attitude toward these two tribes. When Melchizedek (Jesus pre-incarnate, both king and priest) blessed Abraham as a possessor of heaven and earth, He placed in him that priesthood and that kingly order. This was preserved in Isaac and manifested in two of Jacob's sons, Judah for the king and Levi for the priest.

Jeremiah 36:30, *"Therefore thus saith the LORD of Jehoiakim king of Judah; He shall have none to sit upon the throne of David: and his dead body shall be cast out in the day to the heat, and in the night to the frost."*

This dismal prophecy mentions the throne of David to bring the emphasis on the judgment and insure that the wickedness of Jehoiakim cost him his entire legacy, cursed his posterity, and allowed him no royal burial. His seed tried to exempt themselves from this prophecy and placed his son Jechoniah on the throne. He reigned only for a short and pitiful three months, and he had no successor of his own children. David's legacy lived on, even though his earthly seat was empty.

Ezekiel

Ezekiel 34:23, *"And I will set up one shepherd over them, and he shall feed them, even my servant David; he shall feed them, and he shall be their shepherd."*

This clear prophecy of David's being king of Israel during the millennium seems to be too much for Clark and many other theologians. Therefore, they interpret this to mean Jesus instead of literally meaning David. Why should they stumble at the clear prophetic word concerning David's being raised from the dead to serve in the millennium, and yet embrace their own resurrection at the beginning of the Kingdom age? It is clear from this verse, the following verse, Jeremiah 30:9, and many others, that David will be alive and on the throne in Jerusalem as the king of Israel and as the vice-king of the nations.

Ezekiel 34:24, *"And I the LORD will be their God, and my servant David a prince among them; I the LORD have spoken it."*

Again we have the confirmation that David will be raised from the dead and dwell among the people of the earth during the Kingdom Age. Theologians who interpret David in this verse to be the Messiah may either fail to acknowledge Jesus as God Himself in a human body or fail to take literally David's role in the Kingdom Age. There is no need to doubt or try to transfer David here to be the Messiah, when in fact, the scripture does not say a seed of David or a son of David will be a prince among them but *"my servant David a prince."* The prophecy states, *"And I the LORD will be their God."* That is Jesus Christ the Lord.

Instead of interpreting David to be Messiah, we should see that all of the verses on this matter are saying the exact same thing. The Messiah is God in a human body, Jesus. David, the only King in all of the history of Israel with that name, is resurrected to rule the nation of Israel during the kingdom age!

Ezekiel 37:24, *"And David my servant shall be king over them; and they all shall have one shepherd: they shall also walk in my judgments, and observe my statutes, and do them."*

In this verse and the next, we see more clearly that when the verses talk about all of the nations being as one, the prophecy is speaking of the ruler of the whole world, the King of Kings, the Messiah, the Lord Jesus Christ. Yet when the verses speak of the nation of Israel, the reference is to David himself. *"And David my servant shall be king over them"* (Israel).

Here the prophet is speaking of the two sticks becoming one. He is not speaking of all of the nations, but clearly speaking of Israel and Judah, which had been divided since the days of Rehoboam. The Lord will be their God, as they were told in the previous verse, *"so shall they be my people, and I will be their God."* The reference to God is speaking of Jesus the Messiah who is now Emanuel, or God with us, and the reference to David is, in fact, David.

Ezekiel 37:25, *"And they shall dwell in the land that I have given unto Jacob my servant, wherein your fathers have dwelt; and they shall dwell therein, even they, and their children, and their children's children for ever: and my servant David shall be their prince for ever."*

The perpetual factor of this dynasty should not make one afraid to proclaim that, in fact, the David mentioned here is King David. We all will have perpetual ministries beginning at the millennium. How long will Christ, the King of Kings, have David to be King of Israel in the millennium? How long will we be appointed over cities in the millennium? How long will we, the royal priesthood, serve? Revelation 5:10, *"And hast made us unto our God kings and priests: and we shall reign on the earth."*

Hosea

Hosea 3:5, *"Afterward shall the children of Israel return, and seek the LORD their God, and David their king; and shall fear the LORD and his goodness in the latter days."*

The people of the earth will be subject to the Lord Jesus, who will sit on the throne and rule the earth with a rod of iron. Revelation 12:5, *"And she brought forth a man child, who was to rule all nations with a rod of iron":* The men of the earth will come to seek Him and worship. None will come to worship David, who will be king of Israel at this time.

Again Clark stumbles in doubt of the resurrection of David, while he applauds his own resurrection. Clark writes concerning this mention of David, "Some think that the family of David is intended"; It is true that many think that. There is no danger of David's allowing any worship or glory pointed his way. He will accept this literal physical assignment without diminishing the Messiah in the least. Yes, he will lead the nations in worship of Jesus Christ the Lord!

Amos

Amos 6:5, *"That chant to the sound of the viol, and invent to themselves instruments of musick, like David";*

This shows the fame of David's ability to manufacture musical instruments. An ancient painting shows David guiding a craftsman in the making of some instrument that resembles a cross between a harp and guitar. This painting was expressing the part of David that is often over looked but is actually taught us in several verses, the following being one of them: 1 Chronicles 23:5,

Moreover four thousand were porters; and four thousand praised the LORD with the instruments which I made, said David, to praise therewith." This is not to say David personally crafted each instrument, but rather oversaw the work of making them. Evidently David was creative in his designs.

Amos 9:11, "*In that day will I raise up the tabernacle of David that is fallen, and close up the breaches thereof; and I will raise up his ruins, and I will build it as in the days of old*":

This tabernacle of David is not necessarily meant to be speaking of a tent, as we find mentioned in 2 Samuel 6:17, "*And they brought in the ark of the LORD, and set it in his place, in the midst of the tabernacle that David had pitched for it: and David offered burnt offerings and peace offerings before the LORD.*" The term here in the prophecy is referring to the actual worship and sacrificial system David set up before moving the Ark to the tent, as we see in Isaiah 16:5, "*And in mercy shall the throne be established: and he shall sit upon it in truth in the tabernacle of David, judging, and seeking judgment, and hasting righteousness.*"

David had set in place all of the priests, all of the songs, all of the porters, all of the music, all of the sacrifices, and all of the courses of the service of the Lord. He then decreed a twenty-four hour worship vigil. All of this together is called the Tabernacle of David. This can be seen by the quoting of Amos 9:11 by the Apostle James in Acts 15:16, "*After this I will return, and will build again the tabernacle of David, which is fallen down; and I will build again the ruins thereof, and I will set it up*": It is also clear that the apostles saw the New Testament church as instrumental in the fulfillment of this prophecy!

Zachariah

Zechariah 12:7, *"The LORD also shall save the tents of Judah first, that the glory of the house of David and the glory of the inhabitants of Jerusalem do not magnify themselves against Judah."*

This deliverance is in reference to the glorious victory God will give the Jews at the end of the Church Age and the beginning of the Kingdom Age. He will save the people in the country first, in order to accentuate the absolute amazing gift of victory He is giving the Jews, but also to insure that the people of Jerusalem do not boast in themselves in the matter. This verse and others indicate that the inhabitants of Jerusalem had superciliousness toward other Jews because they dwelt in Jerusalem in sight of the Temple where the Ark was. While the house of David is cited here as a glorious house, they were not allowed to boast in themselves. David would not have done this but would only boast in his God.

Zechariah 12:8, *"In that day shall the LORD defend the inhabitants of Jerusalem; and he that is feeble among them at that day shall be as David; and the house of David shall be as God, as the angel of the LORD before them."*

The Lord will fight for Jerusalem and make even the feeblest into a warrior like David. This is the highest level of combat order that could possibly be ascribed to a mere human. There has never been a greater warrior on the earth than David. Yet, the prophecy proceeds even further by proclaiming the presence of the Angel of the Lord, which is Jesus Christ on that white horse, with a two edged sword coming out of His mouth!

The term *"the house of David shall be as God,"* is referring to the new bloodless bodies that the millennium saints will dwell in. They are not deity, but they are clothed in deity, and their bodies are no longer energized by blood, but by the Spirit of the Living God. This glorious army will never lose a battle; David never lost a battle and certainly the Angel of the Lord can't!

Zechariah 12:10, *"And I will pour upon the house of David, and upon the inhabitants of Jerusalem, the spirit of grace and of supplications: and they shall look upon me whom they have pierced, and they shall mourn for him, as one mourneth for his only son, and shall be in bitterness for him, as one that is in bitterness for his firstborn."*

This prophetic word is climaxing the return of the Lord Jesus Christ, and the House of Israel's final realization of their rejection of His First Advent. The house of David will be restored first, for the Messiah is of the house of David, the branch of Jesse.

Zechariah 12:12, *"And the land shall mourn, every family apart; the family of the house of David apart, and their wives apart; the family of the house of Nathan apart, and their wives apart";*

This is speaking of the tremendous mourning that will take place in Israel when they realize they crucified the Lord! This realization will bring a river of grief and contrition that will begin at the house of David. Out of their deep contrition, they will take an honest look at all of the pain and sorrow they have caused themselves by rejecting Jesus at His First Advent. Many believers seem to think Israel will be restored because they are Israel, and certainly they are a chosen people. However, even God's chosen people are required to repent. When they look on Him whom they have pierced, the nation of Israel will enter into national repentance totally astounded by what they have done to the Messiah!

Zechariah 13:1, *"In that day there shall be a fountain opened to the house of David and to the inhabitants of Jerusalem for sin and for uncleanness."*

The prophecy is now going back to the First Advent and the opening of the fountain of redemption. Jews do not bother to write in chronological order, because their method of study in scripture is "here a little, there a little." The last chapter ended with the scene in which Israel comes to the actual realization of the rejection of the Christ in the First Advent. However, this chapter begins at the work of redemption purchased at the cross and paid for at the mercy seat in heaven, with the blood of Jesus which He Himself took there. This is the fountain opened up to David first, then to the Jews, and then on to the Gentiles. God used the Messiah of the House of David to purchase our redemption, and He opened up the fountain first to the House of David!

Matthew

Matthew 1:1, *"The book of the generation of Jesus Christ, the son of David, the son of Abraham."*

This verse simply begins the genealogy of Jesus as King. However, the verse also establishes the order of the Messiah as Davidic, not just as the suffering servant, but also the ruling King of Kings. Matthew reveals Jesus as a King. Mark reveals Him as a servant. Luke reveals Him as a man filled with the Holy Ghost. John reveals Him as God almighty. Therefore Matthew gives his kingly genealogy and Mark gives Him none.

Matthew 1:6, *"And Jesse begat David the king; and David the king begat Solomon of her that had been the wife of Urias"*;

Jesse is the actual father of David, not just his lineage patriarch, as is sometimes the case in some mentions of men in the Bible. However, because of the actual account of genealogy, fathers here are in their correct biological order. The prophet Isaiah spoke of the root of Jesse when he spoke of the Messiah in Isaiah 11:10, *"And in that day there shall be a root of Jesse, which shall stand for an ensign of the people; to it shall the Gentiles seek: and his rest shall be glorious."* So in the case of genealogy, it is David who is said to be the father of Jesus in patriarchal order of the root of Jesse, David's father. Jesse was not a king.

Matthew 1:17, *"So all the generations from Abraham to David are fourteen generations; and from David until the carrying away into Babylon are fourteen generations; and from the carrying away into Babylon unto Christ are fourteen generations."*

This mathematical equation has been the subject of much study. However, it is classic Jewish methodology to number in this manner in order to show the release in the third level. From Abraham fourteen generations later David appears. The second fourteen generations is earmarked by the carrying away of the Jews, or the dismantling of the Davidic physical throne. Yet by the Spirit the third fourteen generations produced the Messiah, the supernatural son of David. The third level is here the significance. In the third level is the release, as in the case of Abraham, Isaac, and Jacob.

Matthew 1:20, *"But while he thought on these things, behold, the angel of the Lord appeared unto him in a dream, saying, Joseph, thou son of David, fear not to take unto thee Mary thy wife: for that which is conceived in her is of the Holy Ghost."*

Both Joseph and Mary were of the house of David. David's actual blood was not in Christ. The scripture teaches us He was *"made of a woman."* The flesh is manufactured by the woman, and the blood is provided by the father. Jesus had no earthly father, and therefore he had perfect blood; yet He is rightly called the son of David, for that is the lineage of both Mary and Joseph. Joseph here is addressed by the angel as the son of David and commanded to go on and take Mary to be his wife, even though she is already pregnant. Notice the preceding verse already declared Joseph to be her husband.

The Jews well knew the lineage of the Messiah would be Davidic, and Joseph is now told by the angels that this son is supernaturally conceived and will be the Messiah. Joseph obeyed, for he was well aware of the amazing prophecy concerning the virgin birth. That is why Joseph never had sex with Mary until after Jesus was born. Matthew 1:25, *"And knew her not till she had brought forth her firstborn son: and he called his name JESUS."*

Matthew 9:27, *"And when Jesus departed thence, two blind men followed him, crying, and saying, Thou Son of David, have mercy on us."*

Before this, only the angel Gabriel had called Jesus by this name, *"Son of David."* This salutation is in recognition of Jesus as Messiah and not just a note concerning His bloodline. Lightfoot declares the salutation of these two blind men was born of revelation because they could not have seen the tribal signet on the side of His tallit! They knew Messiah would fulfill Isaiah 35:5, *"Then the eyes of the blind shall be opened, and the ears of the deaf shall be unstopped."* This is expressly the reason that many began to cry out for healing, utilizing the title *thou son of David.*

Matthew 12:3, *"But he said unto them, Have ye not read what David did, when he was a hungred, and they that were with him";*

This verse is ample proof that Jesus' view of the Davidic realm was both admirable and accurate. He uses the whole instance of David's getting the showbread from Ahemilech the priest to prove His point. The Pharisees twisted the Mosaic Law to exalt tradition above the Word. The amazing thing is that Jesus doesn't mention that David lied to get the bread from the high priest and lied again to get the sword of Goliath that was there. So immense is God's grace that Jesus did not see the sin of David, but only his accomplishments. David's sin had been cast in the sea of God's forgetfulness!

Matthew 12:23, *"And all the people were amazed, and said, Is not this the son of David?"*

This is the height of Jesus' healing ministry and the question could be rendered, "Isn't this the Messiah?" They very well knew that the Messiah had to come from the lineage of David, and that He would operate in the supernatural. The thing they were not prepared for is that He must suffer.

Matthew 15:22, *"And, behold, a woman of Canaan came out of the same coasts, and cried unto him, saying, Have mercy on me, O Lord, thou Son of David; my daughter is grievously vexed with a devil."*

Such salutation, *"thou Son of David",* reveals the extent of both her desperation and her revelation of the Messiah. The hope of Israel in its oppressed state was that Messiah would come and heal all of their sick, then deliver them from their enemies and usher in the everlasting Kingdom. The particular prophecies concerning healings were many and found throughout the prophets, as well as the Psalms, but one of the most quoted was Isaiah 35:6, *"Then shall the lame man leap as an hart, and the tongue of the dumb sing: for in the wilderness shall waters break out, and streams in the desert."*

Matthew 20:30, *"And, behold, two blind men sitting by the way side, when they heard that Jesus passed by, cried out, saying, Have mercy on us, O Lord, thou Son of David."*

This is the second time two blind men cry out beseeching Jesus to heal them by using the title *"Son of David."* The first we find in Matthew 9:27. This time the miracle occurs in Jericho; however, the record of this miracle in Mark 10:46 and Luke 18:35 only tell us of one blind man named Bartimeus. The blind men could see the Messiah in their spirit enough to make a confession with their mouth before they could see Him with their healed eyes! Throughout the gospels, it is apparent that the term *son of David* was of great agitation to the Pharisees and even more the miracles that followed.

Matthew 20:31, *"And the multitude rebuked them, because they should hold their peace: but they cried the more, saying, Have mercy on us, O Lord, thou Son of David."*

The multitude never wants one to cry after Jesus, but against Him. They will certainly eat His miracle bread. Yet when he stands before Pilate they are silent. These blind men refuse to be silent and continued to ask for mercy and profess Jesus to be the Messiah. However, in this verse there is a very important word added to their confession. That word is Lord. *"O Lord, thou Son of David."* This is abundant proof that these blind men were not just referring to Jesus' lineage in David but to His deity!

Matthew 21:9, *"And the multitudes that went before, and that followed, cried, saying, Hosanna to the Son of David: Blessed is he that cometh in the name of the Lord; Hosanna in the highest."*

This scene is one of the most amazing in all of scripture. This multitude was filled with spontaneous revelatory worship for the Messiah. Many had seen Jesus as the Messiah and therefore cried out *"Hosanna to the Son of David."* This event refutes the idea that all of Israel failed to see Him as Messiah. That was not the problem. The problem was the fact that they did not understand the role of the Messiah as the suffering servant. The powerful prelude to this event is when David and the priests brought forth the Ark of the Covenant into Jerusalem. David, the type of Messiah, experienced the same spontaneous worship. Both events were termed by Lightfoot and others as triumphal entries into Jerusalem. However, Jesus is not the type, but in fact He is the Ark, the King, and the Priest all in one!

Matthew 21:15, *"And when the chief priests and scribes saw the wonderful things that he did, and the children crying in the temple, and saying, Hosanna to the Son of David; they were sore displeased,"*

The powerful entry of Jesus into the city, His zeal in cleansing the Temple, the mighty miracles He did, topped by the revelation of Jesus being the son of David, or Messiah, brought the chief priests and scribes much grief. The power surrounding this moment made it impossible to carry out their diabolical machinations at that time. At this point of Jesus' ministry, it was well established that the common people and the recipients of healings and deliverances recognized Jesus, the son of David, as Messiah.

The reason this multitude did not testify in His behalf at the trial is because 1) They were shocked that His supernatural power didn't over rule the religious system in the matter of His arrest; 2) Because of His submitting to the authority of the high priest, they feared their power. They should have known David never lost a battle and neither would Messiah! Jesus opened not His mouth!

Matthew 22:42, *"Saying, What think ye of Christ? whose son is he? They say unto him, The Son of David."*

Jesus here traps the Pharisaical committee sent to accuse Him in His words. They were intent in catching Jesus in blasphemy, but Jesus used David and His relationship to him to totally silence these scribes of Judaism. He asks them, *"What think ye of Christ?"* In this instance, Jesus is not telling them He is the Messiah but rather is asking them to answer whether they believe that the Messiah is the son of David. They take the bait and confess that Messiah is the son of David. They are not speaking this with a revelation like the multitude had but with the head knowledge of religion, the rejection of Jesus as the Messiah, and the jealousy because they full well knew that many of the common people believed Jesus was the Messiah.

The religious leaders were trying to say that the Messiah would be of the lineage of David, but not actual deity. The whole controversy is whether Jesus is God in the flesh or not. The revelation the people were getting was that Jesus is Lord, and this was offensive to the religious leaders. The stage is set for Jesus' next question.

Matthew 22:43, *"He saith unto them, How then doth David in spirit call him Lord, saying,"*

Jesus' question cuts them to the heart. He was basically saying, "If the Messiah is not God in the flesh, but only a man of the lineage of David, then why did David call Him Lord?" Perhaps Jesus was also saying, "The common people know who I am; David knew who I am; what is wrong with you"? This would certainly be in agreement with His treatment of this commitment earlier recorded in John seven and eight.

Matthew 22:45, *"If David then call him Lord, how is he his son?"*

Here is the obvious next question that Jesus asks. "If David called the Messiah Lord, how could He be his biological son?" Jesus knew the blood in His body never came from any man, including David. His lineage was David, yes, but the blood was furnished by the Father by the Holy Ghost through the virgin birth. This question ended their questions and shook their religious doctrine to the core, as well as proving to them they were rejecting His claim of being the Messiah.

Mark

Mark 2:25, *"And he said unto them, Have ye never read what David did, when he had need, and was an hungred, he, and they that were with him?"*

Jesus often referenced the Old Testament to preach. In this case He cites David's revelatory understanding of the showbread in teaching on the Sabbath. Otherwise see commentary on Matthew 12:3.

Mark 10:47, *"And when he heard that it was Jesus of Nazareth, he began to cry out, and say, Jesus, thou Son of David, have mercy on me."*

The title *"Jesus of Nazareth"* is found in seventeen verses in the scripture. It is commonly used to better identify Jesus in His humanity. However, *"Jesus, thou Son of David"* is a much more powerful identification, especially if it is uttered from the lips of one who recognizes Him as the one and only Jewish Messiah.

Mark 10:48, *"And many charged him that he should hold his peace: but he cried the more a great deal, Thou Son of David, have mercy on me."*

The continual confession that Jesus was Messiah seemed to greatly aggravate the religious people, even to the degree that they tried to silence the men who were making it.

Mark 11:10, *"Blessed be the kingdom of our father David, that cometh in the name of the Lord: Hosanna in the highest."*

This record of Jesus' triumphal entry into Jerusalem brings us yet into a deeper insight of the relationship the common people believed existed between the Messiah and David. Lightfoot was correct and so insightful in saying, "These two Kings can never be separated." When the natural dynasty of David failed and there was no throne of David or his sons in Israel, the Messiah, who is the I AM, the son of David, was still alive and well, waiting to fulfill and fill full every jot of very prophecy given to the house of David!

Mark 12:35, *"And Jesus answered and said, while he taught in the temple, How say the scribes that Christ is the Son of David?"*

See commentary on Matthew 22:42

Mark 12:36, *"For David himself said by the Holy Ghost, The LORD said to my Lord, Sit thou on my right hand, till I make thine enemies thy footstool."*

See commentary on Matthew 22:43

Mark 12:37, *"David therefore himself calleth him Lord; and whence is he then his son? And the common people heard him gladly."*

See commentary on Matthew 22:45

Luke

Luke 1:27, *"To a virgin espoused to a man whose name was Joseph, of the house of David; and the virgin's name was Mary."*

It is common not to mention the lineage of the mother. The Jews are careful to follow patriarchal bloodlines, although in this case the actual blood in Jesus had not touched anyone of any man's seed. Mary was also of the Davidic bloodline, but the woman doesn't furnish the blood. It is worthy to note how the Apostle Paul described this matter in Galatians 4:4, *"But when the fulness of the time was come, God sent forth his Son, made of a woman, made under the law."* It is the woman that makes the child. This verse is in perfect agreement with all scriptures concerning the incarnation of Jesus, proving that the blood came from the Father, and the flesh came from the tribe of Judah in the lineage of David!

Luke 1:32, "*He shall be great, and shall be called the Son of the Highest: and the Lord God shall give unto him the throne of his father David*":

The throne of David is totally messianic and represents to the Jews their international dominance under the Messiah, like they had when David defeated all of their enemies. One of the signs of the Messiah is that He will defeat all of His enemies. For this reason the Jews failed to see His First Advent. When Jesus returns, He will absolutely reign over the whole earth and rule with a rod of iron.

Luke 1:69, "*And hath raised up an horn of salvation for us in the house of his servant David*";

This prophetic utterance is coming out of the mouth of Zacharias, who is filled with the Holy Ghost. This is always the mission of the sweet Holy Spirit, to magnify the Christ. The mighty deliverer and King of Kings is coming to the nation of Israel out of the house of David!

Luke 2:4, "*And Joseph also went up from Galilee, out of the city of Nazareth, into Judaea, unto the city of David, which is called Bethlehem; (because he was of the house and lineage of David)*":

This reference to Bethlehem as the city of David instead of Jerusalem is of trouble to some students of theology and even considered an error by some scholars. However, Bethlehem was the home of Jesse and the birth place of David. 1 Samuel 16:1, "*And the LORD said unto Samuel, How long wilt thou mourn for Saul, seeing I have rejected him from reigning over Israel? fill thine horn with oil, and go, I will send thee to Jesse the Bethlehemite: for I have provided me a king among his sons.*"

Jerusalem is the city of the Davidic throne, and Bethlehem is the city of his humble heritage. 1 Samuel 20:6, "*If thy father at all miss me, then say, David earnestly asked leave of me that he might run to Bethlehem his city: for there is a yearly sacrifice there for all the family.*" David came from his home town of Bethlehem where God had prepared him to conquer the city of his throne and the city where God answered him by fire!

Luke 2:11, "*For unto you is born this day in the city of David a Saviour, which is Christ the Lord.*"

Once again Bethlehem is referred to as the city of David.

See commentary on Luke 2:4

Luke 3:31, *"Which was the son of Melea, which was the son of Menan, which was the son of Mattatha, which was the son of Nathan, which was the son of David,"*

It is not a coincidence that Matthew gives Jesus' genealogy through Abraham and David. Matthew reveals Jesus as a King in the lineage of David because Matthew portrays Jesus as King. Luke shows Him as a man and includes some of Mary's lineage which is the same as Joseph's not far back.

Luke 6:3, *"And Jesus answering them said, Have ye not read so much as this, what David did, when himself was an hungred, and they which were with him"*;

See commentary on Matthew 12:3

Luke 18:38, *"And he cried, saying, Jesus, thou Son of David, have mercy on me."*

See commentary on Matthew 20:30

Luke 18:39, *"And they which went before rebuked him, that he should hold his peace: but he cried so much the more, Thou Son of David, have mercy on me."*

See commentary on Matthew 20:31

Luke 20:41, *"And he said unto them, How say they that Christ is David's son?"*

See Commentary on Matthew 22:42

Luke 20:42, *"And David himself saith in the book of Psalms, The LORD said unto my Lord, Sit thou on my right hand,"*

See commentary on Matthew 22:43

Luke 20:44, *"David therefore calleth him Lord, how is he then his son?"*

See commentary on Matthew 22:45

John

John 7:42, *"Hath not the scripture said, That Christ cometh of the seed of David, and out of the town of Bethlehem, where David was?"*

This is the only mention of King David in the entire book of John. Neither does John mention him in his epistles. However, in the Book of The Revelation, John records three mentions of David in messages given to him by an angel, the Lord, and an Elder. Here in this verse, the doctors are disputing over the possibility of Jesus being the Messiah, and in so doing they were referencing the scripture concerning His coming from Bethlehem. It seems from this verse and others that the doctors didn't realize that Jesus was born in Bethlehem.

It seems the providence of God caused Caesar Augustus to make a decree to tax all of the world, causing Joseph and Mary both to travel from Nazareth to Bethlehem to pay their taxes (Luke 2:1-4), at which time Jesus was born. This would have caused the doctors of the law not to consider Bethlehem as His birth place, although the scripture declared it (Micah 5:2). It should be noted that there was no dispute concerning His lineage being Davidic.

Acts

Acts 1:16, *"Men and brethren, this scripture must needs have been fulfilled, which the Holy Ghost by the mouth of David spake before concerning Judas, which was guide to them that took Jesus."*

This verse confirms that the New Testament Church founders considered David a prophet. They carefully searched out every word he wrote and knew that the Lord Himself often quoted the prophetic words of David. For instance the apostle is quoting Psalm 41:9, *"Yea, mine own familiar friend, in whom I trusted, which did eat of my bread, hath lifted up his heel against me."* Yet, they were present at the last supper and heard Jesus quote the same verse concerning Judas Iscariot. John 13:18, *"I speak not of you all: I know whom I have chosen: but that the scripture may be fulfilled, He that eateth bread with me hath lifted up his heel against me."* Jesus called David's words scripture!

Acts 2:25, *"For David speaketh concerning him, I foresaw the Lord always before my face, for he is on my right hand, that I should not be moved"*:

Peter's powerful Pentecost sermon gives reference to David's prophetic words concerning the Lord Jesus! Peter knew the Word, and he knew that David, by the revelation of the Holy Spirit, understood, or *foresaw,* that Christ would not stay dead after he was killed. David also knew that because death could not hold the Messiah, he would also be resurrected. Therefore Peter quotes Psalms 16:8 and expounds on it to convince his hearers that Jesus had in fact raised from the dead, and they could too if they placed their faith in Him like David did. Acts 2:26-27, *"Therefore did my heart rejoice, and my tongue was glad; moreover also my flesh shall rest in hope: Because thou wilt not leave my soul in hell, neither wilt thou suffer thine Holy One to see corruption."* It is clear that through deep revelatory worship, David rested in the hope of the resurrection!

Acts 2:29, *"Men and brethren, let me freely speak unto you of the patriarch David, that he is both dead and buried, and his sepulchre is with us unto this day."*

Peter continues his powerful message and aptly proves that David was not speaking of himself in the Psalm concerning the resurrection, but of the Messiah whom Peter now declares to be Jesus Christ. Yet Peter refers to David as a patriarch. Only in this verse is he called so and yet he was, in fact, a patriarch which Wesley declared to hold more honor than even a king. Peter gives a further proof when speaking of Jesus being the Christ and David being only flesh and blood by quoting a portion of Psalms 110, *"The LORD said unto my Lord, Sit thou on my right hand."* In fact, the very same verse Jesus used to silence the doctors of the law and prove His deity, Peter also used to prove David was flesh and blood. Peter was there the day the Lord Jesus silenced the doctors of Judaism by explaining David's prophecy concerning Jesus being a perpetual priesthood after the order of Melchizedek.

In verse thirty Peter openly declares David to be a prophet. Acts 2:30, *"Therefore being a prophet, and knowing that God had sworn with an oath to him, that of the fruit of his loins, according to the flesh, he would raise up Christ to sit on his throne";* Peter continues to make it clear that David is not the Messiah, but that David prophesied concerning the Messiah, which is Jesus.

Acts 2:34, *"For David is not ascended into the heavens: but he saith himself, The LORD said unto my Lord, Sit thou on my right hand,"*

Peter continues his Holy Ghost empowered message by yet another reference to David. This third reference is complete and total confirmation of David's revelation of the Christ by again quoting from Psalms 110:1. Peter not only knew that Jesus silenced his critics with this verse, but he knew it is the Word of God that brings revelation to his hearers. Therefore, he preached what Jesus preached, hoping that the Daystar would arise in their hearts.

Acts 4:25, *"Who by the mouth of thy servant David hast said, Why did the heathen rage, and the people imagine vain things?"*

In the midst of heavy persecution, the disciples lifted up their cry unto God, and in their prayer they identified with a prophetic utterance David made in Psalms two. They believed that the prophet David saw down through the annals of time, by the Spirit, to prophesy of their demise and the hatred of the kings of the earth for the Messiah. This will yet be fulfilled again, even in a more intense way. Right before Jesus returns, there will be an increased and more intense hatred for Jews and Christians than the world has ever seen.

Acts 7:45, *"Which also our fathers that came after brought in with Jesus into the possession of the Gentiles, whom God drave out before the face of our fathers, unto the days of David"*;

No serious discourse of the history of Israel could possibly be complete without mentioning David. The word *Jesus* here is referring to Joshua. In this verse is a very key phrase, *"unto the days of David,"* which is a reference to the total shift in Israel's sacrificial site. When the Lord answered David by fire at Ornan's threshing floor on Mount Moriah, David knew the house of the Lord would be built there on Mount Moriah, and the sacrifices would be offered there instead of the Tabernacle of Moses.

Acts 13:22, *"And when he had removed him, he raised up unto them David to be their king; to whom also he gave testimony, and said, I have found David the son of Jesse, a man after mine own heart, which shall fulfil all my will.*

There is only one in the scripture to which this description is given *"a man after mine own heart."* This is a quote from 1 Samuel 13:14, *"But now thy kingdom shall not continue: the LORD hath sought him a man after his own heart, and the LORD hath commanded him to be captain over his people, because thou hast not kept that which the LORD commanded thee."*

The Lord removed Saul of Benjamin and installed David of Judah to fulfill all of his will. The tender love and affection the Lord showed David, and the intimate worship David gave God, developed into a fusion that is unequalled except in the Father and the Son. Some remark that this description of David was before he sinned, and that is true. However, there is ample evidence throughout the scripture that David was not only completely forgiven but completely restored to his previous status. Wesley fears stating such might promote the sin of David, or at least a light attitude toward his sin. This cannot happen if one also studies closely David's consequences, contrition, and repentance from his sin!

Acts 13:34, *"And as concerning that he raised him up from the dead, now no more to return to corruption, he said on this wise, I will give you the sure mercies of David."*

This text is referring to Isaiah 55:3, in which the New Covenant with Israel is called *"the sure mercies of David."* This is simply the blessing promised to David that can only be found in Jesus Christ the Messiah. Paul, like Peter, preached the absolute impossibility of interpreting the verses to mean that David himself could have been the Messiah. It seemed necessary to prove this before the doctors could even consider Jesus as being the Christ.

Acts 13:36, *"For David, after he had served his own generation by the will of God, fell on sleep, and was laid unto his fathers, and saw corruption"*:

Paul is again strengthening his position on David's being merely human filled with deity, whereas Jesus was deity, willingly clothed in humanity. In strengthening this point he makes a very powerful statement concerning David, *"after he had served his own generation by the will of God, fell on sleep."* Here David is seen by the apostle as a servant instead of a ruler. The Jews knew that a king was not a dictator, but actually a chief servant, with the very most responsibility, as well as authority.

Acts 15:16, *"After this I will return, and will build again the tabernacle of David, which is fallen down; and I will build again the ruins thereof, and I will set it up"*:

This is a quote from Amos 9:11, *"In that day will I raise up the tabernacle of David that is fallen, and close up the breaches thereof; and I will raise up his ruins, and I will build it as in the days of old."* To the Jew this means that God will restore Israel to the world power that it was when David was king. David was victorious over all of his foes and expanded the nation of Israel to take in all of the land God promised Abraham and more. It is sad that even the disciples could not see the Gentile gap of time existing between the time of the cutting off of the Messiah and of His coming to rule the earth.

The two days of Hosea 6 is clear prophetic evidence that there will be a gap in prophetic time known as "the Gentile gap" or "the church age" but they could not see it. Jesus scolded the two on the road to Emmaus for this very thing. We read in Luke 24:25-26, *"Then he said unto them, O fools, and slow of heart to believe all that the prophets have spoken: Ought not Christ to have suffered these things, and to enter into his glory?"* But David actually could see the suffering servitude of the Messiah and spoke prophetically of it often. Psalms 22 is one example.

Romans

Romans 1:3, " *Concerning his Son Jesus Christ our Lord, which was made of the seed of David according to the flesh"*;

This verse teaches us a very amazing thing concerning the fact that it was Jesus' body, not His blood, that was made by woman. His actual kin to David came through the woman, Mary, because His blood was not from Joseph or any other man. The Jews well knew that the blood is supplied by the father. David had an earthly father, but Jesus didn't. Paul was careful to protect that truth, as we see in Galatians 4:4, *"But when the fulness of the time was come, God sent forth his Son, made of a woman, made under the law."* Made of woman, meaning the flesh!

Romans 4:6, *"Even as David also describeth the blessedness of the man, unto whom God imputeth righteousness without works,"*

This verse reveals the fact that the Apostles understood David to be a recipient of imputed righteousness before the New Covenant was ever instituted. Paul confirms the same concerning Abraham in Galatians 3:6, *"Even as Abraham believed God and it was accounted to him for righteousness."* All of the scripture agrees that imputed righteousness was given before the New Covenant, but very few religionists do!

Romans 11:9, *"And David saith, Let their table be made a snare, and a trap, and a stumblingblock, and a recompence unto them":*

David did not retaliate against Saul or those Saul sent against him. Nor did he have a lack of love for his nation. David is speaking of his heathen enemies. The reason the Apostle quotes these hard words of David from Psalm 69:22-23 is to show the attitude toward Christ rejecters that God delivered to David by the Spirit.

Timothy

2 Timothy 2:8, *"Remember that Jesus Christ of the seed of David was raised from the dead according to my gospel"*:

Some manuscripts do not include the words *"of the seed of David."* However the words should be defended for more than one reason. 1) Most manuscripts do include the words. 2) As Wesley states, *"Of the seed of David,* This one genealogy attend to." 3) It is fitting for Paul's charge for Timothy to be a good soldier to include a mention of the greatest fighting man to ever live on earth!

Hebrews

Hebrews 4:7, *"Again, he limiteth a certain day, saying in David, To day, after so long a time; as it is said, To day if ye will hear his voice, harden not your hearts."*

If the epistle to the Hebrews is not Pauline, then we have yet another New Testament writer who is quoting the words of David, thus recognizing him as a prophet. The writer of Hebrews refers to the familiar passage in Psalm 95 and proves David knew of the rest referred to in the wilderness as well as the rest in the Messiah!

Hebrews 11:32, *"And what shall I more say? for the time would fail me to tell of Gedeon, and of Barak, and of Samson, and of Jephthae; of David also, and Samuel, and of the prophets"*:

We should not expect to find a serious list of the heroes of the faith without finding King David mentioned. Here he is listed before Samuel and the prophets. There is no apparent pattern of reason in Hebrews 11 for the way the heroes of faith are mentioned, but in this section we notice that David is listed before Samuel, who anointed him, and was the only man in the Old Testament to hold the three offices of prophet, priest, and judge. However, this section of scripture is dealing with exploits, and in this respect David could have been listed first of all!

Revelation

Revelation 3:7, "*And to the angel of the church in Philadelphia write; These things saith he that is holy, he that is true, he that hath the key of David, he that openeth, and no man shutteth; and shutteth, and no man openeth*";

The king should have the key to every door and the authority to cause it to remain either shut or open. This is also a reference to the key of David given to one Eliakim (Isaiah 22:22). However, the Spirit of God is declaring this to the church of the Lord Jesus Christ which is apostolic in order. There was a man who while laying prostrate before the Lord was given such a key by the Lord and told, "This is the key of David, and it is apostolic, my son, and I will teach you of it from My Word." This same man was shown of the Lord that He will raise up many in the last days by His sovereign will who will be so consecrated unto Him that they will be entrusted with Kingdom Keys of supreme power and dominion, such as Elijah had over the waters. Those with the *key of David* will be the very nightmare of all who operate in the spirit of Antichrist!

Revelation 5:5, "*And one of the elders saith unto me, Weep not: behold, the Lion of the tribe of Juda, the Root of David, hath prevailed to open the book, and to loose the seven seals thereof.*"

Jesus Christ of Nazareth, the very King of Kings and Lord of Lords, He is the root of David who has the keys of death and hell and is the very Creator of heaven and earth. Revelation 19:16 says, "*And he hath on his vesture and on his thigh a name written, KING OF KINGS, AND LORD OF LORDS.*" This is Jesus Christ, who will now rule the earth with a rod of iron and who will raise up David to be at His side! (Jeremiah 30:9)

Revelation 22:16, "*I Jesus have sent mine angel to testify unto you these things in the churches. I am the root and the offspring of David, and the bright and morning star.*"

In all 968 verses that mention David, and in all of the verses that call him king but do not mention his name, there is none so explicit as this verse concerning David's status in the Kingdom. The people often called Jesus the son of David, and rightfully so. The religious people hated to hear it, and the rulers of the earth, like Pilate, marveled at it. The angel on Patmos told John that Jesus was the root of David! But in this verse Jesus Himself announces to all of the universe that He is in fact the Messiah who came to this earth as a descendant of David in the flesh, as the very root and offspring of David, the bright and morning star, and the One David both prophesied to come and worshipped with all of his heart!

All scriptures taken from The King James Version

ISBN #978-1-937263-97-3

Heart of My Heart Publishing Co., LLC

www.three-sheep.com

No copies may be made without the permission from the author

Contact Ron Miller for permission

http://www.bethelfmi.org/

Other Books Written by Ron Miller:

Walking in the Covenant of Salt "I Am The Bread" "Ye are the Salt"

About the Author and His Wife, Gretchen

Bro. Ron & Sis. Gretchen Miller

Brother Ron Miller has been the pastor of Bethel Fellowship Church in McDaniels, Kentucky since 1980. Bethel is a New Testament church with a worldwide impact.

He and his wife, Gretchen have been involved in numerous visions literally being built from the ground up. They raised their 3 children, plus several foster children on the campus of Bethel Fellowship, educating them with biblical standards. The ministry fought and won a court battle back in the early eighties to establish one of the first private Christian Schools in the state.

In 1987 they began broadcasting a Christian radio station, WBFI, 91.5 fm, a mixture of Christian talk, music and family oriented programming. Brother Ron has become a familiar talk show host of the BBC, (Bible Breakfast Club) heard "live" every weekday morning. He reports the news from a biblical worldview and answers bible questions. He has also interviewed a wide variety of ministers, political figures and businessmen. His syndicated program, "The Sword and Shield" airs daily in the US and several foreign countries.

In the year 2000, Brother Ron authored his first book, "Walking in the Covenant of Salt." This is an ancient Hebrew covenant revealed to him in the scriptures concerning personal holiness. Not afraid to dive in deep, he also wrote "The Book of Balance" tackling the six most controversial issues in the body of Christ.

Pastor Ron continues preaching, teaching and working to Advance the Kingdom. His foot has landed on 33 nations spreading the gospel through mission work, planting and fathering churches and listening close to His voice for the next assignment.

www.ingramcontent.com/pod-product-compliance
Lightning Source LLC
Chambersburg PA
CBHW062035090426

42740CB00016B/2910